COLORADO

GUIDE

BE A TRAVELER - NOT A TOURIST!

OPEN ROAD TRAVEL GUIDES SHOW YOU
HOW TO BE A TRAVELER – NOT A TOURIST!

*Whether you're going abroad or planning a trip in the United States, take Open Road along on your journey. Our books have been praised by **Travel & Leisure, The Los Angeles Times, Newsday, Booklist, US News & World Report, Endless Vacation, American Bookseller, Coast to Coast**, and many other magazines and newspapers!*

Don't just see the world – experience it with Open Road!

ABOUT THE AUTHOR

Larry H. Ludmer is a professional travel writer whose Open Road travel guides include *Arizona Guide, New Mexico Guide, Colorado Guide, Utah Guide, Las Vegas Guide* and *Washington Guide*. His books for other publishers include *Arizona, Colorado & Utah; The Northern Rockies; The Great American Wilderness: Touring America's National Parks;* and *Cruising Alaska.*

COLORADO

GUIDE

BE A TRAVELER - NOT A TOURIST!

Larry Ludmer

OPEN ROAD PUBLISHING

OPEN ROAD PUBLISHING

We offer travel guides to American and foreign locales. Our books tell it like it is, often with an opinionated edge, and our experienced authors always give you all the information you need to have the trip of a lifetime. Write for your free catalog of all our titles, including our golf and restaurant guides.

Catalog Department, Open Road Publishing
P.O. Box 284, Cold Spring Harbor, NY 11724

E-mail:
Jopenroad@aol.com

2nd Edition

Front cover photo courtesy of Aspen Skiing Company. Back cover photo courtesy of Vail Associates, photographer Jack Affleck. Maps by James Ramage.

All information, including prices, is subject to change. The author has made every effort to be as accurate as possible, but neither he nor the publisher assumes responsibility for the services provided by any business listed in this guide; for any errors or omissions; or any loss, damage, or disruptions in your travel for any reason.

TABLE OF CONTENTS

7. BASIC INFORMATION   70

8. SPORTS & RECREATION   83

MAPS

SIDEBARS

COLORADO

GUIDE

1. INTRODUCTION

What is nature's most magnificent sight? A hard question to answer, for sure, but many people would respond to that question with a single word–mountains! And when you think of mountains most of us think of Colorado, the heart of the majestic Rocky Mountains. No other state in the contiguous United States has as many lofty peaks as does Colorado.

In fact, there are over 50 mountain peaks that soar to an elevation in excess of 14,000 feet. Size and quantity, however, don't tell the whole story of Colorado's incomparable mountain scenery. Forested lower slopes, jagged rocks above the timberline, perpetual snow-capped peaks and an ever-changing panoply of light will leave the visitor breathless.

Colorado's scenery isn't limited to wonderful mountains. A variety of unusual and colorful rock formations dot the state, from the Garden of the Gods to the Colorado National Monument. Huge plateaus with overhanging cliffs are common sights here. One of the latter is protected as Mesa Verde National Park and was once home to an ancient Indian civilization.

If the dazzle and excitement of the big city is your cup of tea, then check out cosmopolitan Denver. The towering glass skyscrapers of the city center compete for space in the sky with a mountain backdrop. Denver is home to fine museums, great shopping, historic attractions, cultural venues and loads of recreation. Colorado Springs, the state's second largest city, offers some of the same and adds a host of natural attractions just minutes from the hustle and bustle of the city.

The rest of the state is dominated by small towns, many with their origins in the mining days of the late 19th century. But wherever you are in Colorado, you're never far from the great outdoors, whether it be for the simple pleasure of viewing the sights or testing your skills in a raft against a raging river or speeding down the side of a snow-covered mountain at one of America's greatest ski resorts.

It's all in Colorado, and this book contains all of the information you'll need to plan a short weekend jaunt or a lengthy trip through every corner of the state. There's detailed information on hotels, restaurants, recreation, entertainment, and seeing the sights. I've tried to make this guide as user-friendly as possible. I'm sure it will entice you into taking that trip to Colorado you've been dreaming about. Enjoy your travels!

2. OVERVIEW

Colorado is a large state and is extremely diverse in its scenery, communities and people. Despite a growing population, much of Colorado is wilderness or close to it. Most visitors come to either see the scenery or to take part in the rugged outdoor life that is so abundant throughout the state, even close to the largest cities. It would be a mistake for a nature lover not to at least sample the historic and cultural attractions of Denver and Colorado Springs, and vice versa. In each of the chapters that describe beautiful Colorado I'll try to cover as much of the diversity as possible.

Colorado is a mix of cultural influences. The Native American population is smaller and not as important as in Arizona and New Mexico; the same can be said of the Hispanic heritage. However, each is present and is a worthwhile facet of visiting the state. The stereotype of the American lasso-wielding cowboy is not so much a part of Colorado history as it is in Wyoming, Montana, or some of the other western states but, it too, can be found. A more important historical heritage is that of the miner and prospector. They played a crucial role in Colorado's development around the turn of the century and their influence can still be seen and felt in many former mining towns throughout the state. Their individuality has also left its mark on today's residents. Coloradans, like many other westerners, are friendly but fiercely independent soles, who are staunch defenders of their state's beauty and way of life.

With so much to see and do in Colorado it may seem a daunting challenge to plan the right trip for you. It's not. To make things easier I've begun by dividing the state into six different touring regions–one each for Denver and Colorado Springs, and four geographic regions of varying sizes. Refer to the accompanying regional touring map to get a better picture of how these all fit together. Several other chapters that precede the touring section will provide you with general information on planning your Colorado trip. The remainder of this chapter will briefly highlight each of the regions.

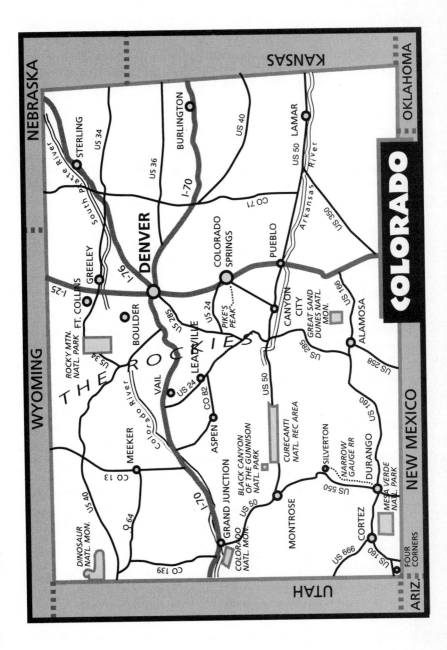

DENVER

Denver, the cosmopolitan capital of Colorado, is the state's largest city and is also the heart of the business and financial community for the inter-mountain region of the west. Soaring glass skyscrapers vie for attention with the towering mountain backdrop provided by the Rockies. The mountains, so close that you feel as if you can reach out and touch them, provide the basis for an extensive system of parks that delight outdoor enthusiasts, both local and visitors.

Born on rumors of gold, which ultimately turned out to be true, Denver saw its share of boom and bust times. But it didn't fade away. Instead, it turned to other business sectors and, combined with the invigorating climate, lured both tourists and residents. This trend still continues right up to the present day. As the city grew so did its cultural and entertainment-based attractions. Today you can visit any number of fine museums, amusement parks, historical attractions, and, of course, the nearby mountains. Lodging choices range from simple motels to luxury resorts and everything in between. The last decade has also seen Denver's emergence as a city of great restaurants.

COLORADO SPRINGS

While **Colorado Springs**, the state's second largest city, is somewhat obscured by the shadow of Denver (which is located only a little over an hour to the north), it is in many ways a much more interesting place to visit. It lacks the impressive downtown core but more than makes up for it with a plethora of wonderful attractions, both within the city and in the adjacent community of **Manitou Springs**.

Nature is at its best in Colorado Springs, which sits at the base of lofty **Pike's Peak**, only a cog railway ride away. Famous attractions such as the eerily beautiful **Garden of the Gods** and fantastic **Seven Falls** are but a couple of the diversions which bring millions of visitors to the Springs. Quality man-made attractions are no less numerous in this area and include several fine museums, a zoo, and America's **Olympic training complex**. A short ride away is the beautiful **United States Air Force Academy** where outstanding modern architecture blends in with the magnificent mountain scenery. Another short excursion will take you to **Canon City** and its fabulous **Royal Gorge**.

Colorado Springs is large enough to feature an excellent choice of places to stay, eat, and be entertained. It is home to one of America's most outstanding resort hotels, **The Broadmoor**, which is also an attraction in its own right.

NORTH CENTRAL COLORADO: HEART OF THE ROCKIES

Nowhere else in America is there an area that is so filled with magnificent Alpine-type mountain vistas than right here. It is in this region, within a short drive of the state's two main population centers, that are found the greatest concentration of 14,000-plus foot mountain peaks. Forever snow-capped, these peaks stand proudly among gorgeous mountain lakes and wildflower meadows. The Continental Divide provides the spine for this part of the state and most points are easily reached by one of the most comprehensive scenic road systems in the world.

Rocky Mountain National Park is the crown jewel of the north-central region, but so much beauty can be found in the mountainous national forests that cover more than three-fourths of this touring region. Summer touring is breathtaking but the north-central is just as popular in winter because it is home to many of the world's greatest ski resorts. Places with names like **Vail**, **Aspen**, **Winter Park**, and **Snowmass** are but some of the resorts that are almost synonymous with skiing. **Georgetown**, **Leadville** and other small towns bring to vivid life the heady days of Colorado's gold rush era.

NORTHWEST COLORADO: OFF THE BEATEN PATH

This is a rugged region of lower mountains that is the most sparsely populated of any part of Colorado. The only major community is **Grand Junction**. Skiing can be found here, too, in **Glenwood Springs**, but it is the unusual side of nature that attracts most visitors to the northwest. The **Colorado National Monument**, a little known wonder of the National Park System is an outstanding example of the effects of erosion with gigantic rock formations spread out beneath your feet. Other scenic areas include even lesser known **Lands End** and the lightly visited but fascinating **Dinosaur National Monument**. Just exploring the little traveled back roads of the northwest region can also be a worthwhile experience.

The northwest isn't nearly as famous as other parts of Colorado for outdoor recreation as there are fewer developed areas. However, nature provides an abundance of opportunities for those willing to work a little harder to find them. Accommodations in this area are mostly of the motel variety and you'll find plenty of places to eat a hearty meal, but not as many fancy restaurants with unreadable menus and high prices.

SOUTHWEST COLORADO: NATURE'S MAJESTY & ANCIENT CIVILIZATIONS

The southwest quadrant of the state has a good deal more natural diversity then the rest of Colorado and, therefore, makes it a place where you can spend a lot of time enjoying some of the finest attractions in the nation. **Mesa Verde National Park** is a place of amazing natural beauty that is enhanced by the well-preserved Anasazi Indian ruins that date back a thousand years. The **Black Canyon of the Gunnison National Park**, deep and narrow, has to rank among the most awesome sights to be found anywhere.

The **Great Sand Dunes National Monument** seems strangely out of place in this mountainous environment, which adds immeasurably to the joy of visiting it. A must-see in the southwest is the world famous **Durango and Silverton Narrow Gauge Railroad**, an exciting journey on vintage trains through the beautiful San Juan Mountains. Or stay in your own car and journey through similar magnificent scenery on the **Million Dollar Highway**. The list of things to see in the southwest goes on and on.

Recreational activities are also one of the biggest draws in the southwest. White-water rafting, jeep tours into the back country, fishing, swimming, and more are the order of the day. **Telluride** and **Purgatory** are the two most famous ski areas in this region. At the end of the day you'll be able to settle into a wide selection of accommodations, mostly motel style, but there are also some luxurious resorts and ski chalets and ranch-style facilities. Because of the large number of visitors the dining and entertainment scenes are unexpectedly active for a region with such a relatively small population. You could come to Colorado and spend all of your time in this touring region and have the vacation of a lifetime!

EASTERN COLORADO: THE GREAT PLAINS

This vast territory is the least visited of any region in Colorado. It is the high plains (with an average elevation of about 3500 feet) that provide a gateway to the magnificent mountains that sit on its western edge. The sights aren't as spectacular as in the rest of the state, but for those who seek out the delights of small towns and shun the crowds, there is much to see and do. The cattle industry is what made this area grow and the history of the mid-19th to early 20th centuries can be discovered in such towns as **Fort Collins**, **Loveland**, **Greeley**, **Fort Morgan** and **Sterling** in the north and **La Junta** and **Lamar** in the south.

Here the choices in accommodations, dining, and entertainment are more limited than in most areas of Colorado, and what you will find is generally of a more simple nature–this is where you'll find "real" people. The region contains long stretches of two of Colorado's longest rivers–the **South Platte** and **Arkansas**, as well as many of the state's largest lakes. These all provide ample opportunity for outdoor recreation.

THE BEST OF COLORADO/1

Decisions, decisions. With so many wonderful places to see and things to do, it hardly seems fair to make a list of Colorado's ten best because so many deserving attractions will be left out and therefore seem less worthwhile. However, such a list also has a positive side, because if you only have time to do the "must sees," then this is a great place to start. If you were to do only what appears on this list on a trip to Colorado, you will have ten of the greatest travel memories of all. This list isn't in any particular order.

    • ***Rocky Mountain National Park:*** *In a state filled with some of the most marvelous mountain scenery, it simply doesn't get any better than this.*

    • ***Mesa Verde National Park:*** *History and scenery combine to make this one of the wonders of the world. You'll wonder how the ancient inhabitants were able to construct their cliff dwellings in this difficult terrain.*

    • ***Durango and Silverton Narrow Gauge Railroad:*** *A joy, plain and simple. Of all the "tourist" railroads in the United States, this is definitely the best. The long narrow gauge trains twist their way through some beautiful scenery. The stopover in Silverton is like going back a century in time.*

    • ***Natural Colorado Springs:*** *No other major urban area in America is so liberally dotted with outstanding scenic wonders. Places like the Garden of the Gods, Seven Falls, Cave of the Winds, Cheyenne Canyon, and many others, make this THE city for the outdoor lover.*

    • ***Colorado National Monument:*** *I can't figure out why this place is still so relatively unknown to travelers. It's convenient to the Interstate highway and contains some of the most impressive scenery to be found in the incredibly scenic American southwest. Reminiscent of some of the unusual sights of Arizona or Utah.*

    • ***United States Air Force Academy:*** *You'll be hard pressed to find a place where beautiful architecture (especially the world renowned Cadet Chapel) blends in so wonderfully with the surrounding scenery. The thrill of a cadet parade or mealtime formation only makes it better.*

THE BEST OF COLORADO/2

• *A drive through the **ski resort corridor** in any season:* The stretch of Interstate 70 between Dillon and Beaver Creek, a distance of about 40 miles, is among the most scenic highways in America (certainly the best on the Interstate system). Brilliant summer sky or snow-covered winter are equally impressive.

• ***Million Dollar Highway:*** Some of the greatest scenery in Colorado (especially with stops at such places like Box Canyon) are the highlight of this road engineering marvel. Easy enough to be done by most drivers and thrilling enough to perk up the attention of the more adventurous.

• ***Royal Gorge of the Arkansas River:*** Although this is a commercial attraction (and some of the surrounding retail activity is a bit overdone), the ride across, or down the forbidding gorge is simply spectacular.

• ***Black Canyon of the Gunnison National Park:*** One of the deepest and narrowest canyons in the world, this is a sight that must be seen to be believed!

Finally, although I didn't include it (because I'm not a skier), anyone who loves the slopes will truly find any of Colorado's major ski resorts to simply be paradise!

3. SUGGESTED ITINERARIES

Colorado is big enough and has enough interesting attractions to keep you entertained for week after week, and that doesn't even count allowing for the time to partake of its splendid recreational facilities. But, since most of us don't have that kind of time to devote to a vacation (even if the money wouldn't run out), you'll probably be looking for a more scaled-down visit. The itineraries that follow range from a few days to a couple of weeks, the time frame that the majority of visitors will spend in Colorado. These aren't meant to limit your imagination. They're simply a guide to give you an idea of where to begin. Of course, if you're the type of traveler that gets a bit befuddled when planning an itinerary, feel free to use them just as they appear. But it's always better to do a little fine tuning to make them more in harmony with the things you like to do best.

Six of the itineraries correspond to the regional touring chapters and allow you to concentrate on a particular area of the state. Others combine two or more and still others are more ambitious trips that cover the entire state. The latter category include "highlight" tours for those short of time as well as the longest of the itineraries for those visitors who have the time and inclination to explore Colorado in detail. The longer trips, especially those not confining themselves to a single region, require moving from one lodging location to another. If you want to minimize that sort of travel, refer to the sidebar on using "home" bases. Keep in mind that these itineraries limit their scope primarily to sightseeing activities. If you just want to relax at a resort, hang around the pool, or spend time pursuing more adventurous outdoor recreation, be sure to add in the time necessary to do that.

Most of the sights in Denver and Colorado Springs can be reached via various forms of public transportation. However, this is not the case in most other parts of the state. Although there is bus service throughout Colorado, and scheduled shuttle service between Denver and some of the resort areas as well as between resort areas, it is not usually the best way to get around for a sightseeing trip. The state's size and generally rural nature make a car, either your own or a rental, almost a necessity once you get out of the two largest cities. Finally, as a matter of practicality, all of the itineraries are based on the likely assumption that if you are flying into Colorado, you will be arriving in Denver and starting around mid-day. The only other alternative destination for most people is Colorado Springs and that isn't all that far from Denver.

One more reminder–play around with the various itineraries. Try combining parts of several different trips. Chances are you'll come up with a highly successful plan.

ITINERARY 1: THE DENVER AREA
(5 Days/4 Nights; Approximately 250 miles)

This first trip is especially for those people who are interested in taking in what large cities have to offer. But since this is Colorado and the mountains are so close you can also explore a bit of mother nature at the same time.

Day 1

Arrive in Denver by the middle of the day and head for downtown to explore the financial capital of the mountain states. Visit the state capitol, historic Larimer Square and do some shopping.

Day 2

Denver's excellent museums and gardens (the Denver Art Museum and Elitch Gardens, for example) can nicely fill up a day. Discover Denver's excellent theater and entertainment scene tonight and other evenings.

Day 3

The western suburbs, especially Golden, have a wealth of sights. Take a ride up to Buffalo Bill's grave and museum and get a fantastic view of city and mountains. Visit the Coors Brewery and Colorado Railroad Museum. Be sure to take a peek at the beautiful amphitheater in Red Rocks Park.

Day 4

Today is a good day to get into the mountains. A loop route can take in Boulder, the Denver Mountain Parks system, historic Central City, and Idaho Springs before returning to town.

Day 5

Some final shopping or sightseeing, perhaps, before departing for home.

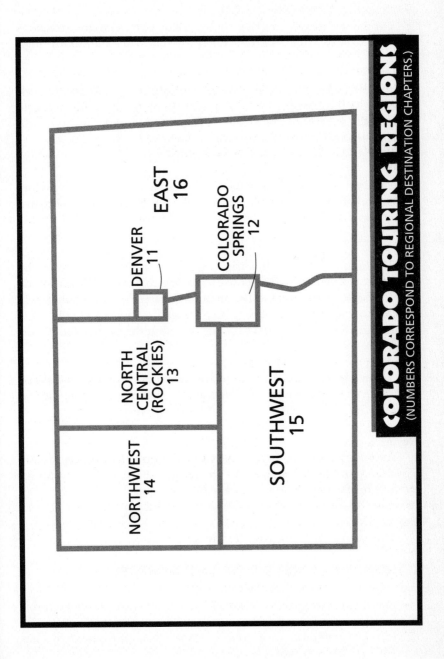

COLORADO TOURING REGIONS
(NUMBERS CORRESPOND TO REGIONAL DESTINATION CHAPTERS.)

EAST
16

DENVER
11

COLORADO
SPRINGS
12

NORTH
CENTRAL
(ROCKIES)
13

NORTHWEST
14

SOUTHWEST
15

ITINERARY 2: THE COLORADO SPRINGS AREA

(6 Days/5 Nights; Approximately 330 miles)

For those who want to strike a better balance between city attractions and natural beauty, there's no place on earth quite like Colorado Springs.

Day 1

It's less than two hours from the Denver airport to Colorado Springs. However, before arriving in town, stop north of the city at the beautiful United States Air Force Academy. Then on to Colorado Springs itself, visiting the Pro Rodeo Hall of Fame in the northern part of town.

Day 2

You can see just about all of the city's man-made attractions, including several museums and the United States Olympic Training Complex, in a single day.

Day 3

The natural part of the trip begins in earnest today. Visit the incredible Garden of the Gods, Cave of the Winds, Seven Falls, Cheyenne Canyon, and more in what will be an unforgettable day. Maybe there will be time to visit the zoo as well. There's a terrific sound and light show during the evening presented on a canyon wall at the Cave of the Winds.

Day 4

Today you'll journey up to the top of Pike's Peak on a cog railway. The four hour trip is a wonderful experience. Spend some time visiting Manitou Springs' excellent shops and historic homes.

Day 5

A short excursion to Canon City to see the attractions of the thrilling Royal Gorge of the Arkansas River. You can get back to Colorado Springs by the late afternoon and take in a few more sights.

Day 6

Return to Denver for your trip home.

ITINERARY 3: HEART OF THE ROCKIES

(6 Days/5 Nights; Approximately 550 miles)

Mountain scenery at its finest will be at every turn throughout this journey that is sure to satisfy the most ardent nature lover. Nowhere else in the United States will you encounter so many beautiful mountain vistas in such a relatively compact area.

Day 1

Take a couple of hours to see the highlights of downtown Denver before making your way to Boulder for the first night's lodging.

Day 2

After exploring the sights of Boulder, home to the University of Colorado, your route will take you through the forested mountains adjacent to the Continental Divide to the resort town of Estes Park, your home for tonight. Ride the aerial tramway and visit some of the local museums and historic ranches.

Day 3

A certain highlight of your trip will be today's jaunt through magnificent Rocky Mountain National Park, then via Grand Lake and Hot Sulphur Springs to Dillon, where you will spend the night.

Day 4

The mountain scenery doesn't get much better than in this area. Make stops to visit such well known historic towns and resorts such as Breckenridge and Vail before proceeding to your final destination of the day–Aspen. Few places can compare with the beauty to be found here. Be sure to visit the Maroon Bells.

Day 5

Retrace your route for a while to Leadville, one of Colorado's most interesting historic communities, before returning to the Interstate and proceeding east to Georgetown, another town from the wild mining era. Then visit Central City and Idaho Springs before arriving back in the greater Denver area.

Day 6

Depending upon how much time you have before heading home, you'll be able to visit some of the excellent sights in Golden and Denver's other western suburban areas.

ITINERARY 4: CITY & MOUNTAIN
(7 Days/6 Nights; Approximately 475 miles)

A combination of parts of the first three trips, this itinerary covers the state's two largest cities as well as some of its best mountain scenery.

Day 1

Arrive in Denver and use the afternoon to hit the sights of downtown.

Day 2

The morning and early afternoon will be devoted to some more sightseeing in Denver and the suburban areas. Then explore Boulder before arriving in Estes Park for the evening.

Day 3

Today you will visit Rocky Mountain National Park, then travel through the breathtaking Berthoud Pass, reaching Georgetown by the end of the Day.

Day 4

Explore Idaho Springs and then head south through the scenic Pike National Forest, arriving in Manitou Springs by mid-afternoon. See the sights here and settle in for the night either in Manitou or Colorado Springs.

Day 5

The cog railway to Pike's Peak in the morning and the natural attractions of Colorado Springs in the afternoon.

Day 6

Visit some of Colorado Springs' many museums, especially the Pro Rodeo Hall of Fame before heading north. Stop at the Air Force Academy and try to catch the noon meal formation when you get there if school is in session. You'll arrive back in Denver by late afternoon and have a little time for some more sightseeing or shopping.

Day 7

Fond memories await you on your return trip home.

ITINERARY 5: THE NORTHWEST

(6 Days/5 Nights; Approximately 950 miles)

Outstanding scenery, both mountains and unusual geologic formations, will highlight this adventure into Colorado's most sparsely populated region.

Day 1

Leave Denver via Interstate 70 westbound and travel through the highly scenic heart of the Rockies and arrive in Glenwood Springs, your first overnight stop. There should be some time to take in some of the local sights.

Day 2

The morning will take you through wilderness country dominated by mountains, hills, and valleys. You'll arrive at Dinosaur National Monument, a most fascinating spot. You'll have to cross the border into Utah for a short time if you want to visit both sections of the Monument. Spend the night in Rangely.

Day 3

One last wilderness drive will bring you to the town of Fruita, along the Interstate, and the eastern entrance to the wonderfully scenic Colorado National Monument. At the western end of the Monument is Grand Junction, your home for the night and the locale for a few minor attractions to fill the late afternoon.

Day 4

Visit eerily beautiful Lands End before making your way through the scenic White River National Forest. Stop at Carbondale and other historic communities before reaching Interstate 70 once again. Head east, arriving at your overnight destination of Vail. Take some time to walk around and see the sights and shops of this famous resort town.

Day 5

Return via the Interstate to Denver, which you should reach in about two hours. You can take the rest of the day to hit the high points of the state's capital city and the surrounding area.

Day 6

Some last sightseeing time, perhaps, before heading home.

ITINERARY 6: THE SOUTHWEST

(8 Days/7 Nights; Approximately 1,100 miles)

Colorado's most diverse region of natural beauty, the Southwest is ideal for those who want to see beauty and experience adventure and history. It's another world!

Day 1

It's a good hike to reach this region from Denver (if you can fly into Colorado Springs, that's closer). So, we'll head straight there upon arrival. From Denver's western side pick up U.S. Highway 285, and head for your first overnight stop, the town of Salida. The drive is a highly scenic one that will take you across the Continental Dive and into the Sangre de Cristo Range.

Day 2

From Salida head west on U.S. 50, crossing the Continental Divide once again at majestic Monarch Pass. At the Curecanti National Recreation Area you'll have the opportunity to see some beautiful mountain and lake scenery as well as take a boat ride. Your final attraction for the day is the incomparable Black Canyon of the Gunnison National Park. This unforgettable day ends at the community of Montrose.

Day 3

Travel south through pleasant scenery to the town of Ouray and its Box Canyon. Then retrace your route for a few miles and head around to the resort town of Telluride. Now the route takes you through the beautiful San Juan National Forest and to the town of Cortez, your home for this third night of the trip.

Day 4

It will take you at least a half day to explore the wonders of Mesa Verde National Park's cliff dwellings and other sights. Then it's on to the quaint community of Durango, your home for the next two nights.

Day 5

Another highlight type day. An all-day excursion on the scenic Durango and Silverton Narrow Gauge Railroad. Time is allowed in Silverton to explore this old mining town that has come back from the mining bust to become a major tourist attraction.

Day 6

Head west from Durango for a lengthy but pleasant drive to the town of Alamosa. After relaxing there for a while and seeing the local sights use the afternoon to visit the impressive sights at the Great Sand Dunes National Monument. Return to Alamosa for the evening.

Day 7

Less than two hours east of Alamosa is Interstate 25. That road will take you back north to Colorado Springs and on to Denver. Do take some time to stop in Colorado Springs and see some of the main sights. In fact, to allow the most time in this interesting city, you should spend the night here.

Day 8

An early morning ride back to Denver, in time to either take in a few sights or to catch your flight home.

ITINERARY 7: THE EAST PLUS DENVER & COLORADO SPRINGS

(8 Days/7 Nights; Approximately 815 miles)

The sights in the east are interesting but more scattered than in other parts of the state, so we'll spice things up a bit by including some things in Denver and Colorado Springs.

Day 1

Drive north from Denver and visit the towns of Loveland, Fort Collins, and Greeley before heading east along the banks of the South Platte River to Fort Morgan, your home for this first night. All of the aforementioned towns have a number of interesting historic sites as well as local museums.

Day 2

The last town to visit along the South Platte is Sterling. Ramble south through the High Plains to several towns in central-eastern Colorado–Limon, Stratton, and Burlington, the last of which will be where you spend your second night.

Day 3

Traveling south one last time through the Plains you'll reach the eastern section of the Colorado portion of the Arkansas River. Stops today include Lamar, Bent's Old Fort National Historic Site, and La Junta. The final destination of the day is Pueblo.

Day 4

It's only a short ride from Pueblo along Interstate 25 before you reach Colorado Springs. Use today to take in the city sights.

Day 5

You can use a half day to take the journey up to Pike's Peak and visit some other scenic attractions in the afternoon, or skip the train ride to do more shorter attractions, of which the Colorado Springs area has many.

Day 6

Pay a visit to the Air Force Academy before proceeding north on the final leg of your journey to Denver. You'll have the whole afternoon to explore downtown, the state capitol, and some of the city's fine museums.

Day 7

More exploration of Denver and the surrounding suburbs. Or take a brief journey into the nearby mountains if scenery is more to your liking.

Day 8
A day for traveling home.

ITINERARY 8: THE SHORT HIGHLIGHT TRIP
(9 Days/8 Nights; Approximately 1,300 miles)
Colorado has so many highlights that can be considered "must sees," that it's difficult to do them in a short trip. But if you have only a limited amount of time, this itinerary can be the perfect solution.

Day 1
Get right to work exploring the highlights of Denver on this first afternoon. You'll spend the night in town.

Day 2
A lovely ride this morning will bring you through Boulder and Estes Park and on into Rocky Mountain National Park. By the end of the day you'll have left the park and reached your overnight destination, the historic town of Breckenridge.

Day 3
A little to the south of Breckenridge is Leadville, one of the most historic of all Colorado mining communities, and now a resort as well. A scenic route leading further south will bring you to the town of Poncha Springs where you'll head west on another scenic route–US 50. Overnight will be in the town of Gunnison.

Day 4
Visit the lovely Curecanti National Recreation Area, followed almost immediately by the mind boggling Black Canyon of the Gunnison National Park. At the town of Montrose you'll begin to travel south, stopping for the night at Ouray. Visit Box Canyon in town.

Day 5
Along the stunning Million Dollar Highway this morning, stopping at the town of Silverton, before proceeding with this highly scenic route and arriving at the town of Durango, home for tonight and tomorrow.

Day 6
A big choice to be made today. Spend a full day on the Durango and Silverton Narrow Gauge Railway or take an excursion to fascinating Mesa Verde National Park. Of course, you could simply do both by adding another day to the trip. (The indicated itinerary mileage includes the 115 miles for the round trip to and through Mesa Verde.)

Day 7

A long drive this morning and early afternoon through scenic mountain and forest terrain before arriving at Canon City. Visit the Royal Gorge before calling it a day.

Day 8

On to Colorado Springs, just a little over an hour's drive away. Spend the entire day visiting the highlights.

Day 9

Depending upon your travel connections you may have a little time in the morning to continue exploring the Colorado Springs area before heading back to Denver.

ITINERARY 9: COLORADO LONG HIGHLIGHT TOUR

(11 Days/10 Nights; Approximately 1,600 miles)

This trip is similar to the previous itinerary but adds a few more delights for those of you who have some more time to devote to Colorado's wonders.

Days 1 and 2

The same basic itinerary as above except that after completing Rocky Mountain National Park on the second day, you'll head to Georgetown to explore that historic town and then proceed to Vail for the night.

Day 3

An easy drive along the Interstate west to Grand Junction where you'll visit the Colorado National Monument. Then it's on to Montrose for the night.

Day 4

A short side trip to visit the Black Canyon of the Gunnison National Park in the morning. The afternoon is for the ride to Ouray, your overnight stop. There's lots to see and do in Ouray.

Day 5

Back track to Ridgway and head south through the San Juan National Forest, stopping at the picturesque resort of Telluride before reaching Cortez. Just east of town is the magnificent Mesa Verde National Park. On to Durango for the next two evenings.

Day 6

An entire day is devoted to the relaxing pleasure of touring the Animas River Valley on the Durango and Silverton Narrow Gauge Railroad.

Day 7

You're heading east today to Alamosa. However, in the afternoon take time to visit the Great Sand Dunes National Monument.

Day 8

In about three hours you will reach the famous Royal Gorge of the Arkansas River. A few hours time is well spent here and then you can head on into Colorado Springs for the night.

Days 9 and 10

This longer trip allows you to spend two full days exploring the area. Choose from a plethora of natural and man-made attractions. You have time to take the cog railway to Pikes Peak if you so desire. Visit the Garden of the Gods and the Air Force Academy.

Day 11

Return to Denver in time for your connections home.

ITINERARY 10: COLORADO EXPLORER

(13 Days/12 Nights; Approximately 1,750 miles)

While this trip doesn't add that many destinations to the previous itinerary, it does allow for more time to take in additional sights, or to just spend additional time at places you really like.

Days 1 and 2

The same as the previous itinerary.

Day 3

We now divert from Itinerary 9 by heading south and visiting Leadville and Aspen, which encompass some of the state's most spectacular scenery, before returning to the Interstate and spending the night at Glenwood Springs.

Day 4

Visit the Colorado National Monument and then proceed to Montrose. Explore the Black Canyon of the Gunnison before returning to Montrose for the evening. These two spectacular monuments will make this a most memorable day.

Days 5 through 9

See Days 4 through 8 in Itinerary 9. However, since you will have already done the Black Canyon you will be able to stretch things out a bit and devote more time to such places as Mesa Verde.

Day 10

Before exploring Colorado Springs itself you should see some outstanding attractions in the outlying area. These include the historic town of Cripple Creek and the Florissant Fossil Beds National Monument. The rest of the day can be spent adding some additional attractions in Colorado Springs that there wouldn't be time for in Itinerary 9.

Days 11 and 12

Colorado Springs and Manitou Springs in all their glory!

Day 13

Head back to Denver. You may have time for some additional sightseeing if your return home isn't until late in the afternoon.

ITINERARY 11: COLORADO IN DEPTH

(17 Days/16 Nights; Approximately 2,100 miles)

Here's an itinerary that will satisfy the most ardent traveler's desire to explore. You'll be a Colorado pro after this trip.

Days 1 and 2

Arrive in Denver and spend the first afternoon and next morning exploring the capital city and surrounding area. Spend the second night in Boulder.

Day 3

Head north and visit both Fort Collins and Greeley before arriving in Estes Park for the night. This gateway community to the national park has many attractions, including an aerial tramway.

Day 4

Rocky Mountain National Park in depth. You could spend days here, but one full day will have to do it. Overnight in Georgetown.

Day 5

See Day 3 in Itinerary 10.

Day 6
Tour the Colorado National Monument and head north to Rangly for the evening.

Day 7
An unusual visit to isolated Dinosaur National Monument before returning to Grand Junction for your second stay here.

Day 8
Visit the Black Canyon of the Gunnison and the Curecanti National Recreation Area. Then return to Montrose, head south and arrive at Ouray for the evening.

Day 9
Through Telluride to Cortez and then Mesa Verde National Park. Arrive in Durango, your home for the next two nights.

Day 10
The Durango and Silverton Narrow Gauge Railroad is on the agenda for today.

Day 11
Through southern Colorado in an easterly direction. Visit the Great Sand Dunes National Monument and stay overnight in Alamosa.

Day 12
On to the town of Canon City and the Royal Gorge. Then head into Pueblo and explore this interesting town in the late afternoon before settling in for the night.

Days 13 through 15
The same as days 10 through 12 in the previous itinerary except that you have to make the short ride from Pueblo into the Colorado Springs area.

Day 16
Return to Denver and allow the remainder of the day to explore suburban Golden and other areas that you didn't do upon arrival.

Day 17
It's been a long trip so you'll be heading home today.

SEEING COLORADO FROM A "HOME" BASE

Some travelers don't mind living out of a suitcase, spending a night or two in one place and then moving on to the next destination. Certainly this allows you to see the most. But, for those of you who feel more comfortable being settled into a nice hotel and staying there, Colorado offers a number of possibilities for seeing a great deal through a series of day trips. The regional tour concept is especially well suited to this approach. The following chart should help you plan a trip using this concept.

You can also combine the home base method with the more traditional point to point method. After several days at one base, go on to another and perhaps more, depending upon the total length of your trip.

TOURING AREA BASES

Denver: *Denver or any suburban location*

Colorado Springs: *Colorado Springs or Manitou Springs.*

(Note: Denver and Colorado Springs are close enough to one another that you can stay in one and see the other, but it is far less convenient because you'll probably have to do it for a few days.)

North-Central: *Boulder; any I-70 corridor resort (Dillon, Keystone, Georgetown, or Vail); or Denver.*

Northwest: *Grand Junction or Glenwood Springs.*

Southwest: *Durango or Montrose are best; Cortez is also a possibility.*

East: *The east regional touring chapter is already divided into a home base approach.*

4. LAND & PEOPLE

LAND

Colorado is the epitome of mountain country. While it's true that mountains are the principal geographic feature of the state, they are most certainly not the only significant landform. Grasslands cover much of the Plains portion of the state while the lower portions of the mountains are generally thickly forested. About one-third of Colorado's land area is owned by the United States government, mostly in the form of national forests and parks. Covering an area of just over 104,000 square miles, Colorado is the eighth largest state in the union. It is almost perfectly rectangular in shape, measuring about 385 miles from east to west and 275 miles from north to south. The highest point is 14,433-foot Mt. Elbert while the lowest is a still high 3,350 feet along the Arkansas River. The mean elevation of almost 6,800 feet is the highest in the United States.

Colorado is bordered by Wyoming and a small section of Nebraska to the north, Nebraska and Kansas to the east, by New Mexico and a tiny part of Oklahoma on the south, and by Utah to the west. The extreme southwestern corner is known as the **Four Corners**, the only point in the United States where the borders of four states converge. (In addition to Utah and New Mexico, you can enter Arizona if you cross the border diagonally.)

Colorado can be divided into four distinct sections from a geologist's point of view. The eastern third of the state is the **Great Plains**, more commonly referred to by locals as the High Plains. It slopes from nearly 7,000 feet in altitude on the western edge of the Rockies to about 3,500 feet on the Kansas-Nebraska border. The land is fertile and overlies hard sedimentary rock. However, it requires artificial irrigation in order to make it productive for agriculture.

The second section is the **Rocky Mountains**, a huge swath of land that covers about forty percent of Colorado in the center of the state. It is one of the highest regions in North America with 54 separate mountain peaks topping 14,000 feet in elevation. The Colorado Rockies are comprised of

BACKBONE OF THE NATION

*The **Continental Divide** is a term that most of us have heard of but have only a vague idea of exactly what it is. Perhaps the most majestic portion of the Divide is located in Colorado. The Divide runs at or near the highest parts of the Colorado Rockies. The term comes from the fact that it "divides" the direction in which rivers flow. Rivers originating on the western side of the divide flow in a westerly direction while those on the east side flow towards the east. In reality, the Continental Divide runs from the northern part of Canada all the way into Mexico and Central America. In a sense it continues into South America through the Andes Mountains.*

Some of the greatest scenery in the world is located along either side of the Divide. In Colorado, the Continental Divide enters from Wyoming and zig-zags its way on into New Mexico in a generally southerly direction. Although it sometimes diverges far to the east or west, if you were to draw a straight line through Colorado the entry and exit points would almost be even.

*Among the many passes on mountain roads where you can and will cross the Continental Divide are: **Rabbit Ears Pass** (9,426 feet near Steamboat Springs); **Willow Creek Pass** (9,683 feet north of Granby); **Milner Pass** (10,759 feet in Rocky Mountain National Park); **Berthoud Pass** (11,307 feet at Winter Park); **Tennessee Pass** (10,474 feet near Leadville); **Independence Pass** (12,095 feet near Aspen); **Monarch Pass** (11,312 feet west of Salida); **Wolf Creek Pass** (10,550 feet north of Pagosa Springs); and the **Cumbres Pass** (10,022 feet at the New Mexico border north of Chama).*

the **Front Range** (facing the Plains), the **Sawatch** and **Park Ranges** in the north, **Sangre de Cristo Mountains** in the south, and the **San Juan Mountains** in the southwest. Most of the ranges are forested, except at the higher elevations. There are quite a few lakes within the mountains, including the state's largest natural lake, Grand Lake. Another prominent feature of this region is the **Continental Divide** (see the sidebar below).

Another one-fifth of the state is part of the **Colorado Plateau**. This covers the western portion of the state except for the extreme north. Mostly at elevations exceeding 6,500 feet, the Colorado Plateau is an area of mesas, deep canyons, and broad valleys. The greater portion of the Colorado Plateau extends into Arizona and Utah. The final section is the smallest. The northwest is a region of hilly highlands and lower mountains known as the **Wyoming Basin**.

Several major American rivers have their origin in the snow melt of the Rockies. These include the **Colorado, Arkansas, North** and **South Platte**, and **Rio Grande** rivers. Most lakes are relatively small in size with the majority of natural lakes being in the mountains. The Great Plains contain several significant man-made lakes, especially along the South Platte and Arkansas Rivers. Both natural and man-made lakes are important parts of the state's extensive recreation system.

PEOPLE

Contrary to the expectations of many first-time visitors to the state, Colorado does not have a large Native American population like in the neighboring states of Utah, Arizona, and New Mexico. In fact, less than one percent of the population was classified as Native American in the last census. There are only two significant sized Indian reservations in the state. These are the Ute Mountain and Southern Ute Reservations, located adjacent to one another in the extreme southwestern corner of the state along the New Mexico border. Both reservations are home to members of the Ute tribe.

The Hispanic influence, both from the days of the Conquistadors and Mexican, is also weaker than in other southwestern states. However, the population of Mexican origin is large and growing. They are concentrated in the southern half of the state but also have an important presence in Colorado's large population centers.

About 80% of Colorado's more than four million people live in urban areas. The Denver and Colorado Springs areas alone account for approximately seventy percent of the state total. Colorado's population growth, while not as explosive as some other southwestern states, has been above the national average for the last several decades and is likely to continue.

Because of the influx of people from just about every part of the country it isn't possible to say that any one group or characteristic is dominant. The cities, especially, are a microcosm of contemporary American society, and even the more sparsely populated areas are quite diverse. Certainly a number of people who shun big crowds are drawn to Colorado's rural areas to make their homes, but so are a lot of other people who find that the sunny and invigorating climate make Colorado a great place to live.

COLORADO PROFILE: FACTS AT A GLANCE

Entered the Union: *August 1, 1876, becoming the 38th state*

Area: *104,091 square miles, ranks 8th*

Number of Counties: *63*

Number of State Parks: *32*

Number of areas administered by the National Park Service: *11*

Population: *4,391,261 (official 2001 Census Bureau estimate), ranks 24th*

Population Growth (1990-1999): *23%, about 2-1/2 times the national average*

Population Density: *38.9 persons per square mile (U.S. average is 73)*

Largest Localities *(1999 population in excess of 50,000):* *Denver, 532,066; Colorado Springs, 350,181; Aurora, 258,008; Lakewood, 143,201; Fort Collins, 113,508; Pueblo, 102,995; Arvada, 102,782; Westminster, 99,081; Boulder, 91,971; Thornton, 77,633; Greeley, 73,826; Longmont, 66,303. (Note: Aurora, Lakewood, Arvada, Westminster, and Thornton are all part of the greater Denver metropolitan area.)*

Nickname: *The Centennial State*

Motto: *Nil sine Numine (Nothing without Providence)*

State Flower: *Rocky Mountain columbine*

State Bird: *Lark bunting*

State Tree: *Blue spruce*

State Song: *"Where the Columbines Grow"*

Highest Point: *Mt. Elbert, 14,433 feet*

Lowest Point: *Along the Arkansas River, 3,350 feet*

Tourism Industry: *$7.5 billion annually*

Major Agricultural Products: *Wheat, corn, hay, cattle, milk*

Major Natural Resources: *Petroleum, natural gas, coal*

Major Manufactured Products: *Machinery, instruments, electronic equipment; transportation equipment, printing and publishing*

5. A SHORT HISTORY

COLORADO BEFORE THE EUROPEANS

The ancient cliff-dwelling master builders commonly known as the **Anasazi** (now starting to be referred to by the more cumbersome term **Ancestral Puebloans**), who settled over vast spaces of the southwest, moved into Colorado sometime before 800 A.D. They developed an advanced civilization that survived for centuries before disappearing suddenly. Various theories exist as to their demise, but the most commonly accepted theories are a period of prolonged drought or over-farming, perhaps a combination of both. Somewhat later they were followed by the **Ute Indians** from the desert regions of what now comprise parts of Utah. Both groups lived together in relative harmony in the southwestern quadrant of contemporary Colorado, often in settlements above the 10,000-foot level.

The Utes always settled in mountainous areas and defended the passes on the eastern side of the mountains from encroachment by the Plains Indians. Later on, after the Utes had acquired horses from the Spanish, they moved further eastward into the Colorado Plains and came into conflict with newly arriving bands of Cheyenne and Arapaho, as well as Comanche and Kiowa. It is likely that many or all of these tribes were being pushed westward by other tribes. It is known that they often fought among themselves. Smaller incursions into Colorado were made by groups of Pawnee, Sioux, and Navajo as well as the Blackfoot and Crow. Today, the Hopi tribe claims to be direct descendants of the Anasazi. They along with the Plains Indians all slowly bowed to the increasing power of European and later American settlement.

FROM THE CONQUISTADORS TO STATEHOOD

By the later part of the 16th century Spanish explorers from bases in Mexico journeyed northward in search of gold treasure. They didn't find any in Colorado at that time and must have been disappointed in discovering only beautiful scenery which, from their accounts, went totally unappreciated. However, they at least took note of the reddish-brown hue of the landscape and named the area *Colorado*, which meant the "color red."

The Spaniards did develop a few settlements but they never colonized the area to the extent that they did in New Mexico and other areas of the southwest. Events in Europe affected the ownership of North American possessions and the area of Colorado east of the Rockies passed to the control of the French. Other than several small southern settlements, most of Colorado was largely unexplored and still controlled mainly by Native Americans.

With the Louisiana Purchase of 1803, Colorado became a territory of the United States. **Colonel Zebulon Pike** (of Pike's Peak fame) led an expedition up the Arkansas River in 1806 and explored new territory. In 1820 **Major Stephen Long** led an expedition which tracked the South Platte River and reached the present site of Denver. Brave fur trappers were responsible for the exploration of most of the western portions of Colorado. It was not until the establishment of Bent's Fort on the Arkansas River in 1832 that the Colorado territory actually opened up to settlement by large numbers of Americans.

The first permanent American settlement was in San Luis in 1851. Growth was painfully slow until the discovery of gold in the Rocky Mountains in 1858. This led to a tremendous gold rush characterized by the slogan "Pike's Peak or Bust." Land that had been given to the Cheyenne and Arapaho tribes was taken back to lay the foundations of Denver. Relations with the Indians had been good until the gold rush. But the taking of land formerly promised to the Indians and a later massacre ended years of relative peace.

The **Colorado Territory** was officially proclaimed in 1861 and coincided with the start of open hostilities with the Indians. It was not until 1867, when the end of the Civil War freed up troops, that the United States forced the removal of the Colorado Plains Indians to reservations in Oklahoma. By that time the initial gold rush and most of the people who had come to make their fortune had, indeed, gone bust. Colorado likely would have stagnated were it not for the dawn of the cattle industry. Large herds were moved north from Texas and by the 1870's had replaced mining as the territory's most important industry. There was a clamor for statehood although many people were also opposed to it because they figured it would mean higher taxes. Sound familiar? Despite that opposition the statehood enthusiasts, who had support in Congress, prevailed and Colorado was admitted to the union in 1876. Because it coincided with the hundredth anniversary of the United States, Colorado became known as the **Centennial State**, its official nickname to this day.

MODERN COLORADO

The last quarter of the nineteenth century was one of significant economic growth for the young state. Cattle ranching continued to grow rapidly. A new mining boom also began with the discovery of rich silver lodes in the mountains as well as additional sources of gold. Unfortunately for the local economy, the latter did not last for long. By the early years of the 20th century it was once again ranching that sustained the state.

A new source of income was also beginning to have an impact— **tourism**. The sights of Colorado were a draw for some early visitors but the healthy mountain air and sunshine quickly made it an important destination. Colorado Springs first developed as a spa resort and several other contemporary resort areas were originally tuberculosis sanitariums. Another mining boom also developed during the days of World War I and continued for a few years afterwards. However, it was not to last for long. When the Depression came to America it hit the ranchers, miners, and farmers of Colorado with great severity. The state was finally helped by numerous large federal projects as well as a reform of the Colorado state taxation system.

World War II, of course, ultimately had the biggest impact on the revival of the Colorado economy as the federal government established many facilities to support the war effort. When peace came the facilities remained and even continued to expand, complementing the growing aerospace and electronics industries. These new industries, continued growth in tourism, and a general movement of the United States population towards the west in the decades from 1950 through the present have kept Colorado humming. Despite the hectic pace of modern life, Colorado residents are sure to take plenty of time to enjoy the magnificent environment in which they live.

That, of course, includes facing the challenge of growth versus environmental concerns. The majority of Coloradans favor a balanced approach but they often seem to be caught in the middle between the more vocal supporters of all-out growth and the most rabid environmentalists who are ready to tear down Denver! Hopefully, the large middle will prevail in the end.

6. PLANNING YOUR TRIP

WHEN TO VISIT

Colorado is definitely a popular destination regardless of the time of the year. However, when to go is entirely dependent upon the nature of your visit. It's simply not possible, for example, to combine the type of outdoor activities and sightseeing done in warmer weather with a ski trip to Vail or Aspen. Perhaps the easiest method to assist you is to discuss each season one at a time.

Summer

I'll begin with the summer because, except for the aforementioned ski trips, this is when the majority of you probably wind up going. The range in altitudes from one part of the state to another creates a big difference in temperature as well as precipitation. Mountains are cooler and generally wetter. During the summer most rainfall occurs in the form of thunderstorms. These can be frequent in mountain locations and less so in other parts of the state. They tend to occur late in the afternoon or early evening and fortunately tend to be brief. As such it isn't often that rain tends to be a major hindrance to a Colorado trip during the summer, although occasional major storms do make their way through all parts of the state. If you are going to be doing a lot of outdoor activity in the mountains keep in mind that some thunderstorms can be extremely violent and dangerous. More about that later when we discuss safety.

Finally, the definition of summer varies. In Denver, Colorado Springs, the Plains, and lower mountain elevations (less than 7,000 feet) summer is pretty much like most other places–June through early September. You can count on warm and mostly sunny days and pleasant sometimes chilly evenings. Higher than that, though, summer often arrives quite a bit later–sometimes as late as July, and it can be over by August. It's not that unusual for a late spring snowfall to keep some mountain passes and roads closed through mid-June.

Fall & Spring

Fall is a beautiful time of the year in most of Colorado. The fall foliage colors can be extraordinary in such places as Aspen and other mountain resort areas. Fall arrives in most places by the middle of September, but temperatures can be quite comfortable in the lower elevations through at least the end of the month. By October most higher altitudes will see their first snow and "regular" touring can start to become a problem, not only because of weather but early closing of many attractions. The pattern for spring isn't much different from the Fall–just the opposite. It can be lovely in the later spring months but still cold and snowy in the earlier part. Most ski resorts, for example, consider their normal season to be from November through April, although this can vary from year to year based on snow conditions.

Winter

While winter brings its own sort of special beauty to the mountains, a beauty which is well worth seeing, I wouldn't recommend it for the first time visitor due to poor travel conditions and closed attractions. And it is cold; if you don't believe me look at the chart below. Leadville is an excellent example of the temperatures in the higher altitudes.

However, it is the ideal time for that ski trip. There is good skiing available throughout the cold weather months in all parts of the Rockies, including resorts located close to the major cities, as well as in the southwest portion of the state.

AVERAGE TEMPERATURE & PRECIPITATION
Highs/Lows, & Precipitation

	Jan.	April	July	October	Annual Precip.
Alamosa	36/1	59/25	83/47	64/25	7.8"
Colo. Springs	43/14	59/31	85/55	60/35	16.3"
Denver	43/17	61/34	87/59	67/38	15.4"
Durango	38/12	60/30	83/51	64/32	17.0"
Estes Park	39/17	54/27	78/47	59/30	14.0"
Fort Collins	42/15	61/34	85/57	64/35	15.2"
Grand Junction	35/17	65/40	93/64	67/43	8.9"
LaJunta	43/16	69/38	94/63	71/39	11.5"
Sterling	38/11	63/34	90/60	66/34	16.1"
Vail	33/2	51/21	80/40	59/24	16.5"

Don't forget that many activities, regardless of season, will be in the mountains near many of the above localities at an elevation several thousand feet higher than the town or city. There is a drop of approximately three degrees for each rise in altitude of a thousand feet. So, for example, if it's a pleasant 80 degrees in Colorado Springs, up on the 8,000-foot high summit of nearby Pike's Peak it will be about a chilly 56 degrees! Bring your jacket.

WHAT TO PACK

The key to proper packing on any vacation is to take only what you are going to need and use. Excess baggage only weighs you down and makes packing and unpacking more of a chore. This is even more important if you're moving from one location to another every night or almost every night. An even more important consideration is to pack appropriate to the climate you can expect to encounter and appropriate for the types of activities you're going to be participating in.

Colorado, like just about all of the western and mountain states, is generally informal and casual style clothing prevails. This is especially true during the warmer months. However, the finer restaurants in larger cities and some of the fancier resorts may impose a dress code so if you plan on that type of dining you will want to bring along some fancier dinner attire.

For the warmer summer weather you should dress in lightweight clothing that breathes, such as cotton. Lighter colors are the best. Even though the temperature in Colorado doesn't get that hot, especially in higher altitudes, keep in mind that the rays of the sun are stronger in the thinner mountain air. Therefore, it is a good idea to keep as much skin covered as possible and also wear a hat. Sunglasses are equally advisable. Long pants and shirts also comes in handy when dealing with some of the rough rocks you'll encounter while exploring in the mountains. Comfortable but sturdy shoes that have good traction are a must in mountain environments. Don't go hiking in a pair of sandals, for instance, or even a loose pair of loafers.

As there is a significant change in temperature in most Colorado localities from one part of the day to another and especially because of changes in altitude, you are likely to encounter a variety of conditions at different times of the same day. Therefore, it is important that you dress in layers. This way you can peel off or add on layers as dictated by the current conditions. While this is of critical importance for those who are going to engage in strenuous outdoor activity, it is strongly recommended even for more casual touring. Experienced skiers already know this but others can learn from their example.

It's very important to make sure that you not only bring a sufficient supply of any prescription medication that you're taking, but to have a copy of the prescription as well. An extra pair of glasses (or, again, a copy of your prescription) also makes sense. At the risk of overstating the obvious, make sure that before you leave home that your tickets and any other documents are in your possession and that you have plenty of film and tape for your cameras or video recorders. I have always found that the best way to make sure that you have everything you need is to make a packing list in advance of your trip and check things off as you pack them. Getaway day is always hectic and even confusing so it's easy to forget something if it isn't written down.

TIPS FOR FOREIGN VISITORS

Tourists from other countries, especially Europe and Japan, are in love with the American west and Colorado isn't an exception.

American customs regulations and formalities are generally quick and easy. Most of the paperwork is done on the plane before arriving in the United States. However, the American embassy or consulate in your home country can familiarize you with the exact requirements, which can vary from one country of origin to another. Passports are always required except for visitors from Canada and Mexico; visas are only needed in a small number of cases. Also find out what the limitations are on what you can bring in or take out of the United States without tax and duties. If you plan to rent a car be sure to have a valid International Drivers License since the only foreign licenses recognized here are those from Canada or Mexico.

A common annoyance to overseas visitors is the fact that America doesn't use the metric system that almost the entire world has adopted. Formulas for conversions vary so much from one type of measurement to another that you shouldn't count on memory. It's best to have quick reference conversion charts for such things as temperature, distances, weights and clothing sizes if you plan to shop. One important item that you should commit to memory is the relationship of kilometers to miles–that will help you avoid a speeding ticket. One kilometer is equivalent to about 6/10 of a mile. So, those 55 and 65 mile per hour speed limits aren't as slow as you might think. Remember that 100 kilometers per hour is equal to 60 miles per hour.

Finally, all of the United States uses 120-volt AC current, so you might well need a transformer for any electrical appliances you bring with you. American plugs have two flat prongs, often with a third round prong for grounding. Inexpensive adapters are the solution to this problem.

COLORADO TOURISM INFORMATION

The idea of this book is to make sure that you have all of the information that you need for a great trip. However, I have never limited myself to a single source of information, so I wouldn't find any fault with you if you wanted to look elsewhere too. Going straight to the source isn't a bad place to begin. Both the state of Colorado as well as many specific resort and tourist destinations are quite happy to provide you with lots of information in the way of brochures, maps and so forth.

Here's a quick rundown on some of the more general sources. Contacts for specific locations can be found in the regional destination chapters.

• **Colorado Travel & Tourism Authority**, *Tel. 800/265-6723*
• **Colorado River Outfitters Association**, *Tel. 303/369-4632*
• **Colorado Ski Country USA**, *Tel. 303/837-0793*
• **Colorado Division of Parks & Recreation**, *1313 Sherman Street, Denver CO 80203. Tel. 303/866-3437*

Good maps are an essential ingredient for any driving trip. While the city maps in this guide are sufficient to get you to many major sights, a statewide road map showing all highways and complete city street maps are beyond the scope of what can be included here due to space limitations. Therefore, make sure you procure the right maps before you begin your trip (or at least no later than your arrival in the state).

Members of the AAA can get an excellent Colorado map from their local office; other good maps are published by a number of companies (Rand McNally and Gousha, for example) and can be found in the travel section of your favorite bookstore. The official state road map provided by the Colorado tourism office is also good. If you are arriving in Colorado by air you can always pick up a map at the airport. Those of you who drive into the state via one of the two Interstate highways will find official visitor information centers not too far past the state line.

BOOKING YOUR VACATION

There are two basic ways of approaching any trip. Pick a destination, get there and then decide what you want to do and where you should stay. The other is to plan in great detail and know exactly where you'll be each night and have room reservations in hand. Of course, there's a wide range in between if you want to combine methods. While there's definitely something positive to be said for the flexibility and spontaneity of the day-to-day or "ad hoc" approach, there are potential serious pitfalls. You can't always count on rooms being available when you show up. NO VACANCY signs are all too common in Colorado's major tourist destinations and

CYBER TRAVEL THROUGH COLORADO

I admit to being guilty of computer heresy–I don't like the Internet. However, there is plenty of information available out there for those of you who are fond of tickling your computer keyboard and giving the ol' modem a workout. Like anything else on the Internet and World Wide Web, there's good stuff available and there's junk. To be safe, stick to the official tourism sources. They have a lot of things to offer and the information will be reliable and up to date. The following are some of the more important addresses you need to know in order to get information high-tech style:

Colorado Travel & Tourism Authority: *http://www.colorado.com*
Colorado Ski Country USA: *http://www.skicolorado.org*
Southwest Colorado Travel Region: *http://www.swcolo.org*
Summit County: *http://www.summitnet.com*
Aspen: *http://www.aspen.com*
Canon City: *http://www.databahn.net/canoncity*
Colorado Springs: *http://www.coloradosprings-travel.com*
Denver: *http://www.denver.org*
Glenwood Springs: *http://www.glenwoodchamber.com*
Grand Junction: *http://www.grand-junction.net*
Pueblo: *http://www.pueblochamber.org*
Vail: *http://www.vail.net/chamber*

Today most hotels and travel-related organizations have their own web sites, many of which will be included in the hotel listings. The sites for airlines, hotel chains and local tourism offices also will be indicated in the text.

resorts, especially in the peak season for each particular area. Not having a place to stay can really be a bummer. So unless you have a great deal of time and are willing to risk the consequences of not having reservations I strongly suggest at least some degree of advance planning for any Colorado trip. If you do want to go "ad hoc" try to avoid traveling during the peak season.

Planning can be a lot of fun and the whole family can get involved. Reading about what you're going to do and see creates a greater sense of anticipation–at least it always does for me. More importantly, for most people it makes it possible to ensure the best use of time you have available for your vacation. Advance reservations are also often a good way to save money on travel and hotels, although I won't deny that when there is space available at the last minute it, too, can be had at a substantial discount.

In this section I'll offer advice on what to book in advance and how to go about doing it, first in a general sense and then on items specific to

Colorado. After you've come up with an itinerary that you like you should be prepared to make advance reservations for (1) air transportation (or other form of common carrier) to and from Colorado–probably Denver but maybe Colorado Springs; (2) lodging, and (3) car rental, unless you're driving your own car to Colorado. In that case hotel reservations are the only thing that you generally have to worry about.

If your itinerary does include any guided tours or unusual activities such as rafting, historic train trips and so forth, be sure to ascertain whether or not advance reservations are required for these things. I'll mention them in each destination's *Seeing the Sights* section where appropriate. If reservations are "suggested" read that as being "required" for peak season travelers. You might save yourself from some big disappointments.

DO YOU NEED A TRAVEL AGENT?

Once you're ready to book your trip, the first question that you have to address is whether to use a professional travel agent or do it on your own. Securing and reading airline schedules isn't at all difficult nor is getting information about hotels, car rentals and other things. That adds up to my own preference of self-booking. (I can feel the glare from all those irate travel agents right now). However, many people simply feel uncomfortable about doing that–they figure why not let a travel agent do the work–they're professionals, know the travel world better and do it for no cost to the consumer. I don't always agree with those assumptions, but it generally boils down to your level of confidence.

Even when using a travel agent you shouldn't always assume that they know so much more than you do about the places you want to go. When selecting a travel agent make sure that they're reliable. Go on references from friends and relatives who were happy with the services of a particular agent. A good indication of their reliability is if the travel agency is a member of the American Society of Travel Agents (ASTA). Membership in that group or other industry organizations should be considered as a minimum requirement when choosing a travel agent.

Regardless of which travel agent you choose, their services should be free of any cost to you. This almost always used to be the case. However, with many airlines cutting back on the commissions they pay agents, some have resorted to the imposition of fees claiming that is the only way they can make a profit. I have no reason to doubt that but why should you pay a fee for something that can be done at no charge? The only time you should have to pay is for special individual planning which is commonly referred to as F.I.T. Although travel agents have on-line access to the best rates I have always found that it's a good idea to check the rates on your own first. You may find that it's better than what the agent tells you. If so, advise him or her of what rate you were quoted and from where. They should easily be able to get the same rate or lower.

It is sometimes difficult if not impossible to, as an individual, book a reservation on certain organized tours. These are often exclusively handled through travel agents. If this is the type of trip you're planning to take then you are probably best off going immediately to a travel agent. Organized tours usually include discounted air options.

INDIVIDUAL TRAVEL VS. ORGANIZED TOURS

I almost always opt for travel on my own instead of being herded into a group. Many tourists do like the group situation for its "people interaction" and the expertise of the guides. However, there are a lot of shortcomings. The first one is that you are on a schedule that someone else sets. And that schedule has a lot of built in down-time to accommodate what will be the slowest person in the group. Organized tours generally dictate where and when you will eat, which is not always to everyone's liking. Careful reading of an organized tour itinerary will show that you do not always spend a lot of time seeing what you want to see. In fact, finding an itinerary that suits your own interests can be the single biggest problem with an organized tour.

While you may feel uncomfortable about being on your own in some exotic foreign destination where the food is strange and people may not speak English, you won't have any such problem while in Colorado. In short, organized tours for Colorado visitors aren't necessary or even advisable for most people, especially those who take the time to read a book like this and get all the information they need to do things on their own. The primary exceptions are for people who do not drive and those who will be traveling alone. Having a group tour, even the worst planned one, is far better than not being able to see anything because you can't drive. It's also better than trying to get around the vast expanse of Colorado with a limited public transportation system. Likewise, while some people don't mind solo travel (and may actually prefer it) I think the majority of you would agree that it's better to share your experiences with someone else, even if that person sitting next to you on the bus was previously a stranger.

Many airlines offer individual travel packages that include hotel and car rental in addition to the airfare. Sometimes these plans can save money but often you can do even better still by arranging everything separately. You see, package "deals" are coordinated by a wholesale tour package company and that middleman has to make a profit too. So the savings that are gotten by bulk purchase of airline seats and hotel rooms aren't always passed on to you like they say in the travel brochures. Also, you should be careful about how restrictive "fly-drive" type packages are. Some are quite flexible but others have a lot of rules regarding which cities you can stay in or the minimum number of nights required. If they fit into your plans, fine; if not, simply build the pieces of your trip block by block.

TOUR OPERATORS

Having said all this, I will give readers who are going to opt for organized tours a few suggestions on who to contact. Travel agents, of course, will be able to provide you with brochures on lots of itineraries covering Colorado. However, I don't care where in North America you travel–if you're going to go the organized bus tour route, the absolute best operators around are Tauck Tours and Maupintours.

Tauck Tours, *Tel. 800/468-2825,* offers an eight day tour beginning and ending in Denver. It emphasizes scenery. The highlights are the Royal Gorge, Durango & Silverton train ride, Mesa Verde National Park, Colorado National Monument, Aspen, Vail, and Rocky Mountain National Park. It gives short treatment to Colorado Springs and nothing to Denver but you can do either or both of those on your own via public transportation either before or after the guided bus tour.

Maupintour, *Tel. 800/255-4266,* has a nine-day Denver to Denver routing. It visits Colorado Springs, Royal Gorge, Durango, Mesa Verde National Park, rides the narrow gauge train to Silverton and tours Colorado National Monument. A unique aspect of this tour is that it crosses the Rockies from Denver to Grand Junction via Amtrak's *California Zephyr* rather than by bus. It, too, can be enhanced by allowing some more time on your own in Denver and Colorado Springs.

In addition to the above operators, visitors can see many attractions through local tour companies in Denver, Colorado Springs and many resort areas. Probably the best known of this genre is Gray Line Tours. **Gray Line of Denver**, *Tel. 800/348-6877 or 303/289-2841* and **Gray Line of Pikes Peak/Colorado Springs**, *Tel. 800/345-8197 or 719/633-1181,* have tours ranging from a few hours to several days. They both have tours that go well beyond the immediate metropolitan areas of their names.

GETTING THE BEST AIRFARE

Even travel agents have trouble pinning down what the best airfare is on a given flight on a given day. It's like trying to hit a moving object. If you call one airline ten times and ask what it will cost to fly from New York to Denver on the morning of July 10th and return on the afternoon of July 20th you'll probably get several different responses. I wouldn't even rule out the possibility of ten different fares, although that's probably an exaggeration. Unfortunately, such is the state of the airline fare game.

There are, however, a couple of things to keep in mind about getting a good rate.

Midweek travel (Tuesday through Thursday for sure, but may include Monday afternoon and Friday morning depending upon the route and airline) is lower priced than weekend travel. Holiday periods are, of course, higher. Fares are also higher during peak travel seasons. Denver wouldn't generally vary as much from month to month as a resort destination would. Night flights are considerably less expensive than daytime travel if you don't mind arriving on the "red-eye" special.

Advance confirmed reservations that are paid for prior to your flight are almost always the cheapest way to go. The restrictions on these low fares vary considerably. In general you must book and pay for your tickets at least seven to 30 days in advance. In most cases they require that you stay over a Saturday night. They usually are non-refundable or require payment of a large penalty to either cancel or even make a change in the flight itinerary. So be sure when and where you want to go before reserving.

You can sometimes find big bargains by doing the opposite strategy– waiting for the last minute. If the airline has empty seats on the flight you select they're often willing to fill it up for a ridiculously low price–after all, they figure that some money in their pocket is better than none at all. The problem with this is that you don't know if there will be an available seat at the time you want to go. If you have definite reservations for everything else during your trip this can be a most dangerous game to play. If you do get a ticket at the last minute it can also wind up being at the full price, which is quite high in most cases.

In this era of deregulation, airfares from one airline to another can sometimes be radically different, although carriers flying the same routes will often adjust their fares to the competition more often than not. Some of the low-cost carriers are as good as the major airlines. Read that as meaning they have an equally impressive safety record. In the case of travel to Colorado the most prominent discount airline that you should definitely consider is **Frontier Airlines**, *Tel. 800/432-1FLY.*

One thing you should always be on the lookout for regardless of who you plan to fly with are promotional fares. Scan the newspapers or just call the airlines. It's always best to phrase your inquiry something like "What is the lowest available fare between x and y on date z?"

Finally, I know that those accustomed to first class air are going to squirm in their seats at this but the cost of first class is simply not worth it–you're only going to be on the plane for a few hours. Given Colorado's location it is unlikely that your flight would be much more than three to four hours and considerably less in many cases. That's obviously not the same as being on a week long cruise where you want to be pampered every minute. Go tourist class, or whatever name a particular airline calls it, bring along a good book and enjoy the flight.

FLYING TO COLORADO

Colorado's busiest airport and the one with the greatest choice of airlines and flights is **Denver International Airport.** You shouldn't overlook the possibility of using **Colorado Springs Municipal Airport.** Many Colorado vacations will encompass both cities, which are less than two hours apart. The latter is far less congested (and therefore subject to less delays). In addition, in order to promote use of Colorado Springs as a flight destination you may be able to find it easier to get lower fares to that location than to Denver. Some major airlines and a host of regional carriers have flights (generally from Denver) to many other locations in Colorado for those who will be skipping the big city scene altogether. Another way to avoid the big city airport scene is by flying into one of many of the state's numerous regional airports. Details will be found in the regional destination chapters, but among the places you can get to are Aspen, Durango, Montrose, Telluride and Vail. These are served directly from Phoenix via America West Airlines, while Skywest can take you into Grand Junction from Salt Lake City.

Here's a more detailed look at all of the carriers serving Denver and Colorado Springs:

DENVER

• **America West**, *Tel. 800/2-FLY AWA, www.americawest.com.* Non-stop service to Las Vegas and their system hub in Phoenix.

• **American Airlines**, *Tel. 800/624-6262, www.aa.com.* Flies non-stop from Denver to Chicago, Dallas/Fort Worth, Los Angeles, Miami and San Jose.

• **Continental Airlines**, *Tel. 800/525-0280, www.flycontinental.com.* Non-stop service to their hubs in Houston and New York (Newark) as well as to Cleveland.

• **Delta**, *Tel. 800/221-1212, www.delta-air.com.* Non-stop service to their hubs in Atlanta, Cincinnati, Dallas/Fort Worth and to New York and Salt Lake City.

• **Frontier Airlines**, *Tel. 800/432-1359, www.frontierairlines.com.* This Denver based carrier (and one of the biggest at DIA) flies non-stop to Albuquerque, Atlanta, Baltimore, Chicago, Dallas/Fort Worth, Kansas City, Las Vegas, Los Angeles, Minneapolis/St. Paul, New York, Omaha, Orlando, Phoenix, Portland (OR), Salt Lake City, San Diego, San Francisco, Seattle and Washington.

- **Northwest Airlines**, *TEL. 800/225-2525, www.nwa.com.* Non-stop service to their system hubs in Detroit, Memphis and Minneapolis/St. Paul.
- **TWA**, *Tel. 800/221-2000, www.twa.com.* Non-stop service to their system hub in St. Louis.
- **United Airlines**, *Tel. 800/241-6522, www.ual.com.* Denver's largest carrier has one of their biggest hubs at DIA. The list of non-stop destinations that follows includes some, but not all, of the smaller United Express services. Albuquerque, Amarillo, Atlanta, Austin, Baltimore, Boise, Boston, Calgary, Cedar Rapids, Chicago, Cleveland, Columbus (OH), Dallas/Fort Worth, Des Moines, Detroit, Fresno, Hartford, Houston, Indianapolis, Jackson, Kansas City, Las Vegas, Lincoln, Los Angeles (also Burbank, Ontario and Orange County airports), Memphis, Miami, Minneapolis/St. Paul, Nashville, New Orleans, New York, Oakland, Oklahoma City, Omaha, Orlando, Philadelphia, Phoenix, Portland (OR), Rapid City, Reno, Sacramento, St. Louis, Salt Lake City, San Antonio, San Diego, San Francisco, San Jose, Seattle, Sioux Falls, Spokane, Tampa, Toronto, Tucson, Tulsa, Vancouver, Washington and Wichita.
- **USAirways**, *Tel. 800/428-4322, www.usairways.com.* Non-stop to Charlotte, Philadelphia and Pittsburgh.

Other notable carriers with service to Denver are ATA, Mesa Airlines and Midwest. Foreign carriers include Air Canada, British Airways, Lufthansa and Mexicana.

COLORADO SPRINGS

See the listings above for airline telephone numbers and web sites. Seven major carriers provide non-stop service from Colorado Springs to a dozen different cities (where you can make connections to many other destinations). These are **AmericaWest** (Phoenix); **American Airlines** (Dallas/Fort Worth and Los Angeles); **Continental** (Houston); **Delta** (Atlanta, Cincinnati, Dallas/Fort Worth and Salt Lake City); **Northwest Airlines** (Minneapolis/St. Paul); **TWA** (St. Louis); and **United Airlines** (Chicago and Denver). The Colorado Springs airport is also served by Delta's **Skywest** affiliate and **Mesa Air**.

See the *Getting Around Colorado By Air* section for more information on the latter two.

GETTING AROUND COLORADO

BY AIR

The major intra-state carrier in Colorado is United Airlines. They serve eight regional airports in addition to Denver and Colorado Springs. There are flights from Denver via their United Express air shuttle service to Aspen, Cortez, Durango, Eagle County Airport (Glenwood Springs and Vail), Grand Junction, Gunnison, Montrose and Telluride. If you are flying to one of these "express" locations from out of state it is generally less expensive, if you can, to book entirely with United than to take another airline into Denver and then transfer to United Express or one of the other local carriers. United Express reservations can be made through the regular United system, *Tel. 800/241-6522.*

Other carriers in Colorado are Mesa Airlines and Skywest. They have much more limited networks within Colorado although both have some direct flights into some of the state's smaller localities from Salt Lake City and Phoenix. **Mesa Airlines**, *Tel. 800/637-2247*, is affiliated with America West and allows for smooth transitions between the two company's extensive southwest route system. **Skywest**, *Tel. 800/453-9417*, has working relationships with both Delta (the "Delta Connection") and United.

BY BUS

Greyhound, *Tel. 800/231-2222, www.greyhound.com,* is the only interstate carrier with service to Colorado. They serve many smaller communities in addition to the major cities. It is the only form of public transportation to a lot of places. Information on routes, schedules, and fares can be obtained by calling them. Local bus station telephone numbers are included under *Practical Information* in the regional destination chapters only where the station is staffed. This also applies to train stations.

BY CAR

I'll say it one last time–the best way to get around Colorado is by car, whether it's your own or a rental. Besides being the most time and cost effective method, it also offers the traveler a degree of flexibility that cannot be matched by any form of public transportation. While it isn't necessarily true for getting around in the heart of Denver, it does apply to just about every other urban area in Colorado and certainly once you get out into the more lightly populated regions.

Driving in Colorado shouldn't be a problem for most people if you stick to the main tourist routes. The Interstate highways are excellent even when they pass through high mountain terrain. Most of the major United States and Colorado secondary highways are almost as good although there may be brief sections that can be said to be mountain roads.

Once you leave the major roads in the higher elevations you'll likely encounter steep grades, hairpin turns and switchbacks, and narrow traffic lanes. Often the roads are on the edge of a precipice and may or may not have comforting guard rails. If you are inexperienced on such roads it doesn't mean that you can't take your Colorado dream vacation. Even experienced mountain motorists know to take it slow and always keep your eye on the road, not on the scenery. Many routes have pullouts where you can stop to admire nature's handiwork. When traveling on unpaved roads, of which there are quite a few in the mountains, go even slower to avoid having objects fly up and hit your windshield. High clearance vehicles and four-wheel drive are usually advisable on such roads and absolutely necessary on the more difficult ones. In the touring sections I'll let you know if you should not attempt to reach a specific location with an ordinary car (that is, two-wheel drive and regular clearance).

Colorado has 36 major mountain passes that range in altitude from about 8,700 feet to more than 12,000 feet. A sign that you're approaching a pass needn't be cause for panic even for the relative newcomer to mountain driving. Most of the passes are quite easy, with grades of 7% or less. Although these will usually require lower gear and decreased speed, that's the only difference from regular driving. There are some pass grades in the steep 8-9% range and only a few in excess of that.

Be prepared at any time of the year for sudden changes in weather. Thunderstorms, besides making the roads slippery, can temporarily reduce visibility to the point where seeing ahead becomes difficult. Winter travelers should have snow tires at a minimum, even if you're going to be sticking to the main routes. Chains are essential winter gear in the back country. Never attempt to negotiate an unpaved road after a heavy rain unless you have checked locally about driving conditions. Likewise, you shouldn't head out on unimproved roads if the weather is threatening. You can get current **road condition information** by calling *Tel. 303/639-1234*. Information on roads within a 50-mile radius of Denver can be obtained by calling *Tel. 303/639-1111*.

In the lower elevations (or at least on terrain that isn't mountainous) driving in Colorado is like any other place in America. Expect heavy traffic in Denver and even in Colorado Springs as well as in popular resort destinations where the road system wasn't designed to handle the huge tourist crush. Once you get away from the most populous and most

COLORADO'S BYWAYS

One of the nicest ways to explore the beauty of Colorado is by traveling on some of the state's more than 20 designated scenic and historic byways. Some of the best are listed here. You'll find additional information on most in the regional destination chapters as shown below.

COLORADO SPRINGS *(Chapter 12):*

• **Gold Belt:** *131 miles. History and scenery come alive along the route through Florissant, Cripple Creek, Victor, Florence and Canon City. Portions require 4WD.*

NORTH CENTRAL ROCKIES *(Chapter 13):*

• **Colorado River Headwaters Byway:** *80 miles. Here one of America's mightiest rivers is little more than a picturesque creek amid the mountains.*

• **Mount Evans Byway:** *56 miles. The highest paved road in the United States. It's always cold up here so dress warm! 4WD is suggested.*

• **Peak to Peak Byway:** *55 miles. Easy and highly scenic drive with the great wall of the Continental Divide mountains immediately to your west.*

• **Top of the Rockies:** *75 miles. You'll see Colorado's highest peaks and rich mining heritage in this stretch of the Rockies between Granite and Minturn.*

• **Trail Ridge Road:** *48 miles. Traverses beautiful Rocky Mountain National Park.*

NORTHWEST *(Chapter 14):*

• **Grand Mesa Byway:** *63 miles. "End of the world" scenery in this remote area of mountains and plateaus.*

SOUTHWEST *(Chapter 15):*

• **Alpine Loop Back Country Byway:** *63 miles. Glorious mountain passes and numerous ghost towns. A difficult road that requires 4WD and is for experienced mountain drivers only.*

• **Highway of Legends:** *82 miles. An easy drive past the Spanish Peaks and the Sangre de Cristos through historic Trinidad, La Veta and Waslsenburg.*

• **San Juan Skyway:** *236 miles. Connecting Durango, Ridgway, Telluride and Cortez, this route is a cornucopia of delights through the magnificent San Juan range.*

• **Trail of the Ancients:** *114 miles, From the Utah line at Hovenweep National Monument, the drive is all on "US" highways through the historic Four Corners region.*

• **West Elk Loop:** *205 miles. A relatively easy drive between Carbondale and Crested Butte through magnificent mountain meadows that most visitors never get to see.*

popular areas, Colorado is a lightly traveled place and you'll often find that you have the road more or less to yourself.

This book will use several prefixes to designate various roads. The letter "I" before a number indicates an Interstate highway. "US" will precede a United States highway while Colorado state road numbers are indicated by "CO." Roads that don't fall into any of the preceding three categories will also be identified by names such as "Forest Route" or for "County Route."

When it comes to familiarizing yourself with Colorado's road system there's simply no substitute for carefully studying a good road map. However, you should know a few major routes and that I can do for you here. It makes more sense to read this section with a map in front of you. I-70 crosses Colorado from east to west, generally just above the middle of the state. Exit numbers indicate the mileage from the western border. I-25 traverses the state from north to south just east of the Rocky Mountain ranges with exit numbers corresponding to the mileage from the southern border. The two interstates cross in Denver. A third Interstate, I-76 crosses into Colorado in the northeast corner from Nebraska and ends at I-70 in the Denver area.

The major east-west United States highways are **US 40** in the central and north; and **US 50** in the south and middle. Other important US roads are 24, 34, and 36. **US 6** also cuts across the entire state but it is coincidental with **I-70** for most of its route. Significant north-south highways are **US 550** in the southwest, **US 285** in the center, and **US 385** in the east.

Renting a Car

If you thought that trying to get a straight answer on airfares was difficult you'll be disappointed to learn that things won't be much easier when it comes to renting a car. Here, too, there are a jumble of rates depending upon a host of factors. However, a few basic rules apply at most rental companies that will put things into sharper focus. First of all it is almost always less expensive to rent a car if you return it to the same location. In other words, a loop trip is more economical than renting in one place and returning the car somewhere else. There are exceptions to this rule so be sure to check it out both ways if a one-way itinerary seems to be better for you. Typically only the major car rental companies will allow a one-way rental, and if it is in the same state (say Colorado Springs to Denver or vice versa) they may not impose a "drop off" charge.

The second thing to look for in a rental is whether there's a mileage charge in addition to the basic daily or weekly rate. If there is, avoid it unless you plan to only use the car minimally. Colorado is big enough that the miles add up fairly fast. When you tack on what you're paying per mile

COLORADO DRIVING DISTANCES

	Colo. Springs	Denver	Durango	Grand Junction	Lamar	Sterling	Vail
Alamosa	165	235	150	263	205	354	174
Aspen	150	163	274	134	310	394	95
Colo. Springs	–	70	313	291	161	190	169
Denver	70	–	370	258	206	120	99
Durango	313	370	–	170	352	490	226
Fort Collins	132	62	432	316	268	100	161
Glenwood Springs	235	166	232	92	348	288	232
Grand Junction	291	258	170	–	405	378	150
Lamar	161	206	352	405	–	245	305
Limon	75	90	388	348	118	127	189
Montrose	230	261	110	60	345	381	182
Pueblo	42	112	270	285	120	232	211
Salida	100	140	230	191	215	260	101
Steamboat Springs	245	175	367	197	380	270	94
Sterling	190	120	490	378	245	–	219
Vail	169	99	226	150	305	219	–
Walsenburg	90	160	223	334	130	280	260

to the rate that you were quoted it won't be the great buy you thought it was. You should always inquire about weekly rentals because these are often less expensive than if you take a simple daily plan. Often you can wind up getting one or two days per week for free when you go weekly.

MAJOR CAR RENTAL COMPANY PHONE NUMBERS

	Nationwide Toll-Free	Denver Airport/Local	Colo. Springs Airport/Local
Alamo	800/327-9633	–	719/574-8519
Avis	800/831-2847	303/389-1280	719/596-2751
Budget	800/227-3678	303/342-7212	719/473-6535
Dollar	800/800-4000	303/342-9099	719/637-2620
Enterprise	800/325-8007	303/757-7242	719/636-3900
Hertz	800/654-3131	303/355-2244	719/596-1863
National	800/227-7368	303/342-0717	719/596-1519
Thrifty	800/367-2277	303/342-9400	719/390-9800

Other things to keep in mind are having the proper insurance. Every rental company will try to sell you coverage at significantly inflated prices. Check with your insurance agent at home if you can't determine whether or not your auto insurance covers a rental car. If it doesn't, then you have to decide whether or not to take a chance and waive the rental insurance coverage. Turning to another area, if more than one person is going to be driving, tell that to the renting agent because that has to be put on the agreement. Some companies charge a small fee for this, although I can't figure out what their justification is other than trying to make a few extra bucks.

Finally, ask about what discounts the car rental company offers. Members of AAA, AARP, some car insurance companies, as well as many major employers and other organizations that you may belong to have agreements with some of the biggest car rental firms. The savings in these cases are usually about ten percent off the regular rates.

Renting a car in either Denver or Colorado Springs is no problem. All of the major companies are represented. The sidebar on the previous page covers reservation numbers for the largest rental companies.

Despite the money-saving names of many of the major companies, there are few bargains. If you want to save some money it's worth looking into the rates offered by some local or regional renters. These will almost certainly require that you return the car to the same location. A couple of possibilities within Colorado are **Advantage**, *Tel. 303/342-0990*, and **Value**, *Tel. 800/GO-VALUE.*

BY TRAIN

Scheduled passenger train service in Colorado is better than in many other parts of the west. Although it can't be relied on to see most places in Colorado because of the limited number of routes and stations, you can get to a number of locations throughout the state and make your way from there by rental car or local tours. The main line through Colorado does provide a pleasant way to view the passing scenery.

Once daily service in each direction is provided on Amtrak's *California Zephyr* which runs from Chicago to San Francisco. Colorado stations are located at Fort Morgan, Denver, Winter Park, Granby, Glenwood Springs, and Grand Junction. The *Southwest Chief*, same frequency of service between Chicago and Los Angeles, touches the southeastern portion of Colorado with stations at Lamar, La Junta, and Trinidad. Amtrak also has connecting bus service between the two lines (Trinidad and Denver stations and north to Wyoming) which more or less parallels I-25.

Schedule, fare, and other information is available by contacting **Amtrak**, *Tel. 800/USA-RAIL.* If you intend to do quite a bit of travel by Amtrak then you should look into their **North America Rail Pass** which allows unlimited travel within a thirty day period for a fixed price. In addition, Colorado does have a number of unconnected railroads that cater to tourists. See the sidebar on the next page.

SCENIC RAILROAD EXCURSIONS

Whether you reach the starting points of these train excursions by air, car, or bus, they all represent a great way to see some of Colorado's most beautiful scenery. You'll find more information in the appropriate destination chapters.

Cumbres and Toltec Scenic Railroad: *Runs along the Colorado/ New Mexico border area from the town of Antonito through pleasant mountain scenery.*

Cripple Creek Narrow Gauge Railroad: *Short ride on restored train through historic mining and ghost towns.*

Durango and Silverton Narrow Gauge Railroad: *The grand-daddy of America's scenic railroads is one of the great rides in all the world. See the San Juan Mountains, Animas River Gorge, old town of Silverton, and more.*

Georgetown Loop Railroad: *Another short mining country tour highlighted by an engineering wonder–the train track circles over itself!*

Leadville, Colorado & Southern Railroad Company: *ditto above but with some of the best scenery in the Rockies.*

Pike's Peak Cog Railway: *Swiss built cars ascend 8,000 feet on a 26% grade. Pass through several climatic zones and reach the top where a wonderful panorama awaits you.*

Royal Gorge Route: *A powerful diesel locomotive reminiscent of those once used in luxury cross country rail travel traverses wonderful scenery through the famous Royal Gorge of the Arkansas River.*

Winter Park Ski Train: *Operates only during ski-season weekends. Fun way to get from Denver to the ski slopes, or just for winter sightseeing. Crosses the Continental Divide and goes through nearly 30 tunnels.*

ACCOMMODATIONS

Once you've decided upon where you're going in Colorado and come up with an itinerary, the next biggest decision for most people is picking out places to stay. An unpleasant hotel or motel experience can be a big downer while an unusually nice place will become part of your fond vacation memories. Giving advice on where to stay is difficult because different travelers are looking for very different things when it comes to lodging.

The cost of lodging is only one factor. Some people just want a clean and comfortable room to plop themselves down for the night while many others want to be pampered in luxurious surroundings and take advantage of many of the amenities of either a first class hotel or resort. I have selected a total of 179 hotels that run the gamut from simple budget motels to some of the most renowned resorts in the world. There is an emphasis on the higher end of the scale because there's a lot more that needs to be said about them than for a small roadside motel. Colorado lodging prices tend to be on the higher side in the big cities and in the resorts.

This section will point out several things that should be kept in mind about lodging. Most are generic to travel anywhere. Colorado lodging tends toward the casual side although there are several resorts that would certainly appeal to the rich and famous. Ski resorts are, by nature, especially informal although you wouldn't necessarily realize it from the prices.

Regardless of what type of lodging you choose it is plain common sense to have advance reservations in all popular resort and tourist areas. Even those places that are more off the beaten track often fill up fast during the summer months. Finding rooms in or near the major national parks can be especially difficult. And in winter the ski resorts are often booked solid just by group ski package tours, so always try to secure your room as soon as you have definite dates in mind.

Most chain properties do not require that you pay in advance so long as you arrive before 6:00pm. However, it's a good idea to guarantee a late arrival with your credit card. Many times the reservations agent will ask you for this information. Smaller and independent establishments and many resort properties require that you do pay in advance, at least for the first night's stay. Be sure you understand and comply with payment regulations and cancellation rules at the time you make your booking.

Reservations can be made in a number of ways All major chains and many independent hotels accept reservations made through travel agents. You can make reservations on your own by contacting the hotel directly or via a chain's central reservation system. It is also becoming increasingly common for independent establishments to belong to associations which handle reservations through a toll-free number.

There are many general and specialized reservation services for hotels throughout Colorado, most of which can also be made free of charge. For specific areas (e.g., Aspen, Vail, Estes Park, etc.), see the listing under "Hotel Hot Line" in the Practical Information section of each regional destination chapter. Many of these reservation services will also be happy to arrange complete package tours in addition to lodging.

A few of the statewide or specialized reservation services are listed below:

- **Bed & Breakfast Innkeepers of Colorado**, *Tel. 800/265-7697; : www.innsofcolorado.org*
- **Bed & Breakfast Rocky Mountains**, *Tel. 800/825-0225*
- **Colorado Dude & Guest Ranch Association**, *Tel. 970/724-3653; www.coloradoranch.com*
- **Colorado Central Reservations**, *Tel. 800/224-8359*
- **Colorado Hotel & Lodging Association**, *Tel. 303/297-8335; www.coloradolodging.com*

Hotel prices for the same room can vary tremendously depending upon the time of the year, the day of the week, and whether or not you can qualify for discounted rates. Don't be bashful when making reservations. Balk at what you believe to be a high price and they may well do better by miraculously finding that they have one more room left at a special price!

The recommended lodging listings in this book are arranged by location. They are further broken down in each touring chapter alphabetically by city. In larger cities they're divided by the area as well. Then they'll be broken down one last time by price category. The category is based upon the price during the peak season but if there is a substantial variation then prices will be shown for peak and low seasons and the dates of each season will be given. The rates shown are known as the rack rate. That means what the normal rate for the room is.

Furthermore, the quoted price will always refer to the room rate (not the per person) rate but are based on double occupancy unless otherwise indicated. Single rates are often the same or only slightly less than the double rate. Hotel policies concerning additional charges, if any, for children in the same room vary considerably. If you plan to have your children stay in the same room as you, then it's wise to inquire with the individual hotel as to the charge.

All prices listed in this book are for the room only (no meals) unless otherwise indicated. The majority of hotels, with the exception of a few resorts, charge on this basis, often known as the **European Plan**. When another plan is involved it will be indicated. A **Continental Plan** includes a small breakfast consisting primarily of pastry and beverage. Depending upon the hotel and your appetite this may or may not be sufficient to satisfy your morning hunger pangs. A Breakfast Plan includes a full breakfast. The **Modified American Plan** (MAP) includes breakfast and diner and is rarely found these days outside of resort facilities. Some hotels, however, do offer optional plans where you can add on meals for a fixed rate.

On-premise restaurants will be indicated and also mentioned if there is a separate listing for it in the "Where to Eat" section. The hotels listed in this book have private baths in every room (except for two with some shared baths that will be so noted). The quoted prices are for what can be termed "regular" guest rooms. More elaborate facilities, especially in luxury hotels and resorts, are almost always available at even higher prices (sometimes running into as much as four figures for a single night!). Because many facilities have a wide variety of accommodations, price ranges aren't an exact science–they may overlap two or three categories. Prices were accurate as of press time but keep in mind that hotel rates have been rising faster than the rate of inflation over the past several years and will likely continue to do so.

Since virtually all hotels now have at least a portion of their rooms designated as "non-smoking" I haven't made any indication of this policy in the individual hotel listings. Many facilities, especially Bed and Breakfast inns and small hotels are entirely smoke free.

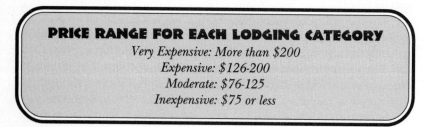

PRICE RANGE FOR EACH LODGING CATEGORY

Very Expensive: More than $200
Expensive: $126-200
Moderate: $76-125
Inexpensive: $75 or less

MAJOR HOTEL CHAINS

In each destination chapter you will find many suggested places to stay, most of which are independent establishments or upscale chains. Many travelers do, however, prefer the convenience of making reservations with nationwide hotel companies and like the "no surprises" rooms and facilities of these chains. I myself often use them. Thus, this list will help supplement the destination chapter listings. The more upscale chains (such as Doubletree, Hilton, Hyatt, Marriott, Radisson and Sheraton) aren't included here because many of their Colorado properties will be found in the suggested hotels in the chapters that follow. Other chain properties are generally only listed in the main text if they are among the best choices in a given location.

The following are major nationwide chains that have a strong presence throughout Colorado. An asterisk (*) next to the location indicates that it is described in greater detail in the appropriate *Where to Stay* section.

BEST WESTERN, *Tel. 800/528-1234, www.bestwestern.com*. Properties in Alamosa*, Basalt, Boulder, Brush, Canon City, Castle Rock, Clifton, Colorado Springs*, Cortez, Craig, Delta, Denver*, Dillon, Durango, Eagle, Englewood, Estes Park, Fort Collins, Fort Morgan*, Frisco, Glenwood Springs*, Grand Junction*, Greeley, Lakewood, Lamar, Las Animas, Limon, Loveland, Monte Vista, Montrose*, Nederland, Ouray, Pagosa Springs, Pueblo*, Salida, Steamboat Springs*, Sterling*, Stratton, Trinidad, Vail, Walsenburg* and Winter Park.

CHOICE HOTELS: The general reservation number and web site for any Choice property is *Tel. 800/4-CHOICE, www.choicehotels.com* **Comfort Inn**, *Tel. 800/228-5150*. Alamosa, Aurora, Avon, Brighton, Burlington, Canon City, Carbondale, Colorado Springs, Cortez, Delta, Denver, Dillon, Durango, Eagle, Estes Park, Fruita, Fort Collins, Golden, Grand Junction, Highlands Ranch, Lakewood, Limon, Longmont, Louisville, Loveland, Monte Vista, Montrose, Ouray, Pueblo, Salida, South Fork, Steamboat Springs and Westminster. **Econolodge**, *Tel. 800/553-2666*. Colorado Springs, Cortez, Durango, Fort Morgan, Gunnison, Limon, Pueblo and Salida. **Quality Inn**, *Tel. 800/228-5151*. Boulder, Castle Rock, Colorado Springs, Denver, Durango, Englewood, Evergreen, Fort Collins, Glenwood Springs, La Junta, Lakewood, Louisville, Pueblo and Wheat Ridge. **Rodeway Inn**, *Tel. 800/228-2000*. Colorado Springs, Denver and Durango. **Sleep Inn**, *Tel. 800/753-3746*. Aurora, Colorado Springs, Evans, Fort Collins, Greenwood Village, Pueblo and Thornton. There are no Clarion hotels in Colorado; however, Choice's new **Mainstay Suite** brand has several locations in the Denver area.

DAYS INN, *Tel. 800/329-7466, www.daysinn.com*. Alamosa, Boulder, Canon City, Carbondale, Castle Rock, Colorado Springs, Cortez, Denver, Durango, Fort Collins, Fort Morgan, Golden, Grand Junction, Greeley, Gunnison, Lamar, Longmont, Montrose, Northglenn, Pueblo, Salida, Silverthorne, Steamboat Springs, Sterling, Trinidad and Walsenburg.

HAMPTON INN, *Tel. 800/426-7866, www.hamptoninn.com*. Aurora, Colorado Springs, Denver, Durango, Englewood, Fort Collins, Glendale, Glenwood Springs, Golden, Lakewood, Longmont, Louisville, Loveland, Pueblo Thornton and Westminster.

HOLIDAY INN, *Tel. 800/HOLIDAY (Including Crowne Plaza & Holiday Inn Express), www.holiday-inn.com*. Alamosa, Aurora, Boulder, Broomfield, Canon City, Castle Rock, Colorado Springs, Cortez, Craig, Cripple Creek, Denver, Dillon Lake, Durango, Eagle, Englewood, Estes Park, Fort Collins, Frisco, Glenwood Springs, Golden, Grand Junction, Greeley, Gunnison, Henderson, La Junta, Lakewood, Littleton, Loveland, Montrose, Northglenn, Pagosa Springs, Pueblo, Salida, Steamboat Springs, Trinidad, Westminster and Wheat Ridge.

LA QUINTA INNS, *Tel. 800/NU-ROOMS, www.laquinta.com*. Aurora, Colorado Springs, Denver, Englewood, Golden, Grand Junction, Lakewood, Louisville, Pueblo and Westminster.

MARRIOTT: Courtyard by Marriott, *Tel. 800/321-2211, www.courtyard.com*. Boulder, Colorado Springs, Denver, Fort Collins, Lakewood and Louisville. **Fairfield Inn**, *Tel. 800/228-2800; Web site: www.fairfieldinn.com*. Aurora, Colorado Springs, Denver, Greeley, Highlands Ranch, Lakewood, Loveland and Steamboat Springs. **Residence Inn**, *Tel. 800/331-3131; Web site: www.residenceinn.com*. Boulder, Colorado Springs, Denver, Durango, Englewood, Fort Collins, Highlands Ranch, Lakewood and Westminster. Note that actual Marriott Hotels can be found in the destination chapter listings.

MOTEL 6, *Tel. 800/466-8356, www.motel6.com*. Aurora, Colorado Springs, Denver, Evans, Fort Lupton, Fort Collins, Grand Junction, Greenwood Village, Lakewood, Pueblo, Thornton and Wheat Ridge.

RAMADA INN, *Tel. 800/272-6232, www.ramada.com*. Boulder, Colorado Springs, Craig, Denver, Durango, Englewood, Frisco, Glenwood Springs, Grand Junction, Gunnison, Keystone, Lakewood, Northglenn, Pueblo and Sterling.

SUPER 8, *Tel. 800/800-8000, www.super8.com*. Alamosa, Aurora, Boulder, Brighton, Buena Vista, Burlington, Canon City, Castle Rock, Cedaredge, Colorado Springs, Cortez, Craig, Cripple Creek, Denver, Dillon, Durango, Englewood, Estes Park, Fort Collins, Fort Morgan, Florence, Fountain, Fruita, Georgetown, Grand Junction, Greeley, Gunnison, Henderson, La Junta, Lakewood, Lamar, Leadville, Limon, Longmont, Loveland, Manitou Springs, Montrose, Pagosa Springs, Parachute, Pueblo, Ridgway, Salida, Steamboat Springs, Sterling, Trinidad, Westminster, Wheat Ridge and Winter Park.

TRAVELODGE, *Tel. 800/578-7878, www.travelodge.com*. Colorado Springs, Cortez, Craig, Denver, Durango, Estes Park*, Evans, Lamar, Longmont and Salida.

CAMPING & RECREATIONAL VEHICLES

Camping sites or places to hook up an RV are in as much demand these days as hotel rooms. So, once again, early advance planning is an absolute must. Reservations are not always accepted for camping on public lands. Inquire as to whether or not they operate on a first come, first served or reservation basis. Campsites and RV facilities range from back to nature "roughing it" to, in some commercially run establishments, facilities that have almost as many amenities as an average motel. Also, be sure to check if the facility is open when you plan to travel. Many are restricted to the summer season.

Aside from commercial RV parks that are often located near natural areas you'll find both camping sites and RV facilities in almost all national parks. Campsites are a part of many Colorado state parks except for "day use" type facilities that are generally located near to the larger cities. Most also have RV hookups. Many sites are also located in the numerous national forests that cover Colorado. Only a small fee is charged in these places. However, while you can just show up at sites within national forests, a permit is required for camping in national parks. The permits are free and can be obtained at the visitor center of the park you are visiting.

General information on camping and RV hookups in state parks can be obtained by contacting either individual parks or the Colorado Division of Parks & Recreation. For national parks it is best to contact each facility directly. The major national forests and their Supervisor Office phone numbers can be found in a sidebar in Chapter 8.

For a sampling of commercially operated sites at major localities throughout the state, see the listings in each regional chapter. Major chain operators of campgrounds, such as KOA, offer nationwide directories and reservation services. You can also get camping information from the **Colorado Agency for Campgrounds**, *Tel. 888/222-4641,* or the **Colorado Campground & Lodging Owners Association**, *Tel. 303/659-5252.*

7. BASIC INFORMATION

This chapter is for potpourri lovers. It covers a wide range of useful information, most of it specific to Colorado. Entries are arranged alphabetically.

ADVENTURE TRAVEL

Adventure travel has become one of the most significant trends in the travel industry during the last decade. More and more people are no longer content to just "see" the world–they want to be physically thrilled by their travel experience. Growth has been fueled to a large extent by the increasing number of tour operators specializing in out of the ordinary activities. Of course, individual adventure travel is also extremely popular, in part due to the exponential increase in the number of four wheel and off road vehicles.

To put it simply, a lot of people simply aren't satisfied with keeping their feet planted solidly on the ground and walking or riding by car from one sightseeing attraction to another. If you like to get involved in the action and aren't frightened by vigorous activity and means of transportation that have an element of risk (at least in the minds of more traditional travelers) then you are ready for adventure travel. There are few places in the world that are more suited to this type of experience than Colorado.

Adventure travel includes a diverse number of activities such as rock or mountain climbing, river running, mountain biking, horseback trips, overnight camping (and not in a comfortable RV), hot air ballooning, dude ranching, and much more. All of these are readily available in Colorado, its rugged mountain terrain and large wilderness areas a natural draw for the outdoor enthusiasts who comprise the biggest section of the adventure traveling public.

General information on the most popular types of adventure travel in Colorado can be found in the next chapter on Sports & Recreation. In addition, reputable operators can be found under specific categories in the various destination chapters. All regions of Colorado have their own share of adventure travel opportunities, although they are much more severely limited in the eastern High Plains portion of the state.

Among the many excellent sources of information on adventure travel in Colorado are:

• **American Wilderness Experience**, *Tel. 800/444-0099*
• **Colorado River Outfitters Association**, *Tel. 303/280-2554*
• **Rocky Mountain Holiday Tours**, *Tel. 970/482-5813*

ALCOHOLIC BEVERAGE LAWS

The minimum age for drinking in Colorado is 21. Anyone driving with a blood-alcohol concentration in excess of 0.10 percent is considered to be under the influence. DUI law enforcement in Colorado is among the toughest in the nation. Penalties for first time offense can include jail or community service. Visitors aren't likely to get the latter and I'm sure you don't want to spend your vacation in one of Colorado's prisons.

ALTERNATIVE TRAVEL

Over the past few years another new industry has grown up within the overall travel industry. Going under various different names, I refer to it as alternative travel. It covers an enormously large range of possibilities–everything from trips designed for specific segments of the population (e.g., senior citizens, gay and lesbian travelers, singles, etc.) to people interested in specific aspects of travel such as the environment, social history of various ethnic or national groups and so forth. The possibilities are so specialized and endless that you could probably find a group for single females between the ages of 20 and 30 who want to combine their travels with doing work for the underprivileged in poverty stricken rural areas. You might think I'm going a bit too far with that last group but the point is that there is virtually no limit to what can be put together in the category of alternative travel.

I am by no means the expert in the needs and interests of all these special groups and, frankly, in most cases don't even see a great need for many aspects of "alternative travel." A broad-based vacation experience provides more than enough opportunity for intellectual improvement and interpersonal communication. However, at least a part of the traveling public is asking for this type of information and like the focus that these types of vacations can bring to a trip. So, I would be remiss if I didn't provide you with at least some basic information. For most people who would like to travel within their own "group" it is simply best to contact an organization comprised of individuals with similar interests. For example, seniors who want to travel with other seniors simply look to an organization like AARP which would sponsor alternative travel opportunities.

CHILDREN

I won't mislead you and say that Colorado is the ideal place for a vacation with children, especially small ones, because it isn't. Much of the attraction of Colorado is, of course, its gorgeous scenery and abundance of outdoor recreational activity of a more grown up nature. However, there is plenty that will appeal to the young ones as well so you don't have to avoid Colorado because you want to bring the children along. Some of the scenery can be appreciated by children, too, once they reach about the age of eight or so. The unusual type of scenery such as is found in the Colorado National Monument is more to the liking of little ones than the awesome beauty of a snow-covered mountain.

Regardless of the destination there are three situations that have to be addressed when it comes to satisfying the needs of children during your travels. These are what do to do with the little tykes when you and your spouse (or whoever) decide that it's time for a night out on the town; keeping the kids busy during long drives (also known as avoiding the "are we there yet?" syndrome); and, finally, finding the right attractions and activities for them. Hopefully, those activities will be enjoyable for the adults as well.

Starting with the first situation, how do you go about finding a good baby sitter in a place you've never been before? One of the best sources of information is from the staff at the hotel where you are staying. They have experience, having made recommendations in the past and getting feedback from their guests. This is especially true in the better hotels. Some larger hotels and resorts provide first class care facilities for children. In the Denver area you can get referrals to reliable child care providers by contacting the **Mile High United Way Child Care Resources & Referral Service**, *Tel. 303/433-8900.*

Road activities don't have to be elaborate and shouldn't be a major hurdle. You know best what will occupy your children while riding in a car. It may be a coloring book, a small hand-held computer game, a favorite doll or toy or even something that doesn't involve bringing something along with you, such as a sing-along or word games. It's easy to get children involved in simple little games that make the time go faster. For example, keeping track of license plates from various states can be both fun and an education in geography.

The list of places to see and things to do in Colorado that will appeal to both adults and children is considerable. Some of the very best are listed right here while each of the regional destination chapters will make special mention of what should appeal most to children.

My personal selections of the best places to see and activities for children follows. What's especially nice about this is that a considerable number overlap with the Best of Colorado list that I set out for you earlier. So not only will you be able to have a good time at the same time your children are doing likewise, but children will get an opportunity to experience some of the greatest wonders our nation has to offer.

- **Bent's Old Fort National Historic Site** will give children a chance to use their imagination as they visit a real "cowboy and Indian" era site while at the same time being educated about the true facts of that era.
- The **Children's Museum of Denver** is one of the best museums of its type.
- Likewise, the **Denver Zoo** is a fine facility that children of all ages are sure to love.
- The **Durango & Silverton Narrow Gauge Railroad** will delight children ages 2 through 102 with its old time flavor as it snakes through countryside that is nothing short of awesome. Other old time railroads that can be ridden in Colorado will have the same effect on children if your trip doesn't get you into the southwest.
- **Mesa Verde National Park** is a living lesson in history about the people who lived in American before the appearance of Europeans. Exploring the ancient ruins will also be a lot of fun for kids.
- **Santa's Workshop-North Pole** is a sure winner for the little ones. Another amusement park that is special is Denver's **Elitch Gardens**. More mundane amusement parks, of which there are quite a few, are listed in the Sports & Recreation section of the regional destination chapters.
- Children who are at least eight years old will probably be able to appreciate the **United States Air Force Academy**, and not just the boys. Little girls will be delighted to hear about the lady cadets of the Academy.
- Any tour of an old gold or silver mine will be an unforgettable adventure for children, especially boys. Similarly, exploration of some of the old mining towns is both educational and fun. While the candidates for the latter are many I unhesitatingly recommend **Leadville** as the best of the lot.
- Finally, don't overlook the magnificent great outdoors of Colorado as something that children will enjoy. While the scenery of Rocky Mountain National park, the Black Canyon, or Great Sand Dunes, for example, may be beyond the comprehension of a four year old, pre-teens can and do understand the awesome majesty of nature. Combine seeing scenery with the adventure of a rafting trip or a ranch style vacation and it's even better for children.

CREDIT CARDS

Each hotel and restaurant listed in the regional destination chapters indicates whether credit cards are accepted. Where four or less cards are accepted the names of the valid cards are listed. If five cards are taken (and include American Express, MasterCard and VISA) the listing will indicate "most major credit cards accepted." When "major credit cards accepted" is shown it means that the establishment takes a minimum of six different cards.

Because the admission price to many visitor attractions has become so high in recent years, many of these businesses are also now accepting credit cards for payment. However, acceptance of cards at these locations will only be mentioned if the admission price is $15 or more. If so, the listing will state "credit cards."

FOOD & DRINK

Colorado has an almost endless list of places with great food. However, those of you who like to sample the local cuisine when traveling may be in for a bit of a disappointment. You see, there really isn't anything that can be called "Colorado cuisine." Denver, Colorado Springs, and the major resort areas are all quite cosmopolitan in nature and you can find just about any type of cooking from around the world.

However, this is not to say that there aren't certain types of food that are especially popular in most parts of Colorado. Beef, in all of its forms, is probably number one. You could almost say that, at heart, Colorado is a "meat and potatoes" kind of place. Tex-Mex is quite popular, too, as Colorado was one of the first places outside of Texas to adopt this kind of cuisine as its own. The southwestern style of cooking popular in Arizona and New Mexico can also be easily found throughout Colorado. Although many restaurants serve up first quality southwestern cuisine it does lack the originality of what is found in New Mexico.

Buffalo is a popular Colorado dish. While it may sound unappetizing to the uninitiated, it is actually quite tasty and is a favorite among health conscious Coloradans because it is high in protein, lower in fat, calories, and cholesterol than chicken let alone beef. Colorado wild game dishes and native trout are also found in abundance in the state's restaurants.

All of the usual beverages found throughout the United States will be found in the bars and cocktail lounges of Colorado. It may be significant to note that *Coors* beer is native to Colorado as are an almost countless selection of local micro-brews.

The destination chapters contain descriptions of 157 different restaurants. The descriptions are geared towards dinner but if a place is especially suitable for lunch I will certainly say so. The inexpensive

THE BEST OF COLORADO DINING

After careful evaluation of my tastebud sensory records, I have chosen the establishments below as the best of Colorado's places to eat. However, this is not simply a list of gourmet restaurants. While that's one category, it ignores the importance of finding places which are most representative of Colorado-style dining. So, I've broken them into two groupings depending upon whether you are seeking culinary masterpieces or a true western experience.

The Gourmets
- **The Bayou** *(Glenwood Springs): Cajun*
- **Beano's Cabin** *(Beaver Creek): American*
- **Briarhurst Manor** *(Colorado Springs): Continental*
- **Cafe Alpine** *(Breckenridge): Continental*
- **Kevin Taylor Restaurant** *(Denver): American*

Colorado & Western
- **Buckhorn Exchange** *(Denver)*
- **Casa Bonita** *(Denver): Mexican*
- **Denver Buffalo Company** *(Denver)*
- **Fancy Moose** *(Boulder)*
- **Outlaw Steakhouse** *(Ouray)*
- **Trail Dust Steak House** *(Denver)*

category usually encompasses what is termed "family" dining, but also is generally good for lunch. I have tried to provide a sampling of as many different cuisines as possible to reflect the great diversity of the state's dining industry. That cross section also applies to price so you'll find that the restaurants, besides being divided up by area, are classified according to the price for a dinner entree exclusive of alcoholic beverages, tip and taxes.

Fast food chains aren't mentioned but you can almost always find one for lunch in all big towns and along the major interstate highways. Likewise, nationwide restaurant chains aren't generally listed (unless they're the best dining opportunity in a given area) but can be found throughout Colorado, especially in the Denver and Colorado Springs areas.

During your travels, most importantly in smaller towns, don't hesitate to try a place simply because it may not look like what you expect a good restaurant to look like from the outside. More often than not you will be pleasantly surprised. Then you can write to me and tell me about it so I can include it in the next edition. Asking hotel employees about a good place to eat is almost always an excellent way to find out about unusual dining places.

RESTAURANT PRICE GUIDELINES

Very Expensive: $31 or more
Expensive: $21-30
Moderate: $11-20
Inexpensive: $10 or less

Prices are for the entree (but include a full course dinner if specified) and are exclusive of tax, tip and beverage.

It will surprise a lot of people to learn that Colorado has become something of a wine connoisseur's destination, albeit on a rather limited scale. Many of the state's finer restaurants are proud to present local vintages for your dining pleasure. And, numerous wineries and tasting rooms are open for public visitation. The largest number of the state's nearly thirty wineries are located in the area around Grand Junction, especially in the community of Paradise. There are also several wineries in the Aspen and Boulder areas. Details will be in the appropriate regional destination chapter

GAMING

Colorado hasn't been left behind in what seems to be the mad scramble by many states to have some form of legalized casino gaming. In Colorado it takes two forms, Indian Gaming and other casinos. Unlike most western states which have a lot of Indian reservations and, hence, probably a lot of Indian casinos, Colorado only has two reservations. They both offer casino action of a limited nature. Other venues with limited gaming are **Blackhawk** and **Central City** in the Rocky Mountains near Denver, and **Cripple Creek** which is not far from Colorado Springs (about 90 minutes away).

"Limited gaming," is, according to Colorado regulators, restricted as to the amount that can be wagered and the hours of operation for casinos. The maximum bet in any game is $5. This may sound like it means you can't lose too much money. That isn't necessarily so. Five dollars a pop can add up if you stay at the table so it is still necessary to budget an amount that you're willing to part with. Casinos are generally open from 8:00am until 2:00am, seven days a week. Among the games allowed, in addition to slot machines, are "21" (blackjack), and poker.

The minimum age for gambling is 21

HEALTH

There isn't any place in the United States that's unsafe to travel from a health standpoint. If anything, Colorado is one of the healthiest places in the country. There are no unusual health risks for the overwhelming majority of visitors. With a few simple precautions and situations to be aware of, it shouldn't present a threat to anyone. The availability and quality of health care in the more populated portions of the state is excellent. Care in less developed areas is also quite good–the only potential problem may be the time it takes to reach the care facility in case of an emergency. Always dial 911 for any medical or other emergency throughout Colorado.

If you are taking prescription medication be sure that you have an adequate supply for your entire trip with you. It's also a good idea to have a copy of the prescription. If you're going to be staying in one hotel for more than a day then leave your medicine in the room, only taking with you what you have to use during the course of the day. Otherwise, do what you can to keep all prescriptions out of excessive heat. Don't leave them in a closed car for any length of time; it's better to carry them with you even if it's extremely hot outside.

Most potential health problems you might encounter in Colorado are related either to the altitude (and climate associated with high altitudes), outdoor activity, or a combination of these factors. Let's take a closer look at each one.

Acute Mountain Sickness affects some people who are not accustomed to high altitudes, so if you live in an area that is close to sea level, pay special attention. AMS can occur in altitudes as low as about 8,000 feet although it is more frequent at levels of 10,000 feet or more. There are plenty of locations in Colorado that are well above these levels. Symptoms include difficulty in breathing, dizziness, and disorientation. It can usually be avoided by increasing altitude slowly, preferably over a period of a couple of days. It is also helpful to eat lightly and to avoid drinking any alcoholic beverages for the first day or so that is spent at or above 8,00 feet. Individuals with cardiac or pulmonary disorders are most susceptible. If you are unsure about whether the high altitude might be bad for you check with your doctor. Should you start to experience the symptoms of AMS you should immediately descend to a lower altitude as quickly as possible. That will almost always effect a quick cure with no lasting complications. However, if symptoms persist upon your return to a lower altitude you should go to the nearest emergency room.

Sunburn is quite common in Colorado because the thinner air at high altitudes doesn't shield you from the rays of the sun as much as the atmosphere at lower altitudes do. So don't be fooled by what appears to be cool weather. Colorado is generally sunny during the summer months and you can get a sunburn quicker than you think. Because it usually isn't that hot **heat exhaustion** and **heat stroke** are not that likely to occur. But they too can happen if you are taking part in strenuous outdoor activity and do not protect yourself from the sun. Limit your exposure to sun to short periods to the extent possible for a few days. Also, wear clothing that covers most of your skin and always wear a hat if you're going to be outdoors a lot. A good sun screen (not sun tan lotion) is advisable for everyone but especially if you are fair skinned.

While visitors to Colorado don't usually have to concern themselves with exotic illnesses, those who will be spending a lot of time in the back country of the southwestern Four Corners region should be aware that there have been isolated cases of **bubonic plague** and **hantavirus**. Avoid contact with wild animals but especially rodents. If, during or shortly after an outdoor trip to these areas, you come down with flu-like symptoms be sure to see a doctor promptly.

Camping or hiking in the back country can expose you to **water contamination** and **hypothermia**. Although the mountain streams of Colorado are sparkling and crystal clear, they are still likely to contain dangerous micro-organisms that can ruin your vacation or, worse, even be fatal. Never drink water from lakes or streams without first purifying it. The best method is to boil the water but special filters and purification tablets can also be purchased. Hypothermia is a strong possibility in any season, not just the cold winter months. The latter can result just from being out in the cold too long without the proper clothing. But during the summer it is most likely to be caused by wearing wet clothing and is made worse by the sudden drops in temperature that can occur in the mountains. The best protection is to wear layered waterproof clothing. Your outfit should also protect against insect bites and stings. Contact between dangerous animals and humans is fairly rare but always assume that all animals in the wild are just that even if they appear to be tame.

When hiking in remote areas it is always advisable to go with someone else. Hiking alone is often asking for trouble. Besides being with a partner you should **tell someone else about your hiking plans**–where you plan to go and when you expect to be back. In national and state park facilities you are encouraged to leave this information with park rangers or officials. At other times you may want to tell someone at the hotel front desk. It may seem silly but an ounce of prevention can help to ensure that you won't have any problems. At a minimum it will make certain that someone else is aware of the fact that you may be in trouble when you don't return as scheduled.

NEWSPAPERS & MAGAZINES

Since both newspapers and magazines are published frequently they offer the most up-to-the-minute information on special events and what's going on in a particular area. They are especially useful in large cities such as Denver or Colorado Springs. Popular magazines geared towards visitors are distributed free of charge in most hotels and motels. *The Denver Post* is the state's largest and most respected newspaper. Colorado Springs' *Gazette Telegraph* is also an excellent daily.

Several magazines that might be of interest to potential Colorado visitors are *Denver Magazine (Tel. 303/455-6463), Rocky Mountain Sports Fitness (Tel. 303/440-5111),* and *Trail And Timberline (Tel. 303/922-8315).* The latter two publications are, obviously, intended for the outdoor enthusiast.

NIGHTLIFE & ENTERTAINMENT

The full gamut of nightlife, from heavy metal clubs to opera, is available in Denver and, to a lesser extent, in Colorado Springs. Outside of these two large metropolitan areas the pickings are slimmer but more diverse than you might think. Because there are so many small towns like Vail and Aspen that draw throngs of tourists year round, the entertainment scene is fairly active. The latter locale, for instance, is home to a world famous annual music festival.

Once you get away from populated areas and places off the main tourist paths, there is little in the way of nightlife save for what is available in lounges of some of the bigger lodging facilities and some annual events. Colorado doesn't actually have any form of entertainment that can truly be said to be "native" to the state, however, western style entertainment is popular. Native American dances are also a worthwhile vacation entertainment experience and can be seen in several places. Details will appear in the entertainment section of each regional destination chapter.

SAFETY

Safety from crime should always be on your mind when traveling. The typical tourist, always occupied, sometimes appearing perplexed, and usually carrying more than a little cash and other valuables, is often a target for savvy thieves. This is true whether you're in a big city such as Denver, in a national park, or even in a small town in the proverbial middle of nowhere. Minimize such situations by always having a firm plan as to what you're doing next. Plan your route in advance whether it's by foot or by car. Don't carry much cash. Use credit cards or travelers checks whenever possible. Record credit card and travelers check numbers and keep them in a separate place.

Don't leave valuables lying around exposed in your car, even for a short time. Cars with trunks that hide luggage completely are better than hatchbacks where you can see into the storage compartment. Many car rental companies have removed identifying stickers that show the vehicle to be a rental since that makes it known to a potential thief that you are a visitor. You might want to inquire with the car rental company beforehand if their vehicles are so marked.

Hotel security is also important. Keep your door locked and don't open it unless you are absolutely sure about the identify of the person seeking entry. Call the front desk to verify that someone has been sent to your room if you aren't sure. Use the deadbolt where provided. Also be sure to familiarize yourself with the location of fire exits. If you must have expensive jewelry with you inquire as to the availability of safe deposit boxes in the hotel. While hotel safety is important in any location, it is especially true in metropolitan areas such as Denver. When outside in the city avoid narrow and deserted locations, especially at night. Don't hesitate to ask hotel personnel about how safe a certain area is if you plan to walk around. Be wary on public transportation. Women should be sure that the clasp on their purse or handbag faces toward their body. Hold on to children at all times.

SHOPPING

Shopping while on vacation is a major enterprise for a lot of travelers, especially when the destination offers unusual or unique items that are representative of the area. Unfortunately, for the most part, this doesn't make Colorado one of the country's big shopping destinations. Oh, for sure, there's no problem in finding a big mall or factory outlet stores in the important urban areas and all of the national chains are well represented, but something that's uniquely Colorado is much harder to come by. The former are too mundane for me to waste vacation time shopping in since the same thing is available near to home. However, no doubt many visitors will want to go to them anyway so I won't ignore them. Each destination chapter will point you to the main shopping venues, especially Denver and Colorado Springs.

Despite the limits on Colorado items there are some things to be sought out that are at least representative of the southwest region of the United States. Western handicrafts as well as Native American goods are found in Colorado much more readily than in most of the rest of the country. The shopping for these items isn't nearly as bountiful as in

Arizona or New Mexico but is decent in a lot of the tourist locations in the southwestern quarter of the state as well as in urban areas.

TAXES

The statewide sales tax rate is only 3% but that doesn't begin to convey the confusing nature of the tax situation in Colorado. In addition to the state sales tax localities, cities, towns and/or counties can levy rates of from 1% to 4.5%. The unfortunate visitor is also confronted with county lodging taxes of anywhere from 1% to 2%. However, an exception is Denver, which assesses an 8% lodging tax and an additional 4% fee on food and beverage in restaurants. Then there are other taxes such as the Regional Transit District tax and others. So, all in all, you can expect to pay anywhere between 4% and 9.5% on non-lodging purchases and up 17.5% on lodging. Although there are many items that are exempt from the sales tax, these do not generally apply to anything a traveler might be purchasing. So, have your calculator handy and be prepared to pay.

TELEPHONES

At latest count Colorado has four different area codes. With the way they've been exploding in recent years this information can become out of date real quick. But right now the lineup looks like this. The Denver metropolitan area has the **303** and **720** area codes, with more about that in a moment. Colorado Springs and the southeastern part of the state are in the **719** area code. The remainder of the state has the **970** area code and looks like an upside down letter L that covers a wide band across the northern and western sections of the state.

The 720 area code was added in mid-1998 and is what the phone company calls an "overlay" of the 303 code. All phone numbers in the Denver area issued prior to creation of the 720 code will keep their 303 designation. Any number issued after that date will use the 720 area code. Thus, you may have to dial a ten-digit number to make a local call when in Denver. So when checking out Denver area telephone numbers in this book pay close attention to which area code to use.

Calling from one Colorado area code to another requires the use of the "1" prefix (except from 303 to 720 and reverse) and then the area code. Long distance calls in the 719 and 970 area codes may also require a "1" prefix if they are outside the local calling area. Toll charges may also apply in these cases. As always, the "1" prefix is also required for all toll-free calls in the 800, 877 and 888 exchanges.

TIME OF DAY

All of Colorado is on **Mountain Time** (two hours earlier than the east coast and one hour earlier than the west coast). The entire state observes Daylight Savings Time.

TIPPING

The general rules of tipping, if there is such a thing, are the same in Colorado as anywhere else in the United States. Tipping is strictly a personal decision and, while I don't feel that it's appropriate to tell folks how to tip, for those of you looking for some generally accepted guidelines, it's standard to tip 15% on the total bill for meals (before tax), 10% for taxis, and $1-2 a day for maid service. And of course, if people provide exceptionally good service or go out of their way for you, a more generous tip is often given.

Keep in mind that most people who are employed in the tourist industry, specifically hotels and restaurants, don't get great salaries. They count on tips for a significant part of their income.

TRAVELERS WITH PHYSICAL DISABILITIES

If you are physically challenged you'll be glad to hear that most facilities in Colorado, including lodging, restaurants, and many attractions, are designed to accommodate you. Of course, depending upon the nature of your physical limitations, some of the outdoor activity so important in Colorado may be limited. Outfitters for more strenuous types of recreation also try to include those people with physical limitations. Make inquiry as to what types of handicaps can be accommodated and, most important, realize the extent to which you are limited.

I've tried to convey some indication of the degree of physical abilities required where appropriate in the destination chapters. Information and assistance for travelers with disabilities is available from a number of national organizations for the physically challenged, but you should also make inquiry with Colorado's **Commission on People With Disabilities**, *Tel. 303/575-3056.*

8. SPORTS & RECREATION

Few places in America are as "into" outdoor recreation as Colorado is. So whether you're planning only an occasional physical activity for your trip or a vacation based solely on taking part in them, Colorado is certain to have something to your liking. Because of the big difference in climate from one part of the year to another many activities are, of necessity, seasonal in nature. General information on a host of the most popular pastimes are listed alphabetically in this chapter while specific listings can be found in the *Sports & Recreation* section of each destination chapter.

BALLOONING

The climatic conditions in much of Colorado aren't as well suited to hot air ballooning as in a lot of other parts of the southwestern United States. However, there are several venues in the state that offer balloon rides. By necessity most of them are limited pretty much to the summer months. For readers who are interested simply in watching the colorful spectacle of a mass balloon ascension, some of the more notable affairs are listed in Chapter 9, *Major Events,* as well as in the destination chapters.

BICYCLING

Because there is relatively light traffic on many of Colorado's highways and back roads, bicycling is a popular sport during the summer months. In many parts of the state, including the Denver and Colorado Springs areas, the spring and fall are also available to the bicyclist. A lot of the terrain in Colorado is, to say the least, quite challenging so you may want to carefully plan exactly where you are going to ride unless you're in great shape and used to pedaling up a steep grade.

If you are bringing your own bicycle into Colorado by air be sure to check with the airline for packaging requirements and possible restrictions. **Bicycle Colorado**, *Tel. 719/530-0051, www.bicyclecolo.org,* is a useful source of information for those who are interested in a biking vacation

BOATING

Pleasure boating is available on many natural as well as man-made lakes throughout Colorado with some of the mountain settings being nothing short of spectacular. State and federal recreation areas frequently have launch sites and other facilities for boaters. Among the most popular areas for boaters are the **Curecanti National Recreation Area** and **Grand Lake**, the latter in the shadow of Rocky Mountain National Park.

FISHING

For the angler Colorado is a dream come true. In addition to well stocked lakes throughout every part of the state, Colorado's mountain streams and rivers are teeming with fish. Despite the popularity of the sport you can almost always find a secluded spot to cast your line. Among the fish commonly found in Colorado are several varieties of trout (especially rainbow, brown, and eastern brook), pike, catfish, white bass, and perch.

For information on how to get a fishing license and regulations concerning size and quantity limits you should contact the **Colorado Division of Wildlife**, *Tel. 303/297-1192*. A non-resident fishing license costs about $6 per day, $19 for five days, and about $45 for the entire year. Specific information on fishing sites, in addition to what is found in the destination chapters, can be obtained from the **Colorado Parks and Outdoor Recreation Department**, *Tel. 303/866-3437*. Another place to go for information is a hot line on fishing conditions and other items of interest, *Tel. 303/291-7533*.

GOLF

There are loads of golf courses in the Denver and Colorado Springs areas and a good number as well in important resort destinations. However, golf is not the paramount sport in Colorado by any means. Unlike some other states which attract people just to play golf, that is not the case in Colorado. Terrain and climate are the two factors which limit Colorado as a hub for this sport. It isn't easy to build a golf course on a mountain. However, if there's room in a resort valley or meadow then they'll likely be one there and it will have a most dramatic backdrop! But the weather is of equal importance. Summer is really the only season that you can play golf in almost all of the state. Although the temperature might be alright in spring the snow will still be covering the course in a lot of places and in the fall an early snow could bring a sudden halt in play that cannot be resumed until seven months later.

A selective list of golf courses is given in each destination chapter. Further information on golfing in Colorado, including golf vacations, is available from the **Colorado Golf Association**, *Tel. 303/366-4653, www.golfhousecolorado.org,* and the **Colorado Golf Resort Association**, *Tel. 303/699-GOLF.*

HIKING

There are few places in America or the world, for that matter, that can reward the hiker as Colorado can. As in the case of bicycling, however, the altitude and terrain can present a great challenge. For some that makes it all the better but if you aren't in shape be forewarned. Take it easy until you acclimate yourself to the altitude and avoid the most difficult areas if you aren't an experienced trekker. Opportunities for hiking are so widespread throughout most parts of Colorado that it would be impossible to list even a fraction of them.

Some of the more notable and popular hikes will be mentioned in the *Seeing the Sights* section of each destination chapter, but you would be best advised to contact the local chamber of commerce or visitor bureau to secure maps and find out about all of the hiking trails in a given area.

HORSEBACK RIDING/GUEST RANCHES

Novice riders may find the task of guiding their mount through the mountains of Colorado on the difficult side and would be better off riding in the lower elevations or at least on some of the easier horse tracks near Colorado Springs and Denver or at a dude ranch. However, for the experienced rider, horseback exploration of the Rockies is one of the best ways to discover the true serenity of the Colorado mountain wilderness. Stables where horses can be rented and guided tours on horseback can both be found in the destination chapters.

Guest (or dude) ranches are such an integral part of the Colorado scene that the final chapter of the book is largely devoted to them.

HUNTING

The mountains of Colorado are home to a wide variety of game including bear, bobcat, deer, duck, elk, geese, grouse, mountain lion, and pheasant. Pronghorn antelope can also be hunted on Colorado's high plains. Some guest ranches offer guided hunting trips. Other outfitters also conduct hunting expeditions. Hunting licenses are required. Information on hunting is also available from the **Colorado Division of Wildlife**, *Tel. 303/297-1192.* Hunting licenses cost between $45 and $260 depending upon the size of the game. Again, air travelers flying into the state should make sure they are in compliance with airline regulations concerning the transportation of firearms.

OFF-ROAD & FOUR-WHEEL DRIVE VEHICLES

The possibilities for exploring the back country of Colorado are virtually unlimited. There are many areas that cannot be reached with ordinary motor vehicles. Some are almost as pristine today as they were a hundred years ago. Dirt roads and no road areas range from simple to the most challenging. National forest areas are among the most popular for four-wheel drive enthusiasts. Each area's Forest Supervisor can provide you with maps showing the roads and other areas that can be traveled on. Jeep rentals and jeep tours are popular in many of the state's most mountainous areas, but are especially numerous in and around Ouray and the San Juan Mountains of the southwest.

PUBLIC LANDS

There are almost 130 natural and historic areas in Colorado administered either by the federal or state government. These include both well known and off-the beaten track localities. Almost all of the best natural scenery along with outstanding recreational facilities are encompassed in these areas. This section can serve as a checklist of places you want to see or as a means of categorizing what recreational activities you want to partake in.

National Park Service (NPS) Facilities

See the appropriate regional destination chapter for details on *all* National Park Service facilities.

- **Arapaho National Recreation Area**: North Central (Rockies) Region. Varied recreational facilities in an area of scenic mountain peaks and lakes.
- **Bent's Old Fort National Historic Site**: East Region. Historic. No recreational facilities.
- **Black Canyon of the Gunnison National Park**: Southwest Region. Scenic (deep and narrow gorge cut by river). Recreation limited to hiking and climbing, mostly of a difficult variety.
- **Colorado National Monument**: Northwest Region. Scenic (unusual eroded and colorful rock formations). Recreation is mainly hiking and climbing ranging from basic to advanced level.
- **Curecanti National Recreation Area**: Southwest Region. Scenic (mountains, lakes, river). Varied recreational opportunities that are mainly water-based.

- **Dinosaur National Monument**: Northwest Region. Historic and scenic (pre-historic fossils and canyons). Varied recreation including hiking, climbing and rafting.
- **Florissant Fossil Beds National Monument**: Colorado Springs Region. Pre-historic fossil remains. Limited recreation consisting solely of hiking.
- **Great Sand Dunes National Monument**: Southwest Region. Scenic (large wind-deposited sand dunes with mountain background). Some recreational opportunities, mostly hiking and climbing the dunes.
- **Hovenweep National Monument**: Southwest Region. Historic (early Native American ruins). No recreational facilities.
- **Mesa Verde National Park**: Southwest Region. Historic and scenic (early Native American ruins and outstanding mountain and plateau scenery). Recreation consists primarily of hiking and climbing.
- **Rocky Mountain National Park**: North Central (Rockies) Region. Scenic (Alpine mountains and meadows). Varied recreational opportunities of all kinds including winter sports.
- **Yucca House National Monument**: Southwest Region. Historic (early Native American ruins). No recreational facilities.

National Forests (Department of Agriculture)

National Forests are especially popular with hikers and campers because of the wide variety of recreational opportunities which are available. While recreation is usually extensive in National Parks, the primary objective in those facilities is preservation. National Forests, on the other hand, tend to be more "user" oriented when it comes to recreation. Few states have more National Forest land than Colorado, so the list that follows is a sports person's heaven. Contact the Forest Supervisor's office for further details on recreation.

- **Arapaho National Forest**: North Central (Rockies) Region. *Tel. 970/498-2770*
- **Grand Mesa National Forest**: Northwest Region. *Tel. 970/641-0471*
- **Gunnison National Forest**: Southwest Region. *Tel. 970/641-0471*
- **Pike National Forest**: Colorado Springs & North Central (Rockies) Regions. *Tel. 719/684-9383*
- **Rio Grande National Forest**: Southwest Region. *Tel. 719/852-5941*
- **Roosevelt National Forest**: North Central (Rockies) Region. *Tel. 970/498-2770*
- **Routt National Forest**: Northwest Region. *Tel. 970/879-1722*
- **San Isabel National Forest**: Southwest Region. *Tel. 719/545-8737*
- **San Juan National Forest**: Southwest Region. *Tel. 970/247-4874*
- **Uncompahgre National Forest**: Southwest Region. *Tel. 970/641-0471*
- **White River National Forest**: Northwest Region. *Tel. 970/468-5400*

Other Federal Lands

Including the NPS and national forests listed above, the federal government administers a total of 86 separate areas within Colorado. More than 20 are under the jurisdiction of the **Bureau of Land Management**, a large agency responsible for a bewildering variety of sites in the western United States. BLM-managed areas in Colorado cover a staggering 8.3 million acres of land. Most of their sites are not developed and are visited primarily by adventure travelers and other hardy outdoor enthusiasts. Some of the more notable sites are described in the regional destination chapters.

For further information you should contact the BLM office nearest to the site you are considering. BLM's Colorado offices are:
• Canon City: *Tel. 719/269-8500*
• Craig: *Tel. 970/826-5000*
• Dolores: *Tel. 970/882-4811*
• Durango: *Tel. 970/247-4874*
• Glenwood Springs: *Tel. 970/947-2800*
• Grand Junction: *Tel. 970/244-3000*
• Gunnison: *Tel. 970/641-0471*
• Kremmling: *Tel. 970/724-3437*
• Meeker: *Tel. 970/878-3601*
• Montrose: *Tel. 970/240-5300*

State Lands

The state administers a system of 40 parks covering the length and breadth of Colorado. The majority are located in unusually scenic areas but the emphasis is on outdoor recreation. Lake boating is an especially popular activity at many of these parks. Details on recreational opportunities will be found in each of the destination chapters under Sports & Recreation. Places of scenic interest are described in the appropriate regional touring sections. General information on Colorado's state parks is available at either *Tel. 303/866-3427* or *www.parks.state.co.us.*

Fees

Almost all National Park Service and many other federal areas have a per vehicle admission charge. The prices shown in this book for the individual parks were accurate as of press time but have been increasing frequently during the past few years. Despite this, national park lands remain a bargain considering the wonders that are contained within their borders. And the new prices are based on regulations that aim to keep the money collected for use within the park and not to panel the office of some official in Washington.

If you are only going to be visiting a few NPS facilities you can simply pay the entrance fee at each one. On the other hand, if your itinerary includes several, then one of the available "passports" is your best bet. The basic multi-park pass is the **National Park Pass** which costs $50 and is good for one year from the date of issue. It allows entry to all National Park Service fee areas. The $65 **Golden Eagle Pass** covers the same ground but also allows access to about 50 additional fee areas administered by other agencies such as the Forest Service and Bureau of Land Management. National Park Passes can be upgraded to Golden Eagle level at any time by purchasing a $15 sticker that you can affix to your park pass. The **Golden Age Passport** allows the same access as the Golden Eagle but is for persons age 62 and older. There is a one time fee of $10. The free **Golden Access Passport** allows entry to all fee areas and any disabled individual is eligible to get one. All of the passes can be obtained at the first fee area you enter.

You can also get them in advance via the Internet at *www.nationalparks.org* or by calling *Tel. 888/467-2757*. The passes are also available at Automobile Club offices and KOA campgrounds.

ANOTHER TYPE OF PARK PASSPORT

Visitors who plan on seeing lots of park service areas in Colorado as well as other states may wish to "collect" passport stamps as proof of their visit. Each National Park Service facility (at the Visitor Center) provides a place where you can stamp your passport upon entry in a manner similar to going into a foreign country. The stamp contains the name of the facility as well as the date of your visit. You can collect the stamp on any paper or book of your choosing but most people like to use the official park service passport booklet that is sold for a reasonable price just for this purpose. It looks like a real passport and makes a good record of your travels as well as an interesting conversation piece.

Everyone traveling with the passport holder in a private vehicle is entitled to be admitted. But remember that the passport only covers the fee to enter the park or other federal area. It does not cover the cost of camping, tours (such as caves) or other concessionaire charges. Sometimes discounts are offered to passport holders, especially the Golden Age Passport. Finally, there is another charge you may sometimes have to pay even with the passports and these are called "user fees." You will encounter them most often in supposedly "free" areas like National Recreation Areas and they are assessed to cover the costs of things like boat ramps and the like. The problem is you have to pay the fee regardless of whether you will be a user or not. While the basic park entry fees don't bother me this little gimmick does raise my temperature more than a little!

User fees at Colorado's state parks are generally modest, never more than a few dollars for a full day. However, if you plan to make extensive use of their system then it makes sense to purchase an annual pass for $40. You can get it at any state fee location, by mail or via the internet at the state park web site listed earlier.

RAFTING

Almost any river of significance in Colorado is well suited to rafting. For the less adventurous serene float trips are available while white-water rafting ranges from beginner to he most challenging. Among the most popular areas for rafting are on the Arkansas River in Canon City, Buena Vista, and Salida; the Colorado River in the Glenwood Springs area, and the Animas River in Durango and Ouray. Rafting on the Green and Yampa Rivers in the more remote northwest corner of the state in and around Dinosaur National Monument is also excellent.

A selected list of operators will be found in several destination chapters. Any operator which I mention has met all requirements and safety protocols as established either by the National Park Service, Forest Service, or state authorities, depending upon where they operate. If you select another company be sure that you verify their credentials. Accidents can always happen, but established outfitters have a remarkable safety record.

It is standard operating procedure in this industry for the price to include all protective gear and transportation to and from either the tour operator's office or local hotels to the raft launch site. Trips can range from an hour or so to several days. Full-day and longer trips usually include appropriate meals. Most rafting trips are of the white-water variety. If you're hesitant about being able to handle it, keep in mind that white-water is officially designated by "class," or the degree of whitewater. Class I is the most gentle, with it becoming progressively wilder through Class V.

Float trips, on the other hand, involve mostly tame stretches of river and sometimes throw in a short segment of near-Class I rapids. These trips tend to last no more than a couple of hours although a few longer ones do exist. When planning you're rafting adventure, don't be afraid to ask the operator as many questions as you need to determine if it's the right one for you.

SKIING

While many states have a large skiing industry, nowhere in America is the quantity and overall quality of skiing sites as wonderful as in Colorado. Next to mountains, skiing is one of the images that quickly comes to mind for a lot of people when they think of Colorado. Whether you just want to spend a single afternoon on the slopes (you only have to travel a short distance from either Denver or Colorado Springs, for example, to reach some great snow) or an entire week, the facilities are there to do so. Both downhill and cross country skiing are popular. The majority of the best known ski resorts are in the north-central part of the state with many being in national forest areas. However, there are some fine ski resorts in areas of the northwest and southwest as well.

SKI COLORADO

There's no mistaking that the slogan "Ski Country USA" certainly applies to Colorado. There are more than two dozen major ski areas in Colorado and this list will direct you to the chapter where you can get more information on each. Locations marked with an asterisk (*) are within 75 miles of Denver.

North-Central (Chapter 13): Arapahoe Basin*, Aspen Buttermilk, Aspen Highlands, Aspen Mountain, Aspen Snowmass, Beaver Creek, Berthoud Pass*, Breckenridge*, Copper Mountain*, Eldora*, Howelsen Hill, Keystone*, Loveland*, Silver Creek*, Ski Cooper, Steamboat, Vail, Winter Park*.

Northwest (Chapter 14): Powderhorn, Sunlight.

Southwest (Chapter 15): Cuchara, Crested Butte, Monarch, Purgatory, Telluride.

Several of these areas lie in an area near where I separate the North Central, Northwest, and Southwest regions, so you can be in one region and take advantage of ski resorts in adjacent regions too.

Because of the importance of skiing in Colorado each destination chapter that has significant skiing venues will have detailed information. See the sidebar below for a quick reference about Colorado's major skiing areas. A good additional source of information about skiing is the annual *Colorado Ski Country USA Guide*. You can contact them at *1560 Broadway, Suite 2000, Denver, CO 80202; Tel. 303/837-0793*. Most areas operate from the middle of November through mid-April but there are a few that start in October and may stay open as late as May or even early June. Details will be found in the destination chapters.

Ski-boarding has become increasingly popular during recent years. A majority of Colorado's major ski resorts have facilities for this variation on the sport. In addition, ski instruction is almost universally available.

Ski lift ticket prices can be a considerable expense. While there are some moderately priced exceptions you can count on spending around $30 for a half-day ticket or $45 and up for a full day ticket, especially in the better known resorts along the I-70 corridor. Resort package plans, however, often include lift privileges.

Directions in the skiing listings are from Denver. Abbreviations used are:

Types of skiing & related activities:
DH=Downhill skiing
XC=Cross Country
TM=Telemarking
SS=Snowshoeing
SB=Snowboarding

Terrain:
The numbers refer to the approximate percentage of runs for each level of skiing skill.
B=Beginner
I=Intermediate
A=Advanced/Expert

SPECTATOR SPORTS

Professional and major college athletics are an important part of the Colorado sports scene. Major league teams in baseball, basketball, and hockey are franchised in Denver and, therefore, that destination chapter has the biggest section on spectator sports. The **University of Colorado** in Boulder has a full program of intercollegiate athletics and is the best known among the state's college teams. **Colorado State University** in Fort Collins and several other smaller schools also participate in intercollegiate athletic contests. Professional rodeo is popular in all parts of the state.

SWIMMING

Swimming can be dangerous in many mountain streams and rivers because of rapids, hidden rocks, and cold water. As a result most swimming is limited to several major lakes. Several also offer water skiing and other water related sports. Of course, if you're just looking for a dip in the swimming pool, most hotels and motels have at least one. All larger communities and many smaller ones have municipal pools that are open to visitors. Check the local telephone directory.

TENNIS

Outdoor tennis is popular in all locations during non-winter months and bigger cities as well as a few smaller towns have indoor tennis courts for during the colder weather. Many large hotels as well as most resorts have some tennis facilities. They are sometimes available only to registered guests. Public courts at reasonable prices are common in Denver, Colorado Springs, and many other communities. Some tennis facilities will be listed in the destination chapters but if your hotel doesn't have a court then it is a good idea to simply peruse the local yellow pages for the location nearest to you.

9. MAJOR EVENTS

The cities and towns of Colorado from end to end are jam packed with special events at all times of the year. Many are geared to the particular season and so there is tremendous diversity in the nature of the events. The events range from the ridiculous to the sublime (for example, the Rubber Duck Race and the Aspen Music Festival). It is entirely impossible to list all of these events in this book so I'll concentrate on those that have the broadest appeal and throw in a few of the more unusual ones. Some of the events are so well known that a lot of people deliberately coincide the time of their visit to be able to partake in a particular event. Good sources of additional event listings are magazines and newspapers in the areas you are visiting as well as local chambers of commerce or visitor bureaus.

Music festivals and rodeos are especially popular in Colorado. Only a few of the most significant ones are mentioned here because there will be more about them later. For a bigger listing of music festivals see the sidebar in Chapter 13. Those looking for more rodeo choices will want to peruse the rodeo section in Chapter 17. In addition, additional information on many of the most important events that are summarized in this chapter will also be found in the regional destination chapters.

As the events listed below are all annual affairs, the exact dates often vary from one year to the next. It is best to contact the local chamber of commerce for the precise dates and times.

JANUARY

The **Winter Festival** in Poudre Canyon is typical of events found throughout the mountains during January and the rest of winter. Skiing and other winter sports expositions are highlighted. This one, in particular, is notable because it doesn't concentrate solely or even mainly on skiing. Other winterfests during this month are in Aspen, Breckenridge and Winter Park.

FEBRUARY

Two winter carnivals are the top attractions during this month. **Carnivale** in Manitou Springs and the **Crystal Carnival** in Leadville are outstanding. The Carnivale includes a Mardi Gras style parade and a Cajun cook-off contest. A parade and magnificent palace of ice highlight the Crystal Carnival, usually held at the end of the month.

Winterfest is another sports celebration, this one held in Pagosa Springs. Races, old time Follies entertainment and a pancake breakfast are notable features.

MARCH

Granby's **Firefighters Feud** is an entertaining event that features actual firefighters in full gear competing in various races including a ski slalom, all while carrying heavy fire hose. Those who love to ride or even watch snowmobiles will want to see the annual **Colorado Snowmobile Association Convention**. Call *Tel. 800/235-4480* for venue.

APRIL

The **Center Yourself Week** in Cortez benefits a local college. Events include theater presentations, Native American dances and other activities, arts and crafts show, and a race. Several weekends during the month are used to present **Murder Mystery Weekends** in Leadville. A number of separate lodging establishments play host to these who-done-its.

MAY

The **Canon City Music and Blossom Festival**, held early in the month, is comprised of a number of events including several school bands, concerts, rodeo and parade and arts and crafts show. Up in Vail is the popular **Whitewater Festival**. This kicks off the resort's summer season in fine style with various river activities, food festival, and music. **A Taste of Breckenridge** gives that town a chance to strut its stuff with many restaurants participating in cuisine samplng and tastings. Sounds delicious.

The **Grand River Indian Artists Gathering** in Grand Junction during mid-month is one of the largest Native American arts and crafts show and sale. Also on the agenda are Indian dancers and story tellers as well as demonstrations of music and cooking. **Bluegrass on the River** in Pueblo will delight lovers of this music genre as two stages and almost non-stop music performances are held along the banks of the Arkansas River. Many visitors to this festival like to camp out right on the river. Estes Park holds a **Duckfest Race** for the benefit of charity. On a more esoteric note, Telluride holds its **Mountain Film Festival**.

Denver's Latin heritage is celebrated with many events throughout the year but none is larger or more fun than the **Cinco de Mayo** festival that fills Civic Center with thousands of people and, it sometimes seems, almost as many mariachi musicians. Not too far away in Boulder, one of the premier people races takes place with the colorful **Bolder Boulder 10K Race**. More than 30,000 runners participate.

JUNE

The world renowned **Aspen Music Festival and School** (mid-June through mid-August) has been drawing crowds for half a century. Great music, including chamber music, opera, and symphony is the main attraction but numerous other events that the whole family will enjoy have also become part of a summer in Aspen. Just preceding the music festival in Aspen is the annual **Food and Wine Magazine Classic**. Food and wine tasting as well as cooking demonstrations by some of the world's great chefs are given. Wine lovers and others will also savor the late month **Telluride Wine Festival**. World famous sommeliers and chefs lend their expertise.

Cripple Creek's **Donkey Derby Days** are held the last weekend of the month and, besides donkey races, features music, a parade and even a watermelon eating contest. A fun event for the whole family. A **Scandinavian Midsummer Festival** in Estes Park closes out the month with folk dancing, music and more.

The **Greeley Independence Stampede** has been a favorite event for almost 80 years. Running from late June through early July, the Stampede is an early start to the Independence Day celebrations. Parades, barbecues and rodeo are the highlights.

In Salida the annual **Fibark Boat Races and Festival** features competitions of different types of water vessels including canoes, kayaks and rafts. On land there's a parade, art show, food fair and entertainment.

A good time to ride the Cumbres & Toltec scenic train is in mid-month during Antonito's celebration of the **Spring Steam Festival**. Music, a wild west show and other events commemorate the train's season opening.

JULY

The early part of the month is dominated by Fourth of July related celebrations. These include Buena Vista's **July 4th Weekend** (art show and sale, quilt show, parade, fireworks); the **Cowboy Roundup Days** in Steamboat Springs which date back almost a hundred years and features rodeo, parade and fireworks; the **Old Fashioned Celebration** in Ouray with family style fun (especially the water fight); and a similar event in Silverton called the **Old Tyme 4th of July Celebration**.

Other events on and around the fourth that don't have the usual fireworks and western style of celebrating the holiday are Denver's **Cherry Creek Arts Festival** and Colorado Springs celebrated **Pike's Peak Hill Climb**. The Arts Festival is one of the largest in Colorado and is considered to be among the nation's best by art experts. Even more famous, the Hill Climb goes back to the 1920's as thousands watch car and motorcycles race to the top of the mountain.

The period after the Independence Day holiday also has plenty of activities. Telluride has a **Celebration Arts Affair** with arts and crafts as well as entertainment; and the **Southfork Logger Days** with various logging events, sports and games, and arts and crafts. The **National HS Finals Rodeo** is one of the largest in the world and also features a major trade show. The host city is Pueblo and the week-long event usually is held in mid-month. Silverton's late month **Blair Street Arts & Crafts Festival** has judges picking the best artists in various categories. The festival also features street entertainment and other events.

Several other major musical events are the **Winter Park Jazz Festival** with top jazz performers captivating the audience in the beautiful setting of a natural amphitheater on the slope of a mountain. Opera buffs will certainly want to see the **Colorado Opera Festival** held in Colorado Springs at around the same time. A different major opera is performed each year.

Finally, wrapping up the month's busy calendar are the annual **Mountain Fair** in Carbondale with arts and crafts, food booths and games for children; and **Aerial Weekend** in Crested Butte. Hot air balloons are joined by airplanes and gliders. Parachute demonstrations are given. Another balloon event is Steamboat Springs' **Rainbow Weekend** in mid-month which features more than 50 of the colorful airships along with a huge craft show.

AUGUST

The town of Buena Vista celebrates **Gold Rush Days** with everything from gold panning to toilet seat races! Yes, that and other esoteric events such as a burro race, old time melodrama and other forms of entertainment will be sure to delight.

If you love mushrooms like I love mushrooms, then you'll savor the weekend when **The Mushroom Foray** is held in Creede. Mushroom experts preside. Later in the month the same town hosts the **Salsa Fiesta**, a spicy way to spend the day. They sure know how to eat in Creede. While we're on the topic of food, head out to Frisco for the "official" state barbecue cookoff in the **Colorado Barbecue Challenge**.

Music in August is featured in Westcliffe with the **Jazz in the Sangres**, Canon City's **Fiddler's on the Gorge** (actually held downtown and not in the gorge but featuring the country's top fiddlers), and the **Great Western Rocky Mountain Brass Band Festival** in Silverton. How's that for musical diversity?

Other interesting events are the **Lake County Boom Days** in Leadville, highlighting the town's Victorian heritage and mining days and the **Colorado State Fair** in Pueblo which runs from about the middle of the month into early September. Several parades, rodeo, and big-name entertainment supplement the usual state fair fare of livestock exhibits and the like. Closing out summer is Denver's **Festival of Mountain and Plain**. Typically almost a half-million people will attend this event in Civic Center Park. There's a carnival, arts and crafts booths, food booths, and free name entertainment.

One of my favorites is Winter Park's **Chocolate Rodeo** where you can sample the most sinful desserts you could ever imagine. It is part of a larger wine, beer and food festival. A definitely more esoteric event is **'Vettes on the Rockies** where Corvette lovers get a chance to check out the wheels during a skill driving event and car show. If you like more vintage cars then go to Steamboat Springs at the end of the month for the **Steamboat Vintage Auto Race and Concours D'Elegance**.

Last, but certainly not least for August, is Breckenridge's annual **Rubber Duck Race**. Thousands of rubber ducks "swim" down the Blue River followed by a huge town-wide party with entertainment and food for everyone.

SEPTEMBER

Several weekends in Estes Park are used to celebrate **Festival Month**. Diverse events include a Scottish festival with international championship pipe bands, jousting, whiskey tasting, and other things Scottish, music, and food fair. The **Colorado Springs Balloon Classic**, held over Labor Day weekend, begins with illumination of tethered balloons in the pre-dawn darkness, followed by a balloon race. The **Colorado Mountain Winefest** in Grand Junction features wine sampling, seminars and tours of different wineries along with music and entertainment.

The majority of events in September center around a fall theme and the spectacular color associated with Colorado's fall foliage. The events usually feature, besides bringing in people to see the change of color, music and entertainment, arts and crafts, and food booths. Among the many such events during the month are **Colorfests** in various venues in the Four Corners region, Pagosa Springs, **Fall Colorfest** in Winter Park, and the **Downtown Boulder Fall Festival**.

Rounding out the many festivals of September is Denver's **Festival of Mountain and Plain**, a celebration of the entire state with just about every kind of entertainment and activity you can think of.

OCTOBER

Octoberfests are popular in Colorado, too. Among the events celebrating the season are **Coloradofest** in Canon City (starts late September), the **Octoberfest and Jeep Raffle** in Ouray, and one in Vail (sometimes in late September).

Other October celebrations are the **Apple Jubilee** in Grand Junction where, in addition to craft displays and entertainment, visitors are invited to join in a local apple harvest. The Denver Botanical Gardens holds its annual **Pumpkin Festival**. Children will enjoy the hayrides as well as the four-acre pumpkin patch. A crafts show is also part of the event. And I couldn't conclude October without mentioning the king of the suds events — the always fun- (and glass-) filled **Great American Beer Festival** in Denver.

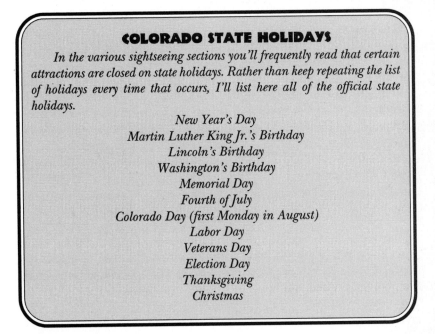

COLORADO STATE HOLIDAYS

In the various sightseeing sections you'll frequently read that certain attractions are closed on state holidays. Rather than keep repeating the list of holidays every time that occurs, I'll list here all of the official state holidays.

New Year's Day
Martin Luther King Jr.'s Birthday
Lincoln's Birthday
Washington's Birthday
Memorial Day
Fourth of July
Colorado Day (first Monday in August)
Labor Day
Veterans Day
Election Day
Thanksgiving
Christmas

NOVEMBER

Most events are late in the month and combine celebration of Thanksgiving with an early kickoff of the Christmas season. These include the **Old Fashioned Christmas, Day After Thanksgiving** in Alamosa, **Come Catch the Glow Christmas Parade** in Estes Park (one of the most popular events in the state), and **Christmas Mountain USA** in Salida where the town is crowded with people who want to witness the lighting of what must be the world's tallest Christmas tree. It's followed by a parade of light and the arrival of Santa Claus.

DECEMBER

More holiday season events are on tap this month. Two of the best are Grand Junction's **Country Christmas** where visitors partake in Christmas events on a farm reminiscent of those that were actually held in the early part of the century, and Denver's **Blossoms of Light**. Held in the Botanic Gardens, thousands of lights bring a special atmosphere to the beautiful gardens.

10. COLORADO'S BEST PLACES TO STAY

A lot of travelers are merely looking for *"a"* place to stay when they're on the road, because they see it mainly as a spot to sleep before they hit the road once again. I'm often in that category. However, many other travelers are searching for *"the"* place to stay. If you fit into the latter group all of the time, or only once in a while, then this chapter will be of special interest. With accommodations in Colorado being so numerous and so diverse it is a real challenge to pick out ten that are absolutely the best. Obviously, it would be almost impossible to get two people to agree. But since I'm writing the book you'll have to settle for my list!

Now don't get frightened away because you think that the "best" places all have to be synonymous with the most expensive. That is true in many cases but certainly not all. I've tried to cut across several price ranges in this list as much as possible. Similarly, not all of the best will be big-city high-rise type facilities or resorts. You'll find both of those as well as other types of accommodations represented here and in each regional touring chapter. The only category I've deliberately omitted from this chapter is dude ranches. This isn't because none of them qualify as being among the best. In some ways almost all of them could be considered special. It is because only a fairly limited group of travelers will find that kind of experience of interest to them. To make up for that I've devoted considerable detail to each guest ranch that I have selected for inclusion in Chapter 17.

Some of the factors that go into my selections are, of course, luxury of accommodations, service, facilities, and general ambiance. But uniqueness is an important consideration too. If a lodging establishment has something about it that says "Colorado" in a special sort of way, it has a big edge on breaking into the top ten. Indeed, the spectacular setting of a few special properties was a significant factor in their inclusion.

So let's get on with it–here is my award winning list. (I should mention that many of them have won awards from all sorts of raters.) They are in alphabetic order and no ranking within this list is implied.

THE BROADMOOR, *One Lake Ave, Colorado Springs. Tel. 719/634-7711, Fax 719/577-5700. Toll free reservations 800/634-7711; www.broadmoor.com. 704 Rooms. Rates: High season (May 1st to October 31st): $295-455; Low season (November 1st to April 30th): $190-345. Most major credit cards accepted. Located three miles west of I-25, Exit 138, via Lake Avenue. From the Manitou Springs area take US 24 to 21st Street and proceed south to Lake Circle, which becomes Lake Avenue.*

There are relatively few hotels that are extra-special in every way and the world famous Broadmoor is definitely one of them. Elegant surroundings and impeccable service are noted hallmarks of this distinguished and sophisticated full service resort. Playing host to the rich and famous since 1918 (and in recent times to a much more diverse clientele), The Broadmoor has managed to remain timeless–it constantly reinvents itself to keep up to date but retains the best features of an earlier time. Their slogan of "European grandeur in the Colorado Rockies" is as good a capsule description as you can come up with.

The first thing you'll notice about The Broadmoor is its excellent location–situated in the heavily forested area of Colorado Springs that now goes by the hotel's name, it is within a short distance of a magnificent backdrop of vividly colored and rocky Cheyenne Mountain. The driveway leading up to the main entrance is flanked by gardens, fountains and statues. The massive stone walls and red roof of the original building tower before you. Once inside the lobby areas of the old part are small and dignified, almost like a grand European villa. Newer wings flank the main building to the left and right while other buildings are set further back on the grounds. Amidst all of the structures is a large open area mainly occupied by The Broadmoor's own lake. Surrounded by pathways and crossed by bridges, there are few more enjoyable walks anywhere in Colorado Springs. Ducks and other feathery creatures seem to like it here too! The hotel's magnificent golf courses and other recreational facilities are all located off of this immaculately kept park-like domain that covers several acres.

The accommodations at The Broadmoor are varied. There are single rooms and suites. Large rooms and some more modestly sized. But all are exquisitely furnished in a traditional style and have many modern amenities. Mini-bars and in-room safes are standard. Such things as coffee makers, Jacuzzi's and refrigerators vary according to the type of room. Plush towels and robes and specially selected soaps and toiletries are par for the course. The room service is outstanding.

Dining at the Broadmoor is as renowned as the hotel itself. **The Penrose Room** and **Charles Court** are both featured in the *Where to Eat* section. Other choices are **The Tavern** featuring grilled specialties and **Spencer's**, which is known both for fine food and beautiful views. Something that all guests should take advantage of is the fabulous brunch available at the splendid **Lake Terrace Dining Room**. Afternoon tea is a time honored tradition that you must do at least once. Then, after you've finished eating there's plenty of opportunity to be entertained at the Broadmoor. Among the lounges and nights spots are **The Golden Bee**, **Julie's** and **Stars**. The latter has nightly dancing.

As a resort you would expect first class recreational facilities but The Broadmoor outdoes itself here. It has three championship level golf courses, over a dozen tennis courts including two that are inside and available for play during winter, four swimming pools, complete exercise facilities, skeet shooting and horseback riding. You can also rent paddleboats to cruise along their lake or bicycles to explore the magnificent surrounding area. The Broadmoor also arranges fly-fishing trips to neighboring areas or anywhere in the state of Colorado for that matter.

For children, in addition to a playground where the kids can entertain themselves, the hotel offers a full range of supervised programs during the summer months. Finally, almost thirty fine stores grace the corridors of the hotel and separate village-like shopping area. These upscale businesses range from golf and sporting goods to jewelry. No matter what the activity or service is, it will be sure to exceed your expectations.

BROWN PALACE HOTEL, *321 17th Street, Denver. Tel. 303/297-3111, Fax 303/293-9204. Toll free reservations 800/321-2599; www.brownpalace.com. E-mail: marketing@brownpalace.com. 230 Rooms. Rates: $225-295 all year; suites from $300-1,000. Major credit cards accepted. Located in the heart of downtown, four blocks north of the intersection of Colfax Avenue and Broadway.*

The Brown Palace has had an almost legendary reputation since its inception more than a hundred years ago. That reputation has been built on luxurious service and beautiful surroundings. The Palace has been host to many American presidents as well as scores of other dignitaries from around the world since its debut way back in 1892. It has been and remains the place to stay in Denver for those who seek perfection and are willing to pay more for it. The Brown Palace, a member of the prestigious *Preferred Hotels & Resorts*, doesn't rest on its past laurels, however– frequent renovation has kept it up to date as far as modern amenities and facilities are concerned. Nor does it forget its important links to the past, a foremost example of which is the wonderful afternoon tea service.

Long before the atrium became a popular design feature for hotels and other public buildings, the Brown Palace had it. The large open area is the focus of the hotel's outstanding public areas. The furnishings and style bring you back to the days of the Victorian era although the dominant architectural style of the building itself is classic Italian Renaissance. The atrium lobby is as comfortable as your living room at home is with big and plush red leather chairs that have become almost as famous as the hotel itself. Oriental rugs and a magnificent stained glass ceiling towering above complete the beautiful picture of opulence and luxury.

The 230 guest rooms make the Brown Palace a relatively small hotel for the city center but that, too, is part of what makes it special. It allows the service to be tailored to each individual guest. And each of those rooms, including an even smaller number of elegant suites, are distinctively appointed in a timeless style that is sure to please the most discriminating visitor. But it is the little things that often make a place stand out in one's mind and that is certainly true at the Brown Palace. In that category are the impeccable 24-hour room service, plush terry cloth robes that are provided to each and every guest and the nightly turn-down service by a cheerful maid. Some rooms have their own refrigerators. The Brown Palace also has what has to be the most unique water supply system of any hotel. It is connected to a 720-foot deep artesian well that provides the purest of Rocky Mountain water–sort of like having your own private reservoir!

Dining at the Brown palace is a great experience as well. The **Palace Arms** and **Ship Tavern** are two outstanding restaurants which are described in more detail under Denver's Where to Eat section. Another excellent choice is the fine contemporary cuisine served at **Ellyngton's**. After dinner the **Churchill Bar** is a wonderful spot for socializing and is well known for its large selection of premium cigars. An air filtration system keeps it from becoming a smoke-filled room. Sitting around with a good cigar in the luxurious surroundings is perhaps the single finest example of how the Brown Palace provides a taste of how the other half lived in a time gone by.

Recreational facilities at the Palace are on the limited side, consisting of a well equipped exercise room. A lovely floral and gift shop are also located on the premises.

CLIFF HOUSE AT PIKES PEAK, *306 Canon Avenue, Manitou Springs. Tel. 719/685-3000; Fax 719/685-3913. Toll free reservations 888/212-7000; www.thecliffhouse.com. E-mail: information@thecliffhouse.com. 57 Rooms. Rates: $129-189 for standard rooms (studio units); $169-400 for suites. All rates include full breakfast. Major credit cards accepted. Located in town via US Highway 24 to the Manitou Avenue exit and then west to Canon and right to the inn.*

Dating back all the way to 1873, the Cliff House is one of the Colorado Springs area's oldest lodging establishments. However, it hasn't been continuously operated having been closed for quite a few years due to the need for renovation. Well, after a $9 million facelift, the Cliff House is now once again open for business and I'm certainly glad about that—it is one of the most delightful places to stay in all of Colorado.

Listed on the National Register of Historic Places, this elegant and luxurious old country inn is a sprawling white Victorian structure topped by a big cupola and surrounded by greenery in full view of the glorious mountains. The gracious public areas feature rich, dark woods and all the cozy warmth of an era that has passed most other places by. The service from every staff member, check-in to check-out, is nothing short of impeccable. It seems as if their mission in life is only to assure their guest's enjoyment. The concierge staff is especially helpful. Public facilities are not that extensive but do include a beautiful dining room with an award-winning chef (see the separate listing for the **Dining Room at Cliff House** in the *Where to Eat* section) and the refreshing **Music Lounge** where guests gather to relax. Drinks are served in the lounge. There is also a limited exercise facility.

However, you don't stay at the Cliff House for the facilities of a full service resort. Besides the look and feel of the place, the biggest attraction is the outstanding accommodation, that while not inexpensive, costs considerably less than many other places of lesser quality. Even the standard unit (which is called a studio) is of upgraded quality with its airy spaciousness, delightful period furnishings and a host of modern amenities such as mini-refrigerator, high quality imported toiletries and plush terry cloth robes. Beyond the standard room are Junior Suites (some with vaulted ceilings), two-story Deluxe Suites and all the way up to the highest priced Celebrity Suites. The latter once were used by such notables as Clark Gable, Teddy Roosevelt and even Buffalo Bill. That guy sure got around! Many suites feature two-person spas and wet bars.

GRAND LAKE LODGE, *US Highway 34, Grand Lake. Tel. 970/627-3967; Fax 970/627-9495; www.grandlakelodge.com. 58 Rooms. Rates $79-144 with higher rates for larger units accommodating up to as many as 14 people. Lower rates may be available during shoulder periods at beginning and end of season. Open only from early June to mid-September. American Express, Discover, MasterCard and VISA accepted. Located a half mile north of Grand Lake Village; look for sign to lodge's private entrance on the northbound side of US 34.*

There is quite a bit of history associated with the Grand Lake Lodge which is now listed on the National Register of Historic Places. Overlooking stunning Grand Lake, the Shadow Mountain Reservoir and the beautiful Middle Park Valley, the lodge was built in 1920 and sits on the western edge of Rocky Mountain National Park. The main lodge building (totally rebuilt seven years after a disastrous fire in 1973) is a long two story wooden structure built of native lodgepole pine and surrounded by a veranda and balcony. It's topped by a green roof that blends in nicely with the hundreds of trees on all sides of the building. On the descending terrain beneath the Lodge are several decks and recreational facilities. Beyond that steps lead down to the shore of Grand Lake. Most of the guest accommodations are hidden in the trees near the Main Lodge. In all there are almost a hundred different buildings at Grand Lake Lodge. The James family has been operating the Lodge for three generations.

Inside the main building you'll find an attractive and large lobby with a big and most unusual circular fireplace surrounded by comfortable rocking chairs. The lobby features bare wooden beams for a true western feel. It also has an excellent gift shop that specializes in Colorado and western crafts. Guest facilities are quite varied. All of the accommodations except for the multi-bedroom Elk Lodge and Ford Cabin are classified as either Spruce Rooms or Aspen and Pine Cottages. The Spruces are the smallest and they work their way up in size through Aspen and Pine. All are rather rustic but attractive in appearance with simple wood furniture and nicely paneled walls. Both the Spruce and Aspen type rooms have baseboard electric heat while the Pine Cabins feature an old time stove for keeping warm. And you'll likely need some heat during the cool evenings of even mid-summer. While the accommodations certainly aren't in the elegant class there is definitely something special about them. Perhaps it's because they epitomize Colorado so well.

The excellent restaurant offers delicious food and good service. Large picture windows look out on a beautiful lake view. Lunch is served outside on the patio. There's also a bar and lounge that offers live entertainment. The large swimming pool and adjacent hot tubs are located in a nicely landscaped area between the Main Lodge and the lake. The mountain and lake vistas from this point are nothing short of dramatic. Other facilities and activities at the Grand Lake Lodge include hiking and riding trails, a recreation room with ping-pong tables, volleyball, horseshoes, picnic area with grills and a playground. Another worthwhile activity is to just sit in one of the old time swings on the spacious veranda and enjoy what the Colorado Rockies has to offer–refreshment for the senses.

HOTEL BOULDERADO, *2115 13th Street, Boulder. Tel. 303/442-4344; Fax 303/442-4378. Toll-free reservations 800/433-4344; www.boulderado.com. E-mail: info@boulderado.com. 160 Rooms. Rates: $150-185 all year; suites up to $285. Major credit cards accepted. Located downtown at corner of Spruce, one block north of the Pearl Street mall.*

A real winner that's almost worth going to Boulder just to see, for even if you don't stay here. This historic edifice is listed on the National

Register of Historic Places. It has been pleasing guests since it debuted on New Year's Day back in 1909. The name is a combination of Boulder and Colorado. At that time Boulder wasn't much of a town and the owner apparently thought it would be a good way to make sure that his guests remembered where they stayed–sort of an inexpensive way of advertising, I guess. The place has been meticulously restored in the finest tradition of Victorian style and is a delight in every way. Let's take a quick tour.

The exterior of the five story structure is a dignified red brick highlighted by green canopies over each window around the first floor. The central part of the front facade has deeply indented balconies. But the best part is the beautiful and elaborate interior. The three-story high lobby has a brilliant stained glass ceiling which curves slightly along the two longer edges, a richly cantilevered cherry wood staircase, and Victorian furnishings, both antique and reproduction which exude warmth and charm. White columns around the lobby perimeter complete this impressive scene.

Guest rooms are divided between the original building (42 units) and a newer north wing (118 units). Both feature Victorian furnishings and modern amenities. They're equally charming, but if you like more space then go for the north wing. Some rooms have whirlpool tubs and/or refrigerators. The hotel also prides itself on the warm and helpful attitude of its staff, from check-in and room service all the way to check-out.

For fine food and service you can enjoy the hotel's dining room for breakfast, lunch or dinner; **Q's Restaurant** (which I describe more fully in the Where to Eat section), or the casually pleasing **Teddy Roosevelt's American Grille**. The Bouldlerado is also home to some of the city's best entertainment and nightlife. Whether it's the **Mezzanine Lounge** that overlooks the beautiful lobby, the English pub-like ambiance of **The Corner Bar** (including a sidewalk cafe during the warmer months), or the live blues and jazz entertainment in the basement located **Catacombs Bar**, a good time is sure to be had by one and all.

If there is any knock that you could make against the Boulderado it would have to be the lack of recreational facilities. However, keep in mind that the Boulderado has never tried to compete as a resort hotel where you come to spend time swimming and sunning yourself by the pool (which it doesn't have). It is more of a nightime sort of place where you can relax in elegant surroundings after enjoying the sights and recreation of Boulder. However, Boulderado guests are offered free privileges at a nearby full service health club. The hotel also rents bicycles which, with Boulder's extensive network of biking paths, makes a great way to see the town and get some exercise at the same time.

KEYSTONE LODGE, *Keystone. Tel. 970/468-2316; Fax 970/468-4260. Toll free reservations 800/842-8072; www.keystoneresort.com. 152 Rooms. Rates: High season (summer and winter): $180-275; Low season (spring and fall): $130-187. Major credit cards accepted. Located on US 6 approximately six miles east of I-70, Exit 205.*

Prior to 1971 when Keystone first opened its doors there was no town on the site. Even today it doesn't really qualify as being a town in the usual sense of the word. The population of about 300 people is more like a large family devoted to operating the resort. Someone had the foresight to see that this gorgeous location in the heart of the Rockies but convenient to everything because of its proximity to the Interstate highway would make a great skiing and year-round resort. The Lodge looks like a village rather than a hotel and it always seems to have a festive atmosphere with its many shops and street activities.

The accommodations in this self contained resort community are housed in a modern and attractive six story building. All of the rooms are extra large by most standards and are comfortably furnished. The standard amenities include mini-bar, coffee maker and in-room safe. Some rooms have refrigerators.

When it comes to dining you're going to have a tough time choosing where to eat. Although the Keystone Lodge isn't that big there are, including the surrounding village, more than a dozen restaurants. Among them is an authentic beer *stube* located atop the mountain for those who want an incredible view to accompany their food and drink. The cuisines run the entire culinary gamut. Two of the best, the **Garden Room** and the **Snake River Saloon** are described separately in the Where to Eat section. There are several cocktail lounges with entertainment, mostly during the winter season.

The recreational facilities and programs of the Keystone Lodge are almost endless. A sampling from the lengthy list would include the heated swimming pool, sauna, steamroom, Jacuzzi, fitness center, a dozen tennis courts (some indoor and lighted), and an 18-hole golf course. One of the more unusual facilities available at the Keystone is their very own hot air balloon. What a way to take in the panorama of the heart of the Rockies as you gently soar over the mountains for a bird's eye view! Fee programs that are available to guests in addition to ballooning are horseback riding, boating, biking, and professional massage. On the more mundane side the hotel also offers a video rental library. Keystone Lodge has supervised child care as well as a sizable playground and a small petting zoo.

THE LITTLE NELL, *675 E. Durant Avenue, Aspen. Tel. 970/920-4600; Fax 970/920-4670; www.thelittlenell.com. 92 Rooms. Rates: High season: $525-750 for rooms & $895-3,920 for suites; Low season: $215-500 for rooms & $500-2,000 for suites. Three night minimum stay during some winter periods. Major credit cards accepted. Located at the base of Apsen Mountain immediately beside the ski gondola.*

A prestigious and highly awarded fine lodging establishment, the Little Nell is one of the most unique hotels in the world. Everything about it (except the rates) is wonderful and a stay here will be something you will likely remember for a long time to come. It combines the homey warmth, luxury and personalized service of a small grand hotel or country inn with the amenities and facilities of a much larger hotel. Nestled at the very base of Aspen Mountain and literally within a few short steps of the Silver Queen Ski Gondola, even the setting is almost picture postcard perfect. The structure itself almost defies description containing, as it does, elements of Victorian architecture as well as hints of a French country manor and Alpine ski chalet. The blending is done so well that everything is lovely and harmonious. The many peaks and odd shaped windows, trimmed in pink, contrast with brown roofs and white walls. It has more corners and crevices than you can count.

No two rooms are exactly alike but each and every one is a spacious and luxurious retreat. Standard in all are a gas-burning fireplace, plush sofas and chairs filled with down, built-in bar with refrigerator, rich Belgian wool carpeting, and huge beds with down-filled comforters. And that's just the living and sleeping areas. The bathrooms feature rich marble vanities and sinks with solid brass fixtures. Some have whirlpools. There are at least two telephones in each unit. Suites, of course, are even more elaborate. The highest prices listed above are for the one-bedroom Little Nell and Paepcke Suites (don't ask me how that one is pronounced) as well as the two-bedroom Pfeifer Suite. Regular guest rooms are classified (according to increasing price) as Town View, Mountain Side, Premium Town View, and Premium Mountain Side. There are also some junior suites.

The Restaurant is almost as outstanding as the hotel is and is described in more detail in the Where to Eat section. For a nice place to have a drink check out **The Bar**. Continuing with the Little Nell's simple naming of facilities, it is a most pleasant room with fine leather panels covering the walls and historic photographs of Aspen. There is occasional live entertainment. Summer visitors can take advantage of the pretty swimming pool that is surrounded by immaculate flower gardens as well as the majesty of Aspen Mountain. A whirlpool and exercise room are also on the premises but guests receive privileges for golf and tennis at nearby facilities. The Little Nell will rent you a bicycle to explore the area, a good way to get around during the summer months. And the whole town of Aspen with its many excellent shopping, dining and entertainment venues is literally at your feet.

The Little Nell offers outstanding service at every turn as evidenced by its 24-hour room service and attentive Concierge staff. The hotel offers many package plans during the winter season that include various amounts of skiing.

Some readers are obviously asking whether the Little Nell is worth the steep price. It depends on your outlook. For people who demand the best and are willing to pay for something special, it isn't a difficult question to answer. As the old saying goes, if you have to ask the price you probably can't afford it. Suffice to say, however, that when evaluating what a hotel has to offer, the Little Nell easily fits the bill as one of the very best places to stay.

THE STANLEY HOTEL, *333 Wonderview, Estes Park. Tel. 970/586-3371, Fax 970/586-3673. Toll free reservations 800/976-1377; www.stanleyhotel.com. 133 Rooms. Rates: High season (late May to mid-October): $169-209 for rooms and $269-299 for suites; Low season (mid-October to late May): $139-179 for rooms and $219-249 for suites. Most major credit cards accepted. Located on a hillside just east of downtown via US 34.*

You probably have seen the Stanley Hotel and don't even know it. That's because it served as the inspiration for Stephen King's classic horror story, *The Shining*. Many people think that is was pictured in the film starring Jack Nicholson, but it wasn't. However, when King filmed his 1996 six-hour television mini-series version, five long months of production did take place at The Stanley. That aside, The Stanley has a long and interesting history.

It first opened its doors in June of 1909 after more than two years of construction under the personal direction of owner Freelan Oscar Stanley, of Stanley Steamer fame. Mr. Stanley had moved to Colorado because his doctor thought it would be good for his tuberculosis condition. Being an astute businessman, Mr. Stanley immediately saw the potential of Estes Park as the location of a great resort hotel. It was built for the then staggering sum of a half million dollars and guests were brought there from Denver in, of course, specially designed Stanley Steamers. Theodore Roosevelt was among the many famous people who stayed there. It was listed on the National Register of Historic Places in 1977. After that, though, it did go downhill for quite a few years. Fortunately, people with the same kind of foresight as Mr. Stanley didn't let it continue on into oblivion. It has recently been restored to all of its original glory. In fact, in 1995 it became a member of the prestigious

Grand Heritage Hotels International, a unique collection of less than a hundred historic properties that dedicate themselves to traditional hotel hospitality and elegance.

Enough history. Let's see what The Stanley has to offer. The first things to impress visitors are the location and awesome physical presence of the building. Approached through extensive grounds of magnificent lawns, hedges and topiary, the long white facade of the four story Georgian styled structure with its high central tower and equally white pillars sits majestically in front of a towering sheer wall of granite. It is separated from the latter by a hilly knoll of pine and aspen trees. Whether in summer or in the white covered days of winter it is a sight that is worth seeing even if you don't stay at The Stanley. The rooms range from spacious to small and from quaint to elaborate but all have a pleasant blend of traditional and contemporary styling with many modern amenities. Then there are the added touches such as quality fabrics and linens, fine furniture and superb service. Most units have excellent views no matter which direction they face.

Dining and entertainment choices are also certainly abundant. The **Dunraven Grille & Bar** features excellent cuisine along with live entertainment and dancing in the adjoining lounge. During the summer you can have a casual meal at the **Front Veranda** which overlooks not only The Stanley's immaculate lawn but a stunning vista that extends far beyond. The **MacGregor Ballroom & Dining Room** is used mostly for meetings and affairs but is also the scene of a fabulous Sunday champagne buffet brunch which I highly recommend. The beautiful room features spectacular mountain views through large windows. Speaking of that, many of the hotels business function rooms are quite elaborate and have equally impressive vistas. You should try to get a glimpse of some of them, especially the **Music Room** with its wide arched windows and doors leading out onto the veranda, and the mirrored **Billiard Room** with its rich dark wood paneling.

Although much of The Stanley's clientele is there for business conferences, vacationing guests will appreciate the recreational facilities. There's a heated outdoor swimming pool, volleyball court and sizable picnic area. It is located close to golf, horseback riding, fishing and many other outdoor activities which can all be arranged by The Stanley's gracious and helpful staff. You might also want to learn more about the Stanley family by visiting the newly opened Stanley Museum on the lower level. Museum curators also offer guided tours of the hotel and its interesting history, including many behind the scenes looks.

STREAMSIDE...A VILLAGE OF CABIN SUITES, *1260 Fall River Road, Estes Park. Tel. 970/586-6464; Fax 970/586-6272. Toll free reservations 800/321-3303; www.coloradodirectory.com/streamsidecabins. 19 Rooms. Rates: High season (mid-May to mid-October): $125-260; Low season (mid-October to mid-May): $80-190. American Express, Discover, MasterCard and VISA accepted. Located a mile west of downtown on US 34.*

An award-winning property that is quite a change of pace from the big resort hotel scene. The 19 individual cabin style suites are located on 17 spacious acres of meadow as well as pine and aspen trees in a secluded setting that is located about 600 feet from the road. Many of the cabins are adjacent to a gentle rolling stream whose quiet babbling is like a nightly lullaby to ease you into sleep. The overall effect is one of tranquillity. Lovely flowers and landscaping further enhance the serene atmosphere. You're even likely to see some elk or deer wandering calmly about the property. (They're on the tame side but be sure not to let children approach them.) The grounds are beautifully manicured and feature several life size topiary plantings.

On the inside is a pretty lobby, impressive in a rustic sort of way. However, you don't come to Streamside to be dazzled by man-made beauty. Nature is king here and everything about Streamside is designed to complement that. On the other hand, the accommodations are surprisingly superb. Besides being large and beautifully furnished with custom made items, the western architecture is highlighted by dramatic cathedral ceilings and skylights that make it bright and cheerful. There again the intention, and result, is to increase the feeling of being out in the wild. Add in a warm fireplace and a large outside deck and you have just about everything you need for your own private retreat. All units also feature full kitchen facilities with coffee maker and microwave oven. Some rooms have whirlpool tubs. Families or groups can opt for one of several multi-bedroom units.

The central outdoor activity point is the pretty "Swim Spa" with its heated pool, hot tub and sundeck, steamroom and gas barbecue grills. There's also a children's playground. A video rental library is on the premises (all rooms have television but no telephone). Anglers can fish either on the grounds or the staff will gladly direct to one of many nearby rivers and streams. Nature trails complete the outdoor picture. Several good restaurants are located within a five minute drive.

SHERATON TAMARRON RESORT, *40292 US Highway 550 North, Durango. Tel. 970/259-2000; Fax 970/259-0745. Toll free reservations 800/ 678-1000; www.tamarron.com. 310 Rooms. Rates: High season (May through mid-October and mid-December through early January): $139-459; Low season (mid-October to mid-December and early January through April): $99-339. Full breakfast is included during the winter months. Major credit cards accepted. Located on the main highway between Durango and Purgatory.*

Whether you spend a night or two at Tamarron during a whirlwind sightseeing tour through southwest Colorado or a week long vacation at any time of the year, this resort will provide an experience that would be hard to surpass anyplace in the world. Now that's a strong statement, I know, but let's look at why I'm willing to make it.

The setting along the San Juan Skyway is in one of the most scenic sections of the San Juan National forest. It is one that few hotels can compare with. Snuggled into the narrow Animas River Valley between towering peaks on each side, the verdant green spaces of the 750-acre resort are like jewels in a magnificent crown. The lodge style buildings perched either on the grassy carpet or atop jagged rock outcroppings are dwarfed by the trees and mountains, yet the manage to blend in with a grace and style all their own. Nothing can quite compare with nature at this level but the facilities and accommodations of Tararron offer strong competition. So does the service. In fact, the Tamarron was always consistently rated in the top five of all the hotels in the well-respected Hilton chain while it had that affiliation. I don't suspect that the recent change to the Sheraton label will have a negative affect on the quality.

The guest rooms are located either in the main lodge or scattered among the spacious and meticulously landscaped grounds in one of three other separate lodges. The "standard" room is categorized as "Deluxe" and, depending upon location, can be up to 900 square feet. It has a separate sitting area. Some have kitchenettes and many have balconies. The Executive Suites are 1,600 square feet in an open loft with living, dining and kitchen areas as well as two baths. All have private balconies. The largest unit classification is the one bedroom deluxe suite with 2,200 square feet of space. Bigger than most single family houses, these loft units have bedroom, living, dining room and kitchen with three baths and a private balcony. Families or groups traveling together can stay here in this manner at an affordable price. All accommodations have iron and ironing board, beautiful furnishings and decorator items. And there are plenty of little things like ample closet space and generous lighting. Many have whirlpool tubs.

For your dining pleasure there is the casually elegant **Antlers Lounge & Grille** and the simpler fare of the **San Juan Mountain Cafe**. Quick snacks and lunches are available at a deli and there is a nice cocktail lounge. People who stay for more than a few nights will certainly be interested in the wide range of recreational and other activities available at Tamarron. To start off there is an indoor/outdoor swimming pool and a complete health club and spa with sauna, steamroom and hot tub. Such extra fee services as professional massage, skin care treatments and aroma therapy are available for those who want to improve their appearance. Some people claim these things will improve your life, too. Then you can work out on three tennis courts or go horseback riding, fishing, rafting on the wild Animas River, take a jeep tour, hike or mountain bike.

Skiing at nearby Purgatory Ski Resort can be arranged through the hotel's activities desk along with seasonal sleigh and snowmobile rides. The latter can be with or without meals (breakfast or dinner). The 18-hole championship level golf course known as *The Cliffs* is worthy of special attention. A challenging course with plenty of water, it is considered to be one of the best in America. Certainly the views are striking. There's a summer golf institute for those seeking to better their game.

Rounding out the scene at Tamarron are several specialty shops and even a general store for those who plan to make use of the in-room cooking facilities. Children aren't overlooked here either. The "Kids Korral" is a full program of daytime activities. While you're out for the evening the little ones can be entertained in Tamarron's "Kampfire Kids" program. They also have less structured child care programs and a playground. Various package plans are offered year round. These include some of the services and facilities at Tamarron and adventures in the surrounding areas that usually cost extra.

11. DENVER

The Mile High City. Kind of has a nice ring, doesn't it? While most of the city lies at an altitude of approximately one mile, the name is more exact when you consider that the fifteenth step to the west entrance of the state capitol is exactly 5,280 feet above see level. Something tells me that bit of engineering wasn't by accident. Regardless of this trivia lover's morsel, **Denver** is something special. It's location near the eastern edge of the Rocky Mountain foothills is nothing short of marvelous. A mountain wall stretching as far north and south of the city as you can see is one of the most imposing backdrops for any city in the world. The mountains are literally Denver's playground.

Denver had a rather inauspicious beginning. When gold was reputedly discovered in Cherry Creek in 1858 prospectors flocked to the area along with plenty of unsavory types who figured they could make a buck in other ways. The boom soon turned to bust but was refueled in 1860 with a real good strike on nearby Clear Creek. The town was designated as the territorial capital in 1867. Originally going by other names, two towns merged and took the name Denver in honor of one of Colorado's early territorial governors, **James Denver**. During its early years Denver managed to come back time and time again from fires and floods, always rebuilding bigger, just like many other frontier settlements. And like many of those it, too, was wild and often lawless. For a good many years it was on a par with such notorious places as Dodge City or Tombstone.

The coming of the railroad spurred more growth which continued until the collapse of the silver market in 1893. But subsequent discoveries of more gold in nearby locales, such as Cripple Creek, restored and even enhanced the city's prosperity. Today's Denver is a modern metropolis although many Victorian structures from its earlier days still exist and blend in nicely with the surroundings. The multinational city (Hispanic and Japanese communities, for example, are sizable) is the financial and business capital of the intermountain states and is an important center of manufacturing, transportation, and distribution. The cattle and sheep markets are among the biggest in the country. Research and development in energy and high technology industries are also of importance. The city shares characteristics of eastern sophistication and western spirit in an interesting blend that is probably unique in America's urban areas. It is the largest city in a 600-mile radius.

Despite Denver's soaring altitude, the urban landscape is relatively flat. Downtown grew up around the confluence of the South Platte River and Cherry Creek. The metropolitan area, all of which lies within the shadowy presence of the nearby Rocky Mountains, is spread out in all directions. To the north are the suburbs of Arvada, Northglenn, Westminster, and Thornton. To the east is Aurora; and to the south is Cherry Hills and Greenwood Villages, along with Englewood and Littleton. The western suburbs are closest to the mountains and are situated higher than Denver itself. Among the major towns here are Golden, Lakewood, and Wheat Ridge. The Great Plains lie to the east of Denver.

While the majority of visitors to Denver are eager to at least venture into the mountains, if not spend the biggest portion of their time in Colorado there, the city itself has much to offer. Many fine museums and cultural venues are located here. Denver has 16 institutions of higher education, many which contribute significantly to the cultural vitality of the city. And then there are the parks–not just your ordinary city parks, but 17 municipally owned mountain areas in the foothills of the Rockies that cover more than 140,000 acres and delight both visitors and residents. So let's get to know Denver better.

ARRIVALS & DEPARTURES
By Air
A far-cry in both architectural aesthetics and passenger comforts from the old Stapleton Airport, the ultra-modern **Denver International Airport** is located 23 miles northeast of downtown. Depending upon your point of view it looks something like a sailing ship or a spaceship. One of the busiest airports in the nation, DIA is served by more than 25 airlines and is an important hub for several major carriers. Non-stop flights to more than 150 destinations are available and its location in the middle of the country (more or less) makes possible convenient connections to anywhere.

Every major car rental company has an office at the airport and there are many local firms to go along with them. The latter are good if you're going to be returning the car to DIA. The route into the city from the airport is simple—just follow the airport connector road (Pena Blvd.) to I-70. From there it is a short ride west into downtown. Public transportation from the airport to Denver and the surrounding areas is extensive.

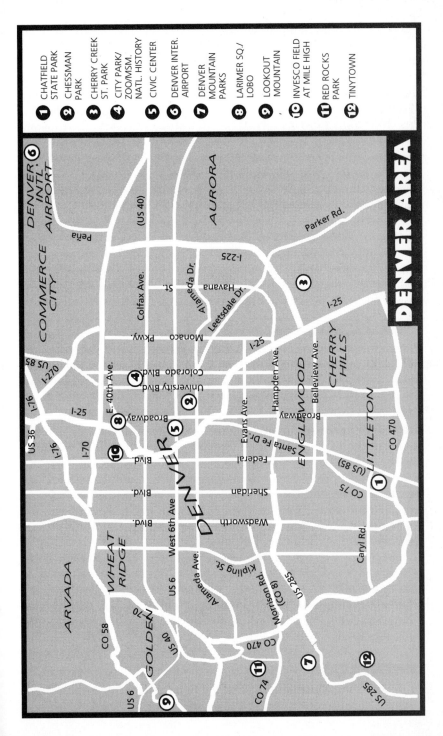

DENVER AREA

Legend:
1. CHATFIELD STATE PARK
2. CHESSMAN PARK
3. CHERRY CREEK ST. PARK
4. CITY PARK/ ZOO/MSM. NATL. HISTORY
5. CIVIC CENTER
6. DENVER INTER. AIRPORT
7. DENVER MOUNTAIN PARKS
8. LARIMER SQ./ LOBO
9. LOOKOUT MOUNTAIN
10. INVESCO FIELD AT MILE HIGH
11. RED ROCKS PARK
12. TINYTOWN

There are many limo and bus services that connect to ski resorts in season and to area communities year-round. These will be described in some of the regional destination chapters.

The options into Denver include many private operators, of which some of the better known are the **Airporter**, *Tel. 303/333-5833*, cost about $20; the **Dash Shuttle**, *Tel. 800/525-3177*, $15; and **SuperShuttle**, *Tel. 303/370-1300*, $15-20. A taxi ride into downtown will cost approximately $35 before the tip. The Regional Transit District has several regular lines that serve the airport but I wouldn't suggest hauling your luggage on them. A better choice is their special **skyRide** service. There are five different routes that go all over the region but two routes (designated AF and AT) serve downtown. The fare ranges from $6 to $8.

By Bus

The main bus terminal is located downtown at *1055 19th Street, corner of Arapahoe Street*. All out of state bus service is through **Greyhound**, *Tel. 800/231-2222*. Gray Line Tours also operates out of the same terminal.

By Car

For those of you driving into Denver from other parts of the state or just about anywhere else in the country, arrival is likely to be via one of the two major Interstates that meet in Denver. I-70 is the primary means of approach from either east or west, while I-25 is the north-to-south artery. They converge near the northwest corner of downtown. I-76 is an alternative means of approach for some. It comes in on an angle from the northeast, crosses I-25 for access into downtown, and finally ends at the junction with I-70 in suburban Wheat Ridge. CO 470 and I-225 form a partial belt around the southern, eastern and western parts of the metropolitan area. I-70 runs along the northern part of the city and, in effect, completes the belt. The primary downtown highway exits are 275 and 276 on I-70, and 209 through 213 on I-25.

By Train

Amtrak, *Tel. 800/USA-RAIL*, serves Denver at **Union Station**, *1701 Wynkoop Street at 17th Street*, on the northwest edge of downtown. Amtrak provides daily service on its Chicago to San Francisco route. The station's location is convenient to all of the downtown area attractions and connections via public transportation to the rest of the Denver metropolitan area. Car rentals are available.

ORIENTATION

The Rocky Mountains eliminate the need for walking around with a compass even for those who get lost if someone turns them around a few times. If you're in the city, anywhere in the city, and you're facing the mountains, then you are looking west. To your right is north, and to your left is south. Obviously, then, east is behind you. Simple!

Within the urban loop formed by the aforementioned I-70, I-225, and CO 470, you need be familiar only with a few major routes. Colfax Avenue (US 40) is the primary east-west thoroughfare and runs along the southern edge of downtown. Other important east-west streets are 6th Avenue (US 6 on the west side of town) and Alameda Avenue. There are many north-south streets that traverse most of the metropolitan area. These include (from west to east) Wadsworth Boulevard, Federal Boulevard, Broadway, and Colorado Boulevard. All of these streets form a neat grid pattern. To make things easier avenues always run east to west and streets go north to south.

Unfortunately, the exception to all of this is downtown itself, which has its own neat little grid pattern. Downtown is roughly bordered by the Cherry Creek to the west, the South Platte River to the north, Broadway on the east, and Colfax Avenue on the south. In the triangle formed by the latter two streets and the rivers, numbered streets run diagonally from southeast to northwest and named streets diagonally from southwest to northeast. All streets within this downtown grid are alternately one-way.

Finally, most streets are designated by directional quadrant (north, south, east, or west). Streets on the mountain side of Broadway have a west prefix while those on the Plains side of Broadway are east. Ellsworth Avenue is the dividing point for north and south designations. All in all Denver is really quite easy to figure out so you don't have to be a professional navigator.

GETTING AROUND TOWN

Like most big cities, Denver has lots of traffic. So if you're going to be exploring downtown it is best to walk. Many attractions as well as hotels, restaurants, and cultural facilities are located downtown so you'll probably be spending a good deal of time in what is a fairly small area that lends itself to the shoe leather method of transportation and exploration. However, there are many things to see and do in the far flung reaches of what is a large metropolitan area, so other forms of transportation will become necessary at some point.

Denver's **Regional Transportation District**, or **RTD,** operates a comprehensive system of buses and light-rail trains throughout the metropolitan area and covers portions of six different counties. Happily, Denver offers inexpensive public transportation. The basic fare is $1.25 for bus or light rail during the rush hours (6:00am to 9:00am and 4:00pm to 6:00pm) and 75 cents at all other times. Routes designated as "Express" charge $2 but these generally connect downtown with some of the suburbs during the weekday rush hours so most visitors won't be using them. Most regular routes operate at all times except between the wee hours of 1:30 and 4:30am. Transfers are available between routes and between modes (i.e., from bus to light rail or vice-versa).

In addition to single fare (paid by cash or transit token), you can purchase a ten-trip ticket book which will save you about $3. There are also monthly passes (beginning at $35) but most visitors will not have a need for this. Information and tickets are available at all transit stations and at the RTD's downtown headquarters at 1600 Blake. For information on routes and schedules contact the RTD at *Tel. 303/299-6000* or *Tel. 800/366-7433* outside the 303 area code.

By Bus

The RTD operates more than 170 different routes that can you bring you to just about any part of the metropolitan area. The main downtown bus station is located adjacent to the Civic Center at the intersection of Broadway and Colfax Avenue. You can get route maps and other information there. That is also the departure point for many Express Routes. Some of these may come in handy if you plan to use the bus to get to some of the suburban locations or you're staying away from the city center.

If you're taking in a concert at the city's Performing Arts Center, the RTD operates a shuttle route for 50 cents that circulates through downtown and stops at the Center. Unfortunately, this service doesn't operate during the day so it can't be used for your sightseeing tour of Denver. However, the bus option is still available via the **Cultural Connection Trolley** (a bus made to look like an old-time trolley) which completes a loop from Larimer Square, through downtown, along Colfax Avenue and on to Cheesman and City Parks. This covers most of the attractions on Tours 1 and 2 that will be described later. Check with the RTD first, however, since the route is seasonal and hours of operation vary frequently.

By Car

As we alluded to earlier, try to avoid driving in downtown. If you must bring the car into the city center, you should leave the car in one of the many lots or garages. Rates are fairly high for short term parking (up to $3 an hour) but aren't that bad for the entire day (almost always under $10). There is limited on-street metered parking. Pay close attention to day and hour restrictions as the Denver police are quick to ticket or tow-away illegally parked cars. There is a $10 fine for overstaying at a meter which means it would be cheaper to have parked in a garage in the first place. Two of the major downtown parking garages are the **Larimer**

Square Parking, *1422 Market Street,* and the **Tremont Parking Center**, *400 15th Street.*

Once you get away from downtown most streets are two-way. Broad avenues help with the traffic flow and the only problems are usually during the morning and afternoon rush hours. The same is true for the freeways which are frequently bumper to bumper during busy commuting times. If you can avoid rush hour driving throughout the metropolitan area there shouldn't be any big problem negotiating a car through Denver. Parking isn't usually a big problem at points of interest outside of the downtown area. If they don't have a parking lot of their own there is on-street parking available close by.

By Light Rail

The new centerpiece of the RTD's comprehensive plan to relieve traffic congestion in Denver, the clean, fast (up to 55mph through the city center) and efficient Light Rail system can be a major part of your getting around. The 5.3 mile long Central line runs from 30th Avenue and Downing (northeast of downtown) and then through the central business district before continuing south to Broadway and I-25. In the downtown section the trains run northbound via California Street and southbound on Stout Street. With stations at 14th, 16th and 18th Streets, you can make a nice little loop through the city center. The newest section of Light Rail is the 8.7 mile long Southwest line which begins at the Broadway/I-25 station and extends through Englewood and other areas before terminating at Littleton. Further lines are planned and construction could begin on some of it as early as 2002, but it won't be complete until at least 2008.

If you are staying quite a way from downtown it is a good idea to take your car to the nearest station with a park-and-ride lot and then continue into the city center via light rail in order to avoid traffic and parking hassles. Stations with park-and-ride facilities on the Central line are 30th/Downing, 29th/Welton, and Alameda. On the Southwest lines you can park at either of the two stations in Littleton or at Englewood. There is also parking where the two lines converge at I-25 & Broadway.

You must purchase your ticket before boarding the train. Vending machines are located at each station and will guide you through the process. Monthly and other passes are also valid for fare on the light rail system. There are heavy fines if you are caught riding without a valid ticket. Random inspections are made. The Light Rail is accessible to the disabled.

If your sightseeing activities are going to take you alongside the South Platte River then you may well be able to take advantage of the **Platte Valley Trolley**, *Tel. 303/458-6255.* Operated by the Denver Rail Heritage Society, this service has five stops between its northern terminus located at Platte & 15th Streets, just north of the confluence of the Platte River and Cherry Creek) and the Denver Children's Museum. The line runs daily during the summer from 11:00am until 5:00pm and costs $2 for adults, $1 for seniors and children. Call for operating hours at other times of the year.

By Taxi

Oh, find me a city with inexpensive cabs. Denver isn't the answer, although it isn't as bad as some places. Taxi rates start at $1.40 for the first drop of the meter and add a like figure for each mile. Most often cabs are ordered by phone although you can sometimes get lucky enough to find one on the street. The most important cab companies are as follows:
• **Metro Taxi**, *Tel. 303/333-3333*
• **Yellow Cab**, *Tel. 303/777-7777*
• **Zone Cab**, *Tel. 303/444-8888*

WHERE TO STAY

Chain properties in the moderate and inexpensive categories have not been included. However, they are among the few good choices available within Denver itself for those who wish to find accommodations in those price ranges. Refer to the listing in Chapter 6 to locate which chains are represented in the Denver area.

DOWNTOWN

The downtown accommodations zone is bordered by Colfax Avenue, Broadway, 22nd Street, the South Platte River and Cherry Creek. It includes the Larimer Square and LoDo districts.

Very Expensive

BROWN PALACE HOTEL, *321 17th Street, Denver. Tel. 303/297-3111, Fax 303/293-9204. Toll free reservations 800/321-2599; www.brownpalace.com. E-mail: marketing@brownpalace.com. 230 Rooms. Rates: $225-295 all year; suites from $300-1,000. Major credit cards accepted. Located in the heart of downtown, four blocks north of the intersection of Colfax Avenue and Broadway.*

An almost legendary hotel now into its second century of operation, the Brown Palace combines the conveniences and amenities of a modern hotel with the atmosphere and service of a Victorian era grand hotel. It's dramatic atrium lobby with soaring stained glass ceiling was, in a sense, a prototype for this architectural style that is so popular in modern hotels and public buildings. The atrium is the gateway to the elegant public areas and contains the lobby lounge with its famous plush red leather chairs.

The Brown Palace isn't that big for a city center hotel which allows the attentive staff to deal with every guest as an individual. Outstanding service is a long-standing tradition at the Palace, just like their afternoon tea service. Little things make the guest rooms special–like the plush terry cloth robes and the nightly turn-down service. Even the drinking water is special at the Brown Palace as they have their own Rocky Mountain water supply via an artesian well.

There are three excellent restaurants, two of which are described in the Where to Eat section. For drinks and socializing, Churchill Bar is a great spot. It's known for its superior cigar selection and relaxing ambiance.

Selected as one of my Best Places to Stay (see Chapter 10 for more details).

HYATT REGENCY DENVER, *1750 Welton Street. Tel. 303/295-1234; Fax 303/293-2565. Toll free reservations 800/233-1234; www.hyatt.com. 511 Rooms. Rates: $200-220 all year with lower rates available on weekends. Major credit cards accepted. Located a block northwest of the 16th Street Pedestrian Mall.*

What can you say that isn't good about almost any Hyatt Hotel? The downtown Denver version falls nicely into that category with its dramatic and modern architecture and spacious public areas. The most attractive feature in the lobby is the large sandstone fireplace. While the price level makes it most appealing to the businessman on a generous expense account, it isn't that overpriced when you consider the level of luxury compared to many other big city hotels that are centrally located.

The guestrooms at the 26-story high Hyatt are generally quite large and are furnished in an attractive modern style that isn't particularly distinguished. There are also luxury level rooms available. All rooms feature a mini-bar and coffee maker.

Among the facilities are a good restaurant as well as a pretty dining room that features an excellent breakfast and lunch buffet each day. For those looking to keep in shape after all that eating, the Hyatt also has a health club with heated indoor swimming pool, tennis court, and an outdoor jogging track. Night owls can spend some time in one of two lounges.

THE TEATRO HOTEL, *1100 14th Street. Tel. 303/228-1100; Fax 303/ 228-1101. Toll free reservations 800/996-3426. 116 Rooms. Rates: $179-225. Major credit cards accepted. Located at the intersection of Arapahoe Street, just northeast of Speer Blvd. and the Cherry Creek. Convenient for theater district.*

This is one of several new boutique style hotels that have sprung up in Denver over the past couple of years. The Teatro is a member of Wyndham's prestigious "Grand Heritage" hotels. The surroundings are elegant and the accommodations are luxurious. Pampering of guests is the order of the day, although you'll hardly need it considering the many amenities that you will find in all of the guest rooms. Although this new facility is first rate and doesn't lend itself to complaints, I think you will find that the Hotel Monaco, described below in the Expensive section, provides a better value. There is an outstanding restaurant and lounge on the premises called Kevin Taylor. See the *Where to Eat* section for further details. Downtown transportation is provided.

WESTIN HOTEL AT TABOR CENTER, *1672 Lawrence Street. Tel. 303/572-9100; Fax 572-7288. Toll free reservations 800/228-3000; www.westin.com. E-mail: denver@westin.com. 420 Rooms. Rates: $225-285 weekdays and $89-129 on weekends, all year. Major credit cards accepted. Located adjacent to the 16th Street Pedestrian Mall at Tabor Center, 2 blocks northeast from Larimer Square.*

Overlooking the bustling 16th Street Pedestrian Mall, the Westin is a beautiful modern building that is part of the gleaming glass and steel city-within-a-city framework that is the Tabor Center. The lobby and other public areas are all luxurious in an elegant but understated sort of way.

Each of the oversized guestrooms features an excellent view of either the city or mountains. The list of amenities provided to guests is long and impressive and include such things as coffee makers, an iron/ironing board, mini-bar, plush towels, a wide assortment of deluxe toiletries and even some free movies. The responsive service provided by an attentive staff is also well above the usual.

The Westin has two restaurants. One of them, Augusta, is listed separately in the *Where to Eat* section below. There is also a cocktail lounge with entertainment. Other facilities include a heated indoor and outdoor swimming pool and a full service health club with whirlpool, sauna, exercise equipment and racquetball.

Expensive

ADAMS MARK HOTEL DENVER, *1550 Court Place. Tel. 303/893-3333; Fax 303/623-0303. Toll free reservations 800/444-ADAM; www.adamsmark.com. 1,230 Rooms. Rates: $169-184 all year. Major credit cards accepted. Located two blocks northeast of Civic Center between 15th and 16th Streets.*

The Adams Mark, a member of a small chain of superior hotels, has long been considered to be one of the finest hotels in Denver. It consists of an older section and a much newer 500-room tower. However, the accommodations are first-rate in either section. The extensive meeting facilities and business services have made the Adams Mark a favorite of the business traveler. Although expensive, it is less so than some of the other top hotels in town so that all except those on a tight budget could find themselves staying in the heart of downtown. In fact, the Adams Mark's imposing presence on the 16th Street Mall adds to the dramatic architectural landscape of Denver's beautiful city center. The public areas aren't designed to dazzle but certainly are spacious and attractive.

The guestrooms best feature is their generous size and comfortable furnishings. That's important because after a busy day of touring the town you're likely to be just as tired as that businessman or woman. More luxurious accommodations are available at higher rates if you want to stay in one of the hotel's more than a hundred suites or take a room on the deluxe Concierge Level. Many rooms have coffee makers and refrigerators. Suites and Concierge Level rooms often feature whirlpools.

Guest facilities include three restaurants at various price levels, a complete health and fitness center that boasts sauna and exercise room, several lounges (one with live entertainment), and a heated outdoor pool located on the roof. The Adams Mark has an underground parking garage.

DENVER MARRIOTT CITY CENTER, *1701 California Street. Tel. 303/297-1300; Fax 303/298-7474. Toll free reservations 800/228-9290; www.marriott.com. 613 Rooms. Rates: $149-169 weekdays and $79-99 weekends, all year. Major credit cards accepted. Located 5 blocks northeast of the Convention Center between 17th and 18th Streets.*

Another of Denver's many fine hotels that usually cater to the business traveler but that are also well suited to the leisure travel because of their proximity to so many important visitor destinations. (There's even a station on the light rail system right at the hotel.) The 20-story hotel tower is modern and attractive even though it lacks any particular unique style. But you do get a large, well-equipped room with ironing facilities and a hair dryer as well as a refrigerator and, just what you need while on vacation–voice mail service.

Besides having two good restaurants I like the Marriott's pizza joint (even though it's a national chain parlor) for a quick lunch or nightime snack. Besides, it gives a needed shot of under sophistication for what is essentially an upscale hotel experience. A cocktail lounge that sometimes features live entertainment is also on the premises. The recreational opportunities include a heated indoor pool and health club with sauna and whirlpool.

HOTEL MONACO, *1717 Champa Street. Tel. 303/296-1717; Fax 303/296-1818. Toll free reservations 800/397-5380; www.monaco-denver.com. 189 Rooms. Rates: $169-209; suites from $215-380. Rates about $30 lower are available between January and March. Major credit cards are accepted. Located at the intersection of 17th Street in downtown, one block away from the middle of the 16th Street pedestrian mall.*

Monaco is a small but growing collection of moderately sized European-style boutique hotels, and this new addition is a fine example of why the Monaco name will soon be easily recognized to travelers. It nicely combines traditional styling with a host of amenities and modern conveniences that will make you think you're still at home—or maybe in the office. Each room has a CD player, fax and copy machine, honor bar, coffee maker and hair dryer amongst other little touches. And, oh yes, the furnishings are all tastefully done. The seven-story structure also has 32 suites, over two dozen of which have two-person whirlpools for that romantic weekend! Plush terry cloth robes are also a standard feature.

On the services side Monaco won't disappoint either. There is a good restaurant called Panzano that serves northern Italian cuisine. The hotel also boasts a complete fitness center that includes an Aveda spa and salon. All guests are invited to partake in a wine reception that is held every evening. There is concierge service available. In fact, the level of service at the Monaco is excellent. A gift shop is on the premises and downtown area transportation is provided free of charge.

The Monaco is a little too new for me to be able to include it with the best places to stay. However, it wouldn't surprise me if it makes it to that category by the next edition of this book.

OXFORD HOTEL, *1600 17th Street. Tel. 303/628-5400; Fax 628-5413. Toll free reservations 800/228-5838; www.theoxfordhotel.com. 81 Rooms. Rates: $169-299 all year. Major credit cards accepted. Located just south of Union Station at the intersection of Wazee Street.*

Situated astride the Larimer Square area and near to LoDo and Coors Field, the Oxford is an attractively small and historic property that provides a delightful alternative to some of the big modern high rise lodging establishments of downtown Denver. The five story high Victorian style structure looks more like a stately old luxury apartment building than a hotel. It was built in 1891 and for a time back before the Renaissance of the old downtown area was not the most desirable place to stay. However, it has been carefully restored to its original elegance and the furnishings, both in public areas and guestrooms, feature a large number of authentic French and English antiques. It also boasts a considerable art collection for a property of its size.

The guestrooms, besides having an old world flavor, have been updated with a host of modern amenities including mini-bar. The Oxford's service is outstanding and features many nice touches such as afternoon sherry served in the lobby along with a daily newspaper. They'll also provide luxury limousine service in the downtown area.

Because the hotel isn't big it doesn't have a lot of public facilities. However, it does have two dining rooms and a cocktail lounge. Guests receive privileges at the nearby Oxford Aveda Salon and Health Club.

Moderate

   HOLTZE EXECUTIVE PLACE, *818 17th Street. Tel. 303/607-9000; Fax 303/628-0201. Toll free reservations 888/4-HOLTZE; www.holtze.com. 244 Rooms. Rates: $99-129; suites available at higher prices. Most major credit cards accepted. Located in the heart of downtown at the intersection of Stout Street, one block off of the 16th Street pedestrian mall.*

   Considering the location and the quality, this may well be the best value in downtown lodging. Although the luxury level isn't quite up to the standards of some of the preceding listings, the Holtze manages to create a boutique style atmosphere and delivers excellent service at a price considerably below the competition. The types of accommodations available are quite varied, ranging from spacious rooms to apartment-like suites. All but about two dozen of the rooms have a full kitchen so you can even save more money by having some meals in (especially breakfast). Room amenities are numerous and the decor is pleasing to the eye. There is no restaurant or lounge on the premises but there are plenty of places to choose from within a short walk.

NEW DIGS FOR DENVER

   As you read through my hotel suggestions for Denver you will see several establishments that have opened within the past year or two. But the Denver hotel building boom continues. Following are a few hotels that weren't complete as of press time but are sure to be places worthy of your consideration.

   ***Marriott** and **Westin**, two of the most respected upscale hotel chains, are both adding to their existing presence in the Denver area. Marriott is constructing a hotel as part of the expansion of the Denver Convention Center, while Westin is building a new facility at Denver International Airport. You can check out these company's web sites to find out when they're ready.*

   *The **Executive Tower Hotel**, conveniently located near the Denver Performing Arts Center, was a favorite of mine and was listed in the first edition of this book. It is now temporarily closed for renovations. When it reopens in the summer of 2001, it will do so under the **Hilton Hotels** banner.*

AROUND THE CITY
Very Expensive

   HYATT REGENCY TECH CENTER, *7800 Tufts Avenue. Tel. 303/779-1234; Fax 303/850-7164. Toll free reservations 800/223-1234; www.hyatt.com. 450 Rooms. Rates: $204; lower rates available on weekends.*

Major credit cards accepted. Located just north of the Denver Technological Center off of the I-25/I-225 interchange.

An impressive modern architectural work, the Hyatt Tech Center caters mostly to the business traveler but is in a good location for getting into downtown as well as other points of interest in the Denver area. The public areas boast the elegance and soaring open spaces so associated with the Hyatt name as well as fine service. The guestrooms are large and quite comfortable and are, of course, well equipped but aren't anything that special from an aesthetic standpoint. There are two restaurants with decent food including one on the rooftop as well as several lounges. Other facilities include a complete fitness center, indoor swimming pool, Jacuzzi, and outdoor lighted tennis court.

WARWICK HOTEL, *1776 Grant Street. Tel. 303/861-2000; Fax 303/832-0320. Toll free reservations 800/525-2888; www.warwickhotels.com. 194 Rooms. Rates: $225-285 all year. Lower rates available on weekends. All rates include full breakfast. Major credit cards accepted. Located slightly to the east of downtown at the corner of 18th Avenue. Drive east from downtown on 19th Avenue and turn right on Grant.*

The Warwick is, considering the price, an elegant upscale hotel in the style of Europe's small grand hotels. The lobby and other public spaces aren't big but they exude warmth and richness. The guest rooms are absolutely huge and feature a European theme with classic Thomasville furniture adding to the luxury. The upper stories of the 15-floor high Warwick afford good views of the mountains as well as of downtown. Most units have refrigerator, wet bar and a balcony. A smaller number of rooms have microwave ovens.

The hotel has a good restaurant as well as a cocktail lounge. Privileges at a nearby health club are extended to all guests. There is also a small heated swimming pool. Courtesy transportation is provided to downtown and other destinations within a five mile radius of the hotel.

Expensive

CAPITOL HILL MANSION, *1207 Pennsylvania Street. Tel. 303/839-5221; Fax 303/839-9046. Toll free reservations 800/839-9329; www.capitolhillmansion.com. E-mail: info@capitolhillmansion.com. 8 Rooms. Rates: $90-175, all year including full breakfast. American Express, Discover, MasterCard and VISA accepted. Located about a half mile from downtown and state capitol via Colfax Avenue east and then south on Pennsylvania.*

The Capitol Hill Mansion is one of the foremost examples of the Victorian 1890's architecture in an area noted for such buildings. It was built in 1891 for Jeffrey Keating, a noted investor and lumber company owner. It became a hotel in the early 1920s but has more recently been restored to its original style and converted into a B&B. It is registered on national and state levels as a landmark building. The Romanesque building has several turrets, high chimneys, balconies and a curved porch. Once inside you'll encounter a graceful staircase and stained glass. All of the public areas are richly decorated and have helped to earn this inn the highest award granted by the American Bed & Breakfast Association.

Even the names of the eight rooms are indicative of the delights that await you. The Gold Banner, Shooting Star, Elk Thistle, Pasqueflower, Paintbrush, Bluebell, Snowlover, and Forget-Me-Not rooms and suites all feature coffee maker and refrigerator, plush towels, color cable TV and designer decor. No two are alike but they're all spacious and airy, bright and cheerful. Many feature fireplaces, whirlpool tubs, wet bar, balcony, and oversized beds. All rooms except one are air conditioned. When making reservations inquire as what floor a particular room is on if you don't want to walk up a lot of steps since there is no elevator in the three-story structure.

Your host, Kathy Robbins, will be glad to assist you in making your Denver stay more entertaining. The bountiful breakfast can be taken either with other guests or in the privacy of your own room, something not often found in B&B's. Games, puzzles and books are provided to fill in some time if you haven't made plans for an evening out on the town but prefer to relax in this tranquil and romantic setting.

DENVER MARRIOTT SOUTHEAST, *6363 East Hampden Avenue. Tel. 303/758-7000; Fax 303/758-6305. Toll free reservations 800/228-9290; www.marriott.com. 590 Rooms. Rates: $139-169 weekdays and $69-89 on weekends. Major credit cards accepted. Located immediately to the east of I-25, Exit 201, approximately 10 miles from downtown via I-25 and Colfax or Hampden Avenue west to Broadway northbound.*

This large full service hotel is quite typical of the high standards usually found at Marriott properties. About the only thing negative you can say about this place is that it doesn't have much that differentiates it from dozens of other places like it. But if you're looking for deluxe facilities at a rate that is affordable, the Marriott Southeast definitely fits the bill. The rooms are a nice size and well equipped. Refrigerators, safes and whirlpools are among the options in some rooms. Rooms on the top four floors that face towards the west have excellent mountain views.

There are two restaurants, a pizza shop, and cocktail lounge. Karaoke (yech!) is featured two nights a week. Recreational facilities take the form of two heated swimming pools (one outdoors and one indoors), whirlpool and exercise room.

CASTLE MARNE–A LUXURY URBAN INN, *1572 Race Street. Tel. 303/331-0621; Fax 303/331-0623. Toll free reservations 800/92-MARNE; www.castlemarne.com. E-mail: diane@castlemarne.com. 10 Rooms. Rates: $115-230, all year including full breakfast. Major credit cards accepted. Located slightly to the southeast of Downtown via Broadway south to 16th Avenue, east to Race and then just north.*

Like the nearby Capitol Hill Mansion, Castle Marne is another Victorian jewel that is a registered historic landmark. It also provides a wonderful combination of old world elegance and charm with many modern amenities. I don't have any complaints about the appearance but it is a touch below Capitol Hill in eye catching architecture both outside and inside. The service is, as you would expect, friendly and personalized.

The rooms are each unique although some are on the smallish side. Some units are on the third floor and there is no elevator. All rooms have ceiling fans but no air conditioning. That isn't often a problem in Denver although it is always possible to encounter an unexpectedly hot spell. The furnishings are authentic period pieces and about a third of the rooms have hot tubs, whirlpool and balconies. The breakfast is excellent. Castle Marne also offers an afternoon tea. Lunch and dinner can be arranged by prior request and are best suited for those in a private romantic mood.

LOEWS GIORGIO HOTEL, *4150 E. Mississippi Avenue. Tel. 303/782-9300; Fax 303/758-6542. Toll free reservations 800/345-9172; www.loewshotels.com. 191 Rooms. Rates: $169-259 weekdays and $99-124 on weekends, all year. Most major credit cards accepted. Located about a half mile north of I-25, Exit 204 via Colorado Boulevard to Mississippi and then just east; or about three miles south of East Colfax Avenue via Colorado Blvd.*

The Giorgio is an elegant moderate sized hotel built in a traditional Italian style. It's like taking a little trip to Europe but instead of shopping by the fashionable shops near Rome's Spanish Steps, you'll be within minutes of hundreds of stores in the Cherry Creek shopping district. Both public areas and guest rooms are beautifully decorated and give off a home-like warmth that you can't find in bigger hotels. The Giorgio has received many awards from a multiplicity of sources and the outstanding personalized service is one of the main reasons. Upon a return from a hectic day you can easily relax and unwind in the gracious surroundings, whether it be the comfortable lobby or lounges or the privacy of your own room. In fact, the glowing fireplace and subdued tones of the public lounging area remind one of the type of living room that would be found in a stately mansion.

The guest rooms carry out the Italian theme and have an old world appearance despite the many modern features. Plush upholstered furniture and fresh flowers are two of the little touches that you'll find. The rooms aren't overly large but are big enough. All feature mini-bar and coffee maker. Some have refrigerators.

There are two restaurants at the Giorgio. One of them, The Tuscany, has very good Italian cuisine and even a harpist to calm you at dinner. A small exercise room is on the premises but you also receive privileges at a nearby full service health club if you're looking for a more vigorous workout. Complimentary transportation is provided within a three mile radius that includes all of the Cherry Creek shopping area.

QUEEN ANNE BED & BREAKFAST INN, *2147 Tremont Place. Tel. 303/296-6666; Fax 303/296-2151. Toll free reservations 800/432-INNS; queenanne@bedandbreakfastinns.org. 14 Rooms. Rates: $115-175 all year including full breakfast. Most major credit cards accepted. Located immediately to the east of downtown intersection of Tremont and Broadway between 21st and 22nd Streets.*

A thoroughly charming facility, the Queen Anne consists of two side-by-side Victorian dwellings that have been combined into a single facility on a most pleasant residential street facing a small but lovely little city park called Eastside Park. Both public areas and guest rooms are furnished in authentic period pieces. I especially like the generous use of flowers and plants throughout the inn.

Each of the fourteen units (four of which are multi-room suites) is quite distinctive as to theme and style. Among the amenities that can be found in some rooms are fireplace, whirlpool tub (although every room has a unique bathtub of some sort) and cable television. The three story building does not have an elevator so you may want to specify a room on a lower floor if you have difficulty negotiating steps. A nice breakfast is served each day and complimentary beverages are available during the evening. The proprietors will be glad to loan you a bicycle to scoot around town.

RENAISSANCE DENVER HOTEL, *3801 Quebec Street. Tel. 303/399-7500; Fax 303/ 321-1783. Toll free reservations 800/HOTELS-1; www.renaissancehotels.com. E-mail: lee_rossiter@rhi.com. 400 Rooms. Rates: $159-185 weekdays and $109-139 weekends, all year. American Express, Carte Blanche, Diners Club, and Discover accepted. Located immediately south of I-70, Exit 278.*

Conveniently located about half-way between downtown and the airport, the Renaissance Denver is a beautiful twelve story luxury hotel with a dramatic atrium lobby. While the public areas are definitely first class, I am especially impressed with the excellent guest rooms. Larger than most hotel rooms in the same price range, they are furnished in a manner that is both tasteful and comfortable–a step up from the too often sterile appearance of modern luxury level hotels. In room conveniences include mini-bar and coffee maker. Some rooms have video cassette players and most have balconies. Unfortunately, the views vary from not too much to so-so, especially for Denver.

The facilities of the Renaissance are extensive. There is a good restaurant and cocktail lounge with live entertainment; two heated swimming pools (both indoor and outdoor); and a health club with steamroom and whirlpool. The staff throughout the hotel is both attentive and efficient in a professional yet friendly sort of way.

Moderate

THE ADAGIO BED & BREAKFAST, *1430 Race Street. Tel. 303/370-6911; Fax 303/377-5968. Toll free reservations 800/533-3241; www.adagiobb.com. 5 Rooms. Rates: $99-140 including full breakfast. Discover, MasterCard and VISA accepted. Located close to downtown via Colfax Avenue east to Race Street. The inn is between 14th Avenue and Colfax.*

"Adagio" is an Italian term widely used in music and means slowly or leisurely. It aptly describes the pace at this lovely little facility tucked away on a quiet street that is remarkably close to the hustle and bustle of downtown. Dating from 1892 the Victorian era inn has a grace and charm that isn't often found in the city. Owners and hosts Jim and Amy Cremmins go out of their way to make sure that your experience at the Adagio is a pleasant one.

The first floor has a spacious living room where guests can gather after a busy day to discuss their activities in Denver. Amy often plays the grand piano and Jim might pick up one of his guitars to strum a few tunes. Guests are invited to make use of them too! The breakfast is a bountiful European style affair and in the afternoon an excellent selection of hors d'oeuvres and beverages is available.

All of the guest rooms are on the second and third floors. The Holst Suite features a four-poster bed, original tile work, and a gas fireplace. The Vivaldi Room is big enough to accommodate up to four people. The Copeland Suite contains some items dating to the original construction and a fireplace. The Handel Room features an indoor fountain and four-poster bed while the Brahms Suite, with its adjoining room and day bed can also accommodate four. The latter also features a hot tub. There is no television in the rooms but one is available in the common area.

BEST WESTERN LANDMARK HOTEL, *455 S. Colorado Blvd. Tel. 303/388-5561; Fax 388-7936. Toll free reservations 800/528-1234; www.interamerika.com/USA-Denver-BestWesternHotel-LandmarkInn.htm. 280 Rooms. Rates: $89-109 all year. Major credit cards accepted. Located a mile north of I-25, Exit 204 or east from downtown on Colfax Avenue to Colorado Boulevard and then south.*

One of the really nice properties in the Best Western family, the Landmark recently remodeled all of the guest rooms and they represent one of the best lodging values in the Denver area. Some rooms have refrigerators as well as mountain views. They aren't exceptional but are clean, comfortable and fairly good size. Country Oak Cafe provides pleasant family style dining while the on premise sports lounge is a lively place well into the wee hours. Recreational facilities include an indoor swimming pool, Jacuzzi and exercise room.

FOUR POINTS HOTEL BY SHERATON, *3535 Quebec Street. Tel. 303/333-7711; Fax 303/322-2262. Toll free reservations 800/328-2268. 200 Rooms. Rates: $79-119. Major credit cards accepted. Located about a quarter of a mile south of I-70, Exit 278, and about six miles from downtown via Colfax Avenue east to Quebec Street northbound.*

Formerly called the Sheraton Hotel Airport (when Stapleton Airport was serving Denver's needs), the place has been nicely renovated and renamed. It is convenient to both downtown and the new airport. The eight story high hotel has some good mountain views, the best one being in the restaurant. The lobby and most public areas are attractive but perhaps a bit too much on the sterile overly modern side. On the other hand, the glass enclosed indoor swimming pool is one of the prettiest in town. The guest rooms are real nice looking and quite spacious but a little short of luxury level. The best rooms have balconies. Microwave ovens and refrigerators are available in some rooms.

Morgan's Food & Spirits serves good food in a dynamic atmosphere and there is also a cocktail lounge. The aforementioned swimming pool is junior Olympic sized. Other recreational facilities are the fitness center and Jacuzzi.

HAUS BERLIN BED & BREAKFAST, *1651 Emerson Street. Tel. 303/ 837-9527; Fax 303/837-9527. Toll free reservations 800/659-0253; www.hausberlinbandb.com haus.berlin@worldnet.att.net. 4 Rooms. Rates: $100-140 including full breakfast. American Express, MasterCard and VISA accepted. Located about 2-1/2 miles south of I-70, Exit 276B via Colorado Boulevard to 17th Avenue and then west to Emerson and then just south.*

Haus Berlin was originally known as the Haskell House when it was built in 1892 for the founder of Colorado College. The Haskell family lived there until 1959. It was added to the National Register of Historic Places in 1983 and was soon after converted to an intimate and delightful B&B that has received recognition from the Bed & Breakfast Innkeepers of Colorado. Your hosts, Christiana and Dennis Brown, will do everything in their power to make your stay a most enjoyable experience. The stately Victorian mansion features a double arched front facade and a steeply pointed roof. Except for the cars on Emerson the quiet tree-lined street hasn't changed that much in appearance since the house was built. Three guest bedrooms are on the second floor and the third floor is entirely occupied by a large suite (no elevator).

While the exterior is classic Victorian, the interior is a wonderful eclectic mixture of European decor with touches from the Caribbean, Mexico, South America and other areas. The furniture is also a mixture of antique and modern which somehow all blends together extremely well. All units have down comforters and the finest linens freshly pressed by hand. The lowest priced room is small but comfortable and is the only one without a television. Another room has a French country appearance while a third features stained glass with a window seat. All four rooms have hair dryers. Fresh flowers are brought in each day. Only the suite is air conditioned. This spacious unit has a lovely view of downtown Denver. Christiana personally prepares the delicious breakfast which may include such delights as crepes, quiche or scones along with a variety of cakes, tarts and German hard rolls. Fine imported hams and cheeses are also a frequent menu item. This place is so good that it just missed making the Best Places to Stay list.

Note that the Haus Berlin is not suitable for children.

THE HOLIDAY CHALET, A VICTORIAN HOTEL, *1820 E. Colfax Avenue. Tel. 303/321-9975; Fax 303/377-6556. Toll free reservations 800/626-4497; bbonline.com/co/holiday. E-mail: holidaychalet@aol.com. 10 Rooms. Rates: $94-160 all year, including breakfast. Weekly rates are available. Major credit cards accepted. Located about one mile east of downtown via Colfax (US 40).*

A carefully restored brownstone mansion conveniently located between downtown and the City Park area of Denver, the Holiday Chalet provides a warm old world home-style stay at a surprisingly low price. Several large chimneys are a prominent part of the exterior architecture which is massive but with a sense of grace. Each unit has its own fully equipped kitchenette so you can cook in and save some bucks over restaurants if you are so inclined. The guest rooms are comfortable and on the cozy side. Guests receive privileges at a nearby athletic club.

MARK I GUEST SUITES, *1190 Birch Street. Tel. 303/331-7000; www.denveronline.com/Mark1/. E-mail: mark1@denveronline.com. 17 Rooms. Rates: $59-139. Most major credit cards accepted. Located near the Cherry Creek shopping district, about three miles east of downtown via Colfax Avenue to Birch Street and then south.*

Situated in a nice residential area with pretty parks and fine shopping nearby, the Mark I features one and two bedroom suites each with a full kitchen. The surrounding area has plenty of good restaurants should you choose not to use the cooking facilities. The suites are located in five separate buildings, four on Birch Street and the last a block away on Bellaire Street. Two of the locations are three stories without elevator.

All of the units are spacious and are furnished in a contemporary motif which is fairly attractive. For families or couples traveling together who plan to stay in Denver for more than a few days, the apartment feeling of the suites makes it an option to be seriously considered. As a "condo" style hotel, the Mark I only provides weekly maid service. There is an outdoor swimming pool and a hot tub.

WYNDHAM GARDENS HOTEL DENVER SOUTHEAST, *1475 S. Colorado Blvd. Tel. 303/757-8797; Fax 303/758-0704. Toll free reservations 800/WYNDHAM. 246 Rooms. Rates: $90-109 all year, with reduced weekend rates. Major credit cards accepted. Located a half mile north of I-25, Exit 204 or south on Colorado Blvd. from East Colfax Avenue.*

This modern 11-story high glass and steel structure differs from the more usual low rises of the Wyndham chain. But it has everything that makes them a good place to stay. Among the guest rooms are a number of junior suites. All rooms have an ample writing desk that's great for sending out those vacation postcards or sorting through the day's paperwork. Each room has a coffee maker. If you don't get a room on one of the upper floors you can try to take a peak from the rooftop ballroom that features a panoramic view of the mountains.

The Garden Cafe is a pleasant eatery serving American cuisine. There's also a lobby lounge which makes a nice place to relax. This is also the locale for a weekly Manager's reception with complimentary refreshments. Among other items of note are the indoor swimming pool and an excellent fitness center. Free transportation is provided to any destination within five miles of the hotel.

SUBURBAN COMMUNITIES
Very Expensive

OMNI INTERLOCKEN RESORT, *500 Interlocken Blvd, Broomfield. Tel. 303/438-6600; Fax 303/438-7224. Toll free reservations 800/THE-OMNI; www.omnihotels.com. 390 Rooms. Rates: $188-329, all year. Major credit cards accepted. Located about 18 miles northwest of downtown via US 36 to CO 128 exit.*

Set against a magnificent Rocky Mountain background, the Omni Interlocken is situated in a quiet area about midway between Denver and Boulder. It's a great location for those who expect to spend a lot of time in the greater Denver area. However, it's not the type of place for everyone. Opened in the fall of 2000, the resort caters to the sophisticated traveler, both leisure and business. It is a full service resort that offers 27 holes of spectacular golf and a complete spa and fitness facility. Guest rooms are large and beautifully decorated. Many have balconies but all feature mini-bar, safe, ironing board and hair dryer. The decor is modern and the furnishings are all of high quality. In addition to regular rooms there are a number of suites in various sizes available.

The Omni features three restaurants, one of which is located on the golf course. Those inside the hotel offer a choice between fine dining in a beautiful room with a huge stone fireplace, or a traditional pub environment. There is also a lounge.

Expensive

INVERNESS HOTEL & GOLF CLUB, *200 Inverness Drive West, Englewood. Tel. 303/799-5800; Fax 303/799-5874. Toll free reservations 800/ 346-4891; www.invernesshotel.com. 302 Rooms. Rates: $89-239 all year. Major credit cards accepted. Located about a quarter mile northeast of I-25, Exit 195, about 17 miles south of downtown Denver.*

In some ways the only true full facility resort in the Denver metropolitan area, the Inverness provides a high level of luxury and service in a fabulous setting. The light gold colored five story building with contrasting dark roof stretches for a long distance along the expertly manicured golf greens and its large pond. Beautiful gardens and pathways are in abundance. Public areas have a style of understated elegance and are spacious.

The large guestrooms are Scandinavian styled and modern in appearance. Many rooms overlook the golf course while others boast mountain views. The best units are those with a balcony so you can take in the fresh air while overlooking the picturesque scene that surrounds you. Amenities are many. All rooms have a mini-bar, some have whirlpools.

The Inverness has three restaurants. The best is called The Swan and is described in the Where to Eat section. A fourth restaurant operates during the summer months and is a most delightful outdoor cafe. An equal number of lounges provide plenty of space to unwind and enjoy live entertainment. As a hotel that also calls itself a golf club you can expect to find many recreational facilities in addition to the excellent 18-hole course in the back yard. The golf facilities also include a driving range. Other facilities are the two swimming pools (one outdoor); complete health club with sauna and whirlpool; three lighted tennis courts; a bocci court and jogging tracks.

SHERATON HOTEL & CONFERENCE CENTER, *360 Union Blvd., Lakewood. Tel. 303/987-2000; Fax 303/969-0263. Toll free reservations 800/ 525-3966. 242 Rooms. Rates: $119-224 on weekdays and $89-129 on weekends. Major credit cards accepted. Located adjacent to the Denver Federal Center, south of the Union Boulevard Exit of US 6. Reach US 6 by heading east from Exit 209 of I-25 or west from Exit 261 of I-70.*

Sometimes called the Sheraton Hotel West, you could almost put this place in the moderate price category. With the excellent facilities, however, it does represent a relatively good hotel value for those seeking something a little better without having to close your bank account. Situated not too far from either downtown Denver or the Rocky Mountain foothills, the Sheraton offers good views of both from most of its eleven floors. Complimentary evening beverages are offered to guests between four and six each afternoon.

All of the large and comfortably furnished guestrooms feature coffee makers. Some have whirlpools. For dining you can choose between a full service restaurant and a coffee shop. There is also a cocktail lounge. Among the many other facilities and services to be found here are a complete health club with exercise room, sauna, steamroom and whirlpool (massage service is available at an extra fee); heated indoor swimming pool; tanning and beauty salon. Free transportation is provided within a three mile radius of the hotel.

TABLE MOUNTAIN INN, *1310 Washington Avenue, Golden. Tel. 303/277-9898; Tax 303/271-0298. Toll free reservations 800/762-9898; www.tablemtn.com. 74 Rooms. Rates: $128-168; specials from $99-119. Most major credit cards accepted. Located a mile northwest of US Highway 6, Exit 19, about a half mile from downtown Golden.*

This is a very pleasantly decorated and comfortable motor inn with a distinctive Southwestern flavor. The exterior looks like a big pueblo, which is appropriate because some rooms face a distinctively New Mexican-looking mesa from which the inn gets its name. The entire property received a thorough renovation in 1999 and was substantially upgraded. All of the rooms have ample space and a lot of amenities including refrigerator, hair dryer and ironing board. Some have balconies and some of the better rooms feature Jacuzzi and fireplace. There is a good restaurant with cocktail lounge on the premises. It, too, is Southwestern.

Moderate

BEARS INN BED & BREAKFAST, *27425 Spruce Lane, Evergreen. Tel. 303/670-1205; Fax 303/670-8542. Toll free reservations 800/863-1205; www.bearsinn.com. E-mail: mail@bearsinn.com. 11 Rooms. Rates: Single room units $95; suites for $175; all rates include full breakfast. Most major credit cards accepted. Located in the Rocky Mountains about 30 minutes west of Denver. Take I-70 to CO 470 south and then west on CO 74 through Morrison, and Kittredge to Evergreen. The inn is just off of CO 74.*

It isn't often that you can experience a true Colorado mountain retreat literally within minutes of the state's largest city. But that's exactly what you'll get at this two-story facility built in the style of a mountain lodge. A canopy covered stairway flanked by rustic stones leads up to the equally rustic wood beamed structure with large plant boxes beneath the big first floor windows. The interior of the 1924 inn has hardwood floors, exposed log beams and many delightful antiques. A lounge area is highlighted by a huge fireplace. Back outside an eight person spa offers a relaxing soak while taking in the fabulous view of towering Mt. Evans.

An attractive flagstone patio separates the inn from the spa. Several times a year the inn hosts "Murder Mystery Get-A-Ways" where guests are given costumes and are invited to participate in helping your hosts solve the heinous crime! ($195 per couple.)

Each of the eleven rooms is unique. I especially like the brightly colored Wildflower; holiday season themed Christmas; the Bunkhouse's western theme combined with a four-poster bed; the Native American styled Dakota; the Colorado's outdoor accessories, and the light hearted English hunt theme in the Fox & Horn. The Suite is classical Victorian with a sitting room separated from the bedroom by elegant French doors.

Proprietors Darrell and Chris Jenkins will also treat you to a sumptuous breakfast each day. While this outlying area doesn't have the variety of restaurants found in closer in Denver suburbs, the adjacent restaurant is quite good.

Please note that Bears Inn is not considered suitable for children under age 12.

CRYSTAL INN, *3300 North Ouray Street, Aurora. Tel 303/340-3800; Fax 303/340-3808. Toll free reservations 888/890-3800; www.crystalinns.com/ denia.html. 157 Rooms. Rates: $89-169 including buffet breakfast. Most major credit cards accepted. Located near Denver International Airport right at Exit 285 of I-70 at the junction of Airport Boulevard.*

A modern four-story pastel colored building, the Crystal Inn provides very good accommodations at a reasonable price so long as you aren't looking for the facilities and services of a large hotel. The guest rooms consist of either a single King or double Queen and Jacuzzi suites along with a few large deluxe and executive suites. All have a separate sitting area which gives you some more room to spread out. Standard amenities include microwave and refrigerator and three telephones with voice mail capabilities. The inn also has an indoor pool, whirlpool spa and a small fitness center. Weekday guests receive a complimentary newspaper and coffee is available all day in the lobby. The hot buffet breakfast is quite good. Movie rentals are available.

DOUBLETREE DENVER SOUTHEAST, *13696 Iliff Place, Aurora. Tel. 303/337-2800; Fax 303/752-0296. Toll free reservations 800/243-3112; www.hilton.com/doubletree/hotels/DENITDT/. 248 Rooms. Rates: $99-179 weekdays and $79-129 on weekends. Major credit cards accepted. Located immediately to the west of I-225, Exit 5 on the Denver metro area's eastern beltway.*

I always have to recommend at least one Doubletree hotel just to plug their great chocolate chip cookies! But seriously folks, those delectable little morsels aside, this is an excellent hotel with real nice public facilities and accommodations. The attractive but undistinguished exterior gives way to a comfortable and warm interior with nicely furnished large rooms. If you get one on the fifth or sixth floor you might have a good mountain view. About ten percent of the units are suites. They, along with some standard units, may feature such extra amenities as coffee makers, refrigerators or whirlpool tubs. There are two restaurants as well as a cocktail lounge on the premises. The Doubletree has a heated indoor swimming pool and whirlpool facility along with a small exercise room. Golf privileges at the nearby Heather Ridge Country Club are available to all guests. Free area transportation is provided within five miles of the hotel.

SHERATON FOUR POINTS HOTEL DENVER WEST, *137 Union Blvd., Lakewood. Tel. 303/969-9900; Fax 303/980-8920. 170 Rooms. Rates: $89-150. Major credit cards accepted. Located adjacent to the Denver Federal Center, south of the Union Boulevard Exit of US 6. Reach US 6 by heading east from Exit 209 of I-25 or west from Exit 261 of I-70.*

This is an attractive and comfortable facility that represents a good value for the money. It doesn't have a lot of the things that you'll find in many larger hotels but if you're looking for a spacious well-maintained room to spend a few nights then this will do quite nicely. There is an on-premise restaurant as well as a heated swimming pool.

RADISSON GRAYSTONE CASTLE, *83 East 120th Avenue, Thornton. Tel. 303/451-1002; Fax 303/452-1962. Toll free reservations 800/422-7699; www.radisson.com. 137 Rooms. Rates: $109-149, including full breakfast. Major credit cards accepted. Located just to the east of I-25, Exit 223, approximately 11 miles north of downtown Denver.*

Conveniently located about half-way between Denver and Boulder, the Radisson Graystone takes its name from the unusual but attractive castle style exterior architecture. The interior is a bit more on the traditional side but still quite nice. The facilities and services are within the expected boundaries of the slightly upscale Radisson chain–toward the luxury side but not quite making it. Then again, the prices don't make the luxury scale either so you're still coming out okay.

Guest rooms are large and modern and have the usual expected amenities. An on premise restaurant isn't anything special but is convenient if you're not going to be taking in any of Denver's nightlife. However, the breakfast buffet spread is better than average. There is a cocktail lounge with occasional live entertainment. The Radisson also has a small pool.

RADISSON HOTEL DENVER SOUTH, *7007 S. Clinton Street, Englewood. Tel. 303/799-6200; Fax 303/799-4828. Toll free reservations 800/422-7699; www.radisson.com. 263 Rooms. Rates: $98-165 weekdays and $69-79 on weekends, all year. Major credit cards accepted. Located immediately southeast of I-25, Exit 197.*

The ten-story high Radisson South is another modern glass structure without any special style but it houses attractively furnished large rooms that almost deserve a luxury prefix. Microwave ovens and/or refrigerators are standard in some units.

The Cafe Galleria is a decent restaurant for dinner but their weekday breakfast and lunch buffets are better. A cocktail lounge is also on the premises. They also have a heated swimming pool, whirlpool and exercise room. Free transportation is provided within a distance of five miles of the hotel.

Inexpensive

WHITE SWAN MOTEL, *6060 W. Colfax Avenue, Lakewood. Tel. 303/ 238-1351; Fax 303/238-0046. Toll free reservations 800/257-9972. 21 Rooms. Rates: $45-69. Most major credit cards accepted. Located about 9 miles west of downtown Denver via Colfax Avenue (US Highway 40) or just east of I-70, Exit 262.*

You can't expect too much these days at the prices charged by the White Swan, but for budget travelers this is a good find. The location is convenient and the property is clean and well maintained. The plain but more than adequate rooms all have a microwave and refrigerator. Some have more complete kitchen facilities. The property doesn't look its age of 50 years. Restaurants are located in close proximity. The only lodging you can get in the Denver area for less is definitely in the flea bag variety.

CAMPING & RV SITES

- **Delux RV Park**, *5520 N. Federal Boulevard. Tel. 303/433-0452*
- **Denver Meadows RV Park**, *2075 Potomac Street, Aurora. Tel. 303/364-9483*
- **Denver North Campground & RV Park**, *16700 N. Washington, Broomfield. Tel. 303/452-4120 or 800/851-6521*

WHERE TO EAT

DOWNTOWN

The downtown dining zone is bordered by Colfax Avenue, Broadway, 22nd Street, the South Platte River and Cherry Creek. It includes the Larimer Square and LoDo districts.

Very Expensive

BROKER RESTAURANT, *821 17th Street. Tel. 303/292-5065. Most major credit cards accepted. Lunch and dinner served daily; dinner only on Saturday and Sunday. Reservations are suggested.*

Feel like a rich Wall Street executive as you dine inside a real bank vault! The service is kind of formal but not too stuffy and the decor keeps to the financial theme quite well. The menu is quite varied and features a good selection of Continental cuisine as well as American style steaks.

Several good seafood choices are also always available. The food is good and the portions are adequate but one of the things that makes the Broker so popular is the complimentary bowl of outstanding shrimp that's placed on each table. In addition to full tableside cocktail service, the Broker has an attractive lounge.

PALACE ARMS, *321 17th Street, in the Brown Palace Hotel. Tel. 303/ 297-3111. Major credit cards accepted. Lunch and dinner served daily, except dinner only on weekends. Dress code. Reservations are required.*

An award winning and time honored restaurant, the Palace Arms is certainly the place to go if you're looking for elegant surroundings. Filled with antiques spanning the 17th century to the American federal period, but mostly concentrating on authentic relics of the Napoleonic era, the Palace Arms is a graceful museum piece as well as a place for first quality cuisine and service. You'll feel like Napoleon or Josephine as an attentive staff offers personalized service that you just don't get too often in even the best restaurants. The cuisine is Continental. Rather than experiment with unique dishes the chef and his staff concentrate on perfecting traditional entrees. Desserts are excellent and the wine list is extensive and served by a knowledgeable person. Cocktail service. The only drawbacks–having to get dressed up. It's also not a great place to take the kids.

Expensive

DENVER BUFFALO COMPANY, *1109 Lincoln Street. Tel. 303/832-0880. Most major credit cards accepted. Lunch and dinner served daily, except dinner only on Sunday.*

Expect more than good food when you dine at this popular Denver eatery–you're in for a good time as well. The DBC is more than a restaurant, it is a tribute to the spirit of the American West. The featured food is delicious, lean and tender Buffalo meat that DBC raises on their own ranch. In case you've never tried it, buffalo meet is exceptional and they really know how to prepare it here. However, to some it might sound unappetizing. If so, the restaurant has an excellent selection of poultry, lamb, fish, veal, traditional beef, and even pasta.

You'll be served by a gracious and efficient staff attired as they would have been in the days of the old west. This helps to give the place a real casual feel and that is also enhanced by the traditional western decor. Dine outdoors on the patio during the summer for even more casual fun. The Buffalo Company has cocktail service, lounge and children's menu as well as a deli with excellent carry-out menu. Before or after dinner take some time to explore their Art Gallery & Trading Post where you can view quality paintings and more as well as purchase authentic Native American and Western goods. A great place for the whole family.

KEVIN TAYLOR RESTAURANT, *1106 14th Street, in the Teatro Hotel. Tel. 303/820-2600. Most major credit cards accepted. Dinner served nightly except Sunday. Reservations are suggested. Dress code.*

One of Denver's most noted chefs has outdone himself with this wonderful restaurant that's sure to be an "in" place to dine for some time to come. The main dining room features a simple but elegant decor but you also have the option of choosing the mezzanine dining area, which is open to the main room below. There's a separate bar on the mezzanine as well. For a special treat you should see if you can take your meal in the spectacular wine cellar, with its vaulted stone tiled ceiling and rich mahogany wine racks that line the walls. Speaking of wine, the cellar holds more than 900 different vintages, something that must have played an important role in the awards the restaurant has received from the respected *Wine Spectator* magazine.

When it comes to the food, you'll be dazzled by the delicious contemporary American cuisine. Select an appetizer from the likes of open ravioli of poached oysters, imported frog's legs "Fricassee" or the finest caviar. Varied entrees represent the fish and meat lines well such as butter poached Scottish salmon, Argentinean beef sirloin in peppercorn sauce or the ranch venison. Desserts are equally spectacular. Go for the liquid center chocolate cake or the Hawaiian pineapple Napoleon.

McCORMICK'S FISH HOUSE & BAR, *1659 Wazee Street. Tel. 303/825-1107. Most major credit cards accepted. Lunch and dinner served daily. Reservations are suggested.*

THE place in Denver for fish and seafood lovers certainly isn't Red Lobster, but McCormick's. Located in a historic building in Lower Downtown, the Fish House & Bar is nicely decorated in a turn of the century style with attractive stained glass windows and a beautiful wooden bar with brass trim. The service afforded by an expert staff of white jacketed waiters with bowtie and black trousers is superb without being overbearing. More importantly, the food is wonderful. Every day a new menu is printed up showing what catch of the day is available. And what a catch it is, always featuring thirty quality and fresh fish or seafood entrees from both coasts of the United States as well as around the world. Cocktail service tableside or at the aforementioned bar which is one of Denver's best restaurant drinking establishments.

THE PALM RESTAURANT, *1201 16th Street, located in the Tabor Center. Tel. 303/825-7256. Most major credit cards accepted. Lunch and dinner served daily. Reservations are suggested.*

A classic steakhouse that has been pleasing the palate since 1926 in several locations throughout the country, it has now quickly become a Denver tradition as well. The Palm is both elegant and romantic with careful, professional service and plush surroundings. During the warmer months you can dine outside on the more casual and attractive patio.

But the food is the main event at the Palm and you'll do well not only with the oversized portions of prime beef but the equally huge jumbo lobsters. They're so big that there's hardly any room on the plate for the veggies. I don't know about you but I like having the option of being so full that I can leave something over rather than having to hunt for the food–something all too common in high priced restaurants. The Palm has full cocktail service as well as an excellent selection of fine wines.

Moderate

AUGUSTA, *1672 Lawrence Street, in the Westin-Tabor Center Hotel. Tel. 303/572-7222. Major credit cards accepted. Breakfast, lunch and dinner served daily. Smoke-free. Reservations are suggested.*

Another elegant place (some entrees spill over into the expensive category) noted for fine food and service as well as great views of the city. The cuisine is American but is served with style and imagination. You won't just find lobster, for example, but you will be served a lobster taco. And so it goes with chicken, beef and veal dishes–they're all a little different than what you're used to but all excellent. Cocktail service tableside or in the separate lounge. A children's menu is available.

DICK'S LAST RESORT RESTAURANT, *1909 Blake Street. Tel. 303/292-1212. Most major credit cards accepted. Lunch and dinner served daily.*

First of all I must make note that this restaurant will not be to everyone's liking. I don't know why but apparently some diners don't like to be insulted by their waiter or listen to a band that doesn't quite know how to get it right. (Do you realize some people actually leave the place not realizing it's all intentional good fun?) Proudly advertising that they need tourists because they've scared off all of the locals (certainly untrue from the crowds I've seen), Dick serves up casual food like ribs, chicken and shrimp in big buckets. It's off-beat LoDo location is perfect for the kind of place it is. Cocktails. Kids also like it.

EUROPEAN CAFE, *1060 15th Street. Tel. 303/825-6555. Most major credit cards accepted. Lunch and dinner served daily. Reservations are suggested.*

Also bordering on the expensive category, the European cafe is a pretty and casual restaurant with excellent service by a warm staff. As the name implies the cuisine is European with an emphasis on such French dishes as rack of lamb and venison. However, you'll also find a nice selection of American entrees including steak and seafood. All are beautiful to look at and delicious to eat. The Cafe is known for its unusual and outstanding desserts. Cocktails are available either tableside or in the comfortable adjoining lounge.

MARLOWE'S, *511 16th Street. Tel. 303/595-3700. Most major credit cards accepted. Lunch and dinner served daily. Reservations are suggested.*

One of Denver's favorite restaurants among residents, Marlowe's serves a wide selection of steaks, seafood and pasta dishes in a pretty but casually elegant atmosphere. A feeling of spaciousness permeates the high ceilinged eatery with bright white columns and overhanging trim. You can also dine outside on the small patio which faces the 16th Street Pedestrian Mall and is great for people watching while you wait for the food. Not that you'll have to wait that long–the service is friendly and efficient. Cocktail service.

NEW SAIGON RESTAURANT, *630 S. Federal Boulevard. Tel. 303/936-4954. Most major credit cards accepted. Lunch and dinner served daily.*

Now approaching its tenth anniversary, the New Saigon has spent most of that time as the top rated Vietnamese restaurant in Denver (and there are several that offer stiff competition). The atmosphere is nice, the food bountiful and on the spicy side, and the service is excellent. Full bar service.

ROCKY MOUNTAIN DINER, *800 18th Street. Tel. 303/293-8383. Major credit cards accepted. Lunch and dinner served daily.*

This is a most interesting casual restaurant that combines elements of the family-oriented east coast diner (you know, simple food nicely prepared in huge quantities at a reasonable price) with western cowboy decor and flair. The fun atmosphere includes a fifties style jukebox and the menu adds several imaginative dishes to the traditional family favorites like Yankee pot roast with mashed potatoes. Among the former are an excellent roast duck enchilada and buffalo meatloaf. They also offer overstuffed sandwiches and whatever is on the menu can be ordered for take-out. Cocktails are served and there is a children's menu.

SHIP TAVERN, *321 17th Street, in the Brown Palace Hotel. Tel. 303/297-3111. Major credit cards accepted. Lunch and dinner served daily.*

Despite the seafood sounding name the Ship Tavern has a lot more to offer than entrees from the deep. Although the fish and fresh seafood are excellent the same can be said for their hefty prime-rib and other selections for land-lubbers. The surroundings are filled with nautical themed items and is quite pleasant. Their selection of beers can rival most of Denver's many brew pubs. Other spirits are also served. The service and atmosphere is warm and friendly and tends towards a leisurely pace.

Inexpensive

CAFE GALILEO, *535 16th Street. Tel. 303/573-7600. Most major credit cards accepted. Breakfast and lunch served daily.*

Whether you're staying downtown or have arrived there to get an early start on a day of sightseeing, the Cafe Galileo is a great choice for either breakfast or lunch. Located on the busy 16th Street Mall, it serves a variety of salad dishes, pizza and other Italian fare, fresh baked items and excellent sandwiches. Dining outdoor on the patio during the warmer weather adds nicely to the pleasant experience you should have here.

CORPORATE DELI & GRILL, *510 17th Street. Tel. 303/825-5353. No credit cards. Breakfast and lunch served Monday through Saturday.*

Generally in the same vein as the Cafe Galileo but with emphasis on overstuffed delicatessen sandwiches. Other good choices are the soups and salads and a good selection of desserts. In the heart of Denver's business district, you'll usually find a big crowd here during lunch hour but the service is fast and things move along pretty well.

THE OLD SPAGHETTI FACTORY, *1215 18th Street. Tel. 303/295-1864. Discover, MasterCard and VISA accepted. Lunch and dinner served daily.*

Almost every big city has an Old Spaghetti Factory and the Denver version isn't much different. If you've never been to one then you probably don't know that they are almost always located in refurbished older structures and are filled with an eclectic collection of items dating from the early 20th century. That, too, holds true at this Factory which is housed in an historic cable-car building. On the food side you get a lot of spaghetti and other pasta served with a choice of sauces at a most reasonable price. It's safe to say that it is the lowest priced full service restaurant in downtown Denver. Children's menu available. Cocktails are served tableside or in a separate lounge.

AROUND THE CITY
Very Expensive
BUCKHORN EXCHANGE, *1000 Osage Street. Tel. 303/534-9505. Major credit cards accepted. Lunch served Monday to Friday; dinner nightly. Reservations are suggested.*

The Exchange is, with excellent reason, one of Denver's most popular restaurants and is now well into its second century, having first been used as a restaurant in 1893. It is now almost like a museum piece as it is richly decorated with hundreds of Old West and Native American artifacts in curio cabinets that line the walls on all sides. Above that are dozens of stuffed animal heads that help make the place look something like a hunting lodge. Bare wood floors and red checkered table clothes let you know that it's a casual sort of place where you can have fun while you dine.

The cuisine includes a little bit of everything but features prime rib and steak along with a selection of western favorites like buffalo, elk and other wild game dishes. The outdoor patio is open year round (don't worry, it is heated). Cocktail service is available tableside but you might want to spend some time at the bar which is a beautiful wood carved masterpiece that is nearly 150 years old. Children's menu. Live entertainment nightly, Thursday through Saturday.

If your preference for dining is usually more in the moderate range, as mine is, if you're going to splurge once or twice than this one is worth spending more for.

CLIFF YOUNG'S, *1702 E. 17th Avenue. Tel. 303/831-8900. Most major credit cards accepted. Dinner served nightly except Sunday. Reservations are suggested.*

This is a casual yet sophisticated eatery that seems to appeal equally to the business traveler or the couple on vacation looking for a romantic evening. The 1930's decor features large and comfortable booth seating, an inviting fireplace and live piano music. The cocktail lounge is also quite inviting. The service is outstanding and all of the staff are extremely knowledgeable about the menu. The extravagant salads are deftly prepared table side. The menu is fairly varied with the highlights including duck and rack of lamb. There is always a good selection of fresh seafood.

FRESH FISH COMPANY, *7800 E. Hampden Blvd. Tel. 303/740-9556. Most major credit cards accepted. Lunch and dinner served Monday through Saturday; brunch and dinner on Sunday.*

A huge selection of fish and seafood is served in this large and busy restaurant that is attractively decorated with a number of colorful and interestingly designed aquariums. Maine lobster and Alaskan crab legs are two of the favorites. There is also a small selection of meat items on the extensive menu. There is cocktail service and a separate lounge. The Fresh Fish Company serves a number of excellent local microbrews. The atmosphere is casual and the service is friendly. Children's menu.

Expensive

CENTENNIAL RESTAURANT, *7800 Tufts Avenue. Tel. 303/779-1234 or 303/850-7164. Major credit cards accepted. Dinner served Monday through Saturday; Sunday brunch. Reservations are suggested.*

Every major city has to have at least one classy rooftop restaurant and this one in the Denver Tech Center is the Mile High City's representative of the genre. It's also better than most which often offer great views but little more. The Centennial serves new American cuisine that is well prepared as you watch the constant activity in the exhibition style kitchen. The knowledgeable service is efficient and attentive. Cocktail service and separate lounge. A children's menu is offered.

TANTE LOUISE, *4900 East Colfax Avenue. Tel. 303/355-4488. Most major credit cards accepted. Dinner served nightly except Sunday. Reservations are suggested. Dress code.*

This fine restaurant is very popular among Denver's gourmet set. The beautiful dining room has the atmosphere of a French country inn and features a fireplace and elegant place settings. The varied menu changes by the seasons but French and French-inspired delights are always in abundance. Typical of the appetizers are escargot, duck liver pate and foie gras. Main courses are highlighted by such entrees as pheasant and venison. Tante Louise has an excellent wine list and one of the best sommelier's in town. During the summer you can dine outside on the patio. Complete cocktail service and separate lounge.

TUSCANY, *4150 E. Mississippi Avenue, in the Loews Giorgio Hotel. Tel. 303/782-9300. Major credit cards accepted. Breakfast, lunch and dinner served daily. Reservations are suggested.*

This is an interesting restaurant that will appeal to a broad spectrum of diners. The atmosphere is a casual and romantic elegance that is good for couples and families. The service is efficient but friendly and never stuffy. The menu is a combination of Northern Italian and American, so most people shouldn't have a problem finding something to their liking. Selections include a good number of health-conscious and vegetarian dishes, and there's even a children's menu. Tuscany is especially popular for their wonderful Sunday brunch which features a harp player. There is also weekend entertainment. Cocktail service and lounge.

Moderate

BABY DOE'S MATCHLESS MINE, *2520 West 23rd Avenue. Tel. 303/433-3386. American Express, Discover, MasterCard and VISA accepted. Lunch and dinner served daily; Sunday brunch. Reservations are suggested.*

The decor has been carefully designed to recreate the look and feel of a late 19th century gold mine even though it isn't necessarily like the one in Leadville whose name it takes. If the idea of dining in a mine doesn't appeal to you then you can try the outdoor patio during the summer with its excellent views. The menu features steak, prime rib and other western meat favorites, all nicely served in ample portions. While I wouldn't put it quite in the same category as Denver's top steakhouses, it is a good value for the price. Cocktails.

IMPERIAL CHINESE SEAFOOD RESTAURANT, *431 S. Broadway. Tel. 303/698-2800. Most major credit cards accepted. Lunch and dinner served daily. Reservations are suggested.*

An almost perennial award winner in the Oriental food category by locals in various restaurant surveys, the Imperial is a little fancier looking than most Chinese restaurants and the service, though typically efficient, is particularly warm and courteous. As the full name implies the emphasis here is on seafood dishes and you will find that many of the usual Chinese restaurant menu selections lacking here. But if you like Chinese and seafood or are just looking for something that is different, you should definitely give this place a try. Carry-out service is available. Cocktails are served tableside or in the separate lounge. Children's menu.

NEW YORK DELI NEWS, *7105 East Hampden Avenue. Tel. 303/759-4741. Most major credit cards accepted. Breakfast, lunch and dinner served daily.*

A popular and almost always crowded place, this is as close as you can get to a kosher New York city deli without going to the Big Apple—right down to the mock semi-belligerent attitude of the owner! (Actually, the staff is warm and friendly.) In case you're not from New York, let me point out that even the name is a great adaptation of an institution in that city—the *New York Daily News* newspaper. The dining room walls are filled with pictures of past customers of note.

The menu has such favorites as pastrami, matzo brei (broken up matzo fried with eggs), cream cheese or lox on bagels, gefilte fish and sable or whitefish. And of course, all sandwiches are served with great pickles. You'll find many of the huge and overstuffed sandwiches to be meals in themselves and often inexpensively priced. There are also hot plate entrees available. Brunch is served on Sunday. Children's menu. Beer and wine only.

PAGLIACCI'S ITALIAN RESTAURANT, *440 W. 33rd Avenue. Tel. 303/485-0530. Major credit cards accepted. Dinner served nightly. Reservations are suggested.*

Serving traditional Italian fare for more than fifty years, Pagliacci's is a most attractive dining room featuring many arches and even a grotto. The ambiance is countrified and on the romantic side. The extensive menu is likely to include all of your favorites. A variety of veal and chicken dishes supplement many pasta entrees. There's also excellent shrimp. Cocktails are served and there is a small but adequate wine list.

SUSHI HEIGHTS, *2301 E. Colfax Avenue. Tel. 303/355-2777. Major credit cards accepted. Lunch and dinner served nightly except Sunday.*

A little bit of Japan in Denver. Reasonably priced and well prepared sushi, tempura and teriyaki as well as many other popular dishes are served by an efficient and attentive staff in a traditional and relaxing Japanese atmosphere. The cocktails include a good selection of Japanese beers and other beverages.

THREE SONS ITALIAN RESTAURANT, *2915 W. 44th Avenue. Tel. 303/455-4366. MasterCard accepted. Lunch and dinner served nightly except Monday.*

A casual and inviting restaurant that has been owned by the same family for about fifty years. The fare is traditional Italian—a bountiful selection of chicken, veal and pasta, all graciously served by a friendly staff. Cocktails; children's menu.

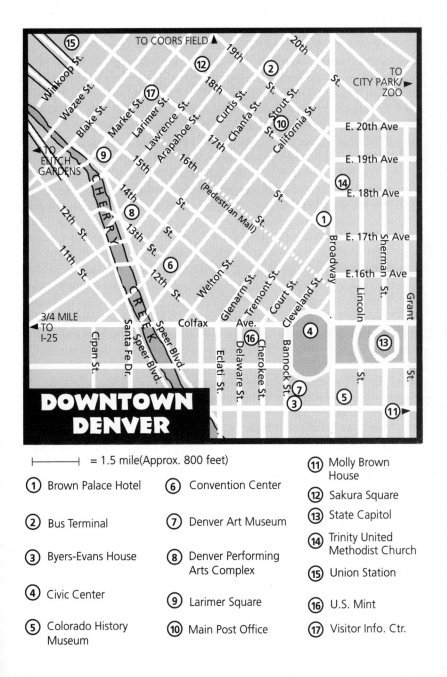

DOWNTOWN DENVER

| | = 1.5 mile(Approx. 800 feet)

1. Brown Palace Hotel
2. Bus Terminal
3. Byers-Evans House
4. Civic Center
5. Colorado History Museum
6. Convention Center
7. Denver Art Museum
8. Denver Performing Arts Complex
9. Larimer Square
10. Main Post Office
11. Molly Brown House
12. Sakura Square
13. State Capitol
14. Trinity United Methodist Church
15. Union Station
16. U.S. Mint
17. Visitor Info. Ctr.

Inexpensive

CASA BONITA, *6175 West Colfax Avenue. Tel. 303/232-5115. Major credit cards accepted. Lunch and dinner served nightly.*

You won't believe your eyes when you see this place and your taste buds will be equally delighted. So will your pocketbook–although Mexican is often inexpensive this restaurant represents one of the best dining values in Denver. The building is huge. The exterior is crowned by a steeple tower that's especially beautiful when lit at night and the interior is designed to resemble a Mexican village. The atmospheric and visual highlight, though, is the thirty foot high indoor waterfall that even features live cliff diving! No, not the patrons, silly–they have employees doing that. If all of that wasn't enough to make this a great place for the entire family, Casa Bonita throws in strolling mariachis to entertain you. Now for the food. They have a large selection of well prepared Mexican and some American dishes. The portions are big, the plate colorful and the heat level nicely prepared to any special request. Cocktail service and bar.

DON JOSE'S AUTHENTIC MEXICAN RESTAURANT, *2200 S. Monaco Parkway. Tel. 303/753-1993. Most major credit cards accepted. Lunch and dinner served nightly.*

Now starting its third decade of service, Don Jose and wife Dona Rosa prepare excellent Mexican cuisine specializing in the regional dishes of Mexico City and Zacatecas. The restaurant is made even more popular by their Sports Cantina lounge. The atmosphere is charming and the service is good and if you're looking for a quieter kind of Mexican (except for the lounge) this could be almost as good a choice as Casa Bonita.

SUBURBAN COMMUNITIES
Very Expensive

BROOK'S STEAK HOUSE & CELLAR, *6538 S. Yosemite Circle, Greenwood Village. Tel. 303/770-1177. Most major credit cards accepted. Dinner served nightly except Sunday. Reservations are suggested.*

An exclusive and elegant setting for steaks and all the trimmings. Exceptional service and careful attention to the preparation of tender prime steaks, lobster tails and more are the hallmarks of this distinctive restaurant. Sizable portions of meat are served along with wonderful salads and often unusual vegetable side dishes. The knowledgeable staff will be glad to help you select from what has to be one of Denver's largest wine lists–there are more than 250 to choose from in all price ranges. Cocktail service. Many guests often like to adjourn to the Cellar after dinner for a drink and a cigar. The tab will definitely set you back quite a bit here but for those seeking the "better things in life" it may well be worth it.

THE SWAN AT THE INVERNESS HOTEL & GOLF CLUB, *200 Inverness Drive West, Englewood. Tel. 303/799-5800. Major credit cards accepted. Dinner served nightly except Sunday and Monday. Reservations are suggested.*

This is another place where you can spend some big time bucks for dinner but the experience is quite unique. The beautiful surroundings are neo-southwestern and the decor features a large number of authentic Native American works of art. The service is first class all the way–knowledgeable, professional, and attentive. Yet, they remain warm and friendly, never stand-offish or stuffy. In fact, the casual nature of the experience (including lack of a heavy handed dress code) are surprising given the overall elegance. The menu features a good balance of traditional American cuisine along with a selection of southwestern fare. Many items are imaginatively prepared. Cocktail service and separate lounge. Entertainment is in the form of a harpist and classical guitar player. How's that for class!

Expensive

AURORA SUMMIT, *2700 S. Havana, Aurora. Tel. 303/751-2112. Major credit cards accepted. Dinner served nightly. Reservations are suggested.*

This is an extremely popular and attractive dining experience. The subdued surroundings are highlighted by bas-reliefs on the walls. The service is without flaw and the food is simply fantastic. While the Aurora is perhaps best known for its prime choice steaks, there is an excellent selection of fish (the salmon and swordfish are wonderful choices), chicken, and lamb. The Aurora has a children's menu, cocktail service and bar with live piano entertainment.

THE FORT, *At the junction of US 285 (Hampden Blvd.) and CO Highway 8, Morrison. Tel. 303/697-4771. Most major credit cards accepted. Dinner served nightly. Reservations are suggested.*

The Fort is a huge restaurant (seating well over 300 people but nicely divided for guest privacy) that is attractively built in the style of an adobe trading post. Some entrees extend into the expensive price category but what else would you expect from a restaurant that was host to a summit of international leaders? Located slightly to the east of the main urban area, the Fort also provides fantastic views of Denver from its high vantage point. The menu specializes in the food of the Old West and includes such game dishes as buffalo, elk and quail besides more traditional beef, fish and chicken. All are nicely prepared. Outdoor dining is available in season. Cocktails.

GOINGS-ON IN LODO

*Back in the early 1990's, an area known as **Lower Downtown** was Denver's skid-row. Today it is a flourishing center of art and entertainment. Called "LoDo" by Denverites, the area covers 26 square blocks to the northeast of the heart of downtown in an area that roughly covers the section between Larimer Square and Coors Field, Denver's baseball stadium.*

How did this sudden transformation occur in this large area of mostly run-down Victorian era structures? It was an area that had been left behind in the shadow of downtown's towering glass skyscrapers. Then came the Colorado Rockies, an expansion baseball franchise, and their new home at Coors Field. The ballpark was built in the brick style of the stadiums of the 1940's. Some merchants in LoDo wanted to take advantage of their new neighbor and the first hint of revitalization quickly surfaced.

The stadium's presence would not have been enough of a push except for an unusual circumstance. When the stadium was built it was done so without adequate parking for the throngs who attended the Rockies' games. Most people had to park their car in one of the many downtown garages and walk to the stadium. This constant traffic through LoDo spurred development and those who walked to and from the stadium became entranced by LoDo's atmosphere. The rest, as they say, is history.

LoDo is alive day and night. It has more than 40 art galleries (they stay open late on the first Friday of each month), countless restaurants and shops, including 80 sports bars and the majority of Denver's popular brew pubs. More is planned, including an Arnold Schwarzenegger Planet Hollywood restaurant.

Even if you don't plan on taking in the shopping and nightlife that is described later in this chapter, it's worth taking a walk through LoDo to see this wonderful example of successful non-government sponsored urban renewal.

Moderate

GUSSIE'S, *2345 W. 112th Avenue, Westminster. Tel. 303/469-5281. Major credit cards accepted. Lunch and dinner served daily. Reservations are suggested.*

The menu in this popular, casual and friendly restaurant is hard to characterize. You can choose from a large variety of entrees from a smattering of numerous different cuisines, including Southwestern, fresh seafood and wild game dishes. Usually when a restaurant tries to be too many things it tends to fail, but Gussie's seems to get it right. They also have an excellent salad bar. The service is efficient. There's live entertainment from Wednesday through Saturday. A children's menu is available. Cocktail service and separate lounge.

THE HISTORIC EL RANCHO VILLAGE, *29260 US Highway 40, Golden. Tel. 303/526-0661. Major credit cards accepted. Breakfast, lunch and dinner served daily.*

Only minutes from the city, the El Rancho is an authentic mountain lodge with a wonderful ambiance and feel. Nestled in the woods with great views of the mountains and city, the wooden building and its solid brick chimney reflect an era gone by. Like The Fort, it specializes in Colorado and Western cuisine although this is a much smaller dining room complete with a cozy fireplace. The service is friendly and personalized. Cocktails are served and there is a separate old time tavern.

TRAIL DUST STEAK HOUSE, *9101 Benton Street, Westminster. Tel. 303/427-1446. Most major credit cards accepted. Dinner served nightly; lunch available on Sunday. (Also opening new location in Denver at 7101 S. Clinton, Tel. 303/790-2420.)*

The menu of thick, juicy steaks along with chicken and ribs might make you think this is an ordinary steak house. Far from it. The food is bountiful and delicious, so you can't go wrong from that standpoint, but what sets it apart from other steak houses is the fun atmosphere that will delight all ages. Oh, yes...I should add something about the food before describing the unique atmosphere. Everything is mesquite-grilled for special flavor, and do try the mountain oysters!

Trail Dust has communal seating but before the evening is out you'll likely be best of friends with your dining neighbors. That's only the start of the Western style and atmosphere which also boasts a huge dance floor, nightly entertainment, an indoor slide that was originally for children but that adults seem to always take over, and a policy that prohibits neckties after five. Now, that's my kind of place.

Inexpensive

GUNTHER TOODY'S, *4500 E. Alameda Avenue, Glendale. Tel. 303/399-1959. Most major credit cards accepted. Breakfast, lunch and dinner served daily.*

A 1950's style roadside diner, Gunther Toody's offers great family fare at a price everyone can afford. They're known for sumptuous breakfasts of hotcakes and Belgian waffles as well as omelets. For dinner, the simple chicken fried steak has been elevated to an art form. Well, almost.

SEEING THE SIGHTS

Because the Denver area is quite large and there is so much to see it's a whole lot easier to plan an attack if you cut the target down in size. I've done that by dividing the sights into three areas. These are downtown; the remainder of the city proper; and the western suburbs.

Tour 1 covers the smallest area and is best done on foot. Tour 2 covers a much bigger piece of real estate and while a car is the best method, just about every point of interest mentioned will be within a short distance of an RTD bus. Taxis can be prohibitively expensive for sightseeing. For Tour 3 a car is almost an absolute necessity although you can reach Golden and several other places on the itinerary by bus. The suggested time frames assume that you will make all of the stops listed. If you don't have that much time just leave out what seems less interesting to you.

The number of the RTD bus route that can be taken to reach each attraction in Tours 2 and 3 will be indicated at the end of each description. Many buses serve the downtown corridor covered in Tour 1, but since this tour will be on foot to begin with the bus routes won't be indicated. Also keep in mind that if you are using public transportation for any of these tours, the time allotment required to see all of the sights will be greater.

Denver has an excellent **visitor information center**, *1668 Larimer Street (Larimer Square area) in the Larimer Square area, Tel. 800/645-3446,* where travelers can walk in and get plenty of brochures and personalized assistance. The hours are Monday through Friday from 8:00am until 5:00pm and on Saturday from 8:00am until 1:00pm.

You can pick up a general guide (but they don't have people available to assist you) at the main office of the **Denver Convention & Visitors Bureau**, *1555 California Street, Suite 300.*

TOUR 1: DOWNTOWN DENVER

Approximate duration (by foot including sightseeing time) is a full day. If you wish to see all of the museums in great detail then it is likely that additional time will be needed. Begin your tour on the north side of Civic Center at the intersection of Colfax Avenue and 14th Street.

To the south of Colfax Avenue is Denver's attractive **Civic Center** area. Several blocks of nicely manicured lawns and colorful fountains are interspersed with mainly neo-Classical style government office buildings housing the city and county administrations. There's a Greek amphitheater that is often the scene of free summer concerts and other events. Several large statues including that of a cowboy and Indian pay tribute to the pioneer spirit. An art museum is also on the campus but more about that later. From just about any part of the Civic Center grounds you can get an excellent unobstructed photo view of the skyscrapers of downtown Denver.

Perhaps the most dramatic structure in Civic Center is the $64 million **Denver Public Library** which opened in 1995 and is one of the largest in the nation with more than five million items in its collection. The colorful exterior gives way to a three-story high atrium interior. In the Western History Room there is an 80-foot diameter rotunda that has outstanding views of the mountains. There's also a gallery of western art. The Library is on the south side of Civic Center park.

Immediately to the east of Civic Center in a continuation of the park-like setting is the Colorado **State Capitol**, *Sherman Street between Colfax and 14th Avenues*. Constructed in 1908 of Colorado granite, the graceful structure is of the ornate Corinthian style of architecture. The impressive dome is covered in gold leaf although time and weather keep turning it to a shade of copper. Inside underneath the dome are beautiful stained glass windows. The 16 panels depict people important in the development of Colorado. There are entrances on each side of the building but most visitors want to use the one on the west side so that they can see the one-mile high altitude plaque on the 15th step. *Tel. 303/866-2604. Open weekdays from 9:00am until 3:30pm, Memorial Day through Labor Day and from 9:30am until 2:30 the rest of the year. During the summer it is open on Saturday from 9:30am to 2:30pm. It is closed on state holidays. Free guided tours are given on the half-hour.*

Go out the south entrance and proceed down Sherman Street for one block to 13th Street. Turn left and walk three blocks to Pennsylvania Street. The **Molly Brown House**, *1340 Pennsylvania Street*, is a pretty Victorian style home dating from 1889. It is not that different from many other such homes in Denver except for the fact that its original owner was one of the survivors of the *Titanic* disaster. That would probably have gone unknown to most of the world save for the musical "The Unsinkable Molly Brown." The decor of the home has been restored to its turn of the century style and guided tours are offered. *Tel. 303/832-4092. The house can be seen only by 40-minute guided tours which are given every half hour daily from 10:00am until 3:30pm (from noon on Sunday) during the summer. At other times of the year it is closed on Monday. Also closed on most major holidays. Tickets can be purchased for use later in the same day. Admission is $5 for adults, $3.50 for seniors and $1.50 for children ages 6 through 12.*

Now walk back on 13th Street, continuing past Sherman, until you reach the **Colorado History Museum**, *13th and Broadway*. This large museum houses an excellent collection of historical artifacts as well as elaborate dioramas that bring history to life. The entire western United States is covered although emphasis is definitely on events in Colorado. Native Americans and the mining era receive special attention. *The museum is open daily from 10:00am until 4:30pm except for Sunday when it opens at noon. Closed on New Year's Day, Thanksgiving, and Christmas. Adult admission is $3, $2.50 for senior citizens and $1.50 for children ages 6 through 16.*

Only a block west of the museum in the southwest corner of the Civic Center is the **Byers-Evans House**, *1310 Bannock Street*, another Victorian dwelling. This one was built in 1883. The two names represent notable

Denver pioneer families. The furnishings reflect the period immediately after World War I when the Evans family occupied it. Also within the house is an interesting little museum on the history of Denver. *Tel. 303/ 620-4933. Guided tours are given on Tuesday through Sunday from 11:00am through 3:00pm. The adult admission price is $3; senior citizens pay $2.50 while students with identification cards and children 6 to 16 are charged $1.50.*

A right turn on Bannock upon leaving the house will immediately bring you face to face with the outstanding **Denver Art Museum**, *entrance at 100 West 14th Avenue at the southern end of the Civic Center.* The first thing you'll notice is that this isn't any ordinary building. It has 28 different sides (try counting them and you'll go crazy) all faced with thousands of glass tiles. The museum is absolutely huge, with ten galleries being devoted to changing exhibits. The impressive permanent collection of the six-story facility has works by notable artists from around the world. True art lovers could get lost here and be in heaven. Non-cultured types like me enjoy the building itself and the excellent collection of Native American arts. The latter is one of the largest in the world with about 18,000 items. *Tel. 303/ 640-4433. The museum's hours are Tuesday through Saturday from 10:00am until 5:00pm and Sunday from noon to 5:00pm, except for state holidays. Admission is $4.50 for adults, $2.50 for seniors, children ages 6-18. It is free to all on Saturday.*

Now take a short walk north on Bannock Street back to Colfax. Turn left and in a block you'll reach the **United States Mint**, *corner of Cherokee Street, entrance on Cherokee.* The Denver Mint makes all values of American coins, but almost three-quarters of the coins produced here are pennies. They pump out the amazing total of 8 billion coins a year, which translates into about 40 million coins a day. The half-hour long tours begin with exhibits on money and the process of making coins, but the highlight of any visit is when you get to look down on the five dozen high speed presses. You'll also see the areas where the coins are counted, sorted and bagged for distribution. There are no samples given no matter how hard you plead! *Tel. 303/405-4761 Tours given Monday through Friday starting at 8:00am with the last tour at 2:45pm. Closed on federal holidays. The mint closes for two weeks every year between June and September but the dates vary each year. Admission is free. Children under 14 must be accompanied by an adult.*

Up until now we've been in what could be termed the "government" downtown. Now it's time to get into the "private enterprise" part of downtown. From Cherokee and Colfax cross over to the north side of Colfax and proceed diagonally down Court Place four blocks to 17th Street. A left turn will bring you to the entrance of the historic and elegant **Brown Palace Hotel**, *321 17th Street.* The hotel dates from 1892 and, with its huge atrium style of construction, foreshadowed many modern hotels. The top of the atrium features beautiful stained glass windows. But what really distinguishes the place from the modern genre of hotels are the richly ornate furnishings. Take a few moments to appreciate the oriental rugs and the fine red leather furniture. Then make your way up to the corner of 17th Street and turn right on Tremont.

After leaving the hotel turn right on Tremont and at the nearby corner is Broadway. Across the street is Denver's oldest house of worship, the **Trinity United Methodist Church**, dating from 1859. The beautiful stained glass windows and the huge pipe organ were added about thirty years later. Of note are the 66 lights above the organ which represent the same number of books of the Bible. *Tel. 303/839-1493. The church is open for visitation Monday through Friday from 8:00am until 5:00pm and admission is free.* 18th Street runs diagonally to the right from across the Church. Take that street for eight blocks (don't complain, this is the first long walk of this tour) to Lawrence Street and the area known as **Sakura Square**. This is the heart of Denver's Japanese community and it reflects in the architecture of several structures. The square block contains gardens and fountains as well as a Buddhist temple.

Then proceed one block further to Larimer Street and turn left. In a few blocks you'll reach fun-filled **Larimer Square**. This is near where Denver got started and was the most important part of the city during the 1880s. Restoration work has returned many buildings to the appearance of that era. They now house an array of eating places, fancy boutiques, gift shops, and more. Larimer Square is also an important part of the city's night time entertainment scene.

Coors Field, *2001 Blake Street*, offers tours of the home field of the Colorado Rockies baseball club. Since many visitors will not be baseball buffs the time for seeing Coors Field is not included in the allocated time for Tour 1. What is of much interest to all is how the modern stadium was given an old-time feel and look to fit in with the surroundings. From the interior there is a beautiful Rocky Mountain backdrop. Tours visit the clubhouse, press box and dugout. *Tel. 303/762-5437. Guided hour-long tours leave from Gate C daily except Sunday on the hour from 10:00am until 3:00pm (until 2:00pm between November and March). There are no tours on days when there is an afternoon game and some tours may be eliminated when there are evening games. Reservations are suggested. The admission is $5 for adults and $3 for those age 13 and under. Fee for parking.*

From Larimer and 14th Street walk southeast on 14th which will soon return you to Colfax Avenue, Civic Center and your starting point. However, along the way you'll pass the **Denver Performing Arts Complex** and the **Convention Center**, both of which can be quickly eyed without stopping. An alternative route back towards Civic Center is via the **16th Street Mall**, a pedestrian only shopping thoroughfare. Of special note along 16th is the **D&F Tower**, corner of Arapahoe, that is a 325-foot high replica of the famous campanile or tower of St. Mark's in Venice. The tower was built in 1910 and was, at the time, the third highest building in the United States. It is not open to the public.

TOUR 2: AROUND THE CITY

Approximate duration (including sightseeing time) is a full day. Begin at Cheesman Park, 8th & Franklin Streets (reached from downtown by taking Colfax east to Franklin and turning right).

Cheesman Park is one of many beautiful parks in the Denver municipal system. However, I haven't brought you here for the park itself, but for the wonderful panorama of the Rocky Mountains. On a clear day you can see Pike's Peak to the southwest and Mt. Evans to the northwest, a distance of 150 miles! The park does have a lovely classical colonnade. To the east of Cheesman and reached by lovely park drives is the **Denver Botanical Gardens**, *1005 York Street*. The facility has five separate garden areas as well as a conservatory that cover 22 acres. The garden styles are Japanese, water, rock, herb, and alpine. The conservatory houses tropical specimens. *Tel. 303/331-4000. The gardens are open daily from 9:00am until 5:00pm with extension to 8:00pm on Saturday through Tuesday, Memorial Day to Labor Day. Admission ranges from $2.50 to $4.50 depending upon the time of the year (highest rates during the summer). Bus 24.*

Another park is our next destination. Go north on Columbine Street (on the east side of the Gardens) until you reach the entrance to **City Park**. Denver's largest park is also the locale of two important attractions, namely the **Denver Museum of Natural History** and the **Denver Zoo**. But first you should allow a short time to take a spin or walk around at least part of the park which is interspersed with pretty gardens, fountains, pools, and several monuments. *The park is free and is open from 5:00am to 11:00pm every day of the year. Bus 20, 24, 32.*

The Museum of Natural History (*east edge of the park at 2001 Colorado Boulevard*) has to be ranked among the foremost museums of this genre in the entire nation. The complex consists of three parts, the first of which is what you would expect to find in a natural history museum–exhibits on animals and minerals, all well done. However, the section known as the "Prehistoric Journey: The History of Life on Earth" is one of the best museum exhibits around. Visitors walk through a complete environment of various prehistoric eras and actually see, hear, and smell what it would have been like during those times. The other parts of the museum feature an IMAX film presentation (topics change periodically) and the Gates Planetarium. *Tel. 303/322-7009, is open daily from 9:00am to 5:00pm except Christmas. The admission is $6 for adults and $4 for senior citizens and children ages 4 through 12. Additional fee for IMAX theater and laser shows. Call Tel. 303/370-6487 for laser show schedules and prices. Bus 20, 32.*

The Zoo occupies a large area in the central portion of the park and is outstanding. There aren't any cages in this zoo where more than 3,000 animals roam freely in large habitats that simulate their natural environment. Among the zoo's sections are Bird World, Primate Panorama, Northern Shores (sea lions and river otters), Sheep Mountain, and Tropical Discovery. The last section recreates a tropical rain forest covering more than 20,000 square feet. *Tel. 303/376-4800, is open every day of the year from 9:00am to 6:00pm, but from 10:00am to 5:00pm from October through March. The admission is $8 for adults, $6 for seniors, $4 for children ages 4 through 12. Bus 32.*

Exit from the park on the west side via West 21st Avenue and travel one block to Gaylord Street and the **Pearce-McAllister Cottage**, located at *1880 Gaylord Street at 19th Avenue.* The 1899 Dutch Colonial Revival style house is a great place for kids as it houses the **Denver Museum of Miniatures, Dolls and Toys**. *Tel. 303/322-3704. The house/museum is open Tuesday through Saturday from 10:00am until 4:00pm and on Sunday from 1:00pm to 4:00pm. Closed on state holidays. The admission fee is $3 for adults and $2 for senior citizens and children ages 2 through 16. Bus 20, 24.*

A few blocks south of the Cottage, via York Street is Colfax Avenue. Turn left (east) and travel a short distance to the intersection of Colorado Boulevard, then turning right. Follow that to CO 83 and bear to the left. A short distance will bring you to the **Four Mile House Historic Park**, *715 S. Forest Street.* The farm house dates from 1859 and has been carefully restored to its original appearance. It was a stock ranch and stop for stage coaches all in one. Several barns can be visited and you can take a stage coach ride (weekends only) on the 14-acre farm. *Tel. 303/399-1859. The farm offers guided tours on the hour Wednesday through Sunday, 10:00am to 4:00pm from April through September, or you can explore on your own. The admission fee is $3.50 for adults and $2 for seniors and children ages 6 through 15. Bus 56.*

Retrace your route back to Colorado Boulevard and head south (to the right). At the junction of I-25 hop on the freeway northbound and take it to Exit 212 (Speer Boulevard). A right off of the exit will quickly bring you to the entrance gate of the **Six Flags Elitch Gardens Amusement Park**. The park was one of the first of its type in this country and is the only one located in what can be said to be the downtown of a major American city. In that respect, as well as its attractive gardens and grounds, it is much like Copenhagen's world famous *Tivoli*. Elitch features about 20 major rides, including a hundred-foot high ferris wheel and several thrill rides. A $25 million expansion completed in 1997 added such hair-raising possibilities as *Shipwreck Falls*, the *Mind Eraser*, and the *Tower of Doom*. The latter lets you experience what it's like to free-fall more than 200 feet at

60 miles per hour. *Twister II* is one of the world's largest wooden roller coasters.

There's also a ten-acre water park called *Island Kingdom* and plenty of tamer rides suitable for small children as well as numerous places to eat and a 3,000-seat outdoor arena. The latter and other venues present six different live acts throughout the day. If you like to spend a lot of time in places like this (that is, you have kids with you), it might be wise to make this the last stop of the day. Then you can stay well into the evening when other attractions are closed. *Tel. 800/354-8247. The park is open daily, June 1st through Labor Day, from 10:00am until 10:00pm and until 11:00pm on Friday and Saturday. Admission: $26 adults; $16 under 48 inches tall. Credit cards. Parking costs an additional $3. Bus 10.*

Just beyond the amusement park via Speer Boulevard is the new **Pepsi Center**, the home of Denver's basketball and hockey teams among other events. This can take ten seconds of your time if you like to see arenas. However, our route after the Elitch Gardens turns left on Speer and proceeds over the South Platte River where you should immediately turn to the left on Water Street and proceed to **Colorado's Ocean Journey**, *700 Water Street*. While Colorado and ocean may seem to be a contradiction in terms, it won't be for long after you enter this new high-tech aquarium that cost almost $100 million before it finally opened in the summer of 1999. Your walk through the facility will take you along two river environments, the Colorado and the Kampar, both of which lead to an ocean in the real world. The Colorado journey passes mountain waterfalls and trout streams before entering a desert world. The Kampar re-creates a tropical rain forest of Sumatra and a coral reef in Indonesia. Both exhibits feature highly imaginative artificial terrains, huge aquariums containing over a million gallons of water and 15,000 fish, plants and animals. Even if you aren't usually enthralled by aquariums, Ocean Journey is worth the trip. *Tel. 303/561-4450. The aquarium is open daily from 10:00am until 6:00pm. From Memorial Day through Labor Day it remains open until 8:00pm on Saturday and Sunday. Closed on Christmas Day. Admission is $15 for adults, $13 for seniors and teens, and $7 for children ages 4 through 12. Credit Cards. Additional fee for parking. Bus 10, 84*

Immediately south of the aquarium via Water Street, bear left onto Children's Museum Drive. A short ride through a pleasant riverside park brings you, naturally, to the **Children's Museum of Denver**. It's great fun for the little ones but, obviously, not worth the bother if your party is only made up of grown-ups. If, however, you want your children to learn how to ski, this is a great place to get some basic professional instruction—the museum has an artificial ski slope. Well, I guess it shows where Coloradans priorities lie when bringing up the little ones! *Tel. 303/433-7444. The museum is open daily from 10:00am to 5:00pm except that it is closed on Monday* *from September through May. The admission is $5 but seniors pay only $3. There are additional fees ranging up to $10 for ski instruction and other special activities. Credit cards. Bus 10, 84.*

This concludes Tour 2. An I-25 interchange is located just north of the museum so you have good access to any point within the metropolitan area. However, sports fans might want to take a look at the new football stadium for the Denver Bronco's on the west side of the South Platte River a little south of the Children's Museum. Set to open for the Fall 2001 season, it replaces venerable Mile High Stadium which was once immediately to the north of this site. The new stadium occupies the former site of the McNichols Sports Arena, a multi-purpose facility which has been replaced by the Pepsi Center. Denver has certainly been on a stadium building binge.

Finally, there are two places that are testaments to the darker side of humanity. One is a place you should visit, while the second should definitely be off- limits. The first is **Babi Yar Park**, *Havana Street and Yale Avenue,* which commemorates the memory of the more than 200,000 Ukrainian victims of the Nazis during their occupation of the city of Kiev. The park covers 26 acres and the use of black granite stones helps to foster a somber atmosphere. The park is open at all times and there is no admission charge. The second is in the suburb of Littleton, immediately to the south of Denver. I've received reports that quite a few people drive or walk past **Columbine High School** where a mass murder took place several years ago. This is not a tourist attraction and I urge you not to go there. It is common for friends and relatives to visit the site as a way of remembering their loss, but visits by the general public, even well intentioned ones, aren't welcome in Littleton.

PUNTING ON THE CREEK

*Kicking a football inside of Mile High Stadium isn't the only way to punt in Denver. A punt is a type of boat similar to a Venetian gondola and used to be quite popular, especially in England. They are almost non-existent in the United States but you can ride on one in Denver. The trip takes you gently down the Cherry Creek through a series of locks immediately adjacent to downtown. It's a relaxing way to take in some of the sights. For information on schedules and fares, call **Punt the Creek**, Tel. 303/698-1322 or 303/893-0750. Tickets are available at Larimer Street at Speer Blvd.*

Before we proceed to the final tour, which goes outside Denver's city limits, I should mention that Denver has many other attractions of interest. The above tours can be considered highlights for people with two days to spare. If you have more time then you should consider adding some of the following:

Black American West Museum & Heritage Center, *3091 California Street. Tel. 303/292-2566.* America's most comprehensive exhibit on the role of Black Americans in the development of the west.

Denver Firefighters Museum, *1326 Tremont Place. Tel. 303/892-1436.* Traces the people who fought fires in Denver's early days and the equipment they used.

Mizel Museum of Judaica, *560 S. Monaco Parkway. Tel. 303/333-4156.* The history, culture, and arts of the Jewish faith.

Museo de las Americas, *861 Santa Fe Drive. Tel. 303/571-4401.* Explores Latin art, culture, and history. Emphasis is on Latin America and northwestern Mexico.

Museum of Contemporary Art, *1275 19th Street. Tel. 303/298-7554.* A new addition to the Denver cultural scene, the museum is designed to inspire an appreciation for contemporary art. Guided tours are available.

Trianon Museum & Art Gallery, *335 14th Street. Tel. 303/623-0739.* A fine collection of 18th century European masterpieces.

Wings Over the Rockies Air & Space Museum, *711 E. Academy Blvd. Tel. 303/360-5360.* Houses a collection of almost three dozen historic aircraft including a B-1 Stealth bomber. There are also model planes, exhibits of uniforms and other items relating to the air force and space.

TOUR 3: GOLDEN & THE WESTERN SUBURBS

Approximate duration (including sightseeing time) is six hours but can be a full day if you want to pursue recreational activities in the mountain parks. Begin in Golden at the Colorado Railroad Museum, reached from Denver by taking I-70 west to Exit 266 and then following West 44th Avenue to the museum.

The **Colorado Railroad Museum**, *17155 W. 44th Avenue*, chronicles the history of railroading in Colorado through documents and artifacts. There is also a sizable collection of rolling stock outside the museum building. The large model railroad collection is also of interest. *Tel. 800/365-6263. Museum hours are daily from 9:00am until 6:00pm from June through August and until 5:00pm the rest of the year. It is closed on Thanksgiving and Christmas. Admission for adults is $4, $3.50 for seniors, and $2 for children under 16. They also have a $9 family rate. Bus 17, 44LTD.*

Continue west on 44th Avenue for a short distance until you reach 13th Street. Turn right and you'll see and smell the **Adolph Coors Company Brewery**. The company just celebrated its 125th anniversary and the classical brewery is known for its large hand-made copper kettles. It is also the largest single brewery operation of its kind in the world (that is, Coors' beer is only made at this location). The forty-minute long guided tours take you through exhibit areas documenting the company as well as the brewery itself. It ends, of course, in the tasting room where you can sample a variety of beers. You've all seen those wonderful commercials touting Rocky Mountain water as the secret of Coors special taste. I don't know if it's true, but those mountains are awfully close to the brewery. *Tel. 303/277-BEER. The free tours are offered daily (except Sunday and holidays) from 10:00am until 4:00pm. Children must be accompanied by an adult. Bus 17, 44LTD.*

MILWAUKEE - WHERE'S THAT?

When it comes to beer that's what Coloradans, especially those living in the Denver area, ask. That's because to them, Denver is the suds capital of America and they can point to lots of things that justify the claim, the first of which is that the **Coors Brewery** *is the single largest facility in the world, with an annual output of some 17 million barrels of beer! Some other facts to consider are:.*

• There are more than 100 beers that are made in and can be bought only in Colorado.

• Denver hosts America's largest beer festival–the **Great American Beer Festival**.

• The two largest brewpubs in America are located in Denver.

A lot of people, especially those from Wisconsin, scratch their heads at this and wonder what could have made it so. After all, there aren't that many Germans in Colorado. The answer is water. Yes, water is acknowledged by all to be the most important ingredient in making a good beer. The simple fact is that nowhere else can you get better beer-making water than in the crisp and cold streams of the Colorado Rockies. And you thought that stuff was just the advertising agency's way of putting Coors on the map!

A few blocks from the brewery at *822 12th Street* is the historic **Astor House Hotel Museum**. The hotel, which opened in 1867, was one of the first in the area. It no longer houses guests, only visitors taking the guided tours, for which reservations are required. *Tel. 303/278-3557. Museum hours are Tuesday through Saturday from 11:00am until 4:00pm, year-round. Admission is $3 for adults and $1 for students with identification and children under 12. Bus 16, 17, 44LTD.*

Now it is only again a few blocks to the next destination, the **Colorado School of Mines Geology Museum** *at 16th and Maple Streets.* In addition to a large and surprisingly interesting display of fossils, gemstones, and minerals, the museum has an exhibit on the early days of Colorado mining. *Tel. 303/273-3823. The museum is open daily from 9:00am until 4:00pm (Sunday from 1:00pm) only during the school year. There is no admission charge. Bus 16, 17, 44LTD.*

Drive west on 16th Street until you reach US 6/CO 93. Turn south and you'll soon reach the junction of US 40. Take US 40 west following signs for **Heritage Square**. The square is a recreation of a Colorado town of the 1880's. The main activities here are numerous shops and shows although children will probably be more entertained by one of several amusement park style rides and the alpine slide. From Wednesday through Sunday (during the summer only) there are humorous Victorian melodramas offered. You might also want to return one evening during that period for the "Lazy H" chuck wagon show and supper. *Tel. 303/278-1938. The square is open daily from 10:00am until 9:00pm Memorial Day through Labor Day and from 10:00am to 6:00pm the rest of the year. Admission to the square is free although there is an admission charge for rides and shows in the music hall. Call Tel. 303/279-7800 for information on the latter.*

Continue west on US 40 until it reaches I-70. Take the highway westbound for three miles to Exit 256 and follow the road for 1-1/2 miles to the **Mother Cabrini Shrine**. From the shrine area a gradual stairway leads up 373 steps (it goes quicker if you don't try to count them) to a 22-foot tall statue of Christ. While the statue is beautiful the main attraction is the incredible panorama of the entire Denver area. To the east is the city and beyond it the plains; in all other directions you are surrounded by towering mountain peaks. *Tel. 303/526-0758. The shrine is open every day of the year from 7:00am to 8:00pm (until 5:00pm from after Labor Day to late May). There is no set admission fee but donations are appreciated.*

If you don't want to make the long climb, or can't, you can get a similar view from the nearby **Lookout Mountain Park**. This sight should be seen even if you do get up to the Shrine because of the park's other attraction, the **Buffalo Bill Memorial Museum and Grave**. To reach Lookout Mountain, go back to Golden and look for the sign off of US 6 that leads to the 66-acre mountain-top park. The museum is at the summit and chronicles the life of William F. Cody, better known as Buffalo Bill. Calamity Jane also gets her due as do plenty of exhibits which depict life in the old west. The grave site of Buffalo Bill is a simple one adjacent to the observation deck which looks out on Denver. *Tel. 303/526-0747. The museum is open daily from 9:00am until 5:00pm May through October and Tuesday through Sunday from 9:00am to 4:00pm the remainder of the year. The admission fee is $3 for adults, $2 for senior citizens, and $1 for children ages 6 through 15.*

Now retrace your route back east on US 6 to US 40 westbound. When you reach the junction of the Interstate go west to Exit 250. Right off the highway the city of Denver maintains a **Buffalo Herd** numbering around 40 animals. It is claimed that they are the direct descendants of the last of America's wild buffaloes. I don't know if any of the beasts has personally confirmed this information. Anyhow, it is one of the best places in the country to get good close up pictures of these powerful animals. Now you can quickly scoot back east on the highway until Exit 260 and then take CO 470 south for only one exit to CO 74 westbound. In a distance of less than two miles you'll pass through the small town of Morrison and reach the entrance to **Red Rocks Park**, one of Denver's premier scenic and cultural attractions. Covering almost 650 acres at the foot of the Rockies, the park features large red sandstone formations that are more than a million years old.

The formations are as high as 500 feet in places and receive their distinctive color from iron oxide in the rock. A large area between the formations, besides providing a great view of Denver, is in the form of a natural amphitheater. It has been converted into a 10,000 seat outdoor theater. Concerts are held frequently during the summer. *Call Tel. 303/ 964-2500 for performance information. The park is open daily from 5:00am until 11:00pm and there is no admission charge (except for shows).*

If you want to spend some more time in Denver's mountain parks many of them are located west of this area and can be reached by I-70. Information is contained in the sports and recreation section later in this chapter.

HERE DINO ••• HERE DINO!

Ever wonder why everyone seems to like dinosaurs? I think it's because you don't have to worry about ever bumping into the real thing! Well, regardless, the Rocky Mountains have proven to be a fruitful area for dinosaur remains and the Denver vicinity is no exception. **Dinosaur Ridge,** *16831 W. Alameda Parkway (Morrison) preserves more than 300 dinosaur footprints, including those of the stegosaurus, allosaurus and ever popular brontosaurus. Interpretive signs follow a mile long pathway along a scenic ridge. Parents should keep a close watch on children as portions of the trail are unprotected from the adjacent road.*

Tel. 303/697-3466. Open on weekdays from 9:00am until 4:00pm; until 5:00pm on Saturday, and from noon until 5:00 on Sunday. It is closed during inclement weather. Admission is free although guided tours for groups of 12 or more can be arranged at a cost of $25.

The last attraction of this final Denver tour is the **Tiny Town and Railroad** located at *6249 S. Turkey Creek Road*. To reach it from Red Rocks, go back to CO 470 and head south for one exit to US 285. Take that road south (although it's actually heading west at this point) for a few miles and turn left on Turkey Creek Road. Tiny Town was built in 1915 by George Turner who started to construct buildings at one-sixth their actual size for his daughter. It was closed down in the early 1940s but was resurrected by volunteers in the late 1980s. It now contains over one hundred miniature buildings representative of a turn-of-the-century community. Children will love the colorful houses, many with full interior furnishings as well as the miniature steam train that winds its way through and around the town on a mile long narrow-gauge track. Adults seem to like it a lot as well. *Tel. 303/697-6829. Town hours are daily from 10:00am until 5:00pm during the period Memorial Day to Labor Day. It is also open on weekends during May before Memorial Day and through the end of September. Admission is $3 for adults and $2 for children ages 3 through 12. An additional $1 is charged for the train ride for all ages.*

Return to Denver by taking US 285 north. You can reach downtown from US 285 by going north on Broadway. US 285 will also intersect with I-25 to give you easy access to whatever point in the Denver area you may be staying in.

As was the case with the city itself, you can't possibly see everything in the suburbs on a single day long tour. So, here are a few places that are worthy of your consideration:

Butterfly Pavilion & Insect Center, *6252 W. 104th Avenue (Westminster). Tel. 303/469-5441.* The more than 1,200 butterflies in the tropical rain forest setting is simply beautiful as well as interesting and educational. Less pleasing from an aesthetic standpoint is the huge collection of insects, including such delights as roaches, centipedes and tarantulas. But your kids will probably love the latter.

Littleton Historical Museum, *6028 S. Gallup Street (Littleton). Tel. 303/795-3950.* The museum contains two working farms with live animals that makes it a good place for small children. A local history museum is also on the pleasant grounds that contain a lake and nice walks.

National Renewable Energy Laboratory Visitors Center, *15013 Denver West Parkway (Golden). Tel. 303/384-6565.* There are interesting exhibits on the practical uses of alternative energy sources such as solar, wind and thermal energy. The building itself is an energy-efficient design.

NIGHTLIFE & ENTERTAINMENT

There isn't any place in Colorado with the quantity and variety of entertainment options that can be found in Denver. To make things a little easier I've divided the possibilities into two sections. "Out on the town" includes nightclubs, dancing establishments, and the like. If you're looking for something more on the cultural side then look under "performing arts."

DRINK IN GOOD HEALTH

In a previous sidebar you found out just how much Denver loves its beer. With all that beer being produced, and not all of it for export outside of Colorado, you might expect to see a lot of pot-bellied folks plodding around. Again, however, conventional wisdom will lead you astray. Studies indicate that Denver's populace is the thinnest among the 33 largest cities in the United States. It seems to me that Denver must be producing the most light beer in the nation, too! Well, maybe not. Obviously the environment and the magnificent recreational opportunities it fosters contributes to the active lifestyle that is so common among Denverites. So, have that beer, light or not, and go jogging along in one of the Denver area's many parks. The calories will be gone before you can say microbrewery.

Out on the Town

BRENDAN'S MARKET STREET PUB, *1625 Market Street. Tel. 303/595-0609.*

One of the favorite places for locals in LoDo. Friendly pub featuring premium draft beers and live entertainment Tuesday through Saturday. The kitchen stays open real late.

COMEDY WORKS, *1226 15th Street. Tel. 303/595-3637.*

Considered to be one of the best comedy clubs in the nation.

GRIZZLY ROSE SALOON & DANCE EMPORIUM, *5450 N. Valley Highway. Tel. 303/295-1330.*

Has live country music every night in a huge dance hall. Free lessons are given so your guy can't give you the excuse that he can't dance. Sunday is Family Night. Good food and gift shop on premises.

POLLY ESTHER'S, *2301 Blake Street. Tel. 303/382-1976.*

Fun but not too wild dance club that features top hits going back to the '70s and '80s era. The inviting atmosphere features interesting tidbits from those years. Good mix of age groups.

SING SING, *1735 19th Street. Tel. 303/291-0880.* Guests are strongly encouraged to make as much noise as they can into the wee hours at this unusual club–a rock and roll dueling piano bar. Great fun. Crowd tends to be fairly diverse–from the 20's through late 40's.

SLUGGERS WORLD CLASS SPORTS BAR & GRILL, *2229 Blake Street. Tel. 303/298-8006.*

The name comes from the establishments close proximity to Coors Field. Has the usual sports bar features but also presents live entertainment along with a game and video room. They serve Chicago style pizza and even have batting cages where you can brush up on your baseball skills. The place is lots of fun and even families have been seen there before the hour gets too late.

STAMPEDE MESQUITE GRILL & DANCE EMPORIUM, *2430 S. Havana, Aurora. Tel. 303/696-7686.* It seems Denver's club owners like their country places to be called emporiums–I guess it lends an air of authenticity. This big (30,000 square feet) hall can accommodate up to 1,800 guests in this popular western nightspot. A good restaurant is located on the balcony that overlooks the dance floor.

TRIOS ENOTECA, *1730 Wynkoop Street. Tel. 303/293-2887.*

A definite hit on the night spot list, Trios Enoteca features excellent rhythm and blues in addition to traditional jazz. They also are noted for having one of the best bars in LoDo that serves up a great selection of wines and top notch martinis. Also has a cigar bar. Lighter drinkers will like their wonderful selection of appetizers, finger foods and scrumptious desserts.

Since I've already alluded several times to LoDo's many brew pubs, I would certainly be remiss if I didn't say anything about them under nightlife. The majority of these pubs also serve food (and sometimes real good food). Besides LoDo you can find brew pubs in the Larimer Square area and on the 16th Street Mall. Among the best are the **Breckenridge Brewery**, *2220 Blake Street,* which markets four brews throughout the Rocky Mountain region (try *Avalanche Ale* or *Mountain Wheat*); the **Champion Brewing Company**, *1442 Larimer Square*, with its award-winning beers and interesting menu along with brewery tours and over 20 televisions; the **Rock Bottom Brewery**, *1001 16th Street*; and **Wynkoop Brewing Company**, *1634 18th Street*. This last place has, besides great beer and excellent pub style menu, an elegant pool hall located on the upper level and a comedy sports program.

Finally, for the guys just looking to look at good-looking women, Denver has a number of "gentlemen's cabarets," a nice way of saying girlie bar. A lot of them are located immediately to the east of downtown along and around Colfax, but most of them are kind of seedy. Two of the more "respectable" places are the **P.T. Showclub**, *1601 West Evans,* and **Shotgun Willie's**, *490 S. Colorado Boulevard.*

Performing Arts

There is little doubt that when you mention the performing arts to a Denver resident the **Denver Performing Arts Complex**, *14th and Curtis Streets*, immediately comes to mind. It is the world's largest arts under one roof (as compared to a multi-building complex like New York's Lincoln Center). The complex is home to eight separate theaters and can accommodate in excess of 10,000 people. All of the venues are connected by an 80-foot high glass arch that stretches for two blocks. The most important venues are:

- **Auditorium Theater**: This historic theater that was incorporated into the complex is the home to the Colorado Ballet and to touring Broadway shows.
- **Boettcher Concert Hall**: An in-the-round setting for the Colorado Symphony Orchestra and other musical events.
- **Temple Hoyne Buell Theater**: Varied performances take place in this, the largest of the complex's theaters. Seats 2,850 people.
- **Garner Galleria Theater**: A small theater used for cabaret style productions.
- **Helen Bonfils Theater**: This unusual facility is actually five venues within a single venue and is used for professional theater and other events.

Although touring productions and visiting celebrities are a significant part of the Arts Complex calendar, among the permanent tenants are the aforementioned **Colorado Symphony Orchestra**, *Tel. 303/830-TIXS;* **Opera Colorado**, *Tel. 303/986-8742;* **Colorado Ballet**, *Tel. 303/837-8888;* and the **Cleo Parker Robinson Dance** company, *Tel. 303/395-1759.* The theater box office number is *Tel. 303/466-4847.*

The performing arts are by no means limited to the Arts Complex as will be evident after you've scanned through this list of other entertainment possibilities:

- **Arvada Center for the Arts & Humanities**, *6901 Wadsworth Boulevard, Arvada. Tel. 303/431-3939.* Year-round theater, dance, concerts, and other programs in separate indoor and outdoor venues.
- **Historic Paramount Theater**, *1631 Glenarm Street. Tel. 303/825-4904.* Presents a wide variety of musical entertainment as well as comedy, and dance.
- **Swallow Hill Music Association**, *1905 S. Pearl Street. Tel. 303/777-1003.* Weekend concerts all year long featuring blues, bluegrass, Cajun, Celtic, and a variety of other forms both popular and little known.
- **Theater on Broadway**, *13 S. Broadway. Tel. 303/860-9360.* A fine resident company puts on worthy productions of both Broadway and off-Broadway drama and musicals.

The Denver area also has a number of family oriented dinner theater venues. Among them are the **Heritage Square Music Hall**, *18301 W. Colfax Avenue, Golden, Tel. 303/279-7800*; and the **Country Dinner Playhouse**, *6875 S. Clinton Street, Englewood, Tel. 303/799-9311.*

Finally, there are few places in Colorado or anywhere else that can compete with the natural surroundings of the **Red Rocks Park Amphithe-**

ater. The 9,050 seat facility is world renowned and each summer is home to as many as 30 different performances ranging from popular recording stars to classical music. *Tel. 303/640-2637 for theater schedule and information.*

SHOPPING

The diversity of shopping in Denver is as large as would be expected from a city of its size. Among the more important trinkets that visitors seem to look for are Native American and western goods. They are, of course, widely available although such items aren't as important in the overall scheme here as in states further west. One of the nicest things about Denver shopping is that downtown and other areas within the city haven't fallen prey to the suburban mall. While there are plenty of the latter to choose from, center city shopping in Denver is alive and well. In fact, it is growing all the time.

So, starting with downtown, shoppers should head for the **16th Street Mall**, a pedestrian-only shopping heaven that stretches for nearly a mile between Cleveland Place and Arapahoe Street. The seemingly countless stores, including many chic boutiques, are located in structures ranging from modern glass office towers to restored buildings from the early part of the century. In fact, two shopping centers are within the 16th Street Mall. These are **The Shops at Tabor Center** (*at Lawrence Street*) with more than 60 stores, and the **Denver Pavilions** (*between Welton and Tremont*). In addition to shops and theaters, the Pavilions features several restaurants. Should you tire of walking on the Mall and its adjacent shopping streets, you can always hop on **The Mall Ride**, a free bus service provided by the Regional Transit District.

At the north end of the mall you're only steps away from another popular shopping area—**Larimer Square**. About 30 stores are housed in Victorian style dwellings and some others that date back as far as the Civil War era. Part of the attraction of Larimer Square is not the shopping, but the environment, the frequent street entertainment and numerous special events. You can even ride around in an old-time horse-drawn carriage. The last few years have seen an extension of great shopping into neighboring **LoDo**. The shops here range from the eclectic to the downright bizarre but you can find just about anything you're looking for. LoDo is also known for its art galleries.

The **Cherry Creek Shopping District** may be the most popular area to shop when it comes to the locals way of doing things. The area is only a few miles from downtown (East 1st Avenue) and consists of numerous shops on lovely tree-lined streets and the **Cherry Creek Shopping Center**, *3000 E. 1st Avenue.* Besides the usual specialty shops it is known for upscale department stores including Saks Fifth Avenue, Neiman Marcus, and Lord & Taylor. Between the mall and the other stores in the area

Cherry Creek has more than 400 stores and over 60 restaurants. There's something for every taste. The area is filled with outdoor sculptures, gardens, and fountains. A big expansion of the mall is planned.

Now that I've introduced the main shopping areas let's take a look at some specific merchants that peddle the goods that travelers are most looking for.

Native American Goods

West Southwest, *257 Fillmore Street*, has fine quality Native American art and jewelry including prized Nambe ware. You ca also try the **Red Rocks Trading Post** on *County Route 470 in Morrison* near the Red Rocks Park.

Western Wear

Miller Stockman, *1600 California Street.*

Art Galleries/Antiques

The Collection, *899 Broadway*, is home to more than 60 area dealers in art and antiques. The **Denver Antique Market**, *1212 S. Broadway,* is a block-long antique district with more than 250 dealers. Also of interest in the antique category is **Wazee Deco Antiques**, *1730 Wazee,* LoDo's upscale gallery. For more unusual works of art, try **Earthzone**, *1411 Larimer Square.*

Colorado Goods

Made in Colorado, *4840, W. 29th Avenue;* **Lokstok-N-Barel**, *1421 Larimer Square.*

Not quite fitting into any of these categories but a definite destination in itself whether or not you're in the market to buy is the **Denver Buffalo Company**, *1109 Lincoln Street.* In addition to housing a well-known restaurant, the mercantile section of this large complex features several retail shops and an art gallery. Both western wear and art are available. Also in the unusual category is the **Mile High Flea Market**, *7007 E. 88th Street* in suburban Henderson. You'll find everything from avocados to zircons in Colorado's largest flea market. It covers 80 acres and is open weekends and Wednesdays only with expanded hours during the Christmas season.

For those of you who just have to visit the regional shopping mall, some possibilities are (in addition to those on the 16th Street Mall and the aforementioned Cherry Creek Shopping Center):

• **Park Meadows Town Center**, *8401 Park Meadows Center Drive, Littleton.* More than a hundred stores including Nordstroms and Dillards.

• **Southglenn Mall**, *6911 S. University Blvd., Littleton.* More than a hundred stores in a typical suburban mall.

Those looking for factory outlets will have to go a little further. Southbound on the way to Colorado Springs are the **Castle Rock Factory Stores** *(I-25, Exit 184).*

SPORTS & RECREATION

Amusement Parks

• **Six Flags Elitch Gardens**, *I-25, Exit 212A. Tel. 303/595-4386.* See Tour 2 for details.
• **Funplex**, *9670 W. Coal Mine Avenue, Littleton. Tel. 303/972-4344.*
• **Lakeside Amusement Park**, *I-70 at Sheridan, Tel. 303/477-1621.*
• **Water World**, *88th Avenue at Pecos, Federal Heights. Tel. 303/427-SURF.*

Ballooning

Life Cycle Balloon Adventures Ltd., *410 19th Street, Golden. Tel. 800/ 980-9272 or 303/216-1900.* Year-round sunrise champagne flights subject to weather conditions. Over 25 years experience.

Looney Balloons, Inc., *Littleton. Tel. 303/979-9476 for pickup.* Regular or champagne flights over the Rockies depart from Chatfield State Park.

Bicycling

It seems that everyone in Denver loves to ride a bike. The parks are usually jammed with riders. The city operates an extensive network of bicycle paths that cover the entire metropolitan area. You can get bike route maps and other information, as well as join in organized rides, by contacting the **Denver Bicycle Touring Club**, *Tel. 303/798-3713.*

Boating

Yes, there is boating available within the Denver metropolitan area. **Chatfield State Park** (*eight miles southwest of downtown via S. Santa Fe Drive, which is US 85*) and **Cherry Creek Lake State Recreation Area** (*S. Parker Road, CO 83, in suburban Aurora*) both contain large lakes and have boat ramps.

Fishing

Each of the areas listed above under boating also are places where you can fish.

Golf

• **Aurora Hills Golf Course**, *50 S. Peoria Street, Aurora. Tel. 303/364-9401.* 18 holes.

- **City Park**, *E. 25th Avenue & York Street. Tel. 303/295-4420.* 18 holes. The closest course to downtown. An excellent public links location, but usually crowded.
- **Evergreen Golf Course**, *29614 Upper Bear Creek Road, Evergreen. Tel. 303/674-4128.* Another fine 18-hole course operated by the city of Denver.
- **Meadow Hills Golf Course**, *3609 S. Dawson Street, Aurora. Tel. 303/690-2500.* 18-hole championship level course.
- **Springhill Golf Course**, *800 Telluride Street, Aurora. Tel. 303/739-6854.* 18 holes.

Hiking

Hiking and related outdoor activities are available in all of Denver's "mountain parks." The two closest ones are:
- **Lookout Mountain Park**, *Golden*
- **Red Rocks Park**, *off CO 74 in Morrison*

Details on getting to the above can be found in the Seeing the Sights section. Nearby portions of the **Clear Creek**, **Gilpin** and **Boulder National Forests** are also excellent places for hiking as are **Coal Creek** and **Golden Gate Canyons** along, respectively, CO 72 and CO 46 to the northwest of downtown Denver.

Horseback Riding

- **Stockton's Plum Creek Stables**, *7479 W. Titan Road, Littleton. Tel. 303/791-1966.* Year round riding. Reservations required.

Spectator Sports

Denver has a franchise in every major professional spectator sport and some of their teams have a strong nation-wide, or at least region-wide following. Here's the rundown on where and when they play.

Baseball: The **Colorado Rockies** of the National League draw fans from a wide radius to Coors Field, located downtown at *2100 Blake Street* to the northeast of the Larimer Square area, from April through the beginning of October. *Tel. 800/388-7625* for schedule and ticket information.

Basketball: Pepsi Arena, located a short distance from the heart of downtown, is the home of the National Basketball Association's **Denver Nuggets**. They haven't been one of the leagues better teams but if you want to join with the local fans in suffering through their woes, ticket information is available at *Tel. 303/893-6700.* The season is from November through April.

Football: The **Denver Broncos** of the National Football League are dear to the hearts of the people of Denver and Colorado. They play to packed houses regardless of the weather conditions. During the 1990's the Broncos were among the league's most successful teams. Their achievements included two Super Bowl championships. Now, in the post-John Elway era, their level of excellence is not the same. However, tickets are still hard to come by. The Broncos play at the spanking new **Invesco Field** at Mile High. For schedules and information, *Tel. 303/649-9000.*

Hockey: The **Colorado Avalanche** of the National Hockey League shares the Pepsi Arena with the Nuggets and play from October through March, plus the playoffs. The team has met with quite a bit of success the last few years. Ticket and schedule information can be obtained by calling *Tel. 303/405-1100.*

Other professional team sports include the **Colorado Rapids** and **Colorado Foxes** (soccer), and the **Colorado Xplosion** (women's basketball).

Racing: Thoroughbred racing is held at Arapahoe Park Racetrack in nearby Aurora. *Tel. 303/690-2400.* The park has live racing during the summer and simulcast at other times of the year. Greyhard racing takes place in Commerce City's Mile High Greyhound Park, *6200 Dahlia Street, Tel. 303/288-1591.* The season runs from mid-June through mid-February. Car racing enthusiasts will enjoy the NASCAR events held at the Colorado National Speedway, Exit 232 of I-25, *Tel. 303/665-4173.*

Skiing

With the snow-capped mountains seemingly at the city gates a lot of visitors to Denver expect to find skiing within the immediate metropolitan area. Well, the slopes aren't quite that close but there are a number of ski areas that are less than a two hour drive which means you can get there and back in a day trip. These locations (described in Chapter 13) are Arapahoe Basin, Breckenridge, Copper Mountain, Eldora, Keystone, Loveland, Silver Creek, and Winter Park.

The two nearest ones are Eldora and Winter Park. A good way to get to the latter is by taking the **Ski Train**. It leaves on weekend mornings from Union Station and gets back in the early evening. The fare is approximately $30-50 depending upon class of travel. For information call *Tel. 303/296-I-SKI.*

Swimming

• **Chatfield State Park**, *S. Santa Fe Drive (US 85)*
• **Cherry Lake State Recreation Area**, *S. Parker Road (CO 983) in Aurora*
• **Eisenhower Recreation Center**, *4300 E. Dartmouth Avenue*

• **20th Street Recreation Center**, *1011 20th Street*

Tennis

The largest number of courts open to the general public can be found in **City Park**. There are numerous private tennis clubs throughout the city.

EXCURSIONS & DAY TRIPS

While I usually describe excursions from the big cities as a separate section like this (and will do so in the case of Colorado Springs), Denver presents an unusual situation because all of the nearby excursion destinations are more appropriately part of another touring region. So, I'll mention the best destinations here but you'll have to look elsewhere for details.

The Heart of the Rockies region (*see Chapter 13*) is close enough to Denver for one or more excursions. The best destinations for a single day or less are Boulder, Idaho Springs, Central City, and Georgetown. These places will get you into some beautiful mountain scenery as well as acquaint you with the history of Colorado's mining era.

A longer trip is a loop through Estes Park, Rocky Mountain National Park, and back to Denver via Winter Park and Idaho Springs. Although I've done this myself I must warn you that it is a fairly ambitious agenda for one day and requires an early start.

It is also possible to see some of the highlights of Colorado Springs (see Chapter 12) in a day trip from Denver but I would only recommend it, as well as the excursions above, if you otherwise don't plan on going beyond the Denver area. The same can be said of the northern I-25 corridor attractions in Loveland, Fort Collins, and Greeley.

PRACTICAL INFORMATION

• **Airport:** *Tel. 303/342-2000*
• **Airport Transportation:** *Airporter, Tel. 303/333-5833; Dash Shuttle, Tel. 800/525-3077; Denver Express Shuttle, Tel. 303/766-7959; and SuperShuttle, Tel. 800/370-1300*
• **Bus Depot:** *Downtown: 1055 19th Street, Tel. 303/293-6555; Aurora: 13179 E. Colfax, Tel. 303/340-0501*
• **Hospitals:** Downtown and central city: *St. Joseph Hospital, 1835 Franklin Street. Tel. 303/837-7111; Denver Health Medical Center, 777 Bannock Street. Tel. 303/436-6000. North: Columbia North Suburban Medical Center, 9191 Grant Street, Thornton. Tel. 303/451-7800. South: Columbia Swedish Medical Center, 501 E. Hampden, Englewood. Tel. 303/788-5000.*
• **Police** (non-emergency): *Tel. 303/575-3127*

- **Public Transportation**: *Regional Transit District (RTD) 303/299-6000*
- **Taxi**: *Metro Taxi, Tel. 303/333-3333; Yellow Cab, Tel. 303/777-7777; Zone Cab, Tel. 303/448-8888*
- **Tourist Office/Visitor Bureau**: *1668 Larimer Street, Tel. 800/645-3446 or 303/892-1112; www.denver.org*
- **Train Station**: *Union Station, 1701 Wynkoop Street. Tel. 303/893-3911*

12. COLORADO SPRINGS

It's likely that if you asked most people about **Colorado Springs** they would definitely be aware of its existence but think that it isn't a very big city. Well, it is the second largest city in Colorado with a population of well over 300,000 and it's growing faster than Denver. Because it's not the capital, not the biggest, and not the finance center, it literally exists in the shadow of Denver, which is less than 70 miles to the north. But it doesn't take second place when you look at it more carefully from the standpoint of a visitor rather than as a business person.

Located on a broad plateau at the foot of Pike's Peak, Colorado Springs is hundreds of feet higher than Denver with an official elevation of 5,980 feet. The city is even closer to the mountains than the former and so it seems that you can literally reach out from your hotel window and touch the Rockies. The area also has an abundance of unusual geologic formations and other natural wonders that make it a delight for those who love scenery. Historic and other man-made attractions are also numerous. It's my own personal opinion that sightseeing opportunities of a first class level are in greater supply here than in Denver. Colorado Springs also offers a multitude of recreational and cultural facilities.

The city was founded in 1871 by **General William J. Palmer**, builder of the Denver & Rio Grande Railroad, on the site of an existing mining community. Because of the natural springs in the area he envisioned the place as a health resort. (Although the mineral spas probably have some therapeutic effect, the health benefits associated with the Colorado Springs area are more likely to be a result of the invigorating climate and its clear, crisp mountain air.) The resort was successful from the beginning but real commercial growth didn't occur until after 1892 when gold was discovered at nearby Cripple Creek. By the early part of the 20th century, Colorado Springs was one of the wealthiest cities in America.

Today, Colorado Springs continues to be a major resort destination, both for health and other reasons, as well as an important manufacturing center for electrical equipment and pottery. There are two colleges plus

THE WILD EARLY DAYS AT THE SPRINGS

It didn't take long after General Palmer established his new resort immediately to the east of the existing town of Colorado City for it to attract a well-heeled clientele. The visitors included a large number of gentrified Englishmen and their families who soon took to playing polo and cricket and building Tudor style homes and business buildings where they could relax at afternoon tea. In fact, the English presence became so entrenched that a portion of the resort came to be known as "Little London."

While the Springs had much to offer it lacked (actually it banned) some of the diversions that were available in Colorado City. Such things as liquor, gambling, and brothels were readily available there and a significant portion of the high-society menfolk of the Springs longed for the theoretically less desirable activities of Colorado City. But, it wouldn't look right for them to be seen traveling there to partake in the action.

It has been alleged, although never been proven, that a series of tunnels were constructed from the resorts in General Palmer's community that connected with the heart of Colorado City, thus allowing unseen passage for those who wished their presence their to go unnoticed. There is little doubt that much of Colorado City's "business" came from the wealthy Springs patrons but it still a matter of argument among local historians if the tunnels ever really existed. But it is definitely the stuff of which historical legends are made of.

the **Air Force Academy**, and several government military installations including the **North American Air Defense Command** (NORAD) operations center inside Cheyenne Mountain.

ARRIVALS AND DEPARTURES
By Air

The modern (1994) **Colorado Springs Airport**, *Tel. 719/550-1930,* is an attractive facility that is large enough to have sufficient service from many localities to make it useful, but still small enough to avoid smothering crowds and the attendant delays associated with too many flights. Located at *7770 Drennan Road,* about a 20 minute ride from downtown, you should seriously consider booking your flight into Colorado Springs rather than Denver if this city is going to be a part of your itinerary. Consolidated information on ground transportation is available at a service booth in the airport lobby.

A taxi to downtown will run you about $17. There is also the **Airport Express**, *Tel. 800/782-7730,* and **Airport Shuttle**, *Tel. 800/222-2112 or 719/578-5232,* both about $11 to many popular locations. The latter also

COLORADO SPRINGS AREA

|——————| = Approx. 2.66 miles

1. The Broadmoor
2. Bus Terminal
3. Cave of the Winds
4. Cheyenne Mtn. Zoo/ Shrine of the Sun
5. Colorado Springs Municipal Airport
6. Garden of the Gods
7. Western Museum of Mining & Industry
8. Manitou Cliff Dwellings Museum
9. Miramont Castle
10. Olympic Training Complex
11. Pike's Peak Cog Railway
12. Pro Rodeo Hall of Fame
13. Seven Falls
14. U. S. Air Force Academy
15. Van Brigele Art Pottery
16. World Figure Skating Museum

serves many ski resorts. The staff at the airport's Ground Transportation Booth can provide complete details on the best means of getting to your destination by public transportation. For those seeking to return to the airport you can contact the booth by calling *Tel. 719/550-1930*.

If you rent a car at the airport, exit via Drennan Road and take that street to Hancock Expressway (a regular street and not a controlled access road despite the name). Turn right on Hancock and take it to Lake Avenue. Another left will bring you to I-25 in a few blocks. From that point you can reach downtown or most other points in the area via the highway.

By Bus

Inter-city bus service to Colorado Springs is provided by Greyhound. Their terminal is located at *120 S. Weber, Tel. 719/635-1505*.

By Car

Travelers coming from Denver and other points north and south will most likely arrive on I-25. If you're coming from the southwestern part of Colorado your access roads could be CO 115 (from the Canon City/Royal Gorge area) or US 24 (from Buena Vista). Access from the east is via I-70 to Limon and then by US 24 on into the Springs area. Exits 138 through 148 on I-25 provide direct access to almost any point in Colorado Springs.

ORIENTATION

Colorado Springs does have a downtown or central business district but it isn't of much importance to visitors on vacation expeditions. Most of the city lies on either side of Monument Creek, which kind of neatly divides things into east and west sides. Fountain Creek runs at an angle from about the middle of Monument Creek, northwest towards Manitou Springs, an important suburb and tourist destination. The greater portion of Colorado Springs is relatively flat and lends itself to a grid pattern. However, this pattern breaks down quickly once you get into the western part of the metropolitan area, such as Manitou Springs, or the southwest section of Colorado Springs around Cheyenne Canyon. This is because of topographical interference from mountains, waterfalls, rock formations, and other natural wonders.

Important routes are, first and foremost, I-25 which runs through Colorado Springs from north to south along Monument Creek; and CO 24, also known as the Midland Expressway, a semi-controlled access highway that runs from I-25 immediately to the west of downtown northwest to Manitou Springs. Major city streets include Cascade and Nevada Avenues, which run north to south on the east side; and 21st and

30th streets on the west side. For east-to-west travel the important city streets are Platte Avenue, Fountain Avenue, and Cheyenne Boulevard.

GETTING AROUND TOWN

Attractions and activities in the Colorado Springs area tend to be in clusters and are primarily in the southwest and in the corridor running to Manitou Springs along the Midland Expressway. Few points of interest are located downtown. Therefore, walking is generally not a viable means of getting from one attraction to another.

Gray Line/Pikes Peak Tours, *Tel. 800/345-8197*, offers the biggest variety of tours for those who aren't going to be driving.

By Bus

Springs Transit has more than 20 different routes that serve Colorado Springs and neighboring communities, including Manitou Springs. Most routes operate between 6:15am and 6:15pm although there are several night routes. The fare is $1.25 (60 cents for children under 11 and seniors age 60 and up). An additional zone will cost non-seniors 35 cents more (Manitou Springs is in another zone). There are free transfers between routes. Exact fare is required. If you are going to be using the bus a great deal then you can realize a small savings and convenience by purchasing a 22-ride punchcard for $25.

The far-flung nature of many of Colorado Springs' attractions (few are in the downtown core) makes using the bus to get around a limited option. In addition, Springs Transit doesn't have as extensive a route system as in Denver. Therefore, I won't bother to list the nearest route to each attraction when we get to the various tours of Colorado Springs. However, the following general route information will be of help to those who do plan to use the bus. Most routes serve the system's downtown terminal at Kiowa Street and Nevada Avenue. Route 11A serves Manitou Springs while 11B goes to the Garden of the Gods. If you want to reach the Broadmoor area then hop on Route 14, 42 or 44.

By Car

The primary means of reaching tourist attractions in the Colorado Springs vicinity. The city is big enough that there is considerable traffic, especially during rush hours along I-25 and the Midland Expressway. Try to avoid those routes at peak hours and you shouldn't encounter any serious congestion. Downtown street parking is by meter although there are many garages charging reasonable rates. Almost every tourist attraction has substantial free parking.

By Taxi

Taxis are considerably cheaper in Colorado Springs than in many large cities but at $3.00 for the first mile and $1.65 for each additional mile it can still add up to be an expensive way of getting around. Should you want to use taxis for a limited number of hops it is best to call for one by phone. **Yellow Cab**, *Tel. 719/635-9907 or 719/634-5000* is the main company. Another possibility is **American Cab**, *Tel. 637-1111.*

WHERE TO STAY

Accommodations in the Colorado Springs area are divided into the following locations: a "city zone" which includes everything north of US 24-Midland Expressway and east of I-25; and a separate section for the southwestern part of Colorado Springs including Manitou Springs. A third section encompasses Canon City, Cripple Creek, and Pueblo for visitors who want to spend more time in the surrounding areas.

CITY ZONE
Expensive

ALIKAR GARDENS RESORT, *1123 Verde Drive. Tel. 719/475-2564; Fax 719/471-5835. Toll free reservations 800/666-9997. 121 Rooms. Rates: High season (mid-May to mid-September): $179; Low season (mid-September to mid-May): $149. Major credit cards accepted. Located about two miles north of I-25, Exit 138 via Circle Drive to Verde.*

This townhome-style hotel has a convenient location whether you want to be near the airport, downtown, or the attractions of the southwestern quadrant of Colorado Springs. Although it isn't far from the city center the property has a much more rural feel because of the spacious tree covered grounds that include lovely fountains, streams and even waterfalls. There's even a picnic area amongst all of this water and greenery that can really make you think you're in the countryside, especially when you look in the direction of Pikes Peak.

All of the guest units are multi-room apartments that have either one or two bedrooms, separate living room, and a fully equipped kitchen including coffee maker and microwave oven. When you take that into account the rates aren't that expensive at all. The furnishings are attractive and home-like. For extended stays you won't even feel like you're in a hotel which can be a big plus if you're traveling with small children. Patios on the ground floor and balconies on the upper floors are also standard.

Recreational facilities include an Italian tiled heated outdoor swimming pool with spa and an exercise room. You can rent videos from the hotel's library but there is a charge for the cassette player. A public golf course is located within walking distance. The Alikar has no restaurant but there are quite a few good ones within a short distance. Weekly and monthly rates are available. The hotel has no elevator so if you have trouble climbing steps don't get a room on the third floor.

ANTLERS ADAMS MARK, *4 South Cascade Avenue. Tel. 719/473-5600; Fax 719/444-0417. Toll free reservations 800/222-TREE; www.antlers.com. 290 Rooms. Rates: High season (summer): $190-220; Low season (winter) $140-150. Major credit cards accepted. Located just off the east side of Exit 142 of I-25 via Bijou to Cascade.*

The 13-story high Antlers replaced an older hotel by the same name that was originally built in the early 1880's. The new version is thoroughly modern in every way. Although it's basically just a rectangular box there is something impressive about the architecture and its blending of darker and lighter colors at the top and bottom as well as the rooftop crown, for lack of a better term to describe this trapezoidal shaped feature.

Each of the large rooms is beautifully appointed with quality furnishings that belie the moderate price. A host of thoughtful amenities are on tap including a coffee maker. Some rooms have whirlpools and a few have refrigerators. If you can swing it try to get a room facing the mountains. Those, especially on the higher floors, offer one of the best views of the Rockies from any Colorado Springs hotel.

Antlers Grille is a new restaurant that is quickly earning a good reputation. A more casual restaurant is also on the premises. For nightlife you should try out Judge Baldwin's Brewing Company, an attractive old west themed microbrewery. They also serve sandwiches and that sort of thing. A separate cocktail lounge offers live entertainment on weekends. For recreation you can take advantage of the heated indoor swimming pool, Jacuzzi and health club. And this is a Doubletree so you know what that means–cookies!

COLORADO SPRINGS WYNDHAM, *5580 Tech Center Drive. Tel. 719/260-1800; Fax 719/260-1492. Toll free reservations 800/962-6982; www.wyndham.com/ColoradoSprings/. 310 Rooms. Rates: High season (mid-May to late September): $149; Low season (late September to mid-May): $135. Located about a half mile west of I-25, Exit 147 via Rockrimmon Blvd. to the Colorado Springs Tech Center.*

I wouldn't say that this is one of Wyndham's best properties, but it does afford the opportunity to stay at a first class chain at a quite reasonable price. The nine story high hotel's rooms usually offer a good view of the mountains or of Colorado Springs depending upon which direction you're facing. The rooms are large and comfortable. The Gratzi Restaurant serves good Italian and American specialties while Chats Lounge is a nice place for a nightcap. The Wyndham has lots of recreational facilities including heated indoor and outdoor swimming pools, Jacuzzi, sauna, exercise center and a volleyball court.

SHERATON COLORADO SPRINGS, *2886 S. Circle Drive. Tel. 719/ 576-5900; Fax 719/576-7695. Toll free reservations 800/981-4012; www.asgusa.com/scsh/index1.htm. 500 Rooms. Rates: High season (summer): $112-160; Low season (winter): $79-89. Major credit cards accepted. Located on the east side of I-25, Exit 138, convenient to downtown and the Broadmoor area.*

The recently remodeled Sheraton is spread out in low and mid-rise buildings over an extensive area with colorful flowers and nicely manicured grounds. The public areas feature a warm European style ambiance with large upholstered chairs, fireplaces and chandeliers. However, it has more of a casual feel than the stuffy atmosphere sometimes associated with better hotels. Guestrooms are large and attractive and all have coffee makers. A complimentary newspaper is delivered to your door each morning.

The public facilities of the Sheraton are first rate. The Cafe Terra Cotta is a good full service restaurant or you can go for something lighter at the whimsically named Relish This Deli. On the nightlife side Rickenbacker's is a popular spot with guests as well as residents as it has live music as well as several local microbrews. The pretty garden filled atrium is also the location of the heated indoor pool and Jacuzzi. There's also an outdoor heated pool, basketball and tennis courts and a putting green.

Moderate

BEST WESTERN LEBARON HOTEL, *314 W. Bijou. Tel. 719/471- 8680; Fax 719/471-0894. Toll free reservations 800/477-8614; www.lebaroncolospr.com/home.html. 206 Rooms. Rates: High season (May 15th to October 15th): $109; Low season (October 16th to May 14th): $79 including Continental breakfast. Located on the west side of I-25, Exit 142, within walking distance of downtown.*

The "LeBarons" are like a mini-chain within the Best Western family. Several of them are located throughout the Southwestern United States and all of them are excellent motor inns. The attractive three-story blue tile roofed hotel has nicely landscaped grounds with well kept lawns and plenty of trees. The pretty pool area features a large courtyard and gazebo.

All of the guest rooms have either a patio or balcony. Because it is low you'll only get partial mountain views. However, if you don't mind hearing people having fun at the pool, then get a room facing in that direction–the scene is an attractive one. The rooms are large, comfortable and attractive although they don't reach a luxury level. All have coffee makers. A few efficiency units are available. The LeBaron's restaurant is called Bijou 314 and has both indoor and outdoor dining in the summer-time. It overlooks the courtyard and is a pleasant place to eat. There is a small lounge in the lobby with live piano entertainment most evenings. A heated swimming pool and small exercise room round out the facilities.

HOLDEN HOUSE, *1102 W. Pikes Peak Avenue. Tel. 719/471-3980; Fax 719/471-4740; www.holdenhouse.com. E-mail: mail@holdenhouse.com. 6 Rooms. Rates: $120-140 all year, including full breakfast. Major credit cards accepted. Located in the Old Colorado City area via US 24 to 11th Street and then north to Pikes Peak Avenue.*

A classic Victorian home and carriage house, the Holden has been beautifully restored. The delightful suites are an antique lover's paradise but even if you aren't an enthusiastic supporter of such furnishings, you'll probably like the warm working fireplaces. And what could be better for a romantic weekend than the hot tub for two in each unit. Thinking about it, huh? It's okay, leave the kids at home. The Holden House is also the home of two cats named Mingoy and Muffin. They're always scampering around the public areas, so if you don't like felines maybe you should find accommodations elsewhere. Breakfasts are a hearty affair featuring a wide variety of freshly made breads, pastries and more.

MECCA MOTEL, *3518 W. Colorado Avenue. Tel. 719/475-9415; Fax 719/520-1215. Toll free reservations 800/634-2422. 21 Rooms. Rates: High season (summer): $110-130; Low season (winter): $50-90. Most major credit cards accepted. Located west of I-25, Exit 142 via Colorado Avenue. Near Manitou Springs and southwest area attractions.*

A good mid-priced motel for people who are looking for clean and comfortable basic accommodations. The family owned Mecca has been around for some time but has recently been remodeled so the rooms have a new look and feel to them. Morning coffee is served in the lobby. The Mecca has an outdoor swimming pool with hot tub. It doesn't have a restaurant but several are located close by. The location on West Colorado Avenue puts it convenient to many attractions as well as the nightlife of Old Colorado City and Manitou Springs.

PAINTED LADY BED & BREAKFAST, *1318 W. Colorado Avenue. Tel. 719/473-3165; Fax 719/4635-1396. Toll free reservations 800/370-3165; www.paintedladyinn.com. E-mail: innkeepers@paintedladyinn.com. 4 Rooms. Rates: High season (summer): $125; Low season (winter): $75, including full breakfast. Most major credit cards accepted. Located west of I-25, Exit 142 via Colorado Avenue. Near Manitou Springs and southwest area attractions.*

An 1894 Victorian home converted to a B&B, the Painted Lady is smaller and less showy than a lot of other similar facilities but it has the friendly atmosphere of home. The units aren't that big but are comfortable. Both individual rooms and suites are available. Here you'll only encounter a single resident cat. Good breakfast served. Don't you just love the name of the place?

OLD TOWN GUESTHOUSE, *115 South 26th Street. Tel. 719/632-9194; Fax 719/632-9026. Toll free reservations 888/375-4210. 8 Rooms. Rates: $95-165 including full breakfast. American Express, Discover, MasterCard and VISA accepted. Located west of downtown via US Highway 24 to 26th Street and then just north.*

As a B&B with the name "old town" and being situated in the architecturally interesting Old Colorado City area, you would think this was an old place. It even has the look of an older European-style brick mansion. However, this delightful inn was constructed in 1997 to perfectly fit in with its surroundings. The spacious and luxurious rooms feature a warm fireplace and lovely traditional furnishings. The rooms are named after flowers (some examples are Moroccan Jasmine, Victorian Rose, Oriental Poppy and Indian Paintbrush) and each has an aroma and style that befits its title. Half of the rooms have a hot tub on their own private porch. The others have steam showers.

The public areas of the Guesthouse are equally nice and quite varied. Breakfast is served in the "dining room" while guests can converse in the library. Both have fireplaces. The game room has a pool table and limited exercise equipment. There is a social hour each evening when beverages are served by the gracious husband and wife owners. They have resided in the Colorado Springs area for 25 years and are most happy to share their knowledge of the area with their guests. Many restaurants are located within a short distance, including some that you can walk to.

RADISSON INN NORTH, *8110 N. Academy Blvd. Tel. 719/598-5770; Fax 719/598-3434. Toll free reservations 800/333-3333; www.radisson.com. E-mail: radisson@citystar.com. 200 Rooms. Rates: High season (Memorial Day weekend through Labor Day): $109-159; Low season (after Labor Day to before Memorial Day weekend): $79-140. Major credit cards accepted. Located just east of I-25, Exit 150A to the north of downtown and convenient to the Air Force Academy.*

This is an attractive low-rise motor inn with nice grounds and good mountain views. The atrium lobby features a lush garden with eye catching fountains. Located off of the atrium are the appropriately named Garden Cafe restaurant and cocktail lounge. Rooms are spacious and nicely decorated in a modern style. Amenities vary quite a bit; among the features in some rooms are coffee makers, refrigerators, microwave ovens and Jacuzzi tubs. The Radisson has a heated indoor swimming pool, sauna, and Jacuzzi as well as a small exercise room. Guests receive privileges at a nearby health club and the hotel provides free transportation in the immediate vicinity, including a major shopping center.

Inexpensive

SATELLITE HOTEL, *411 Lakewood Circle. Tel. 719/596-6800; Fax 719/570-4499. Toll free reservations 800/ 423-8409. 75 Rooms. Rates: $54-64. Major credit cards accepted. Located near the Colorado Springs airport, a mile south of US 24 (Platte Avenue) via Academy Blvd. to Lakewood Circle.*

One of the better values in the Colorado Springs area, the Satellite is located in a high-rise condominium with a small number of units on each floor so you have a sense of privacy. All have a private balcony and are comfortably furnished. There is a restaurant and a cocktail lounge on the premises. Recreational amenities are a heated swimming pool, sauna, tennis courts and a small exercise room.

SOUTHWEST & MANITOU SPRINGS
Very Expensive

THE BROADMOOR, *One Lake Avenue. Tel. 719/634-7711; Fax 719/577-5700. Toll free reservations 800/634-7711; www.broadmoor.com. 704 Rooms. Rates: High season (May 1st to October 31st): $295-455; Low season (November 1st to April 30th): $190-345. Most major credit cards accepted. Located about three miles west of I-25, Exit 138 via Lake Avenue.*

The elegant surroundings and impeccable service have made The Broadmoor one of the most famous destination resort hotels in the world. Providing "European grandeur in the Colorado Rockies" since 1918, the Broadmoor is set in a wonderful location surrounded by heavily forested areas and within close proximity to majestic Cheyenne Mountain. The hotel consists of the stately original building and several other structures all built around a spacious open area that contains the Broadmoor's private lake. Few things can be as relaxing as a walk around the duck filled lake.

Both the accommodations and dining facilities are outstanding. The rooms vary in size but all have wonderful traditional styling and many modern amenities. The award winning dining options include five different restaurants. Two are described in the Where to Eat section. Another, the **Lake Terrace Dining Room** overlooks the magnificent interior open space and is home of the Broadmoor's fabulous brunch. There are several night spots and lounges.

The recreational facilities of the Broadmoor are among the best. Three golf courses, tennis courts, four swimming pools, exercise facilities, skeet shooting and horseback riding are among the options available. Children have their own playground and the hotel offers a full range of supervised programs during the summer months. Shopping lovers will enjoy browsing through the more than thirty upscale stores in the hotel and the adjacent village-like shopping area.

Selected as one of my Best Places to Stay (see Chapter 10 for more details).

ROCKLEDGE COUNTRY INN, *328 El Paso Boulevard, Manitou Springs. Tel. 719/685-4515; Fax 719/685-1031. Toll free reservations 888/685-4515; webcom.com/rockinn. E-mail: rockinn@webcom.com. 3 Rooms. Rates: $195-250 all year, including full breakfast. American Express, Discover, MasterCard and VISA accepted. Located just west of US Highway 24 or east of Manitou Avenue.*

This is definitely one of the more expensive B&B's in Colorado but I think those who appreciate this type of accommodation will find it worth the steep price. I was seriously considering including it in the Best Places to Stay chapter–the only reason I didn't was because with only three rooms it isn't likely that too many people will be taking advantage of this charming hostelry.

It was built of native greenstone in 1912 as a summer retreat for a wealthy businessman before being purchased by a Texan ten years later and expanded. The Smith family that runs Rockledge today are experts at catering to their guests and making a stay there a memorable experience. The outside grounds have beautiful stone terraces and gardens that cover almost four acres. The patio is a great place to get a view of magnificent Pikes Peak as is the huge window by the copper fireplace on the inside.

The luxurious accommodations are all suites with king size featherbeds and separate sitting rooms. The Roxie Highland suite has a view of the inn's grounds as well as the mountains from its twelve windows! It also has a whirlpool tub. The El Ocaso (meaning "sunset") faces Pikes Peak and has two less windows than Roxie does. The Country French style suite has handpainted porcelain fixtures in the bathroom. Spindletop takes the window crown with 17. It has a woodburning fireplace and complete spa.

The morning breakfast at Rockledge is something special indeed. Fresh fruits and juices are accompanied by something special each day, perhaps Belgium waffles, along with fresh baked breads and pastries. In the afternoon your hosts graciously serve wine from Colorado along with Spanish *tapas*, chocolates and cookies. As they say in the commercial, "it doesn't get much better than this."

Expensive

CHEYENNE CANYON BED & BREAKFAST INN, *2030 W. Cheyenne Blvd. Tel. 719/633-1348; Fax 719/633-8826. Toll free reservations 800/633-0625. 8 Rooms. Rates: High season (summer) $145-200; Low season (winter): $95-135, including full breakfast. Most major credit cards accepted. Located in the Cheyenne Canyon section. Use Exit 140 of I-25 south on Nevada Avenue and then west on Cheyenne Blvd.*

The Cheyenne is an attractive little place that was originally built as a mansion in the southwestern mission style, something not seen that often in this part of Colorado. Situated in an idyllic location, this bed and breakfast is quietly secluded among the thick trees and rocky boulders of beautiful Cheyenne Canyon Park. One would never know from the surroundings that you are only minutes away from the city and thousands of tourists.

Each of the spacious suites is decorated in the style of a different country and all have fireplace and Jacuzzi tub plus a lot of other modern amenities that you don't always get in a B&B. The breakfast is good and the public areas are nice and comfortable.

CLIFF HOUSE AT PIKES PEAK, *306 Canon Avenue, Manitou Springs. Tel. 719/685-3000; Fax 719/685-3913. Toll free reservations 888/212-7000; www.thecliffhouse.com. E-mail: information@thecliffhouse.com. 57 Rooms. Rates: $129-189 for standard rooms (studio units), and $169-400 for suites. All rates include full breakfast. Major credit cards accepted. Located in town via US Highway 24 to the Manitou Avenue exit and then west to Canon and right to the inn.*

Listed on the National Register of Historic Places, the fully renovated Cliff House first began serving travelers back in 1873. Today, it is the epitome of luxury living from an earlier era. The ambiance of the property and the fine personalized service are wonderful. Inside this large Victorian style country inn are a variety of excellent accommodations ranging from standard studio units to Junior Suites and up to two-level Deluxe Suites and beyond. While the rooms are tastefully decorated in an old world style, they have all of the modern amenities that demanding travelers expect. You'll find mini-refrigerator, terry cloth robe and quality toiletries to name a few. Some units have their own spa and wet bar.

There's an excellent restaurant on the premises as well as the delightful Music Lounge where guests gather to converse and enjoy beverages. The Cliff House also has a small exercise facility.

Selected as one of my Best Places to Stay (see Chapter 10 for details).

WHEELER HOUSE, *36 Park Avenue, Manitou Springs. Tel. 719/685-4100; Fax 719/685-5937. Toll free reservations 800/685-2399; www.wheelerhouse.com. E-mail: wh@wheelerhouse.com. 18 Rooms. Rates: $50-160. Discover, MasterCard and VISA accepted. Located off of US Highway 24 then west onto Canon Avenue for 2 blocks to Park Avenue.*

From the outside this gracious looking many peaked building looks like a large bed and breakfast facility. It has that feel on the interior as well, but it isn't. (Complimentary morning coffee is served.) Actually, it is a grouping of buildings around a main structure and all of the guest rooms have a private entrance. It is located across the street from the pretty Soda Springs Park and its babbling brook. During the summer you can use the outdoor swimming pool or barbecue facilities located beneath four huge Colorado blue spruce trees.

Accommodations range from small efficiency to one and two bedroom units. There isn't any telephone or air conditioning in the rooms but it isn't likely you'll need the latter. All do contain fully equipped kitchens if you want to cook in. The Wheeler House doesn't have a restaurant but since it's only a couple of blocks to the center of Manitou Springs you won't have any trouble finding a place to eat. Owners and hosts Edd (don't forget the second "d") and Penny Bever are most gracious and will be glad to advise you on local dining and shopping as well as just about anything else.

Moderate

EL COLORADO LODGE, *23 Manitou Avenue, Manitou Springs. Tel. 719/685-5485; Fax 719/685-4645. Toll free reservations 800./782-2246; www.coloradodirectory.com/elcoloradolodge. 26 Rooms. Rates: High season (May 15th to September 15th): $79-105; Low season (September 16th to May 14th): $52-67. Major credit cards accepted. Located just west of US Highway 24.*

If I didn't know better I would think that the El Colorado was in New Mexico with its distinctive pueblo style architecture and interior southwestern decor. Expansive rolling lawns out front are traversed by stone steps that lead up to the wide veranda. Wood beamed ceilings in the public areas and guest rooms protrude to the outside in authentic pueblo manner. The mostly spacious accommodations are quite varied. Although a few units are on the smaller side many have two bedrooms and there are some with efficiency kitchens. Most have working fireplaces.

The El Colorado has a heated swimming pool and large outdoor patio area with barbecue facilities and picnic tables. Morning coffee is served in the lobby. There is no restaurant at the Lodge but several are located in close proximity.

SILVER SADDLE MOTEL, *215 Manitou Avenue, Manitou Springs. Tel. 719/685-5611.. Toll free reservations 800/772-3353; www.silver-saddle.com. E-mail: silver@silver-saddle.com. 54 Rooms. Rates: $74-125. Major credit cards accepted. Located about a quarter mile west of US Highway 24.*

A mostly typical roadside motel with adequate accommodations and facilities located in the heart of town. The rooms are clean and comfortable and all have queen beds and coffee makers. Some have hot tubs. The outdoor heated swimming pool is large and inviting. Kids will love the water slide. There are also hot tubs and a small picnic area. Many restaurants as well as good shopping are located within a short distance.

VILLA MOTEL, *481 Manitou Avenue, Manitou Springs. Tel. 719/685-5492; Fax 719/685-4143. Toll free reservations 888/315-2378; www.villamotel.com. 47 Rooms. Rates: High season (mid-June to mid-August): $87-96; Low season (mid-October through March): $50-59. Most major credit cards accepted. Located on US Highway 24 about 4 miles northwest of I-25, Exit 141.*

This is a pleasant two-story roadside motel with nice mountain views that offers good value in a generally much higher priced area. The rooms are comfortable and nicely furnished. Several efficiency units are available. The motel has a swimming pool and hot tub. Restaurants are located within a short distance.

Inexpensive

EAGLE MOTEL, *423 Manitou Avenue, Manitou Springs. Tel. 719/685-5467; Fax 719/685-0542. Toll free reservations 800/872-2285; www.eaglemotel.com. 25 Rooms. Rates: High season (Late May to late September): $59-89; Low season (late September to late May): $50-69. American Express, Discover, MasterCard and VISA accepted. Located about a half mile west of US Highway 24.*

Definitely one of the better values in the Colorado Springs area. You'll get an adequate size room with king or queen beds that is exceptionally well maintained, comfortable and nicely decorated. The only negative is that there are hardly any recreational facilities (there is an outdoor hot tub but no pool). However, if you aren't the type of person who is going to take advantage of such things, then it shouldn't be a reason not to consider the Eagle. Restaurants and shopping are within walking distance as is a tranquil mountain stream and city park.

AROUND THE REGION: CAÑON CITY, CRIPPLE CREEK & PUEBLO
Moderate

ABRIENDO INN, *300 W. Abriendo Avenue, Pueblo. Tel. 719/544-2703; Fax 719/542-1806. Toll free reservations 800/781-2200. 10 Rooms. Rates: $65-120 all year, including full breakfast. American Express, Diners Club, MasterCard and VISA accepted. Located one mile west of I-25, Exit 97B.*

Occupying a beautiful former estate that dates back to the earliest part of the 20th century, the Abriendo is picturesquely situated in a park-like setting. The large and comfortably furnished rooms feature king and queen beds and many have their own private whirlpool. In addition to a sumptuous breakfast each day, guests are offered complimentary beverages in the evening. Located close to downtown Pueblo, the Abriendo is convenient to restaurants. There is a two night minimum stay imposed.

CANON INN, *3075 East Highway 50, Cañon City. Tel. 719/275-8676; Fax 719/275-8675. Toll free reservations 800/525-7727; www.canoninn. 152 Rooms. Rates: High season (May 1st to September 30th): $70-90; Low season (October 1st to April 30th): $60-85. Major credit cards accepted. Located along the Arkansas River two miles east of downtown on the main highway.*

The biggest lodging establishment in town, the Canon Inn is a slightly better than average motor inn that is a convenient place to stay if you plan on spending a lot of time in the Royal Gorge area. The rooms are a nice size and comfortably furnished; some have refrigerator. It has two restaurants and a lounge which sometimes features live entertainment. For recreation there's a large outdoor heated swimming pool and six hot tubs.

IMPERIAL HOTEL & CASINO, *123 N. 3rd Street. Cripple Creek. Tel. 719/689-7777; Fax 719/689-0410. Toll free reservations 800/235-2922; vhays@worldnet.att.net. 29 Rooms. Rates: High season (summer): $90-145; Low season (winter): $65-75. American Express, MasterCard and VISA accepted. Located in the center of town just north of Colorado Highway 67.*

"The" place in tiny Cripple Creek. The Imperial is a beautifully restored Victorian style hotel in the heart of town. The rooms are kind of small but attractive in an old fashioned sort of way. It has an excellent buffet restaurant (see the *Where to Eat* section). Guests with extra time on their hands will usually be found in the casino, which is one of the biggest in Cripple Creek. It has more than 200 slot machines in addition to table games. During the summer and fall the Imperial is also home to a Victorian melodrama theater. A fun place.

Inexpensive

BEST WESTERN AT PUEBLO WEST, *201 S. McCulloch Blvd., Pueblo. Tel. 719/547-2111; Fax 719/547-0385. Toll free reservations 800/528-1234; www.bestwesterncolorado.com/motel15.htm. 80 Rooms. Rates: High season (May 1st to October 31st): $67-89; Low season (November 1st to April 30th): $55-69. Major credit cards accepted. Located about eight miles west of Pueblo via US 50 (towards Cañon City) and then just south on McCulloch.*

An extremely attractive property that represents an excellent value. Set on almost 15 nicely landscaped acres, the Pueblo West has good views of the mountains. It's located adjacent to an 18-hole golf course (fee charged) All of the rooms are large and many feature private patio. In-room coffee makers are standard. There is a restaurant on the premises as well as a cocktail lounge with entertainment four nights a week. Other facilities include a heated swimming pool, exercise room and a gift shop.

CAMPING & RV SITES

- **Buffalo Bill's Royal Gorge Campground**, *at the Royal Gorge off of US Highway 50. Tel. 800/787-0880*
- **Colorado Springs KOA**, *8100 Brandy Drive, Fountain. Tel. 719/382-7575*
- **Cripple Creek KOA Campground**, *2576 County Road 81, Cripple Creek. Tel. 719/689-3376*
- **Garden of the Gods Campground**, *3704 W. Colorado Ave., Tel. 800/248-9451*
- **Golden Eagle Ranch Campground**, *710 Rock Creek Canyon Road, Tel. 800/666-3841*
- **Peak View Camp**, *4950 N. Nevada Ave., Tel. 800/551-CAMP*
- **Pikes Peak RV Park & Campground**, *320 Manitou Ave., Manitou Springs. Tel. 719/685-9459*

WHERE TO EAT

The dining listings are divided into the same zones as the accommodations.

CITY ZONE
Expensive

PRIMITIVO WINE BAR, *28 S. Tejon Street. Tel. 719/473-4900. American Express, Discover, MasterCard and VISA accepted. Lunch and dinner served daily. Reservations are suggested.*

The "we aim to please" owners of this attractive and quite elegant restaurant opened their business in 1997 because they couldn't find a nice place to have a glass of wine with good food in downtown Colorado Springs. They were right...and have done a fine job of rectifying that situation. Never stuffy but always proper service goes along with the excellent wine and food selection. The menu changes weekly but is Mediterranean style. Fresh seafood is always available. Patio dining is an option during the warmer months.

STEAKSMITH, *3802 Maizeland Road. Tel. 719/596-9300. Most major credit cards accepted. Dinner served nightly. Reservations are suggested.*

One of Colorado Springs' most popular and awarded restaurants, Steaksmith is a casually elegant restaurant beautifully decorated in a southwestern style and featuring large, tender and juicy beef dishes to satisfy the most demanding connoisseur. The service is professional and personal. There is tableside cocktail service as well as a separate lounge. Steaksmith has a fairly good selection of wines. Children's menu.

Moderate

GIUSEPPE'S OLD DEPOT RESTAURANT, *10 South Sierra Madre. Tel. 719/635-3111. Major credit cards accepted. Lunch and dinner served daily.*

This giant sized restaurant occupies an attractive restored depot that was once operated by the Denver & Rio Grand Railroad line. It's a combination of Italian, American and western style restaurants with something for everyone on the menu. Their pizza and lasagna dishes are extremely popular with the local folk but you can also order steak, prime rib and overstuffed sandwiches. The Baggage Cart is the name Giuseppe gives their extravagant salad bar–you can make a meal from that alone.

The prices are certainly reasonable and many items are actually in the inexpensive category. The service is quick and efficient. Giuseppe features a full bar, children's menu and complete take-out service.

LUIGI'S RESTAURANT, *947 South Tejon. Tel. 719/632-0700. American Express, Discover, MasterCard and VISA accepted. Dinner served nightly except Monday.*

Luigi's has been owned and operated by the same family for more than forty years. The traditional Italian menu includes pasta, veal, chicken and fish. The nightly special is always an excellent deal, budget and taste-wise. The atmosphere is casual and the decor attractive. The warm and friendly service make your dinner more enjoyable. You can choose from a decent wine list as well as the complete cocktail service. Some entrees are in the expensive category.

PHANTOM CANYON BREWING COMPANY, *2 East Pikes Peak Avenue. Tel. 719/635-2800. Most major credit cards accepted. Lunch and dinner served nightly; Sunday brunch.*

Popular with visitors and locals alike, Phantom Canyon Brewing is located in a restored building dating back to 1901 in Colorado Springs' old town section. The huge windows provide good views of downtown. The casual and large brew pub and restaurant is a beehive of activity as the wait staff efficiently brings beverages and ample portions of tasty food to diners who always seem to be having a good time. The varied menu includes such English favorites as shepherd's pie and fish 'n chips, German brats and many American favorites. The five in-house ales and beer are excellent. Full cocktail service. Children's menu and take-out are available.

SUEHIRO JAPANESE RESTAURANT, *4331 N. Academy Boulevard. Tel. 719/593-1800. Most major credit cards accepted. Lunch and dinner are served daily. Reservations are suggested.*

Don't let the drab and rather uninviting exterior facade scare you away. This is a really good Japanese restaurant. The simple, traditional Japanese style interior is comfortable and the service is warm and friendly. The varied menu includes a number of teriyaki-style entrees as well as sashimi and sushi. Much of the preparation is teppan-style done at hibachi tables. The combination dinners are a good value and are especially popular. There is table side cocktail service and a full bar. Try some of their special drinks like the Mai Tai Tokyo or the Suehiro. I'll warn you about the latter—it's also called the Flaming Volcano!

SOUTHWEST & MANITOU SPRINGS
Very Expensive

CHARLES COURT, *One Lake Avenue, in the Broadmoor Hotel. Tel. 719/634-7711. Major credit cards accepted. Dinner served nightly. Reservations are suggested.*

One of the Broadmoor's more casual restaurants, Charles Court is a wonderful dining experience served in a beautiful room that sits astride the hotel's private lake. The contemporary atmosphere is relaxing and inviting, the friendly service impeccable but of a far less formal nature than at the Penrose. The menu has a good selection of southwestern and other regional American fare served in some imaginative ways such as smoked duck. The desserts are also something special. Cocktail service and separate lounge.

THE PENROSE ROOM, *One Lake Avenue, in The Broadmoor Hotel. Tel. 719/634-7711. Major credit cards accepted. Dress code. Dinner served nightly; open only on Friday and Saturday evenings from January 1st to mid-February. Reservations are suggested.*

Formal and elegant dining at you would expect from a first class restaurant, the Penrose offers a view as sumptuous as the food from its location atop the Broadmoor Hotel. The plush Edwardian decor is beautiful as is the exquisite table and dinnerware. Much of the food preparation is performed at your table by a staff that provides deft and professional service. The cuisine is Continental with a smattering of American.

All of the entrees are exquisite to look at and are delicately seasoned with the chef's special sauces. Wild game dishes are the most renowned of Penrose's menu items. Full tableside cocktail service as well as a lounge with entertainment. The Penrose has an excellent wine list.

Expensive

BRIARHURST MANOR, *404 Manitou Avenue, Manitou Springs. Tel. 719/685-1864. Most major credit cards accepted. Lunch and dinner served daily (Sundays only from May through October); Sunday brunch. Reservations are suggested.*

While I can't knock anything about the Penrose Room I strongly feel that for quite a bit less money the Briarhurst offers an elegant and delicious alternative for those on a somewhat more limited budget.

Located in an ornate and large stone mansion with intricately carved woodwork that dates from the late 1870's, the Briarhurst manages to convey a sense of privacy and personalized service by being divided into nine separate dining areas. Or, during the warmer months you can opt to eat outside on the beautiful terrace in view of the magnificent natural surroundings of Manitou Springs.

This chef-owned and operated restaurant features Continental cuisine that is prepared with great care and skill. Wednesday evening is buffet night but even then you get a trace of the excellent service which is offered for the sit-down dinners. The Briarhurst has full cocktail service and a separate bar. There is also a wine cellar which not only houses an excellent selection but makes for an interesting place to visit.

CRAFTWOOD INN, *404 El Paso Blvd., Manitou Springs. Tel. 719/685-9000. Discover, MasterCard and VISA accepted. Dinner served nightly. Reservations are suggested.*

If you're looking for a quiet and romantic ambiance along with great food and excellent service than seek no further than the Craftwood. The quality level is comparable to the most exclusive restaurants. It also occupies an historic property with beautifully landscaped grounds that afford wonderful views of the surrounding area. Specialties of the house are Colorado wild game dishes such as wild boar, elk, pheasant, caribou and quail. However, the steaks, fresh seafood and a few vegetarian dishes are also excellent. The Craftwood features cocktail service, separate bar, and a large wine list.

DINING ROOM AT CLIFF HOUSE, *306 Canon Avenue, in the Cliff House at Pikes Peak Hotel. Tel. 719/685-3000. Major credit cards accepted. Breakfast, lunch and dinner served daily. Reservations are suggested.*

Situated in a elegant setting of Victorian design, the Dining Room boasts an original 19th century rock fireplace, the finest china and gorgeous place settings. The atmosphere can only be described as totally charming. To this add the imaginative weekly menu of an award-winning chef and you have a wonderful evening of fine dining that is most appropriate for adults. A fabulous view of the Rockies is the final touch.

The food is Continental in basic style but there is a definite western mountain flair to the preparation. So, while you can always expect to find veal on the menu, you're equally likely to see some bison dish as well. Don't let habit get in your way of trying some of the more unusual menu items. Desserts are simply grand, and none is more delightful than the Grand Marnier Creme Brulee which I urge you not to miss if it is appearing on the menu during the week you're here. There is table side cocktail service and a separate lounge. The wine list is extensive and the sommelier is most helpful.

Moderate

ADAM'S MOUNTAIN CAFE, *110 Canon Avenue, Manitou Springs. Tel. 719/685-1430. MasterCard and VISA accepted. Smoke free premises. Breakfast, lunch and dinner served Tuesday through Saturday.*

An attractive downtown restaurant in Manitou Springs' historic district, Adam's Mountain Cafe serves a good selection of international entrees along with a considerable choice of vegetarian dishes. The service is friendly and efficient and the surroundings cozy and comfortable. Along with full cocktail service the cafe has a surprisingly good selection of fine wines as well as microbrewed beer.

EDELWEISS RESTAURANT, *34 East Ramona Avenue. Tel. 719/633-2220. Most major credit cards accepted. Lunch served Monday through Friday; dinner nightly.*

A delightful restaurant built in Bavarian chalet style and featuring excellent German as well as Continental cuisine. The place is extra casual whether you dine indoors or outside on the patio. Service is friendly and efficient. If you can manage it try to eat at the Edelweiss on either Friday or Saturday evening when strolling musicians in authentic Bavarian outfits complete with lederhosen will entertain you. Full cocktail service and, of course, an excellent selection of beers.

MONA LISA FONDUE RESTAURANT, *733 Manitou Avenue, Manitou Springs. Tel. 719/685-0277. Most major credit cards accepted. Dinner served nightly. Reservations are suggested.*

Take the short journey from Bavaria to Switzerland and savor the tempting delights of Mona Lisa's outstanding fondue dishes. Maybe even better is the cheese and boiled potato dish known as raclette. If you're looking for something delicious and different than why not try this popular and attractive little restaurant. They also boast an excellent selection of wine and beer.

STAGECOACH STEAK & ALE HOUSE, *702 Manitou Avenue, Manitou Springs. Tel. 719/685-9400. MasterCard and VISA accepted. Dinner served nightly.*

One last historic property restaurant for Manitou Springs. The Stagecoach specializes in , as they themselves describe it, "great western fare" such as buffalo, prime ribs, rotisserie chicken and steaks. You can also select from a decent selection of fish (try the excellent Colorado trout), seafood and pasta. The restaurant is cozy and attractive but it's better to dine outside in the sidewalk cafe or on the deck beside the pretty creek. Cocktail service tableside or at the bar.

Inexpensive

MASON JAR, *2925 W. Colorado Avenue. Tel. 719/632-4820. Discover, MasterCard and VISA accepted. Lunch and dinner served daily.*

The Mason Jar is a popular restaurant that always seems to be crowded with locals along with visitors. And with good reason. They offer tempting and deliciously prepared home-style favorites in abundant quantities at a most reasonable price. The service is quick and efficient as well as friendly. The atmosphere is as casual as it gets with tables kind of crowded into a country style decor. A fireplace is in operation during the winter. Beverages are served in, you guessed it, real mason jars which makes it kind of difficult to drink without a straw! The Mason Jar serves cocktails, has a children's menu and take-out. Even waiting for your table is fun because you're given the name of a celebrity when you check in so the hostess is always saying something like, "Mick Jagger, your table is ready."

MISSION BELL, *178 Crystal Park Road, Manitou Springs. Tel. 719/ 685-9089. MasterCard and VISA accepted. Open nightly for dinner (except closed on Monday from September through May). Reservations are suggested.*

Great homestyle Mexican food (no Tex-Mex or ersatz Mexican here) is the hallmark of this popular restaurant, serving Manitou Springs since the early 1950's. It is also one of the most attractive restaurants in town. The indoor dining room is decorated in a most pleasant southwestern style while the patio is kept warm by the active fireplace. Bar service available. An excellent value for enjoyable family dining.

AROUND THE REGION: CAÑON CITY, CRIPPLE CREEK & PUEBLO
Expensive

LE PETIT CHABLIS, *512 Royal Gorge Blvd., Cañon City. Tel. 719/269-3333. Discover, MasterCard and VISA accepted. Dinner served nightly. Reservations required.*

I never fail to be surprised when I find an excellent haute French restaurant in a small town that caters mainly to family vacationers. But here's a good example of what I'm talking about. Le Petit offers two small but attractive dining rooms with a menu featuring country French and cajun cuisine that's appealingly prepared and delicious. They also have an excellent selection of wines. The service is gracious and the atmosphere casual and pleasant. Cocktail service tableside or in the separate bar.

Moderate

GOLD MINE RESTAURANT, *212 E. Bennett Avenue, Cripple Creek. Located in Womack's Casino. Tel. 719/689-0333. Major credit cards accepted. Breakfast, lunch and dinner served daily.*

A casual and attractive restaurant with reasonable prices and friendly service, the Gold Mine's strength is its varied menu. You can get everything from a burger to a New York steak with everything in between, such as shrimp scampi, ribs and Russian scallops. The preparation doesn't break any new ground but if you're looking for a decent meal this is one of the best of the restaurants in Cripple Creek's numerous casinos. On Saturday night they have a very good buffet and brunch is served on Sunday. Located upstairs away from the hustle and bustle. Full cocktail service.

MERLINO'S BELVEDERE, *1330 Elm Avenue (CO 115), Cañon City. Tel. 719/275-5558. Major credit cards accepted. Lunch served on Sunday only; dinner nightly.*

Take a seat in a setting reminiscent of a sunny Mediterranean resort as you select from an extensive menu that specializes in traditional Italian cuisine but also has steaks and seafood. The pasta is made fresh each day as are all of the delicious breads and pastries. The portions are large and everything is delicious. The family which has been operating Merlino's for over fifty years is renowned for their own special brand of apple cider–be sure to try some. Cocktail service and separate lounge. Children's menu and take-out are available.

Inexpensive

NACHO'S, *409 N. Santa Fe, Pueblo. Tel. 719/544-0733. American Express, MasterCard and VISA accepted. Lunch and dinner served daily except Monday.*

Nacho's is a popular spot with the locals and serves authentic Mexican cuisine in a pretty dining room in the heart of Pueblo's historic downtown area. Strolling mariachi musicians add to the fun on Friday and Saturday evenings. Cocktails are served.

SEEING THE SIGHTS

I promised you more to see than in Denver, so here's where I have to offer the proof. The most famous of Colorado Springs' attractions have to do with nature but there won't be a shortage of museums, historical attractions, and other assorted points of interest. Again, to make things easier, the sights will be divided up into three geographic area to minimize travel time and allow the greater portion of your day for taking in the sights you came to see.

The first tour covers what's on the east side of Monument Creek, which includes downtown, and the northern part of the city. The second tour will take you to the south side of town and the west, an area of great natural beauty in the foothills of the Rockies. Some of the region's best known attractions aren't in Colorado Springs itself but in adjacent Manitou Springs. That area is the focus of the third and final tour.

TOUR 1: THE EAST SIDE & NORTH

Approximate duration (including sightseeing time) is a full day. Begin at the ProRodeo Hall of Fame located in the northern part of Colorado Springs immediately off of I-25, Exit 147.

The **ProRodeo Hall of Fame** is a large and modern facility that pays tribute to the heroes of rodeo as well as to the sport itself. Outside the building is *The Champ*, a larger-than-life bronze statue of heralded rider Casey Tibbs aboard the bronco "Necktie," legs kicking high into the air as it attempts to throw its rider. In addition to several multi-media presentations, the main focus of the museum is Heritage Hall with its huge collection of cowboy and rodeo gear and the Hall of Champions where individuals are honored for their contribution to rodeo. An outdoor area contains a small rodeo arena and an interesting sculpture garden of rodeo figures. *Tel. 719/528-4764. The Hall is open daily from 9:00am until 5:00pm except New Year's Eve and Day, Easter, Thanksgiving, and Christmas. Admission is $6 for adults, $5 for seniors, and $3 for children ages 5 through 12.*

After you've finished visiting the Hall of Fame get back on I-25 northbound for the short ride to Exit 150 (South Gate Boulevard) which leads directly into the fabulously beautiful **United States Air Force Academy.** Although the order of most itineraries in this book are somewhat interchangeable, I strongly suggest that you follow this one in the order described if it is during the academic school year. That's because you will certainly want to get to the Academy before 12:00 in order to be on time for the noon formation. The city sized campus sits majestically at the foot of the Rocky Mountains. The modern architecture of the buildings is inexplicably harmonious with the natural surroundings. Visits are facilitated by picking up a map and guide at the visitor center. That makes it easier to find the various points of interest as well as viewpoints on the loop road that provide outstanding vistas of both mountain and campus.

The Barry Goldwater Visitor Center has exhibits that tell the history of the academy as well as depicting cadet life. Movie presentations about the academy are given periodically. The visitor center is also the place where guided walking tours of the academy begin (summer only). You are always welcome to tour on your own. Facilities that are open to visitors include the Field House, Arnold Hall (many interesting paintings, flag displays, medals, and military memorabilia), Falcon Stadium, the planetarium, and the B-52 bomber display. However, the highlight and what probably makes the Academy Colorado's most visited man-made attraction is the famous **Cadet Chapel**. This graceful structure contains 17 soaring steel spires in the form of inverted "V"s that appropriately honor the spiritual tradition of churches reaching toward heaven as well as the air force's very basis–our control of the sky. The interior of this magnificent edifice contains the huge Catholic Chapel on the main floor with its combination of modern and traditional church features, including stained glass windows,. On the lower level are three smaller chapels for Protestant and Jewish cadets as well as an all-faiths worship room.

As I mentioned at the outset, another highlight of an Academy visit is the noontime meal formation held during the academic year (approximately late August through early June). The best viewing is from the promenade on the east side of the Chapel. It is an impressive and stirring sight to watch as the entire cadet corp assembles on the vast quadrangle (so big that the jet fighter at each corner looks like a toy airplane from the vantage point above) and marches off to have their meal, group by group, while flags fly and cadences are shouted. Even without dress uniforms it is a sight to remember and one which will make you proud to be an American. Other parades are held at various times throughout the year. *Tel. 719/333-USAF for information. For general information call Tel. 719/ 472-2025. The academy is open every day of the year from 9:00am until 6:00pm (to 5:00pm after Labor Day to day before Memorial Day). The chapel is open daily from 9:00am to 5:00pm except on Sunday when it opens at 1:00pm. It may be closed periodically for special events. The Visitor Center is closed on New Year's Day, Thanksgiving and Christmas. There is no charge for admission.*

Leave the Academy via the north entrance and you'll immediately be back at I-25. However, before heading back towards downtown, cross the interstate (Exit 156) to the east side of the highway which is Gleneagle Drive. You'll momentarily arrive at the **Western Museum of Mining & Industry**. This fine museum houses numerous exhibits which documents the importance of mining in the area's history. Artifacts include simple gold panning equipment to early steam engines. There are also exhibits which depict life in the mining communities. You can visit the museum on your own or via informative guided tours. *Tel. 719/488-0880. The museum is open daily from 9:00am until 4:00pm (from noon on Sunday) except that it is closed on most major holidays and on Sundays from October through May. Admission is $6 for adults, $5 for seniors and $3 for children ages 5 through 12. Guided tours, lasting 90 minutes, are given at 10, 12:30 and 2:30.*

Back on I-25, drive south to Exit 143 (Uintah Street) and head east to Hancock Avenue. Make a right and follow that street to Boulder Street and the **U.S. Olympic Training Complex**, *1750 E. Boulder Street*. The center, besides being the primary training facility for America's Olympic athletes, is also the headquarters for a number of amateur sports governing committees. *Tel. 719/578-4618. The center is open daily from 9:00am until 5:00pm. Guided tours are given every 30 minutes during those hours except that the last tour on Sunday is at 4:00pm. There is no charge for either admission or tours.*

Now it's time to head to downtown. Take Boulder west to Cascade Avenue, turn right and drive to Colorado Avenue and pick out a garage to dump the car for a while. Downtown Colorado Springs isn't much to look at nor is it a big center of tourist activity but there are a few points of interest that are worth some of your time. The last four attractions on this tour are best done on foot. Go one block east on Colorado to Tejon Street and a block south to the **Colorado Springs Pioneer Museum**, *215 S. Tejon Street*. The museum is located in a former county courthouse that was built at the turn of the century and traces the history of the city and Pike's Peak area from the days of Native Americans to the present. There are also displays of pottery and art. *Tel. 719/578-6650. The museum is open Tuesday through Saturday from 10:00am until 5:00pm and on Sundays from 1:00pm to 5:00pm during the months of May through October. There is no admission charge.*

Now return to Cascade and turn right, going six blocks to the **McAllister House Museum**, *423 N. Cascade*. Major Henry McAllister was an associate of Gen. Palmer in the project to develop the Springs as a resort facility. The house was built in 1873 and is typical of a wealthy businessman's home of the period. *Tel. 719/635-7925. The house is open Wednesday through Saturday from 10:00am to 4:00pm and on Sundays from noon to 4:00pm during May through August. During the rest of the year the hours are Thursday through Saturday from 10:00am until 4:00pm. Admission: $4 for adults; $2 for seniors and children ages 6 through 16.*

Three blocks further north on Cascade will bring you to Dale Street and the **Colorado Springs Fine Arts Center**. The center is a multi-faceted cultural facility on the edge of the Colorado College campus. It includes a theater, library, and school within an attractive building that combines the pueblo and art deco styles–quite an unusual mixture. Of special interest to visitors is the *Sacred Land* exhibit which takes a detailed look at Native American and Hispanic art and culture. In addition to the Hispanic influence, the contributions of Pueblo, Navajo, and Apache cultures are explored. *Tel. 719/634-5581. The museum is open daily except Monday from 9:00am until 5:00pm (opens 10:00am on Saturday and 1:00pm on Sunday). Closed on state holidays. Admission: $4 adults and $2 for seniors and children.*

The **American Numismatic Association Museum**, *818 N. Cascade Avenue,* is across the street from the Fine Arts Center. It houses one of the world's largest collections of currency and medals in nine separate galleries that cover the entire history of numismatics. Many rare and extremely valuable specimens are on display. *Tel. 719/632-2646. The museum is open Monday through Friday from 8:30am until 4:00pm and Saturday from 9:00am, Memorial Day through Labor Day. It is closed on Saturday the rest of the year. No admission fee is charged but donations are requested.*

This completes the tour so you can head back to where you parked the car. As you'll only be a few blocks from I-25 it will be convenient to get to any part of the Springs area from here.

TOUR 2: THE SOUTH SIDE & WEST

Approximate duration (including sightseeing time) is a full day. Begin at The Broadmoor Hotel in the southern section of Colorado Springs. Use the Nevada Avenue exit (#140) off of I-25 and go south on Nevada to Lake Avenue. A right turn onto Lake Avenue will soon run into Lake Circle and bring you to The Broadmoor.

The Broadmoor Hotel is a ritzy place that only a small number of readers will likely be staying at. However, everyone going to Colorado Springs should see it. The Broadmoor is the epitome of classic European hostelry elegance and a work of art. Details are in the Where to Stay section but at a minimum visitors should take the pleasant stroll around the hotel's private lake.

Immediately opposite the main entrance of the Broadmoor at Lake Avenue and Lake Circle is the small but interesting **El Pomar Carriage House Museum**. A number of 19th century coaches are on display, including two used in presidential inaugural celebrations. There is also a Conestoga wagon which was so important in opening up the western United States. Although this museum won't take very long to see, it is likely that you may have to see it later in this tour because of its rather limited operating hours. *Tel. 719/634-7711. The museum is open Tuesday through Saturday from 10:00am until noon and again from 1:00pm to 5:00pm. It is closed on state holidays. Admission is free.*

From the hotel head north on Cresta for a short distance to Cheyenne Boulevard and turn left. Soon after the street changes name to North Cheyenne Canyon Road and will bring you into picturesque **North Cheyenne Canyon Park**. In this forested and rocky area it's hard to believe that you are only minutes away from heavily developed residential areas and within sight of all of Colorado Springs. The canyon (often seen spelled in the Spanish form, canon) has several interesting rock formations and pretty waterfalls. There is a parking area by two of the best, Silver Cascades and Helen Hunt Falls. The park has two visitor centers and miles of hiking trails if you are so inclined. *The park's visitor centers are open daily from 9:00am until 5:00pm during the summer and from 10:00am until 5:00pm at other times of the year.*

Leave the park in the opposite way you came in. Just past the exit is a sharp right turn for South Cheyenne Canon Road and the remarkable **Seven Falls**. The streets around here are a little on the confusing side so be on the lookout for Seven Falls' many directional signs. A long entry road leads to the entrance gate. Take a moment to review the map given to you at the entrance because there are several points of interest on the approach road to the falls area. The road snakes through a narrow canyon (only 42 feet wide at a point known as the Pillars of Hercules) and affords opportunities at pullouts to look at a number of unusual rock formations.

The falls are at the end of the box canyon and drop majestically 181 feet in seven distinct cascades, but I bet you already figured that out from the name. Smart, real smart. The best way to view the falls is from a lookout point known as the Eagles Nest. You walk through a 170-foot long tunnel carved into the mountain before ascending 130 feet in an elevator that lets you out on an observation platform. More adventurous visitors will want to challenge the steep 224-step stairway alongside the falls. At the end of the stairway is a mile long nature trail that leads to another overlook with a panorama of Colorado Springs and the Plains beyond. During summer evenings the falls and canyon are illuminated in an array of colors that shed a whole different perspective on the area. *Tel. 719/632-0765. The Seven Falls park is open daily from 8:00am until 11:00pm from mid-May through Labor Day, and from 9:00am to 4:00pm the remainder of the year. It is closed only on Christmas. Adult admission is $7 for adults, $5 for senior citizens, and $4 for children ages 6 through 15. A small additional fee is charged during summer evenings to see the illumination.*

Retrace your route out of the canyon and stay on South Canon Road until Penrose. Hang a right and that street will lead into Cheyenne Mountain Zoo Road. On the low slopes of the mountain is **Cheyenne Mountain Zoo**, America's highest at an elevation of about 7,000 feet. Located amid a 150-acre forest of oak, spruce, and ponderosa pine, the zoo is home to more than 500 animals many of which can be termed exotic. Of greatest interest are the Wolf Woods and Asian Highlands habitats. The latter is home to tigers, leopards, and red pandas. Also on the zoo grounds are a carousel from the 1920s and a nature trail. During the summer a tram is available to take visitors around the zoo grounds. It is an excellent zoo and the location makes it even better. *Tel. 719/633-9925. Zoo hours are daily from 9:00am until 6:00pm. It closes at 4pm after Labor Day and before Memorial Day. Adult admission is $7 while seniors pay $6 and children ages 3 through 11 get in for $4.*

A toll road leads from past the zoo further up Cheyenne Mountain to the **Shrine of the Sun**, about a thousand feet higher than the zoo. A stone monument to Will Rogers graces the sight which provides one of the most outstanding vistas of Colorado Springs. The road is closed during inclement weather. *Tel. 719/634-5975. Operating hours are the same as for the zoo. No additional admission except for the small toll.*

It's now time to descend from Cheyenne Mountain. Stay on the same road until you get back to Lake Avenue by the Broadmoor. Turn right and go to *20 First Street* and the **World Figure Skating Museum**. The enjoyable facility (I have no interest in skating and found my visit to be entertaining and educational) honors famous skaters from the United States and around the world. Some of the more recognizable names are Peggy Fleming and Sonja Henie. In addition to the skaters, the museum traces the history of skating and has many artifacts and colorful costumes from all over the world. *Tel. 719/635-5200. The museum is open Monday through Saturday from 10:00am until 4:00pm during the summer months and on weekdays from 10:00am until 4:00pm the rest of the year. It is closed on holidays. The admission fee is $3 for everyone age six and up except that seniors pay $2.50.*

Return via Lake Avenue to the main road that came from Cheyenne Mountain and turn right. North of Lake the name changes to Cresta Road and then a little further north changes again, this time to 21st Street. **Van Briggle Art Pottery**, *600 S. 21st Street*, offers tours of the factory which has been making fine pottery according to time honored methods since 1899. They are one of the premier manufacturers in the country and many of their products are available for sale only at their factory. Of course, the tours are the introduction to the large showroom where they hope you'll spend lots of money on their stuff. It is nice and there is a wide range of prices to fit different budgets. *Tel. 719/633-7729. Open Monday through Saturday from 8:30am until 5:00pm and on Sunday from noon until 5:00pm.*

Just north of Van Briggle at the intersection of US 24 is the **Ghost Town Museum**. The museum contains parts of abandoned ghost towns from around the Colorado Springs area that have been restored and put together to create the appearance of a late 19th century village. Among the places you can visit are the print shop, saloon, blacksmith, and Victorian style home. There is also a large general store with a variety of goods looking for turista dollars. *Tel. 719/634-0696. Open daily except New Year's., Thanksgiving and Christmas. Check locally or call for exact hours. There is no admission charge.*

For a little more area history, check out **Magic Town** which is located nearby at *2418 West Colorado Ave, near 24th Street*. Colorado Avenue is a couple of blocks north of US 24. This part of town was known as Colorado City and was a precursor to Colorado Springs. Many interesting shops and restaurants in restored 19th century structures line both sides of several blocks of Colorado Avenue. Magic Town is an interesting miniature village of that era that is made to seem more alive by clever use of mirrors, holographs and other devices. *Tel. 719/471-9391. Magic Town is open daily from 10:00am until 8:00pm (to 5:30 on Sunday) from early June to early September and to 5:30pm every day the remainder of the year. Adult admission is $3 and children ages 7 through 12 pay only $1.*

TOUR 3: MANITOU SPRINGS
& GARDEN OF THE GODS

Approximate duration (including sightseeing time) is a full day. Begin at the Pikes Peak Cog Railway in Manitou Springs which can be reached by taking US 24 (Midland Expressway) to Manitou Avenue. Follow Manitou to Ruxton and turn left.

The Cog Railway, officially known as the **Manitou and Pikes Peak Cog Railway Company**, is one of Colorado's premier attractions. I

PIKES PEAK OR BUST

The famous phrase wasn't originally meant to state the challenge of ascending the peak in the early days of Colorado but rather to the hope of finding gold in the area. Nevertheless, it may now be too easy to get to the top. The cog railway is the easiest method of ascending Zebulon Pike's mountain, but it certainly isn't the only one.

*The **Pikes Peak Highway** allows visitors to take in the remarkable scenery via a 19-mile long unpaved road. Motorists usually like to make frequent stops to explore the alpine meadows and other things seen along the way. While the road is safe despite the absence of pavement and guardrails, it isn't recommended for the novice mountain driver. Bus tours from Colorado Springs are available if you don't want to take the train or drive yourself. Use low gear for the entire descent. Both weather and road conditions effect the operating dates of the highway which usually opens around the middle of June and stays open to the end of October. The beginning of the road is in Cascade, about 11 miles from Colorado Springs via US 24. Call Tel. 719/684-9383 for more information. The Pikes Peak Highway is a toll road costing $10 for each person ages 16 and up.*

*The Highway is always closed to private vehicles on July 4th when the annual Pikes Peak Hill Climb Auto Race is held. I can think of saner things to do then race up the mountain. Bikes aren't allowed on the Highway either, except for the unusual **Challenge Unlimited**. You are taken by van to the summit and then provided with a 21-speed mountain bike to make the thrilling descent. A guide leads the way and another pulls up the rear to make sure everyone is always okay. If you're interested in this way of seeing Pikes Peak which, according to Challenge Unlimited, does not require you to be an experienced rider, call for more information. Their number is Tel. 800/798-5954. Reservations are mandatory and the price includes breakfast.*

Finally, of course, you can climb Pikes Peak by means of the Bra Trail. Although the trail isn't unusually difficult for experienced hikers the real challenge can be the cold, thin air. So be prepared!

suggest that you take the first or second departure of the day because a busy agenda is on tap for you. This spectacular journey takes you on a nine mile long adventure on the world's highest cog railway (and the highest railroad of any type in the United States), starting at 6,571 feet at the base station and increasing more than 7,500 feet to the 14,110-foot high summit. It has been operating a series of Swiss-built cars since 1891 and has a perfect safety record.

Interesting commentary abounds as the train rises through the heavily forested lower part of the mountain until it passes timberline. The higher you get the better the scenery is. Distant mountains, the city itself, beautiful lakes, and plenty of ice and snow are all en route. (Be sure to have a warm jacket with you even on the warmest day because I guarantee you'll definitely need it at the top.) At the summit is a small structure with a snack bar and gift shop but you won't find any full meals, nor will you have the time since only a limited amount of time is spent at the top before you make the descent on the same train you came up in. Do make use of the time to, besides get a cup of hot coffee, take in the remarkable vistas in all directions. You will also see the end of the Pikes Peak Highway (see the sidebar for more information) and a monument to Katherine Lee Bates who was inspired to compose "America the Beautiful" after ascending Pikes Peak. I think you'll understand and share her feelings as you gaze out on the panorama before you.

The round-trip journey on the cog railway, including some time at the summit, takes three hours and ten minutes. *Tel. 719/685-5401. The railway operates daily from late April through October and makes up to eight runs per day beginning at 8:00am. From the beginning of the season through Memorial Day weekend and after Labor Day, the train makes two daily runs at 9:20am and 1:20pm. The fare is $24 for adults and $12 for children ages 5 through 11. Credit cards.*

From the railway base station head back up Ruxton Avenue to **Merriment Castle**, *9 Capitol Hill Avenue off of Ruxton*. This interesting 46-room mansion was built in 1895 on a steep hillside. That, more than the eccentricity of the builder, explains why the front entrance is on the first floor but the rear entrance is on the fourth! But then again, eccentricity does show in the building itself which incorporates nine distinct architectural styles including Gothic, Tudor, and Romanesque, and two-foot thick stone walls. Maybe he was expecting an attack. The interior features some unusual rooms (one eight sided and one 16-sided) with gold ceilings and huge fireplaces. Some rooms have collections of miniatures. Both children and adults will find it fascinating. *Tel. 719/685-1011. The Castle is open daily from 10:00am until 5:00pm from March through Labor Day; 11:00am to 4:00pm from after Labor Day through December; and noon to 3:00pm the rest of the year. The adult admission price is $3 while senior citizens pay $2.50. Children ages 6 through 11 are charged $1.00.*

Manitou Springs is something of an "art town" with many galleries, unusual boutiques, and other shops. These are concentrated along Manitou Avenue. Make a right on Manitou at the end of Ruxton. Then, when you've finished exploring downtown Manitou Springs, turn off of Manitou Avenue on El Paso Boulevard. Make a left onto the US 24 bypass which will lead you directly to the next attraction, the **Manitou Cliff Dwellings Museum and Preserve**. This fine facility has been educating people about the Anasazi culture's Great Pueblo Period (1100-1300 A.D) since it opened in 1907. The site includes several museum buildings as well as the well preserved ruins that encompass over 40 rooms that include a **kiva** used for religious ceremonies and the living quarters.

The Pueblo is a three-story structure which best exemplifies the high point of Anasazi building. In the museums are artifacts and exhibits which explain what is known about the mysterious Anasazi.. An added treat during the summer months are the performances of Native American dance. *Tel. 800/354-9971. The Preserve is open daily from 9:00am to 8:00pm, June through August, to 5:00pm March and April and October through December; to 6:00pm May and September; and on weekends only from 9:00am to 5:00pm during January and February. Adult admission is $6, $5 for seniors and $4 for children ages 7 through 11.*

After the Cliff Dwellings head west for a short time on US 24 until you reach the well signed side road leading up a steep cliff to the **Cave of the Winds**. This 200 million year old limestone cavern in Williams Canyon was discovered in 1881 and opened to visitors soon after that but it's a lot easier to tour it today. Most visitors opt to see the narrow passageways, huge chambers, and graceful stalactite and stalagmite formations on the 40-minute long Discovery Tour which covers about a half-mile. More experienced cavers might be interested in the Lantern Tour which recreates the way tours were given around the turn of the century, including lighting by candles. Spelunkers can also go for the 3-1/2 hour Wild Tour which requires miner's lanterns and goes through some tight places. Summer evenings outside the cave are literally lit up with "Legends in Light, a forty minute laser light and sound show projected on the 150 foot high cliff of Williams Canyon. The show recounts the history of the Pikes Peak region. *Tel. 719/685-5444. Discovery Tours are given every 15 minutes from 9:00am to 8:00pm Memorial Day through Labor Day and until 5:00pm the rest of the year. Adult admission is $12 and children ages 6 through 15 pay $6. Call for schedules and rates on Lantern and Wild Tours. The laser show takes place every summer evening at 9:00pm and costs $6 for adults and $3 for children.*

Now head back east on US 24 until you reach 31st Street. This road runs into 30th Street which will bring you to what is perhaps Colorado Springs' most unusual natural attraction, the **Garden of the Gods**. Enter via Gateway Road. Across from this entrance is the first stop, the **Visitor Center**. The center is much like a natural history museum in that the modern multi-level facility has exhibits and films that explore the geological and human history of the Garden of the Gods area. It also has a pleasant restaurant and a terrace with a great view of some of the Garden's unique forms.

GARDEN OF THE GODS BY HORSE

One of the most fascinating ways to explore the Garden of the Gods is by horseback. **Academy Riding Stables** *is the only stable authorized to offer tours within the park and you can select from either one or two hours on a horse that suits your riding experience level. There's also a three hour trip that circumnavigates the Gardens. If you're interested in exploring this area the way it was done a hundred years ago then contact the Stables, Tel. 719/633-5667, for information on schedules and rates. Reservations are suggested and all participants must be at least eight years old.*

Garden of the Gods is a 1,400 acre preserve with huge red sandstone formations jutting out from forested areas. You can ride through and get out at the more interesting formations or spend even more time by hiking the park's many trails. Among the most unusual rock formations are Gateway Rocks, the Kissing Camels and Balanced Rock. Garden of the Gods Trading Post is an attractive pueblo style structure built in the 1920s. It serves as an Native American art gallery and has a huge gift shop selling authentic high quality Indian crafts. *Tel. 719/634-6666. Grounds open daily from 5:00am to 11:00pm May through October and until 9:00pm the rest of the year. Visitor Center opens at 9:00am and is closed New Year's Day, Thanksgiving, and Christmas. Admission is free but there is a charge for film presentations at the Visitor Center. Guided bus tours of the gardens are also available at a cost of $4 per person.*

Also within the confines of the Garden is the **Rock Ledge Ranch Historic Site** (near the Gateway Road entrance) which depicts homestead and ranch life during the second half of the 19th century. *Tel. 719/578-6777. Ranch open Wednesday to Sunday from 9:00am to 5:00pm from June through August and on weekends from September through December 24th. The admission fee is $3 for adults, $2 for senior citizens, and $1 for children ages 6 through 12.*

This completes the final tour of Colorado and Manitou Springs. Once you leave the Garden's south entrance you'll be in sight of US 24 which will provide access to wherever you're headed. If you leave from the Gateway entrance you can follow Garden of the Gods Road to I-25.

SCENIC DRIVES & OTHER POINTS OF INTEREST

Although each of the three preceding tours can be accomplished in a single day depending upon your pace and level of interest, you could well find yourself running out of time. But even if you manage to complete them all there are sure to be some of you who have more time or have different interests. These attractions are for those of you who fall into either of those categories.

High Drive leads from the western end of Cheyenne Boulevard and climbs to a portion of the Gold Camp Road (see excursions later in this chapter for more information on that road) before descending back towards Bear Creek Road. The scenery is stunning but the steep grades and lack of comforting guard rails makes this road suitable only for those with experience in mountain driving. Just off a portion of the road is the pleasant **Bear Creek Nature Center**. The center has exhibits and nature trails.

Peterson Air & Space Museum, *Peterson Air Force Base, about 7 miles east of downtown via US 24. Tel. 719/556-4915.* This air base once served as Colorado Springs' airport. More important, the exhibits in the museum have, in addition to the usual collection of historic airplanes, an excellent presentation on the North American Aerospace Defense Command (NORAD). This organization is headquartered in Colorado Springs.

NIGHTLIFE & ENTERTAINMENT
COLORADO SPRINGS & MANITOU SPRINGS

First a couple of things that the kids can enjoy along with the grown-ups. The **Flying W Ranch**, *Flying W Ranch Road one mile northwest of the intersection of Garden of the Gods Road and 30th Street, Tel. 800/232-FLYW or 719/598-4000.* Prior to dinner you explore the recreated western village consisting of more than a dozen buildings and shops. A western barbecue dinner is served and then you are entertained by the Flying W Wranglers.

A Colorado Springs tradition for more than 30 years is the **Iron Springs Melodrama Theater** *at Iron Springs Chateau, 444 Ruxton Avenue, Manitou Springs. Tel. 719/685-5104.* Following a family style western dinner, guests are treated to a Victorian era comedy melodrama that encourages audience participation.

For entertainment without the kids, try one of the following:
COWBOYS, *3910 Palmer Park Blvd. Tel. 719/596-2152.* The place in Colorado Springs for country music and environment. They claim to have the largest dance floor in town. It better be because it's usually crowded.

JUDGE BALDWIN'S BREWING COMPANY, *4 South Cascade. Tel. 719/473-5600.* Colorado Springs' most popular micro-brewery, gathering place, and waterin' hole.

Performing Arts
- **Colorado Springs Choral Society**, *219 W. Colorado Ave. Tel. 719/634-3737.* Year round performances including changing venues as part of summer outdoor program.
- **Colorado Springs Dance Theater**, *7 E. Bijou. Tel. 719/630-7434.* Hosts renowned dance companies from all around the world.
- **Colorado Springs Symphony Orchestra**, *619 N. Cascade. Tel. 719/633-4611.* Their season at the Pikes Peak Center runs from September through May.

A number of production companies, both resident and touring, put on Broadway style plays at different venues from time to time. It is best to check with the Visitors Bureau or current publications for what is going on when you're in town.

CRIPPLE CREEK

The primary diversion, other than a few local bars, are the many casinos. Among them are **Bronco Billy's**, **Double Eagle**, **Gold Rush**, **Imperial**, **Midnight Rose**, **and Womack's**. All of them are within the 200 block of East Bennett.

PUEBLO

The **Sangre de Cristo Ballet Theater**, **Pueblo Symphony Orchestra**, and the **Pueblo Choral Society** all have active programs at varying times of the year. It is best to contact the Pueblo Convention and Visitors Council for complete information.

SHOPPING

I briefly touched on the **Garden of the Gods Trading Post** as a great place to get Native American goods in the touring section. It is probably the largest gift shop of its type in the state and a great source of Navajo rugs, Kachina dolls, Pueblo pottery, and jewelry. Less known but equally high in quality are the Santa Clara ware and items from the Acoma and Jemez pueblos of New Mexico. You can also get original paintings by well known western artists. **Blue Mesa Indian Jewelry & Gifts**, *2125 N. Weber Street*, is also an excellent outlet for Native American items.

If you're looking for western wear, try **Lorig's Western Wear**, *31 S. Tejon Street*; or either of two locations of the **Western Warehouse**, *945 N. Academy Blvd.* and *5506 N. Academy Blvd.* Most of the better art galleries in Colorado Springs are located on the west side along West Colorado Avenue, especially around the 2500 block. The **Flute Player Gallery**, *2511 W. Colorado Ave.*, specializes in Indian art of the southwest.

The largest shopping mall in the Colorado Springs area is **The Citadel**, *Academy Boulevard at Platte Avenue (US 24)*. It has 170 stores including four department stores. The **Chapel Hills Mall**, *North Academy Boulevard at Briargate Boulevard,* is only slightly smaller, with 140 stores and four department stores.

Manitou Springs

With all of the visitors that Manitou Springs receives it should come as no surprise that there is plenty of shopping. Everything from cheap souvenir stands to the most upscale boutiques can be found. Things are centered on Ruxton Avenue and along nearby stretches of intersecting streets.

A few places that are especially noteworthy are **Navajo Gallery & Gifts**, *11 Arcade*, which features authentic and beautiful Navajo works of art; the **Taos Trading Company**, *737 Manitou Avenue,* a great place for all types of Native American goods including Navajo, Hopi, Zuni and Kachina items; and the **Commonwheel Artists Co-op,** *102 Canon Avenue*, displaying the works of more than 40 talented local artisans.

SPORTS & RECREATION
Amusement Parks
- **Arcade Amusements**, *900 Black Manitou Ave., Manitou Springs. Tel. 719/685-9815*
- **Champions Golf & Games**, *Chestnut & Fillmore, Colorado Springs. Tel. 719/593-9844*
- **Q-Zar Laser Tag**, *4388 Austin Bluffs Parkway, Colorado Springs. Tel. 719/593-8188*

Ballooning
- **Adventures Out West**, *Colorado Springs. For pick-up Tel. 800/755-0935.* Also does jeep tours.
- **High But Dry Balloons**, *Colorado Springs. For pick-up, Tel. 719/260-0011*

Bicycling
- **Adventure Bike Tours & Rentals**, *22703 W. Colorado Ave., Colorado Springs. Tel. 719/635-3655*

For information on places to ride your own or a rental bike, get a copy of the Pikes Peak Area Trails Map & Recreation Guide. It's available wherever you can rent bikes, at outdoor shops, and at the Colorado Springs Convention & Visitors Bureau office.

Boating
· **Lake Pueblo State Park**, *640 Reservoir Avenue, Pueblo. Tel. 719/561-9320*

Fishing
· **Angler's Covey**, *917 W. Colorado Ave., Tel. 800/753-4746*
· **Lake Pueblo State Park**, *640 Reservoir Road, Pueblo. Tel. 719/561-9320*
· **Schryver Park**, *202 Manitour Avenue, Manitou Springs*

Golf
· **Patty Jewett Golf Course**, *900 E. Espanola, Colorado Springs. Tel. 719/578-6827*
· **Pine Creek Golf Club**, *9850 Divot Trail, Colorado Springs. Tel. 719/594-9999*
· **Valley Hi Golf Course**, *600 S. Chelton, Colorado Springs. Tel. 719/578-6351*

Horseback Riding
· **Academy Riding Stables**, *4 El Paso Blvd., Colorado Springs. Tel. 719/633-5667*
· **Stables at Broadmoor**, *Old Stage Road, Colorado Springs. Tel. 719/448-0371*

Rafting
· **Adventure Quest Rafting**, *Canon City. Tel. 888/448-RAFT*
· **Dvorak's Whitewater Rafting**, *US 50, Canon City. Tel. 800/824-3795*
· **Echo Canyon River Expeditions**, *45000 US Highway 50, Canon City. Tel. 800/748-2953*
· **Raft Masters**, *2315 E. Main St., Canon City. Tel. 800/568-7238*
· **Whitewater Adventure Outfitters**, *1420 Royal Gorge Blvd., Canon City. Tel. 800/530-8212*

Spectator Sports
Auto Racing*:* **Pikes Peak International Raceway**, *off of I-25 in Fountain. Tel. 800/955-RACE*

Baseball*:* **Colorado Springs Sky Sox** (highest level minor league team), *4385 Tuft Boulevard. Tel. 719/597-3000*. The season is from April through September. While it may not be major league quality, it's fun and a lot less expensive. All seats are under $10 and close to the action.

Swimming
· **Lake Pueblo State Park**, *640 Reservoir Road, Pueblo*
· **Memorial Park Pool**, *Pikes Peak Ave. & Union Blvd., Colorado Springs. Tel. 719/578-6634*

- **Mineral Palace Pool**, *1800 N. Santa Fe, Pueblo. Tel. 719/545-5319*
- **Schryver Park (Manitou Springs Pool)**, *202 Manitou Avenue, Manitou Springs. Tel. 719/685-9735*

Tennis
- **Lynmar Racquet & Health Club**, *2660 Vickers Drive, Colorado Springs. Tel. 719/598-7075*
- **Memorial Park**, *Pikes Peak Ave. & Union Blvd., Colorado Springs*

EXCURSIONS & DAY TRIPS

You don't have to travel far from Colorado Springs to get into the wonderful scenery of the Rockies and other nearby marvels of nature. The first excursion combines scenery with a living history of the Colorado mining era along with a chance to partake in some gaming. The second will bring you face to face with one of the most amazing chasms in North America, while the final trip takes you to, after Denver and Colorado Springs, one of the bigger cities in Colorado.

The first two require a full day to complete the entire suggested itinerary and all are designed to be done by car. The final one can be completed in about six hours although it can be extended to a full day as well by doing things in greater detail.

CRIPPLE CREEK & THE ROCKIES

This excursion covers only about 105 miles from start to finish so you'll have most of the day for sightseeing rather than just riding. Then again, even the riding part can be a real treat given the scenery of this area. History is also important. **Cripple Creek** found its way onto the map with the discovery of gold in 1891. Within two years the population boomed to more than 18,000 people. By the beginning of the 20th century the "world's greatest gold camp" had 28 millionaires, 70 saloons and about 90 each of doctors and lawyers. It was ultimately to produce more than $350 million worth of gold. At an elevation of 9,494 feet, Cripple Creek has always seen nothing but high times!

Start out by heading west on US 24 and passing through the towns of Cascade and Woodland Park before reaching the **Florissant Fossil Beds National Monument**, *located off of US 24 via County Route 1, two miles south of the town of Florissant*. The Monument is a 6,000 acre area of thin shale rock strata that dates from the Oligocene epoch which occurred about 35 million years ago. Within the shale are the fossils of beautifully preserved plants and animals. Your tour will also include a stop at the visitor center with its fossil collection and numerous exhibits that explain how the fossil beds came to be. *Tel. 719/748-3253. The Monument is open daily from 8:00am until 7:00pm from Memorial Day through Labor Day and to 4:30pm the* *rest of the year. It is closed only on New Year's Day, Thanksgiving, and Christmas. Admission is $2 but is free for holders of park service passports.*

Leave the Monument via the south entrance and continue southbound until you reach Cripple Creek itself. The town has a permanent population of less than a thousand people so you won't have any trouble finding things since there are only a few streets. The first stop is located on the north edge of town. The **Molly Kathleen Gold Mine** conducts forty minute long tours that take you a thousand feet underground to see how gold was excavated in Cripple Creek's hey-days. It's cold in there but if you forget a jacket it will be provided by Molly Kathleen. *Tel. 719/689-2465. Mine hours are daily from 9:00am until 5:00pm, May through October. Adult admission is $10 and $5 for children ages 3 through 11.*

Next up is the **Cripple Creek District Museum** located in the old railroad depot at *Bennett and 5th Streets*. The museum's Heritage Gallery portrays the history of Cripple Creek through pictures. Also on site is one of the original assay offices used for weighing gold. *Tel. 719/689-2634. Museum hours are daily from 10:00am until 5:00pm from late May to the end of October. It is only open weekends from noon till 4:00pm the rest of the year. Admission is $2.25 for adults and 50 cents for children ages 7 through 12.*

A highlight of the day in Cripple Creek will be the journey on the **Cripple Creek & Victor Narrow Gauge Railroad** which departs across the street from the museum. This authentic locomotive has been meticulously restored and colorfully painted and follows a four-mile long route over trestles and past abandoned mines and ghost towns, all amid spectacular scenery. Frequent photo stops are made. The train goes to Victor, another mining era town that has still survived. *Tel. 719/689-2640. Departures every 45 minutes from 9:30am until 5:30pm, Memorial Day through mid-October. Adult fare is $8, seniors pay $7, and children ages 3 through 12 are charged $4.*

There are a couple of other ways to be entertained while in town. One option is to go see the **Victorian Melodrama** in the 1896 Imperial Hotel, *123 North 3rd Street*. The impressive Gold Bar Room Theater is evidence of the town's wealth at the turn of the century. *Tel. 719/689-2922. Performances Tuesday through Friday at 2:00pm and Sunday at 1:00 and 4:30pm, June through December. Ticket prices range from $9-4 for adults and $4-6 for children ages 6 through 11.* Another fun option is to sample one of Cripple Creek's more than twenty casinos. No, it's not Las Vegas–the casinos are small and so are the stakes but that can make it more enjoyable for some. Details can be found in the *Nightlife & Entertainment* section of this chapter.

It's time to leave Cripple Creek now and you have two ways to get back to Colorado Springs. For the adventurous (and those who have four wheel drive vehicles preferably with high clearance) there is an incredibly scenic and exciting route that will actually cut about 15 miles off the mileage estimate of this excursion. However, it definitely is not for the faint of heart. Take the road south to Victor then go east on the unpaved **Gold Camp Road** that goes over the mountains. Those seeking a more tranquil return can head north from Cripple Creek on CO 67 back to US 24 eastbound.

To make up for the lack of adventure on this route I'll let you add another attraction. **North Pole & Santa's Workshop** on US 24 near Cascade is great for kids and can even be fun for grown-ups who think like kids. The village is decked out in Christmas regalia all the time and even has little elves working at various tasks. In addition to visiting Santa's house, there are also some rides of varying degrees of intensity (the big ferris wheel is popular), magic shows, eating places, and plenty of gift shops. A lot of people like to mail postcards home from this spot because they are postmarked "North Pole, Colorado." How cute. *Tel. 719/684-9432. The amusement park is open from the middle of May through Christmas eve and hours are generally from 9:30am to 6:00pm but call to check if you're coming after Labor Day. The admission is $11 for everyone over two years of age except that seniors get in for $5. Credit cards.*

CAÑON CITY & THE ROYAL GORGE

Although our second excursion is another relatively short trip mileage-wise (about 125 miles), there are so many attractions that you couldn't do all of them in a single day. The options are to return to Colorado Springs or to relocate for the evening to the Cañon City area. Either way, the time you spend in this vicinity will be well spent. Head south from Colorado Springs either via Nevada Avenue from the city center or by I-25 to Exit 140, which is Nevada Avenue. The street becomes CO 115. About 35 miles south of Colorado Springs you'll reach US 50. Go west for ten miles and you'll have reached **Cañon City**, setting for virtually all of the day's activities.

The Royal Gorge, soon to be described, is the main point of interest but its importance as a tourist attraction has spawned a number of other activities and we'll take care of them first. The first is right on US 50 just past Cañon City itself and the other is on the short approach road off of US 50 to Royal Gorge. The **Colorado Territorial Prison Museum & Park** is an interesting if not macabre look into the past. Considered one of the "hell holes" of the west, the prison housed some of the frontier's most notorious criminals during the period from 1871 through 1975. Thirty-two of the prison's cells have been converted into exhibits with life-sized models. You'll also see a hangman's noose, confiscated weapons, and the gas chamber. The gift shop has some unusual items–art work produced by Colorado inmates. *Tel. 719/269-3015. The operating hours are daily from*

8:30am until 6:00pm, Memorial Day through Labor Day; and Friday through Sunday from 10:00am until 5:00pm the remainder of the year. Closed on Christmas. The admission is $5 for adults, $4 for senior citizens, and $2.50 for children ages 5 through 12.

Buckskin Joe is a diverse facility that will certainly delight children and also features a number of activities that adults will like as well. Among the former are horseback and pony rides, a mystery house, and maze. Everyone will like the frequent on-street western shoot-outs as well as panning for gold, exploring historic mining town buildings brought here from all over, and the many stores and shops. Another important reason for stopping at Buckskin Joe is to take the three mile ride on their Royal Gorge Scenic Railroad, a miniature train that takes a 30 minute trip along the edge of the gorge. There is a stop at a scenic vantage point from which there is a fantastic view of both the gorge and its famous bridge. *Tel. 719/ 275-5149. The attraction is open daily from 8:00am until 8:00pm between Memorial Day and Labor Day and from 9:00am to 6:30pm from after Labor Day until October 31st. All inclusive admission is $14 for adults and $12 for children ages 4 through 11. Individual attraction tickets are also available. Credit cards.*

Now you're ready for the **Royal Gorge of the Arkansas River**. Zebulon Pike claimed that no one would be able to cross the forbidding Royal Gorge. Today it's easy. The sheer dark cliffs and the canyon itself, with the murky colored Arkansas River, are almost completely devoid of vegetation, in stark contrast to the forested canyon rims. Rather than stunning, like the Grand Canyon, it is impressive and eerie, a sight that isn't easily forgotten. Spanning this tremendous chasm is the **Royal Gorge Bridge** which is suspended 1,056 feet above the river. It was built in 1929 in the miraculous time frame of six months without a single fatality. It is only one lane wide (wooden roadway at that) and can be crossed by private vehicles but not large campers. Most people, however, like to just walk over it on foot so they can stop and peer down at the canyon or by the trolley that makes frequent crossings. If you do cross by car you have the option of coming back the same way or continuing on the loop road which loops back across the canyon at another but less noteworthy spot.

The surrounding area is a 5,000 acre privately owned amusement park type facility that has numerous small rides, entertainment indoors and outside, plenty of restaurants and shops, as well as viewpoints for seeing the gorge. Although this commercialization of nature may put off some, none of it interferes with the view of the gorge and it is a way to make a natural attraction more palatable to small children. The bridge, awesome as it is, is not the only way (or the best) to explore the Royal Gorge itself.

Another option is to cross the gorge by aerial tramway. This gives you the feeling of actually being suspended in air over mid-canyon along with providing what is probably the single best view of the entire bridge. The best part to me, however, is to descend into the gorge by means of the incline railway. This is reputedly the world's steepest incline (you'll believe it too after making the trip) where passengers are crammed into small cage like compartments as they travel down between the rocks of one of the gorge's small side crevices. At the bottom you can get out and walk alongside the river and stare up at the canyon walls and the bridge that crosses it. A great experience. *Tel. 888/333-5597 or 719/275-7505. Open every day of the year. Hours vary but always at least as early as 9:00am and never closes before 5:00pm. During the summer it operates from sunrise to sunset. The admission price (all means of transportation across and into the gorge as well as entertainment and attractions) is $12 for adults and $9 for children ages 4 through 11. Credit cards.*

Just about everyone who descends to the bottom of the gorge is awe-struck with the stupendous view. If you want more of this type of experience then you should definitely go for the **Royal Gorge Route**, a 90-minute, 24-mile long adventure from Cañon City to Parkdale pulled by an impressive cross-country type diesel locomotive. Although some of the scenery is the same as you would get from descending into the gorge by aerial tram (the train, for example, passes under the Royal Gorge Bridge), this trip does get to other areas that would otherwise only be able to be reached by rafters. For example, one of many highlights is when the train crosses a hanging bridge in a portion of the river canyon that is only 30-feet wide. You have the option of riding inside or on an open air car. *Tel. 888/724-5748. The train operates from mid-May through the middle of October with daily departures at 9:00am, noon and 3:00pm. At other times of the year it departs at 12:30pm on Saturday and Sunday only. The adult fare is $25 while children ages 3 through 12 are charged $17. Credit Cards. Reservations are highly recommended.*

The Arkansas River is one of the great places in the United States for river rafting that ranges, as they say in the business, from mild to wild. Most trips require at least half a day and, therefore, can't be done on a one-day excursion from Colorado Springs if you want to do most of the other attractions. However, there are a couple that are as short as two hours. At the other extreme are multi-day trips. Several of the many Arkansas River outfitters operating from in or near Cañon City are listed in the Sports & Recreation section later in this chapter along with the time-frames of their trips.

One last point to mention before we head back to Colorado Springs. For those readers who are on the adventurous side, the Cripple Creek and Cañon City excursions can be combined into a great overnight trip without returning to the Springs in the middle. The two areas are connected by the famous, or maybe infamous, **Phantom Canyon Road**.

This 36-mile long narrow gravel road twists its way along through the mountains and by fantastic red rock formations of great beauty. There are also some tunnels to make it more exciting. The speed limit is 15 or 20 miles per hour and the trip requires about two hours. Four-wheel drive low clearance vehicles are helpful but any experienced mountain driver not pulling a big trailer could probably handle it. Don't try it in bad weather. Phantom Canyon Road leads directly from Victor (four miles south of Cripple Creek) to US 50 about ten miles east of Canon City.

PUEBLO

The last suggested trip from Colorado Springs heads south approximately 40 miles to Pueblo, one of the state's largest communities with a population of more than 100,000. This excursion covers only a little more than a hundred miles. Use Exit 101 of I-25 and then go west on US 50 for one block to Elizabeth Street. Make a left and at the intersection of 26th Street is the **Colorado Vietnam Veterans Memorial** which has the name of 621 Colorado residents who lost their lives in Vietnam inscribed on three solemn black granite monuments. Continue south on Elizabeth until you reach 14th Street and then make a left.

The **Rosemount Museum**, *419 West 14th Street*, is an outstanding example of Victorian architecture at its best. The elegant 37-room mansion contains almost all original furnishings that convey the lifestyle of the era's most wealthy families. Of special note is the ornate and beautiful woodworking found throughout he house. Also in the home is the unusual collection of curiosities from around the world that has such oddities as kiwi birds and an Egyptian mummy. *Tel. 719/545-5290. Summer hours (June through Labor Day) are Tuesday through Saturday from 10:00am to 3:30pm and Sunday from 2:00-3:30pm. Call for off-season hours. Admission is $5 for adults, $4 for senior citizens, and $2 for children ages 6 through 16.*

The next attraction is the **Greenway & Nature/Raptor Center**. It's a little confusing to get there but here goes–travel west on 17th Street until just before it ends and then go a block north to 16th Street, continuing west until Lambert Avenue. Make a right and then another right on 11th Street. That turns into Nature Center Road and leads to the Greenway. The Raptor Center rehabilitates injured hawks, owls, and eagles. There are also several exhibit areas. *Tel. 719/549-2414 or 719/549-2327. The center is open Tuesday through Saturday from 9:00am until 5:00pm (from 11:00am to 4:00pm for the Raptor Center). It is closed on holidays. Donations are requested.*

Retrace your route as far as Elizabeth Street and then turn right until you reach 1st Street. The **El Pueblo Museum**, *325 West 1st Street*, is run by the Colorado Historical Society and was built on the site of an 1842 trading post. The exhibits document the history of Native and later peoples of the area from prehistoric times through 1900, when Pueblo became a major commercial center. Emphasis is on Native Americans prior to the arrival of the Spanish in 1540. *Tel. 719/583-0453. Museum hours are Monday through Saturday from 10:00am until 4:30pm and on Sunday from noon to 3:00pm. It is closed state holidays. Adult admission price is $3; seniors and children ages 6 through 16 pay $2.50.*

A couple of blocks south of the museum is Union Avenue. The four block stretch from north of the Arkansas River is known as the **Union Avenue Historic District** and has many nicely restored buildings, including the old Pueblo Union Railroad Depot with mosaic floor tiles and stained glass windows. All the businesses in the district will be happy to furnish you with a walking tour map that describes the significance of each building. The area bustles with street sales.

After finishing here cross the bridge over the river and go to the end of the street which is Orman Avenue. Turn right and go to the end. Make a left onto Goodnight Avenue and take that to the **Pueblo Zoo**, *junction Pueblo Boulevard,* in **Pueblo City Park**. The park is one of many in Pueblo that can fill up some extra time if you want to take advantage of the city's many recreational facilities. The Zoo has more than 300 animals in natural settings. The African Lion exhibit at the zoo has won several awards. Also of special interest are the tropical rain forest and a penguin exhibit which you can view from above or underwater. *Tel. 719/561-9664. Zoo hours are daily 10:00am until 5:00pm, Memorial Day through Labor Day; and 9:00am to 4:00pm the rest of the year. Closed New Year's Day, Thanksgiving, and Christmas. The admission is a reasonable $4 for adults and only $2 for children ages 3 through 12.*

Head north on Pueblo Boulevard to the intersection of US 50. Take that road east to I-25 and go south on the highway for one exit, which is US 50 Business. Go east once again to the Pueblo Municipal Airport, home to the **Fred E. Weisbrod International B-24 Memorial Museum**. The museum houses almost 30 historical military aircraft including B-24 and B-29 bombers as well as jet aircraft. The indoor portion of the museum chronicles the history of the famous World War II B-24 as well as the specific units that flew them. *Tel. 719/948-9219. Check for hours. There is no set admission fee but donations are requested.*

You can now head back west on US 50 until reaching the Interstate. Enter northbound to return to Colorado Springs. Should you have additional time available in Pueblo there are other things that you might want to check out. These include the **Hose Company #3 Fire Museum**, **Pueblo County Historical Society Museum**, and **Pueblo Art Guild and Gallery**. Information on these and events in Pueblo can be obtained from the Visitor Information Center, *at the intersection of US 50 and Elizabeth Street.*

PRACTICAL INFORMATION

All listings are for Colorado Springs unless otherwise specified:
- **Airport**: *7770 Drennan Road. Tel. 719/550-1930 or 800/462-6774*
- **Airport Transportation**: *Colorado Springs Airport Shuttle, Tel. 719/578-5232*
- **Bus Depot**
  Colorado Springs: *120 S. Weber Street, Tel. 719/635-6611*
  Pueblo: *Tel. 719/544-6295*
- **Hospital**
  Colorado Springs: *Memorial Hospital, 1400 E. Boulder. Tel. 719/475-5000; Pennrose Community Hospital, 3205 N. Academy Blvd. Tel. 719/591-3000*
  Cañon City: *St. Thomas Moore Hospital, 1019 Sheridan. Tel. 719/725-3381*
  Pueblo: *Parkview Medical Center, 400 W. 16th St. Tel. 719/584-4000*
- **Police** (non-emergency)
  Colorado Springs: *Tel. 719/632-6611*
  Cañn City: *Tel. 719/275-2000*
  Cripple Creek: *Tel. 719/689-2644*
  Pueblo: *Tel. 719/544-6295*
- **Public Transportation**: *Colorado Springs Transit, Tel. 719/475-9733*
- **Taxi**: *Yellow Cab, Tel. 719/635-9907; American Cab, Tel. 719/637-1111*
- **Tourist Office/Visitors Bureau**
  Colorado Springs: *104 South Cascade, Tel. 800/DO-VISIT; www.coloradosprings-travel.com*
  Cañon City: *403 Royal Gorge Blvd., Tel. 800/876-7922; : www.canoncitychamber.com*
  Cripple Creek: *375 E. Bennett Avenue, Tel. 800/526-8777*
  Manitou Springs: *354 Manitou Avenue, Tel. 800/642-2567; www.manitousprings.org*
  Pueblo: *302 N. Santa Fe Avenue, Tel. 800/233-3446; www.pueblochamber.org*

13. NORTH-CENTRAL COLORADO: HEART OF THE ROCKIES

Dreams of Colorado conjure up visions of a brilliant sun shining down on snow covered mountain peaks and colorfully clad skiers whooshing down those same mountains. Either would be an excellent way to characterize the north-central part of the state which is blessed with an abundance of those scenes. The heart of the Rockies *is* Colorado in many ways.

Here you will find more high mountains than in any other part of North America. Certainly the scenery is comparable to that found anywhere in the world and it is just that which has made it famous. Famous, too, are the names of some of its best known resorts–places like **Aspen**, **Keystone**, and **Vail**–names that are synonymous with great winter sports. While you are literally always in the middle of the mountains here and, hence, always amid wonderful scenery, the single greatest natural gem of the region must be **Rocky Mountain National Park**, which contains the highest continuous through-highway in the United States. In fact, almost all of the scenic wonders of the heart of the Rockies are almost too easy to get to via an excellent system of well maintained mountain roads.

Scenery and the wonderful recreational facilities of this outdoor oriented region aren't the only things you'll encounter on a journey through it. The history of Colorado comes alive in many former mining towns some of which are now ski resorts or just living reminders of an era gone by. Whatever it is you're looking for, you're likely to find it at its best in the heart of the Rockies.

ARRIVALS & DEPARTURES

I've chosen **Boulder** as the starting point for a loop tour through the north-central region of Colorado for two reasons. First, it is the largest community in the area and thus has many good transportation and other facilities. Second, its proximity to Denver makes it easy to reach for the large number of visitors who will inevitably be flying into Denver. However, since it can be seen in a loop you can join it from a number of places depending upon where you are coming from. Other likely points are in Vail (if coming from the west), Aspen (from the south), or Estes Park (from the north). Car rentals are available in all of these places.

Boulder is less than 30 miles from Denver and is connected to it by US 36. That road intersects with I-25 just a few miles north of the Denver city line. CO 119 also goes to Boulder from I-25 if you are coming south on that road from Wyoming. Regularly scheduled bus service from Denver to Boulder is provided on a frequent basis by the **Regional Transportation District (RTD)**.

Other easily reached places to begin a jaunt through the north-central are Aspen, Steamboat Springs and Vail. All of these have regularly scheduled service from Denver via United Express. Both Vail (35 miles west) and Glenwood Springs (24 miles east) are served by the Eagle County Regional Airport. Both the Aspen and Eagle County airports pick up additional service from numerous locations by Northwest and America West during the winter ski season.

ORIENTATION

The region is roughly rectangular and is approximately 100 miles from east-to-west and about 150 miles north-to-south. That's a sizable enough chunk to require a car to get from one place to another. There is, however, some bus service between points in this area. During the ski season the major resort areas of Aspen, Vail, Steamboat Springs and the Summit County resorts of Dillon, Breckenridge, and Keystone. All provide bus service between the slopes and town as well as to neighboring communities.

GETTING AROUND THE REGION

I-70 is the primary road artery and bisects the heart of the Rockies about a third of the way through the region from the southern edge. It is probably the most prolonged scenic stretch of road in the entire Interstate system. You can drive across the north via US 34 and US 40. Major north-south routes include CO 72 in the east and CO 9 and 91 in the west. Despite the fact that there are few sizable towns once you leave Boulder, you're never too far from a major highway. And the quality of the roads

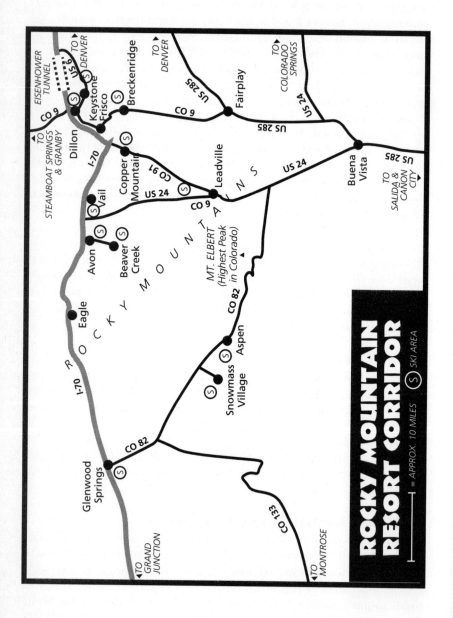

are excellent. If you stay on the paved routes (US and CO designated), all of this mountainous terrain is open to even inexperienced mountain drivers. There are several passes and other areas with steep grades and sharp turns. However, no four-wheel drive or other special vehicles are required. Just watch the road carefully and stay within posted speed limits. The engine should be thoroughly checked before driving in the mountains. And, if you're coming in winter, snow tires are a must and even snow chains should be taken along. It's a different story, of course, once you leave the main roads.

Most communities are quite small and public transportation facilities are usually limited to resort shuttles. They often provide service to and from Denver and Colorado Springs as well as within the resort towns and surrounding areas. They're great during the ski season but have limitations for sightseeing purposes. The best of the resort transportation is via Summit Stage, *Tel. 970/668-0999,* which serves Breckenridge, Keystone, and other resorts within Summit County. Many of the resort transportation services are provided free of charge. Bigger Boulder does have several bus routes that make getting around easy, especially in the downtown area. See the sidebar under Boulder.

WHERE TO STAY
ASPEN/SNOWMASS

I guess it's not really my place to apologize for the fact that there are literally no acceptable accommodations in Aspen that are priced even remotely close to moderate during the ski season. If you want to ski in Aspen, then expect to pay dearly for it. On the other hand, if you're staying overnight during the summer, then you can find some relative bargains by carefully scanning through the low season rates.

Very Expensive
HOTEL JEROME, *330 E. Main Street, Aspen. Tel. 970/920-1000; Fax 970/925-2784. Toll free reservations 800/331-7213; www.hoteljerome.com. E-mail: hjerome@aol.com. 93 Rooms. Rates: $365-2,400 depending upon dates; higher for some suites. Rates vary frequently within each season as do the minimum number of nights. American Express, Diners Club, MasterCard and VISA accepted. Located in the heart of Aspen town on CO 82.*

A luxurious and exclusive small hotel that will satisfy just about the most discriminating traveler even though it is a notch or two below the Little Nell that is described next. The Jerome first opened as a hotel way back in 1869 and the historic property has been meticulously refurbished and restored to its original elegance. The furnishings are exclusively either authentic Victorian antiques or top quality reproductions.

The Victorian decor extends beyond the public areas into each spacious guest room. Mini-bars are standard in all units and many have a Jacuzzi tub. Only the highest quality fabrics and linens are used and the same can be said for toiletries and bath accessories. The Hotel Jerome has two restaurants with good food although the prices are, as would be expected, quite high. An additional summer option is to dine poolside. There is a cocktail lounge with frequent live entertainment. Among other facilities and services are a heated swimming pool, Jacuzzi, exercise room, video rental library, and free transportation within Aspen.

THE LITTLE NELL, *675 E. Durant Avenue, Aspen. Tel. 970/920-4600; Fax 970/920-4670; www.thelittlenell.com. 92 Rooms. Rates: High season (mid-December to late March): $525-750 rooms/$895-3,920 suites; Low season (April 1st to late May and late September to mid-December): $215-500 rooms/$500-2,100 suites. Three night minimum stay during some winter periods. Major credit cards accepted. Located at the base of Aspen Mountain immediately beside the ski gondola.*

This wonderfully unique property combines elements of a small European style grand hotel with that of an American country inn along with many of the amenities and facilities of a larger hotel. Located at the base of beautiful Aspen Mountain and within steps of the ski gondola, the Little Nell's exterior features a mixture of Victorian elegance, French country charm and the appropriateness of an Alpine ski chalet–all in a delightful blend of countless colorful turns and crevices. The rooms are all different but share many common denominators such as spaciousness, fireplace, built-in bar and refrigerator and plush decor that includes things like Belgian wool carpeting and down-filled comforters.

The public facilities are simply named, like The Restaurant (see *Where to Eat*) and The Bar, hardly hints of the luxury contained therein. The Little Nell is a service oriented facility with an attentive staff that is only too glad to attend to your every need. The availability of Aspen's many shops and restaurants within a short walk is a lure to get you away from the hotel's swimming pool and the surrounding pretty flower garden.

Selected as one of my Best Places to Stay (see Chapter 10 for details).

MOLLY GIBSON LODGE, *101 West Main Street, Aspen. Tel. 970/925-3434; Fax 970/925-2582; www.mollygibson.com. 50 Rooms. Rates: High season (winter): $129-399; Low season (summer): $99-249; all including Continental breakfast. Most major credit cards accepted. Located immediately to the west of the center of town on CO 82.*

Not a bad alternative to either of the preceding listings for those who can't afford the steep tab of Aspen's top places. The Molly Gibson is an attractive small motel with a good location, nice rooms, and some recreational facilities. There isn't any restaurant or lounge but you can find plenty of both within close proximity. About a third of the rooms have a working fireplace while all have voice mail telephones and refrigerators. Some room options are efficiency units and whirlpools. The size of the units does vary considerably from kind of smallish to spacious. Out back there is a nice Jacuzzi located amid a plethora of lovely pine trees. Molly Gibson rents bicycles to explore Aspen and provides free transportation within town and to all ski areas.

ST. REGIS ASPEN, *315 E. Dean Street, Aspen. Tel. 970/920-3300; Fax 970/925-8998. Toll free reservations 888/454-9005. 257 Rooms. Rates: High season (various times): $239-775; Low season (April 1st to June 1st and mid-October to mid-November): $135-175. Minimum stays apply during winter holiday periods. Major credit cards accepted. Located south of CO 82 via Durant and Mill Streets.*

The upscale luxury of the St. Regis name fits in well in the high rent district of Aspen. Appealing to a clientele where only the best will suffice, the St. Regis is Aspen's biggest hotel. However, it isn't so big as to sacrifice the personalized attention that is one of its noted hallmarks. And like so many of its sister properties, this Ritz has an understated form of elegance rather than showy glitz. That applies to both the exterior and interior although indoor public areas do have fine works of art and lots of crystal chandeliers.

The guestrooms are large and tastefully appointed with high quality modern furnishings. Standard amenities include mini-bar and in-room safe. Rooms at the upper end of the scale, including those on the separate luxury level, feature whirlpool and video cassette player. There is a nice restaurant at the hotel and in summer you can dine on the patio or have lunch alongside the swimming pool. A distinguished looking cocktail lounge can also be found.

The Ritz Carlton is a full service resort facility. Besides the aforementioned pool there are sauna and steamrooms, Jacuzzis, and health club with massage (additional fee) and exercise room. Golf and tennis privileges are extended to guests at nearby facilities. In addition, the staff will help you arrange skiing, skating, snowmobiling, bicycle rental and even horseback riding. A supervised children's program is also available.

SILVERTREE HOTEL, *100 Elbert Lane, Snowmass Village. Tel. 970/923-3520; Fax 970/923-5494. Toll free reservations 800/525-9402; www/silvertreehotel.com. 262 Rooms. Rates: $250-550 in peak periods and : $99-375 at non-peak periods, both of which vary within seasons. Major credit cards accepted. Located in Snowmass Village, about four miles southwest of CO 82.*

Not quite as fancy or pricey as some of their Aspen counterparts, Snowmass' Silvertree is, nevertheless, a quality and highly attractive modern ten-story property at the base of the skiing area. That's actually putting it rather mildly in view of the fact that you can ski directly onto or from the slopes into the interior of the Silvertree! The rooms are large, bright and cheerfully furnished. It isn't air conditioned (nor is it needed in this part of Colorado) but all rooms have fans and humidifiers along with lots of other amenities such as coffee makers, refrigerators, hairdryers and video games for young children as well as not so young–like about forty! A majority of rooms have balconies and some have whirlpool tubs.

There are two restaurants, including patio dining during the summer, and a cocktail lounge. Live entertainment is offered only during the winter season. In addition to skiing the Silvertree offers a comprehensive program of recreation that includes hiking trails, horseback riding, bicycling (rental fee), and tabogganing. There is also a supervised program of children's activities. Two swimming pools, Jacuzzi, steamrooms, sauna, and tanning facility round out the picture.

WILDWOOD LODGE, *40 Elbert Lane, Snowmass Village. Tel. 970/ 923-3520; Fax 970/923-5490. Toll free reservations 800/525-9402; www.aroomforyou.com/wildwoo. 151 Rooms. Rates: $99-279 depending upon dates, which vary considerably within each season. Continental breakfast included at all times except from the end of May to early October. Closed April to May and mid-October to early December. Major credit cards accepted. Located in Snowmass Village, about four miles southwest of CO 82.*

This is another nice place and, when it's open, is one of the more affordable hotels in the Aspen area. The rooms are beautifully decorated and have coffee makers, refrigerator, fan, humidifier and video games. Better rooms feature Jacuzzis and video cassette players. There is a restaurant open for dinner and a cocktail lounge. A heated pool, whirlpool and health club (fee charged) are on the premises as is a good ski shop. A number of recreational opportunities are also available but there is an additional fee for many of them. Free transportation in and around the village is provided.

Expensive

LIMELIGHT LODGE, *228 East Cooper Street, Aspen. Tel. 970/925-3025; Fax 970/925-5120. Toll free reservations 800/433-0832. 63 Rooms. Rates: High season (mid-December to March 31st): $185-375; Low season (April 1st to mid-December): $84-250, all rates including Continental breakfast. Major credit cards accepted. Located in town just south of CO 82.*

While the price may be "cheap" for Aspen keep in mind that all you get is a rather basic motel. Of course, whether you've come to ski in winter or take in the sights during the summer, that may be more than enough for a lot of people. The rooms are comfortable and well kept. All have refrigerators; a few have whirlpool tubs. The recreational facilities consist of two heated pools, sauna, and whirlpool. The three-story building has no elevator. There also isn't any restaurant but it is within walking distance of many of Aspen's fine dining spots as well as shopping and ski areas. Free transportation to the slopes.

ULLR LODGE, *520 W. Main Street, Aspen. Tel. 970/925-7696; Fax 970-920-4339; www.aspen.com/ullr. 23 Rooms. Rates: High season (mid-December to mid-May): $106-270 including full breakfast; Low season (mid-May to mid-December): $70-150 including Continental breakfast. American Express, Diners Club, MasterCard and VISA accepted. Located about a mile west of central Aspen on CO 82.*

The Ullr is even more basic than the preceding property but it does represent the bottom end of Aspen's price scale. About a third of the units are two-bedroom affairs, making it the best bargain in town if you want a separate room for the kids or are two couples traveling together. About half of the units have kitchens. The lodge has a small heated swimming pool as well as a Jacuzzi. There are several restaurants located close by and free transportation is available within the Aspen area.

BOULDER
Very Expensive

MARRIOTT HOTEL BOULDER, *2660 Canyon Boulevard. Tel. 303/440-8877; Fax 303/440-3377. Toll free reservations 800/228-9290; www.marriott.com. 155 Rooms. Rates: $169-270. Major credit cards accepted. Located near downtown in the Village Shopping Center.*

Boulder's premier business hotel is also well situated for the visitor given its proximity to shopping, dining and the University. The deluxe guest rooms and suites are large, bright and modern. They have all of the amenities that you would expect from a Marriott. Many rooms have a wonderful view of the Flatirons but if your room isn't one of them then just take the elevator up to the roof where a lovely terrace will give you a great vista of the entire Boulder area. For great dining try JW's Steakhouse (described in the Where to Eat section); the hotel also has a good cocktail lounge. Guests can take advantage of the hotel's heated indoor swimming pool, whirlpool, and full service health club. There are a number of fashionable boutiques as well as a gift shop.

Expensive

ALPS BOULDER CANYON INN, *38619 Boulder Canyon Drive. Tel. 303/444-5445; Fax 303/444-5522. Toll free reservations 800/414-2577; www.alpsinn.com. E-mail: alpsinn@aol.com. 12 Rooms. Rates: $125-225 including full breakfast. Major credit cards accepted. Located in Boulder Canyon, about 3-1/2 miles west of town on Colorado Highway 119.*

The natural world of Boulder Canyon is the setting for this log lodge that dates from 1870 and has been graciously restored. Set back from the road behind a low stone wall and a front lawn filled with stately trees, the inn boasts luxurious guest rooms. Among the features are fireplaces, stained glass windows, authentic antique furnishings and ornate bathrooms. Some units have double Jazuzzi tubs as well as porches that are almost literally on the mountainside. There is no television in the rooms but one is available in the common area.

In addition to an outstanding breakfast guests at the Alps Boulder Canyon are treated (and I do mean treated) to sinfully delectable desserts in the evening. Just don't count the calories. Fishing and hiking trails are available or you can rent a bicycle to explore the canyon. Professional massage can be arranged at an additional charge.

COBURN HOTEL, *2040 16th Street. Tel. 303/545-5200; Fax 303/440-6740. Toll free reservations 800/858-5811. E-mail: coburn@nilenet.com. 12 Rooms. Rates: $149-189 all year, including breakfast. Most major credit cards accepted. Located in the heart of downtown.*

This small hotel located right in the middle of Boulder's exciting downtown core is a blend of old world style and western hospitality. It doesn't have a lot of public facilities besides the breakfast room and a small cocktail lounge but that's hardly necessary given the proximity of all the restaurants and other services available within walking distance. What you will get, however, are excellent rooms that have fireplaces and Jacuzzis among the many amenities. They also have balconies that provide good but partially obstructed mountain views.

EARL HOUSE HISTORIC INN, *2429 Broadway. Tel. 303/938-1400; Fax 303/938-9710. E-mail: vicearl@bouldernews.infi.net. 6 Rooms. Rates: $129-189 all year, including full breakfast.. Most major credit cards accepted. Located four blocks from downtown and the Pearl Street Mall.*

An impressive looking stone mansion dating from 1882 and renovated in 1995 to a Victorian style B&B, the Earl House is a simple but pleasant place. The rooms are attractively decorated with period reproductions and some units feature Jacuzzi tubs. If you're going to be staying in Boulder for an extended period you might inquire about staying in one of the two adjacent Carriage Houses that provide lots of space and additional amenities at a higher rate. The morning breakfast is excellent and you can also enjoy an old fashioned afternoon tea service. For other dining you're only a four block walk from the Pearl Street Mall and its many restaurants and other services.

HOTEL BOULDERADO, *2115 13th Street. Tel.. 303/442-4344; Fax 303/442-4378. Toll free reservations 800/4334344; www.boulderado.com. E-mail: info@boulderado.com. 160 Rooms. Rates: $166-216 all year; suites up to $285. Major credit cards accepted. Located downtown at corner of Spruce, one block north of the Pearl Street Mall.*

The name of this 1909 hotel that's listed on the National Register of Historic Places is actually a contraction of Boulder, Colorado. It seems that back in those days Boulder wasn't well known and the owner thought this would be a way for people to remember his hotel. The simple red brick exterior is graced by green canopies over the first floor windows and by many indented balconies. But it is the beautiful interior that catches the most attention. A three story lobby topped by a stained glass ceiling and featuring a rich cherry wood staircase and plush Victorian furnishings is the focal point of all the hotel's public areas.

Guest rooms continue the Victorian theme whether they're in the original building or a newer wing. Comfortable furnishings and modern amenities will be found in all. There are two fine restaurants (Q's is described in *Where to Eat*, below) and three lounges, one of which features jazz entertainment. The Bouldlerado is a service oriented hotel with a professional and attentive staff.

Selected as one of my Best Places to Stay (see Chapter 10 for details).

REGAL HARVEST HOUSE, *1345 28th Street. Tel. 303/443-3850; Fax 303/443-1480. Toll free reservations 800/545-6285; www.regal-hotels.com. E-mail: bzollars@richfield.com. 269 Rooms. Rates: $109-199. Major credit cards accepted. Located close to Colorado University, about a mile south of the junction with US 36.*

The Harvest House is one of the nicest hotels in Boulder. It covers almost 16 acres of well landscaped grounds between the university campus and the foothills of the Flatirons. Pathways for walkers and bicycle riders meander tranquilly through colorful flower gardens. The large, attractively furnished rooms are decorated in a bright and modern style. Most rooms that face the west have a largely unobstructed view of the mountains. Those having balconies are the best. The rooms have the usual amenities; a few have refrigerators for a small additional charge.

An excellent restaurant called the Fancy Moose is highlighted in the Where to Eat section. Champs Lounge provides a relaxed and friendly spot for drinks and chatter as well as occasional live entertainment on weekends. The recreational facilities of the Regal Harvest House are extensive. There are both indoor and outdoor heated swimming pools, 15 tennis courts (including five indoor for winter players), sand volleyball courts, complete exercise facility and whirlpool, and a playground for the children. You can also rent bicycles and mountain bikes to take advantage of the great nearby biking venues.

Moderate

BRIAR ROSE BED & BREAKFAST, *2151 Arapahoe Avenue. Tel. 303/938-1400; Fax 303/938-9710. E-mail: brbbx@aol.com. 9 Rooms. Rates: $89-199 all year including full breakfast. American Express, MasterCard and VISA accepted. Located about a half mile west of US 36 at 28th Street.*

A small and attractive looking Victorian style inn, the Briar Rose features authentic period furnishings and original works of art in each room. Plush down comforters will keep you warm on the chilliest of evenings. Two units have fireplaces for additional warmth, both physical and emotional. No in-room television and only a few units have air conditioning. There aren't any recreational facilities but guests do receive privileges in a nearby health club. The breakfast is ample and delicious. Located on a residential street, the Briar Rose is for people looking for pretty accommodations in a private and quiet setting. If that's all you want then you will be quite content by selecting this B&B. Many restaurants are located within a short distance.

BROKER INN, *555 30th Street. Tel. 303/444-3330; Fax 303/444-6444. Toll free reservations 800/338-5407; www.boulderbrokerinn.com. 116 Rooms. Rates: $118-138 all year, including breakfast on weekdays. Major credit cards accepted. Located west of US 36 via Baseline Road to 30th Street and then just south.*

Combining all the features of a modern motor inn (along with many aspects of a full service hotel) with Victorian style decor, the Broker Inn winds up being a most delightful place at a rate that isn't a bad value. Conveniently located not far from the Colorado University campus, the Broker's Victorian theme extends beyond the public areas to each of the attractive guestrooms. Especially attractive are the real brass headboards and the comfortable leather reclining chair that's just perfect for resting weary toes after a busy day pounding the streets. While all of the rooms in the four story inn are just fine, some have upgraded amenites such as coffee makers and refrigerators or even whirlpool tubs.

The Broker Inn Restaurant is one of Boulder's finest and is described in the Where to Eat section. There's also a cocktail lounge. Complimentary beverages are served each evening in the pretty lobby. A heated swimming pool and whirlpool can be supplemented with a visit to the neighboring health club–Broker Inn guests receive free privileges. Free transportation is provided within five miles of the hotel, an area that takes in most of Boulder's sights. You can also rent bicycles.

SANDY POINT INN, *6485 Twin Lakes Road. Tel. 303/530-2939. Toll free reservations 800/322-2939. 33 Rooms. Rates $69-130 including full breakfast. Monthly rates available. Most major credit cards accepted. Located northwest of downtown via CO 119 to Jay Road, then east to 63rd Street and then east on Twin Lakes Road.*

Situated in the quiet residential Gunbarrel area of Boulder, the Sandy Point sometimes describes itself as a bed and breakfast, but it really isn't even though it has some of the features of that type of facility. It is quite reasonably priced and one of the better values in Boulder. Popular with families, all of the rooms are studio style suites with lots of space and mini-kitchen (that is, a coffee maker, refrigerator and microwave oven). There is also a full kitchen and dining area that can be used by guests. The attractive park like grounds of the inn have a playground. Guests are entitled to free privileges at the nearby RallySport Health Club. Many restaurans are located within a short ride.

Inexpensive

FOOT OF THE MOUNTAIN MOTEL, *200 Arapahoe Avaenue. Tel. 303/442-6600. 18 Rooms. Rates: $65-75 all year. Weekly rates available. American Express, Discover, MasterCard and VISA accepted. Located two miles west of US 36 on the transition between city and mountain.*

A bargain find! Delightfully situated at the entrance to picturesque Bouldler Canyon and at the base of Flagstaff Mountain, the Foot of the Mountain Motel's rooms are designed to look like authentic old time log cabins. The interiors are built of knotty pine and, with the rustic style but comfortable furniture, really can make you feel like you're out in the countryside even though you're only minutes away from all that Boulder has to offer. All rooms have refrigerators. There is no air conditioning (although the location is naturally cool) or swimming pool but you can take in the fresh high altitude air from the spacious yard that is set up with picnic tables.

CRESTED BUTTE
Very Expensive

SHERATON CRESTED BUTTE RESORT, *6 Emmons Road. Tel. 970/349-8000; Fax 970/349-8050. Toll free reservations 888/223-2469. 252 Rooms. Rates: High season (late December through March): $218-240; Low season (April through November): $92-101. Closed during some spring and fall periods. All rates include full breakfast. Minimum stay requirements are imposed during peak periods. Most major credit cards accepted. Located 2-1/2 miles north of town via State Highway 135 at the Mount Crested Butte ski area.*

While this is a nice property in every way, there isn't anything particularly special about it from an architectural or interior design aspect. Perhaps the setting, surrounded by magnificent mountains, speaks for itself and the designers felt that nature didn't need any improving on. The accommodations, in particular, are undistinguished looking although the rooms are spacious and well equipped with just about every amenity you could ask for. Better are the public areas including the large and attractive lobby with its required fireplace (or so it seems in ski country). The views are great and that can be said to apply to most of the rooms as well.

Facilities at the Sheraton include a decent restaurant and a deli for those in a hurry or seeking only a bite to eat. Recreational diversions range from indoor and outdoor swimming pools to whirlpools to a complete fitness center. There are also extensive hiking trails. The hotel is within walking distance of the ski lifts.

Moderate

NORDIC INN, *14 Treasury Road. Tel. 970/349-5542; Fax 970/349-6487. Toll free reservations 800/542-SNOW. 27 Rooms. Rates: High season (mid-November through March): $110-160; Low season (June through late October): $80-90. Closed at other times. All rates include Continental breakfast. Minimum stay requirements may be imposed during parts of high season. American Express, MasterCard and VISA accepted. Located 2-1/2 miles north of town via State Highway 135 at the Mount Crested Butte ski area.*

This isn't your typical ski town resort and maybe that's good, because it's nice to be able to stay in the area without busting the entire travel budget in one evening. For summer travelers that's even more important, although the Nordic Inn is within a stone's throw of the slopes. This small lodge has an attractive semi-alpine style exterior. The large lobby has a Norwegian inspired fireplace and is the place for guests to play games and puzzles or take a book to read from the library. There's a hot tub and Jacuzzi. Guest rooms are a nice size and feature pleasant decor. Many rooms have kitchen facilities and all have hair dryers. Restaurants are located within a short distance.

OLD TOWN INN, *Colorado Highway 135. Tel. 970/349-6184. 33 Rooms. Rates: High season (Christmas/New Year's period and March): $113-125; Low season (April 1st to late December and early January through February): $83-103. Most major credit cards accepted. Located immediately to the southeast of town on the main highway.*

This is a basic roadside motel but is worthy of mention because you don't see prices like this very often in the ski resort areas, winter or summer. The rooms are clean and comfortable and the staff is friendly. Free area transportation is available. Several restaurants are close by. There isn't any swimming pool but the motel does have a whirlpool.

ESTES PARK

Very Expensive

THE STANLEY HOTEL, *333 Wonderview Avenue. Tel. 970/586-3371; Fax 970/586-3673. Toll free reservations 800/976-1377; www.stanleyhotel.com. 133 Rooms. Rates: High season (late May to mid-October): $169-209 for rooms and $269-299 for suites; Low season (mid-October to late May): $139-179 for rooms and $219-249 for suites. Most major credit cards accepted. Located on a hill just east of downtown via US 34.*

The Historic Stanley was named for its original owner of Stanley Steamer fame. He built the lavish resort back in 1909. The hotel has starred in movies and television for its ornate and majestic appearance as well as the magnificent surroundings. The setting must be seen. Sitting on an immaculate and huge front lawn with hedges and topiary, the hotel is backed by a wall of Rocky Mountains. The white Georgian architecture is splendid.

A wide range of rooms all feature quality furnishings in a beautiful traditional style. Guests can choose from one of three restaurants, explore The Stanley's extensive public rooms or relax and take in the beautiful scene from the hotel's spacious veranda. The hotel also has some fine recreational facilities but the area around it offers almost unlimited recreational opportunities.

Selected as one of my Best Places to Stay (see Chapter 10 for details).

STREAMSIDE...A VILLAGE OF CABIN SUITES, *1260 Fall River Road. Tel. 970/586-6464; Fax 970/586-6272. Toll free reservations 800/321-3303; www.coloradodirectory.com/streamsidecabins. 19 Rooms. Rates: High season (mid-May to mid-October): $125-260; Low season (mid-October to mid-May): $80-190. American Express, Discover, MasterCard and VISA accepted. Located a mile west of downtown on US 34.*

A spacious retreat with almost an acre for each guest unit, Streamside is near town but on a secluded site filled with pine and aspen trees alongside a stream. Wildlife freely roams about and there is lovely landscaping. It is delicious refreshment for the soul. The "cabin suites" are large and beautifully furnished. In keeping with the natural surroundings, they feature airy cathedral ceilings, skylights and a private deck. All have their own full kitchen.

On the recreational front Streamside has a pretty "swim spa" with hot tub and sundeck. Or you can fish in their private stream followed by an exploration of their many nature trails. Everything about Streamside complements the wonders of nature that so abound in the Estes Park area.

Selected as one of my Best Places to Stay (see Chapter 10 for details).

Expensive

APPENZELL INN, *1100 Big Thompson Avenue. Tel. 970/586-2023; Fax 970/586-1874. Toll free reservations 800/475-1125; www.appenzellinn.com. 28 Rooms. Rates: High season (April through October): $110-190; Low season (November through March): $95-100. Discover, MasterCard and VISA accepted. Located a mile east of the center of town on US Highway 34.*

This conveniently located inn boasts an attractive Swiss styling and very nice rooms. You can choose from a regular unit or a two-bedroom suite. There are a variety of options in the rooms including efficiencies, whirlpool units and rooms with fireplace. Of course, most of these are limited to the suites but even a few basic rooms have some of the upgraded amenities. The inn has three floors but no elevator, so those with difficulty climbing stairs should request a room on one of the lower floors. For recreation there is a heated indoor swimming pool. The Bier Stuble Pub is a good place for a drink and a light snack but you have to go outside for restaurants. Several are located nearby.

ASPEN WINDS, *1051 Fall River Court. Tel. 970/586-6010; Fax 970/586-4195. E-mail: aspenwinds@aol.com. 16 Rooms. Rates: High season (mid-May to mid-October): $135-270; Low season (mid-October to mid-May): $90-230. Two night minimum stay during summer. American Express, Discover, MasterCard and VISA accepted. Located northwest of town on US 34 Bypass.*

The Aspen Winds gives Streamside a good run for the money. It may actually be a better dollar value but falls just a wee bit short in the overall experience, mainly because of fewer activities and less extensive grounds. But it is a great place to stay and shouldn't disappoint anyone. The naturally attractive reddish brown wooden exterior with dark contrasting roof sits in a quiet area next to a thick pine forested area alongside the pretty waters of the Fall River. It's about halfway between town and Rocky Mountain National Park. You can take in all of the great views of forest, river and mountains from outside or from behind the wall-to-wall windows of your room.

And those rooms are something special. Each unit is a one or two bedroom suite with either efficiency or full kitchen (with coffee maker), oversized Jacuzzi tub, working gas fireplace, high vaulted ceilings, home-style comfortable furnishings and either an outdoor deck or balcony. Video cassette players are also standard. Outdoor activities include barbequing on gas grills and fishing. There isn't any restaurant on the premises but you can get to a number of places to eat by a short car ride.

ROMANTIC RIVER SONG, *just off of Lower Broadview. Tel. 970/586-4666; www.romanticriversong.com. E-mail: river-sng@frii.com. 9 Rooms. Rates: $150-275 all year including full breakfast. Master Card and VISA accepted. Located on a private road reached by US 36 to Mary's Lake Road then about three quarters of a mile west on Lower Broadview to marked turnoff.*

Here's another winner for Estes Park! This wonderful bed & breakfast inn is at the luxury level and is simply great for couples looking for a getaway like the name of the place implies. Situated on 27 acres of forested land with its own mountain stream, the River Song has first class accommodations. Each of the units is beautifully decorated with lots of unusual pieces but all have an authentic oversized antique brass bed. The fireplace may be eiher wood burning or gas operated but the best part is that in most units the fireplace sits immediately behind a whirlpool tub built for two. All units have a cheerful skylight and some have refrigerators as well as either a balcony or deck. There isn't any in-rom telephone, TV or air conditioning and, best of all, it isn't likely that you'll need or want any of them.

The full breakfast is the typically wholesome and bountiful one that you come to expect at a B&B. If you want, by prearrangement only, you can have a romantic and private candlelight dinner for two, expertly prepared and served. Otherwise, it's not too far to the nearest restaurants. The River Song has on premise fishing and nature trails. There may be age restrictions on children so family travelers should inquire in advance before booking. A two night minimum stay is imposed.

Moderate

AMERICAN WILDERNESS LODGE, *481 W. Elkhorn Ave. Tel. 970/ 586-4402; Fax 970/586-7782. Toll free reservations 888/378-3775, Ext. 198. 30 Rooms. Rates: High season (summer) $89-110; Low season (winter) $60-85. Most major credit cards accepted. Located to the west of downtown on US 34.*

An attractive motel type facility located along the Fall River and within walking distance of Estes Park's many downtown restaurants and shopping, the American Wilderness Lodge offers comfortable rooms at an affordable price. The amenities vary but some rooms feature balconies overlooking the river, fireplaces, full kitchens and hot tubs. The Lodge also has a large heated indoor swimming pool located inside a pretty flower bedecked glass enclosure. There's also a recreation area and guests can fish in the river from on the lodge's property.

DEER CREST, *1200 Fall River Road. Tel. 970/586-2324. Toll free reservations 800/331-2324; deercrest@webtv.net. 26 Rooms. Rates: High season (mid-May to early October): $89-99; Low season (early October to mid-May): $71-84. MasterCard and VISA accepted. Located about a mile northwest of downtown on US 34.*

Also situated along the picturesque river that is Estes Park's "back yard," the Deer Crest is a newly redecorated and well maintained property built in a rough hewn wood a la Western lodge style. A lush and vividly green lawn separates the lodge from the riverfront. All rooms have refrigerators and microwave ovens and either a balcony or patio. Some have full kitchens and gas fireplaces. For recreation you'll find a heated pool, picnic area with barbecue grills and a large yard area for lounging located near the water. Fishing is also available.

The Deer Crest doesn't have a restaurant but it is within close proximity to many eating places. No one under 18 years of age is permitted to stay here which means you're probably in for a nice quiet and relaxing stay.

THE SILVER MOON, *175 Spruce Drive. Tel. 970/586-6006; Fax 970/ 586-3151. Toll free reservations 800/818-6006; www.silvermooninn.com. 40 Rooms. Rates: High season (summer): $80-160; Low season (winter): $58-145. Most major credit cards accepted. Located close to downtown via US 34 west and then north just across the river on Spruce Drive.*

The Silver Moon is a nice looking motor inn that has a different style than many of Estes Park's western oriented facilities. This one looks more like a stately mansion with its white columns and walls and red tiled roof fronting a rocky bluff. There are also a couple of cottage units with suite facilities in addition to the motel style rooms. The motel units are fairly basic but clean and comfortable but there are some with king or queen beds and kitchenettes. The property has a small but pretty swimming pool. It is located near downtown and is within walking distance of restaurants and shopping but without the throngs of tourists walking by every thirty seconds. The new owners, Tom and Katy Hochstetler, are eager to please.

TRAVELODGE, *1260 Big Thompson Avenue. Tel. 970/586-4476. Toll free reservations 800/578-7878. 55 Rooms. Rates: High season (summer): $89-159; Low season (winter): $49-119. All rates include Continental breakfast. Major credit cards accepted. Located about two miles east of town center via US Highway 34.*

Until a few months ago this nice motel was known as the Silver Saddle Inn. The name change to a chain property doesn't take away the fact that it isn't exactly cut from the "sameness" mold that plagues chains like Travelodge, a good reason for me to include it here. The rates are attractive for Estes Park and the accommodations are well worth the price. There are a couple of two-bedroom units (in which minimum stay requirements may be imposed during the summer). Some rooms have balconies with good views. Gas fireplaces and kitchen facilities are other available features. The lodge has a swimming pool, whirlpool and a playground. Many restaurants are located within a short drive.

GRANBY/GRAND LAKE
Expensive

INN AT SILVER CREEK, *62927 US Highway 40. Tel. 970/887-2131. Toll free reservations 800/926-4386; www.innatsilvercreek.com. 200 Rooms. Rates: $89-189. Minimum stays may be imposed during peak periods. Major credit cards accepted. Located two miles southeast of town on the main highway.*

Situated practically at the base of the Continental Divide and near the lake shore, the Inn at Silver Creek has postcard surroundings that you would have to try hard to improve on. It consists of regular hotel rooms and condominium units. About three-fourths of the units have kitchenettes while all have either a steam cabinet or whirlpool. Some have fireplaces, deck or patio. The decor is pleasant but nothing too out of the ordinary. There are extensive recreational opportunities in the surrounding area, while the inn itself boasts a heated swimming pool, sauna, racquetball court, lighted tennis, volleyball and a playground for children. There's also a game room and a gift shop. The on-premises restaurant is decent and it also has a separate bar. But what really strikes a note is the small cafe that makes a mean cappuccino.

SPIRIT MOUNTAIN RANCH, *Highway 41, Grand Lake. Tel. 970/ 887-3551. 4 Rooms. Rates: From $130-175 including full breakfast. Discover, MasterCard and VISA accepted. Located slightly north of Grand Lake village and then west on County Route for just under four miles to the gate and driveway..*

Close to the activities of Grand Lake but secluded away in the woods, the Spirit Mountain Ranch is an idyllic Bed & Breakfast that lets you have all of the comforts of home while enjoying the magnificent surroundings of Colorado's high country. The multi-level timber framed home sits quietly amid 72 acres of tall aspen trees which you can enjoy through the wide windows or from the inn's spacious back deck.

All four bright and airy guest rooms are attractively furnished in a simple western style. The common rooms have fireplaces to sit and relax by during a quiet evening inside. You can also make use of the barbecue grill on the deck. A hearty gourmet breakfast is served. Restaurants are within a fifteen minute drive. Guests find hiking on the inn's extensive grounds to be a lot of fun.

Moderate

GRAND LAKE LODGE, *US Highway 34, Grand Lake. Tel. 970/627-3967; Fax 970/627-9495; www.grandlakelodge.com. 58 Rooms. Rates: $79-144 with higher rates for larger units accommodating up to as many as 14 people. Lower rates may be available during shoulder periods at beginning and end of season. Open only from early June to mid-September. American Express, Discover, MasterCard and VISA accepted. Located a half mile north of Grand Lake Village; look for sign to lodge's private entrance on the northbound side of US 34.*

This historic lodge was built in 1920 of native lodgepole pine. Consisting of a main lodge and many other buildings hidden in the woods, it offers a magnificent vista of lakes and mountain. What could be more delightful than to take in that view in the fresh mountain air from one of the old time swings on the large veranda that surrounds the large rectangular shaped main lodge? Inside the big lobby is a huge fireplace surrounded by rocking chairs in a setting of rustic beauty.

That same style applies to the rooms, most of which provide a feeling of privacy and tranquility given their wooded location away from the hub of activity found in the main lodge. The Grand Lake Lodge features an excellent restaurant with splendid views. The varied recreational facilities are mainly located between the main lodge and the lakeshore in a setting of wonderful natural surroundings. The accommodations and facilities of Grand Lake Lodge are first class (if you don't object to rustic styling) but it is mainly a place to enjoy nature at its best. And after all, that is one of the primary reasons to come to Colorado in the first place.

Selected as one of my Best Places to Stay (see Chapter 10 for details).

Inexpensive

BIGHORN LODGE, *613 Grand Avenue, Grand Lake. Tel. 970/627-8101; Fax 970/627-8097. Toll free reservations 800/341-8000. 20 Rooms. Rates: $59-100. Closed most of April and mid-November. Major credit cards accepted. Located approximately a quarter mile east of US 34 via Grand Avenue.*

Not the greatest place but a decent spot if you're looking to save some bucks on lodging. The rooms are standard motel stuff as far as facilities go but are fairly spacious and reasonably attractive. They are clean and well maintained. The Lodge has a whirlpool but no swimming pool. It is located close to restaurants. Free area transportation is provided.

LEADVILLE
Moderate

APPLE BLOSSOM INN, *120 West 4th Street. Tel. 719/486-2141. Toll free reservations 800/982-9879; www.colorado-bnb.com/ab. E-mail: applebb@amigo.net. 6 Rooms. Rates: $99-141 including full breakfast. Most major credit cards accepted. Located downtown about a block west of Harrison Avenue (US 24).*

As you'll quickly see there isn't anything fancy about the lodging available in Leadville. Whether its a motel or B&B, plain and simple is generally the order of the day. Maybe that's not so bad because you'll probably have had your fill of luxury in the many mountain resort areas. However, the Apple Blossom is an attractive and interesting place. It was built in 1879 for a well-to-do banker and is one of the finest examples of Victorian homes in Leadville. Located downtown and close to restaurants, the Apple Blossom is decorated throughout with antiques. Rooms boast feather beds and fireplaces. The one drawback to the Apple Blossom is that some units have shared bath facilities. Opt for one with private bath and it's a delightful place. The delicious breakfast features home baking. The inn doesn't have any recreational facilities but guests do receive privileges at a nearby recreation center.

DELAWARE HOTEL, *700 Harrison Avenue. Tel. 719/486-5650; Fax 719/486-2214. Toll free reservations 800?748-2004; www.delawarehotel.com. 36 Rooms. Rates: $60-120 including Continental breakfast. Major credit cards accepted. Located in the center of town on the main street.*

The Delaware was built in 1886 at the height of Leadville's mining prosperity. The Victorian style edifice has lost much of its glamour over the years and is far from the luxury category that many of these restored properties strive for. But, then again, look at the prices! The three story building has no elevator. There are a half dozen two-bedroom units. All of the rooms are a little on the small side. The traditional furnishings are nice but somehow don't feel authentic enough. Recreation is limited to a hot tub. The hotel has a gift shop. Restaurants are located nearby.

Inexpensive
    TIMBERLINE MOTEL, *216 Harrison Avenue. Tel. 719/486-1876; Fax 719/486-9462. Toll free reservations 800/352-1876. 15 Rooms. Rates: $543-88; family units for $80-127. Most major credit cards accepted. Located in the center of town on the main street.*

    This is the only modern accommodation in the historic center of Leadville. It is quite convenient as you can walk to just about every important attraction in town. The rooms are little more than basic in size and furnishings and amenities are limited, with in-room coffee being about the most upscale feature you'll find. Family units can accommodate up to six persons and are a real bargain. If you're looking for clean and comfortable lodgings at an affordable price, then the Timberline will do nicely. For an experience, try somewhere else.

STEAMBOAT SPRINGS
Very Expensive
    BEST WESTERN PTARMIGAN INN, *2304 Apres Ski Way. Tel. 970/879-1730; Fax 970/879-6044. Toll free reservations 800/538-7519 or 800/528-1234. 77 Rooms. Rates: High season (winter): $169-235; Low season (summer): $75-195. Closed mid-April to late May. Major credit cards accepted. Located about three miles northeast of town via US 40 to Mt. Werner Road and then Apres Ski Way.*

    Rather lofty prices for a Best Western family member but that is to be expected in high priced ski country. At least you will get a beautiful facility that is better than the norm for this chain. Located at the base of the Silver Bullet ski gondola, the four story Ptarmigan is an attractive building but perhaps its snow-white exterior makes it blend in too much with the surroundings during the winter. Inside it has a spacious and pretty lobby dominated by a warm fireplace. The rooms are spacious and attractively decorated. All feature coffee makers while some have refrigerators and air conditioning.

    The Ptarmigan has direct ski-in and ski-out along with a well stocked ski shop. The Snowbird Restaurant has good food at moderate prices and an adjacent cocktail lounge. It also has a small heated swimming pool, hot tub and sauna as well as a playground. There is a three night minimum stay during the ski season. Area transportation within four miles is provided free of charge.

SHERATON STEAMBOAT RESORT, *Mount Werner Road. Tel. 970/ 879-2220; Fax 970/879-7686. Toll free reservations 800/848-8878; www.steamboat-sheraton.com. 273 Rooms. Rates: High season (mid-October to late May): $99-369 with the lower range in the fall season; Low season (late May to mid-October): $79-249. Closed mid-April to late May and mid-October to late November. Major credit cards accepted. Located at the ski area, 2-1/4 miles east on US 40 from town and then a mile north on Mt. Werner Road.*

Steamboat's largest hotel is also the only one that is a complete resort destination. The eight story high building is an undistinguished modern block style but the interior and grounds are much more attractive. However, the best part of the Sheraton are the excellent accommodations. Each large room is beautifully furnished and has a private balcony that affords wonderful views of either the mountain slope, valley or village of Steamboat Springs. There are many amenities including coffee maker, iron with ironing board and hair dryer. Every room is also equipped with a humidifier which can be more important than you might expect in the often dry mountain air.

Public facilities are also varied and extensive. For dining you can choose from a full service restaurant or more casual coffee shop. The Sunday brunch in the restaurant is outstanding. A cocktail lounge offers live entertainment during the winter. I especially like the on-premises bakery shop where you can indulge yourself in fresh and savory baked goods. On the recreational side there is a heated swimming pool, sauna, steamroom, whirlpool and complete exercise facility as well as four tennis courts and a gorgeous and challenging 18-hole golf course designed by the famous Robert Trent Jones. Massage service is also available. The Sheraton offers child care as well as a supervised children's program.

Expensive

THE INN AT STEAMBOAT, *3070 Columbine Drive. Tel. 970/879-2600; Fax 970/879-9270. Toll free reservations 800/872-2601. 32 Rooms. Rates: From $129-189 including full breakfast depending upon exact dates except from April 1st to mid-December when it is $69-97 including Continental breakfast. It is closed for periods during April, May and November. American Express, Discover, MasterCard and VISA accepted. Located about 3-1/2 miles east of town via US 40, north on Walton Creek Road and then Columbine.*

Quite large for a B&B type facility, the Inn at Steamboat is a warm and gracious facility with Alpine style architecture and charm. All of the large rooms have spectacular views of either the Majestic Mountains or Yampa Valley. The accommodations are pretty and feature warm and comfortable furnishings and accessories. You get nightly turndown service and, of course, a mint on your plump pillow. There is also a heated outdoor swimming pool, sauna, game room and bar. Free area transportation is provided during the winter. Multi-night stays are also required during the ski season. The breakfast is more than adequate but perhaps a little below the sumptuous level found at many B&B's.

Moderate
THE ALPINER LODGE, *424 Lincoln Avenue. Tel. 970/879-1430; Fax 970/879-0054. Toll free reservations 800/538-7519. 32 Rooms. Rates: High season (mid-December to March 31st): $87-140; Low season (April 1st to mid-December): $55-75. Major credit cards accepted. Located downtown on US 40.*

Good lodging at affordable prices are hard to come by in Steamboat Springs but this nice little motel fits the bill extremely well. The colorful Tyrolean inspired chalet style building fronts the main street in downtown Steamboat Springs and is well located for restaurants and shopping. The guest rooms are fairly spacious and the furnishings pretty well keep with the Alpine theme although they're a little more on the modern style than the architecture of the building would suggest. All rooms have coffee makers.

There is a multi-night stay required during the winter and free area transportation is provided during the ski season. Although the Alpiner doesn't have a swimming pool or Jacuzzi it is only one block from the municipal hot springs pool.

SUMMIT COUNTY
Breckenridge, Copper Mountain, Dillon, Frisco & Keystone
All of the accommodations in this section are accessible during the winter season via the Summit County Stage bus transportation system.

Very Expensive
ALLAIRE TIMBERS INN, *Colorado Highway 9, Breckenridge. Tel. 970/453-7530; Fax 970/453-8699. Toll free reservations 800/624-4904; www.allairetimbers.com. 10 Rooms. Rates: High season (late November through March): $170-300; Low season (April 1st through late November): $130-230, all rates including full breakfast. Closed late April to late May and mid-October to mid-November. American Express, Discover, MasterCard and VISA accepted. Located a half mile south of town on the main road.*

A pretty little Bed & Breakfast built of native Colorado wood with excellent mountain views. All of the charming units are lovingly furnished and feature a private balcony. Some rooms have whirlpool tubs and gas fireplace. If your room doesn't have its own whirlpool there is one for general use. The inn has a number of decks from which you can also admire the surrounding scenery. An excellent breakfast is served each morning and refreshments are provided in the afternoon. The inn imposes age restrictions so inquire if you are going to be traveling with children. There is also a two night minimum stay on weekends.

COPPER MOUNTAIN RESORT, *Copper Mountain. Tel. 970/968-2882; Fax 970/968-2733. Toll free reservations 800/458-8386; www.ski-copper.com. E-mail: wc@ski-copper.com. 525 Rooms. Rates: High season (early November through March 31st): $195-350; Low season (April 1st to early November): $120-175. American Express, MasterCard and VISA accepted. Located off of I-70, Exit 195.*

The Copper Mountain Resort is a self-contained full service resort community in an imposing setting in a narrow river valley right off of one of the most scenic portions of the Interstate highway. This establishment, like many other resort facilities in the Summit County resort corridor, was built from the ground up with the primary purpose of providing everything a skier could want. As such it is composed of many different buildings in a village like setting rather than having all of the facilities under one roof.

Most rooms are, however, contained in the seven-story high main building and feature spacious accommodations with many luxury amenities, among them being coffee makers and a humidifier. Almost two-thirds of the units have kitchens and many feature Jacuzzi tubs. A large number of two bedroom units are also available.

There are no fewer than eight restaurans within the village to choose from including three cafeterias for those who've busted their budget on the rooms. There is also a cocktail lounge that sometimes offers live entertainment. Besides skiing there's a host of year round recreational opportunities to keep you busy. These include a heated indoor swimming pool, full service health club with sauna and whirlpool, eight tennis courts (two indoor), racquetball and horseback riding. Other options available according to the time of year are exploring the more than 45 miles of bike trails (bicycle rentals are available), nature trails, an 18-hole championship golf course, sleigh rides, river rafting, fishing, paddleboats and skating. Copper Mountain staff will also arrange for area tours, and they conduct a large number of social programs. There is professional child care, children's activity program and a playground so the little ones can be kept just as busy as you.

Expensive

GALENA STREET MOUNTAIN INN, *106 Galena Street, Frisco. Tel. 970/668-5607; Fax 970/668-1569. Toll free reservations 800/248-9138. 15 Rooms. Rates: High season (mid-December to mid-April): $105-170 including full breakfast; Low season (mid-April to mid-December): $95-150 including Continental breakfast. Most major credit cards accepted. Located about a mile east of I-70, Exit 201 to 1st street and then north.*

Galena is an attractive B&B built and furnished in neo-mission style. The comfortable rooms are made extra cheerful with pretty and colorful natural fabrics. The most distinctive feature of the large units are the extra tall windows that feature a window seat offering a great place to view the magnificent mountain scenery that surrounds Frisco.

The spacious common areas of the Galena Street Mountain Inn are the scene for both the bountiful breakfast and an afternoon tea service. On premise facilities include whirlpool and sauna. A number of restaurants are located within a short distance.

KEYSTONE LODGE, *Keystone. Tel. 970/468-2316; Fax 970/468-4260. Toll free reservations 800/842-8072; www.keystoneresort.com. 152 Rooms. Rates: High season (summer and winter): $180-275; Low season (spring and fall): $130-187. Major credit cards accepted. Located on US 6 approximately six miles east of I-70, Exit 205.*

A resort hotel that's a village and a village that's a hotel....that's Keystone, a unique full service facility located in one of the most beautiful Rocky Mountain settings that you can find. The modern accommodations are large and comfortable. There are more than a dozen restaurants covering a wide range of cuisines and styles, including a mountain top beer *stube*. Two restaurants are more fully described in the *Where to Eat* section.

Despite the luxurious surroundings and the fine dining, visitors to Keystone are often there to take advantage of the varied recreational activities that are available at any time of the year. And the lodge emphasizes recreation. The list includes swimming pool, sauna, steamroom, Jacuzzi, fitness center, tennis, golf, horseback riding, boating and biking. Keystone even has its own hot air balloon so you can get a bird's eye view of the Rockies!

Selected as one of my Best Places to Stay (see Chapter 10 for details).

THE LODGE AT BRECKENRIDGE, *112 Overlook Drive, Breckenridge. Tel. 970/453-9300; Fax 970/453-0625. 45 Rooms. Rates: High season (winter): $165-400; Low season (summer): $105-200, including full breakfast. Most major credit cards accepted. Located off of Colorado Highway 9.*

The Lodge is a small hotel built in a rustic style. It has excellent mountain views from just abou any part of the property. The rooms are fairly modest in size but attractive, comfortable, and well kept. Facilities include a quiet little restaurant, swimming pool, health club and small spa.

Moderate

DILLON INN, *708 Anemone Trail, Dillon. Tel. 970/262-0801; Fax 970/262-0803. Toll free reservations 800/262-0801. 30 Rooms. Rates: $70-130 all year but in the higher range except for spring and fall, including Continental breakfast. American Express, Discover, MasterCard and VISA accepted. Located a half mile south of I-70, Exit 205 via US 6 to Anemone Trail.*

There aren't that many of what I would term "normal" motels in the Summit County resort corridor and the ones that do exist are, for the most part, ridiculously overpriced. The Dillon Inn is a rare exception and offers a decent alternative for the budget traveler. This is probably even more so in the non-skiing season when you don't have to have the convenience of being right near the slopes. The Dillon Inn features contemporary decor in what is an average motel. Facilities include an indoor swimming pool, sauna and whirlpool. There is also a bike path that runs right by the inn. Several restaurants are located within a short distance.

VAIL/BEAVER CREEK

Uh, oh, it's time to apologize again for those on limited budgets. If you thought Aspen was high, wait to you take a look at these prices. Again, there are some decent rates to be found if you're coming in summer. Also, most Vail accommodations have multi-bedroom units which can save you some bucks if you're traveling with another family. A few hotels listed in the chain accommodations section earlier in the book are represented in the Vail/Avon/Beaver Creek vicinity. They're usually expensive, too, but a few are moderate. Most rates are broken down by winter and summer only since the rates can vary quite widely within a given season and change often.

Very Expensive

ANTLERS AT VAIL, *680 W. Lionshead Place, Vail. Tel. 970/476-2471; Fax 970/476-4146. Toll free reservations 800/843-8245; www.antlersvail.com. 68 Rooms. Rates: High season (mid-November through mid-April): $225-410; multi-bedroom units from $255-785; Low season (mid-April to mid-November): $125-160; multi-bedroom units from $150-240. Major credit cards accepted. Located a half mile west of I-70, Exit 176 at the Lionshead ski area.*

Several of the recommended lodging spots in Vail are of the condominium hotel variety and this is one of them. The seven story building looks like a modern apartment building and isn't particularly impressive but its location at the base of Vail Mountain about 500 feet from the gondola is. Rooms facing the slope have a clear look at skiers coming down what appears to be a giant white chute in the middle of rows of trees. The summer scene turns the chute to a light shade of green that contrasts with the darker trees. Views of the stream that runs through Vail are also nice. The units are spacious and vary from studio to three bedroom. There are also some nice loft units. All units feature a big balcony, gas fireplace, full kitchen with coffee maker and microwave oven, and video cassette player (video rental library on premises). There is no restaurant but many are located within close proximity. Area transportation is provided.

EVERGREEN LODGE, *250 S. Frontage Road W., Vail. Tel. 970/476-7810; Fax 970/476-4504. Toll free reservations 800/284-8245. E-mail: evergreen@vail.net. 128 Rooms. Rates: High season (winter): $190-280 rooms/ $550-900 multi-bedroom; Low season (summer): $89-180 rooms/$175-275 multi-bedroom. Major credit cards accepted. Located on the I-70 frontage road, about a quarter mile west of Exit 176.*

This one also looks like an apartment building but is more attractive than the Antlers because of its nice beige color and more interesting step architecture–each section of the building is of a differing height. The Evergreen has both hotel and condominium units. All of the ovesized rooms have a refrigerator. There is an outdoor heated swimming pool, sauna and whirlpool. The Cafe Colorado is a good restaurant. The Altitude Billiards and Sports Club has entertainment during the ski season. Even when it doesn't it's still a popular place in Vail because of its 13 big screen televisions and six pool tables. Also on the premises is a ski and bike shop. The Evergreen offers bike rentals and massage.

HYATT REGENCY AT BEAVER CREEK, *136 E. Thomas Place, Beaver Creek. Tel. 970/949-1234; Fax 970/949-4164. Toll free reservations 800/233-1234; www.hyatt.com. 295 Rooms. Rates: High season (winter): $240-650 plus suites at higher prices; Low season (summer): $205-520 plus suites at higher prices. Closed during most of the first half of November. Major credit cards accepted. Located three miles south of I-70, Exit 167 via Avon and Village Roads.*

An exceptionally beautiful full service resort, the Hyatt at Beaver Creek displays a number of architectural styles in a harmonious blend that is quite appealing to the eye. The mostly modern exterior facade is topped by several peaked roofs and large picture windows that are more reminiscent of a small ski chalet. At the base of Beaver Creek's ski slopes, it is one of many Vail area resorts with ski-in and ski-out facilities.

The deluxe rooms and suites are among the most luxurious of any ski resort and many rooms boast excellent mountain or valley views. Some rooms face the hotel's attractive courtyard and only have partial views of the surrounding area. Furnishings are modern but plush. All rooms feature mini-bar and many have microwave ovens and/or refrigerators.

Public facilities at the Hyatt are equally first class. For dining you can choose from the lovely Patina Restaurant (dining on he terrace in summer) or a more casual deli style eatery. There is an attractive lobby lounge with entertainment. During the ski season an additional restaurant and lounge are open. Recreational facilities include heated indoor and outdoor swimming pools, a huge spa facility with sauna, steamroom and whirlpool; completely equipped health club, and an 18-hole seasonally open golf course. Other pursuits, many of which are seasonal by nature, are fishing, skating, tobagganing, snowmobiling, horseback riding, and bicycling (rentals available). Skiing, of course, is right outside the door. The Hyatt has a children's program and a playground.

LION SQUARE LODGE & CONFERENCE CENTER, *660 W. Lionshead Place, Vail. Tel. 970/476-2281; Fax 970/476-7425. Toll free reservations 800/525-5788; www.lionsquare.com. 118 Rooms. Rates: High season (winter): $155-580; multi-bedroom units from $525-1550; Low season (summer): $79-145; multi-bedroom units from $155-270. Most major credit cards accepted. Located a half mile west of I-70, Exit 176 at the Lionshead ski area.*

The Lion Square consists of one to three bedroom condominium units as well as 28 hotel rooms in the main lodge building. Located adjacent to a ski run gondola and express lift, the several attached buildings of the lodge are pleasantly arranged in a clustered setting that has the charm of an alpine village (although the architectural style may be a little too modern to support that claim). It has ski-in and ski-out facilities. Spacious accommodations feature in-room refrigerators. Some rooms have full kitchens, balcony and fireplace. The K B Ranch Restaurant & Lounge is a nice place to take your meals or have a nightcap before returning to your room for the evening. The recreational side of the ledger shows an outdoor swimming pool, Jacuzzi and sauna.

LODGE TOWER, *200 Vail Road, Vail. Tel. 970/476-9550; Fax 970/476-4095. Toll free reservations 800/654-2517. 80 Rooms. Rates: High season (winter): $255-285 rooms/$460-1,000 multi-bedroom; Low season (summer): $89-139 rooms/$199-450 multi-bedroom, all rates including Continental breakfast. Most major credit cards accepted. Located adjacent to the lifts at the base of Vail Mountain.*

The nine story Tower is one of the tallest lodging establishments in Vail and rooms on the top floors have excellent views. The diverse units range from hotel style to studio to condominium apartments with from one to three bedrooms. All units are quite large and nicely furnished in a modern style. Kitchens, refrigerators, balconies and fireplaces are among the features in some rooms. The Lodge Tower's only recreational amenity is a Jacuzzi. Restaurants are located close by.

Expensive

THE CHARTER AT BEAVER CREEK, *120 Offerson Road, Beaver Creek. Tel. 970/949-6660; Fax 970/949-6709. Toll free reservations 800/525-6660; www.thecharter.com. 180 Rooms. Rates: High season (late November through April): $120-175 for standard rooms and $175-425 for multi-room units; Low season (Late May through mid-November): $100-140 for standard rooms and $140-280 for multi-room units. Closed in early May. Major credit cards accepted. Located three miles south of I-70, Exit 167 via Avon and Village Roads.*

This is another one of those combination hotel/condominium resorts that are so popular in the Vail area and other ski resorts throughout Colorado. If you've wondered why, it's because many winter visitors either stay a fairly long amount of time or come with friends on a ski trip. The hotel units in the main lodge represent about a third of the total units and all have washer and dryer and ironing board while many have kitchens. Sounds like they expect you to do a lot of housework! Some units have fireplaces and a few have balconies with nice views. The condominium units range from one to five bedrooms and all have fireplace, balcony or patio and full kitchen facilities. The decor is tasteful and all the units are spacious.

The facilities of Charter are extensive and include two heated swimming pools, whirlpool and playground. The Spa Struck is a complete health club with sauna, steamroom and more. The Charter boasts ski-in and ski-out facilities, gift shop and concierge service. When it comes time to eat you can choose from the TraMonti Restaurant serving well prepared Italian cuisine, or the more family-oriented Pacific Ranch. The latter has a good variety of entrees although the emphasis is on Chinese.

MARRIOTT'S MOUNTAIN RESORT AT VAIL, *715 W. Lionshead Circle, Vail. Tel. 970/476-4444; Fax 970/476-1647. Toll free reservations 800/648-0720. 349 Rooms. Rates: High season (winter): $110-389; multi-bedroom units from $399-1200; Low season (summer): $85-250; multi-bedroom units from $225-275. Major credit cards accepted. Located less than a half mile from I-70, Exit 176 almost adjacent to ski gondola.*

One of Vail's largest and most luxurious properties, the Marriott is a cluster of attractive mid-rise buildings at the base of the mountain. Big rooms seem to be the rule in Vail and this hotel conforms to that general standard. The rooms are quite attractive and have a fresh feel. In-room refrigerators are standard. Many units feature fireplaces and some have full kitchen facilities. A large fire in late November 2000 seriously damaged one building so that capacity will be limited throughout the year 2001.

For dining you can sample the good fare at the Mountain Grille. Their breakfast buffet is absolutely the best in town. Lunch and dinner are casually elegant. The Avalanche Pub is open year round but has entertainment only during the ski season. The extensive recreational facilities include both indoor and outdoor swimming pools, spa with Jacuzzi and sauna, and a full service exercise room.

SITZMARK LODGE, *183 Gore Creek Drive, Vail. Tel. 970/476-5001; Fax 970/476-8702; www.sitzmarklodge.com. 35 Rooms. Rates: High season (mid-December to late April): $135-270 including Continental beakfast; Low season (May to mid-December): $70-105. Discover, MasterCard and VISA accepted. Located in the center of Vail village, south via Vail Road from I-70, Exit 176.*

The Sitzmark is a small, warm and friendly establishment that is also more affordable than most of the bigger resorts. As such it is a good alternative, especially for summer visitors who don't need to be near the slopes. The Tyrol theme carries well beyond the name and Austrian eagle logo that's emblazoned on the front wall of the building. Set against a mountain backdrop, the alpine village architecture is a pleasant change from the cookie-cutter modernity of many of Vail's better resorts. Then again the Alpine style is much more in evidence in town than in the slopeside lodging establishments.

The attractive and comfortable guest rooms all have balconies that overlook either pretty Gore Creek or the pedestrian mall in front of the hotel. Other standard amenities are humidifier and refrigerator. Some rooms have fireplaces and efficiency kitchens. A small restaurant is open except during the spring and fall seasons. The **Left Bank** bar and lounge is one of Vail's more popular establishments. Coffee, tea and hot chocolate are always served free of charge in the lobby. For recreation you try out the heated swimming pool, sauna or whirlpool. The Sitzmark has underground parking.

CAMPING & RV SITES

For camping in the **Arapaho National Forest** contact the U.S. Forest Service reservations number, *Tel. 800/280-CAMP.*

- **Blue Arrow RV Park & Campground**, *1665 Highway 66, Estes Park. Tel. 800/582-5342*
- **Elk Creek Campground & RV Park**, *143 Highway 48, Grand Lake. Tel. 970/627-8502*
- **Estes Park KOA Campground**, *2051 Big Thompson Ave., Estes Park. Tel. 800/562-1887*
- **Leadville RV Corral**, *135 W. 2nd Street, Leadville. Tel. 719/486-3111*
- **Paradise RV & Travel Park**, *1836 Highway 66, Estes Park. Tel. 970/586-5513*
- **River Pines RV Park**, *12082 US Highway 34, Grand Lake. Tel. 800/793-0835*

- **Rocky Mountain National Park**: Open all year: Moraine Park Campground; Longs Peak Campground; Tiamber Peek Campground. Summer only: Aspenglen Campground; Glacier Basin Campground. For these parks, call *Tel. 970/586-1206 for information; for reservations, contact Destinet at Tel. 800/365-2267.* At press time it was reported that the National Park Service would not be renewing its campground reservation contract with Destinet. If so, contact the park headquarters for information regarding the new campground concessionnaire.
- **Steamboat Springs KOA Campground**, *29135 West US Highway 40, Steamboat Springs. Tel. 970/879-0273*
- **Sugar Loafin' Campground**, *2665 County Road, Leadville. Tel. 719/486-1031*
- **Tiger Run RV Resort**, *Breckenridge. Tel. 970/453-9690*
- **Winding River Resort Village**, *1447 Highway 491, Grand Lake. Tel. 800/282-5121*

WHERE TO EAT
ASPEN
Very Expensive

PINE CREEK COOKHOUSE, *off Castle Creek Rd. in Ashcroft, near Aspen. Tel. 970/925-1044. American Express, MasterCard, and VISA accepted. Open daily during summer and winter only for lunch and dinner. Reservations required.*

Guests at the Pine Creek Cookhouse are in for a unique and charming dining experience. The historic building with its glowing fireplace sits tranquilly in an unspoiled setting amid the beauty of the Elk Mountain Range and the Ashcroft Valley. Weather permitting, lunch is served out on the deck. Summer diners can reach the Cookhouse from Aspen via Castle Creek Road. The restaurant is about 1-1/2 miles north of the Ashcroft ghost town. During the winter, you can only reach the restaurant by cross-country skiing (guided by staff carrying old miner's lamps) or by a romantic sleigh ride from Aspen pulled by two elegant Percheron draft horses. Hot drinks await you upon your arrival.

Executive chef Kurt Boucher prepares exquisite menus summer or winter. Prix-fixe winter dinners ($65 if you've skied in or $80 if you've come by their sleigh) are a multi-course affair with entrees like sauteed elk tenderloin, yellowfin ahi, or quail in lingonberry kumquat port wine sauce. Excellent wine list, cocktails. Summer prices feature several entrees in the expensive category.

PINONS, *105 South Mill Street. Tel. 970/920-2021. American Express, MasterCard and VISA accepted. Dinner served nightly. Reservations are suggested. Closed April to mid-June and October to November. Smoke free premises.*

This is one of the most attractive western themed restaurant decors you're likely to encounter. A ranch atmosphere prevails in this high class eatery that features imaginative western cuisine. Wild game dishes are the real stars with such specialties as pheasant quesadilla waiting to entice your taste buds. They have a good selection of other game dishes as well as fish and seafood. Fresh lobster is usually available. Many entrees are mesquite grilled to perfection. Despite the high prices and excellent service, Pinions maintains a casual atmosphere. Cocktails are served tableside or in the separate lounge.

THE RESTAURANT, *675 E. Durant Avenue, in the Little Nell Hotel. Tel. 970/920-6330. Major credit cards accepted. Breakfast, lunch and dinner served daily; Sunday brunch. Smoke free premises. Reservations are suggested.*

The restaurant prices in Aspen, unfortunately, match the hotel rates but in the case of "The Restaurant" it's worth the cost of admission. Featuring what the chefs term as "American Alpine cooking," the delicious meat and fish dishes are enhanced by the use of herbs and spices indiginous to Colorado. Even the soups and salads are something special here. And the surroundings are elegant without being overbearing. A light and airy dining room, The Restaurant has fine provincial furniture and French style doors in beautiful light-wood shades. Rich linens and fine tableware are also in evidence. During the warmer weather you can dine outside in the delightful courtyard with its fragrant trees and flowers and in full view of the magnificent mountain slopes.

The service is everything you would expect from a luxury restaurant but the attentive staff manages to combine friendliness with their expertiese. Cocktails are available tableside or in the separate lounge. Children's menu.

Expensive

THE CHART HOUSE, *219 E. Durant Avenue. Tel. 970/925-3525. Most major credit cards accepted. Dinner served nightly. Smoking in lounge only. Reservations are suggested.*

An excellent restaurant featuring prime rib and seafood, the Chart House has a rustic atmosphere enhanced by aromatic woods. They also have a superior salad bar. Cocktail service and lounge. Children's menu.

Moderate

THE INN AT ASPEN DINING ROOM, *38750 Colorado Highway 82, in the Inn at Aspen. Tel. 970/925-1500. Most major credit cards accepted. Breakfast, lunch and dinner served daily. Closed early April through end of May).*

Decent selection of American and Continental dishes served in an attractive atmosphere by a competent staff. It's main claim to listing here, though, is the scarcity of good restaurants in the moderate price range. Cocktail service.

BOULDER

Very Expensive

THE BOULDER BROKER INN RESTAURANT, *555 30th Street in the Boulder Broker Inn. Tel. 303/449-1752. Major credit cards accepted. Breakfast and dinner served daily; lunch Monday to Friday; Sunday brunch. Reservations are suggested.*

For an old west atmosphere and dining experience it's hard to find anything but good things to say about this restaurant. Fresh seafood and juicy, tender steaks are the main menu attractions and all dinners are accompanied by the Broker Inn's famous complimentary bowl of Gulf Shrimp. Equally famous among the locals is the fabulous champagne brunch and the sumptuous lunch that consists of, among other things, a great soup, salad and dessert bar. Cocktail service and separate lounge with dancing. Children's menu.

Expensive

THE FANCY MOOSE, *1345 28th Street, in the Regal Harvest House. Tel. 303/545-6485. Major credit cards accepted. Breakfast, lunch and dinner served daily; Sunday brunch in lieu of breakfast.*

One of the most delightful places to have dinner that you'll find in Boulder, throughout Colorado, or anywhere for that matter. The Fancy Moose is casual elegance at its best. You can be served in the beautiful mountain lodge inspired dining room but it's even better to eat outside on the fabulous heated dining terrace that has a wonderful little garden and a waterfall, all enhanced by the pleasant sounds of Boulder Creek. Enjoy a sumptuous feast of Rocky Mountain style entrees including certified Angus beef, trout or one of several wild game dishes. Even the vegetables are authentic Colorado fresh. The desserts are equally satisfying and best enjoyed by the open-pit fire with the Moose's top-notch cappuccino. Cocktail service.

FLAGSTAFF HOUSE RESTAURANT, *1138 Flagstaff Road. Tel. 303/442-4640. Major credit cards accepted. Dinner served nightly. Reservations are required. Dress code.*

This is one of the finest dining establishments in a city of fine restaurants. Be advised at the outset that several entrees are priced in the Very Expensive category. The restaurant first opened way back in 1930 but it has been under the talented direction of the Monette family since 1971. It consistently is an award winner. The contemporary New American cuisine menu showcases a variety of excellent entrees with the star usually being a wild game dish. However, the fresh fish is also wonderfully prepared. There are even several vegetarian selections to choose from.

When it comes time for a drink there is full table side cocktail service and a separate lounge but the Flagstaff is best known for its outstanding collection of wines. In fact, there are more than two thousand different kinds so you might want to ask for the sommelier to make a suggestion or two. The service is semi-formal but not so stuffy as to turn off people who don't like that sort of wait staff. During the summer it's delightful to dine out on the patio with the majestic mountains seemingly at the edge of your plate.

JW'S STEAKHOUSE, *2660 Canyon Boulevard, in the Boulder Marriott Hotel. Tel. 303/440-8877. Major credit cards accepted. Breakfast, lunch and dinner served daily.*

A steakhouse with exceptional flair, JW's offers great food in an attractive setting and fine service. There are many unusual dishes. For starters try the escargot in butter sauce or grilled jumbo shrimp in herb butter. Then go on to a main course of beef steaks, prime rib or salmon, all prepared with the chef's special sauces such as Madeira herb, papaya relish or peppercorn crust. Fabulous desserts served with a variety of espresso are the final touch to a satisfying dinner. Be sure to try one of the draft beers or great margaritas. Tableside cocktail service and full bar.

Q'S RESTAURANT, *2115 13th Street, in the Hotel Boulderado. Tel. 303/ 442-4880. Major credit cards accepted. Dinner served nightly. Reservations are suggested.*

I can't explain the reason for the abundance of fantastic restaurants in Boulder, but here's another one for you. This award winner has an atmosphere of casual elegance and fine service by a warm and friendly staff. Owner and chef John Platt has created a wonderful menu that changes each month (not just the main courses but even appetizers and desserts) so you never know exactly what to expect–but it'll always be delicious! Among the things you might see are grilled asparagus or lobster stuffed potato for an appetizer; roasted pheasant breast, fontina and prosciutto stuffed pork loin, or chile crusted trout with spinach for the main course; and fine pastries or rich home made ice creams for dessert. All of the bountiful salads are made with organically grown greens from the area around Boulder. Q's also features an excellent wine list. Cocktail service and lounge.

Moderate

ANTICA ROMA, *1308 Pearl Street. Tel. 303/442-0378. Most major credit cards accepted. Lunch and dinner served daily.*

An authentic trattoria with fine Italian cuisine in a delightful setting on the Pearl Street Mall that has the look and feel of a Roman piazza. From pizza to saltimbocca, from lasagna or ravioli to fiorentina alla griglia, and from veal to seafood, the large menu has the simplest and most complex of Italian cooking. You can also dine outside on the pleasant patio. For dessert try the incomparable tiramisu. Antica Roma features almost two hundred diffeent Italian wines and a large an attractive bar.

ATTUSSO'S ITALIAN CAFE OF BROOKLYN, *1739 Pearl Street. Tel. 303/442-2262. Major credit cards accepted. Dinner served nightly. Reservations are suggested.*

With a name like that how can it be bad? Oops, sorry—my Brooklyn origins are showing. Seriously, though, this is like a bit of Little Italy with its varied menu of two dozen New York style Italian entrees including perennial favorites like shrimp fra diavolo, eggplant parmigiana, veal picatta, and manicotti. The desserts are also delicious and make generous use of spirits and liqueurs. The atmosphere is casual and inviting and the service friendly, knowledgable and efficient. Attusco's also has outdoor dining on the patio. Cocktail service.

THE BOULDER CORK, *3295 30th Street. Tel. 303/443-9505. Major credit cards accepted. Lunch served Monday through Friday; dinner served nightly.*

The Boulder Cork is another excellent steakhouse (Boulder's oldest) that also features a number of delicious southwestern dishes like chicken enchiladas and stuffed chillies. Lighter meals as well as many pasta dishes and sandwiches can be ordered at the bar. They also have an excellent wine list which has received several awards.

DANDELION RESTAURANT, *1011 Walnut Street. Tel. 303/443-6700. Most major credit cards accepted. Lunch served Monday through Friday; dinner served nightly; weekend brunch.*

Relatively new to the Boulder restaurant scene, the Dandelion has a team of chefs that have received national recognition. The cuisine is contemporary American and specializes in lighter fare and fresh fish and seafood. Gourmet's seem to be especially fond of the food although I don't consider it to be as great as many fine food "experts" seem to think. The patio seating area has wonderful views of the Flatiron Mountains. Pleasant atmosphere and good service but more of a romantic dining experience than a family style one. Cocktail service.

LA ESTRELLITA, *1718 Broadway. Tel. 303/939-8822. Most major credit cards accepted. Lunch and dinner served daily.*

La Estrellita is considered to be one of the top Mexican restaurants in the United States by people who should know—in this case, *Hispanic Magazine*. The attractive dining room is supplemented by an outdoor patio along Boulder Creek. Classic Mexican fare such as stuffed sopapillas and a variety of fajitas headlines the menu but you can also choose from a number of vegetarian dishes. The chef comes up with imaginative specials on Friday evenings. Cocktail service and separate bar.

THE MEDITERRANEAN, *1002 Walnut Street. Tel. 303/444-5335. American Express, MasterCard and VISA accepted. Lunch served daily except Sunday; dinner served nightly.*

It's almost standard for a Boulder restaurant to have an outdoor patio and this one is no exception. It's made even prettier by the large central fountain. The charming interior decor is reminiscent of the sunny Mediterranean region. The cuisine of the Mediterranean is well represented by such popular items as authentic Spanish tapas and pizza from wood burning ovens as well as more substantial fare like salmon Costa Brava, paella Valenicia and lamb kabobs. Guests can enhance their already delicious meal by choosing from a list of about 140 different wines and many beers in addition to full cocktail service. The Mediterranean has a separate lounge.

OASIS BREWERY, *1095 Canyon Boulevard. Tel. 303/449-0363. American Express, MasterCard and VISA accepted. Lunch served Monday through Saturday; dinner served nightly; Sunday brunch.*

The biggest brew pub in Boulder, the Oasis features two separate bars, pool tables upstairs from the main restaurant, and a patio with excellent mountain views. In addition to their great ales the kitchen produces light fare such as salads, seafood, pasta and pizza and for the hungrier diner there's steak and southwestern cuisine. And what would a pub be without fish 'n chips? Well, Oasis has that too. For dessert I highly recommend their outstanding mud pie.

Inexpensive

MAMA'S CHICKEN SOUP AND MORE, *2111 30th Street. Tel. 303/413-9343. American Express, MasterCard and VISA accepted. Breakfast, lunch and dinner served daily except Sunday.*

With a name and chief product like Mama's Chicken Soup, need I say more? Another indoor and outdoor dining spot, Mama's features six homemade soups each day. While most of the main courses are simple traditional favorites prepared extremely well (e.g., meatloaf), you can also order some fancier fare, especially for appetizers. The sauteed mushroom caps fall into that category. Homemade pies and cakes are featured for dessert. A friendly family restaurant that everyone can enjoy. Carry-out service available.

NEW WORLD CAFE, *6325 Arapahoe Road. Tel. 303/449-9158. American Express, MasterCard and VISA accepted. Breakfast and lunch served Monday through Friday.*

A small and cozy restaurant that features a big variety of freshly baked goods and gourmet deli style sandwiches. Gourmet coffees and many specialty teas are also hallmarks of the New World Cafe. Take out service.

CRESTED BUTTE

Moderate

IDLESPUR, CRESTED BUTTE BREWERY AND PUB, *226 Elk Avenue. Tel. 970/349-5026. American Express, Discover, MasterCard and VISA accepted. Lunch and dinner served daily. Closed mid-April through late May.*

A western decorated restaurant with a menu to match. The log beamed dining room is filled with stuffed animals with faces as friendly as the efficient wait staff. There's also patio dining in season. Ribs and chicken are the primary culinary delights but there is an ample selection of Mexican dishes as well. Cocktail service and separate lounge. Children's menu. Live entertainment on most weekends.

ESTES PARK

Moderate

COWPOKE CAFE, *165 Virginia Avenue. Tel. 970/586-0234. Most major credit cards accepted. Breakfast, lunch and dinner served daily in summer; schedule varies during winter.*

This is a nice family restaurant with a western style dining room and wonderful views. The menu features a good variety of meat, chicken, fish and other dishes along with daily specials that are an excellent value. The Cowpoke also has a big salad bar. Cocktail service. Children's menu.

ED'S CANTINA, *362 E. Elkhorn Avenue. Tel. 970/586-4416. American Express, Discover, MasterCard and VISA accepted. Breakfast, lunch and dinner served daily. Reservations are suggested.*

Another good place for the whole family, Ed cooks up a big selection of both American and Mexican fare. On the light side they have great burgers and sandwiches. If you're more hungry then go for the barbecued ribs or broasted chicken. Don't overlook the decent salad bar. The service is fast, efficient and friendly. There is full cocktail service but I suggest you go either for Ed's very own microbrewed beer or the best margaritas in Estes Park.

GRUMPY GRINGO, *1560 Big Thompson Avenue. Tel. 970/586-7705. Most major credit cards accepted. Lunch and dinner served daily, except closed Monday from October through May. Reservations are suggested in summer.*

The gringo staff at this restaurant is anything but grumpy. A friendly atmosphere and sunny decor prevail at this reasonably priced Mexican restaurant. The views from their seasonal patio dining area are spectacular and the food is well prepared and authentic. The separate lounge is one of the nicest in town and is a great place for a pre-dinner drink.

THE OTHER SIDE RESTAURANT, *900 Moraine Avenue, National Park Village. Tel. 970/586-2171. Most major credit cards accepted. Breakfast, lunch and dinner served daily except lunch and dinner only on weekdays during the winter. Reservations are suggested.*

Whatever side of this restaurant you're on is the right side. Serving a variety of well prepared American fare such as prime rib, steaks and fresh trout, you can opt for the main dining room or the even more casual coffee shop. I prefer the dining room because of the nice view of a mountain lake through the oversized picture windows and the pleasingly rustic decor. Cocktail service and separate lounge. Children's menu.

GEORGETOWN
Moderate

THE RAM BAR & RESTAURANT, *606 6th Street. Tel. 303/569-3263. Most major credit cards accepted. Lunch and dinner served daily.*

A pleasant atmosphere and friendly service highlight this decent family style restaurant that offers a good selection of American dishes. Emphasis is on Colorado beef, game and fish. Cocktail service.

Inexpensive

THE HAPPY COOKER, *412 6th Street. Tel. 303/569-3166. Diners Club, Discover, MasterCard and VISA accepted. Breakfast and lunch served daily.*

I don't know—maybe I have a soft spot for restaurants with corny names, but this place really does cook up wonderful traditional American favorites without being fancy—just good. Located in a former Victorian style house dating back to the 1920's, the surroundings are delightful and the service is prompt, efficient and exceedingly friendly. Outdoor patio dining is available during the warmer months. Children's menu. Cocktail service. Since the Happy Cooker is open until 3 pm and on weekends until 5pm, it is possible to make this a place to have an early dinner. I do myself when I'm in Georgetown, because it's that good – especially considering the budget prices.

GRAND LAKE
Expensive

THE RAPIDS RESTAURANT, *201 Rapid Lane, in The Rapids Lodge. Tel. 970/627-3707. American Express, MasterCard and VISA accepted. Dinner served nightly. Closed in April, November and on Monday and Tuesday from after Labor Day through May.*

Occupying an historic 1902 log structure, the Rapids is a pleasant place to enjoy well prepared cuisine that is mostly Italian. However, you will find other items on the menu. There's a good selection of beef, fresh seafood and pasta. A tasty highlight is their shrimp appetizer tray—don't miss it. The restaurant overlooks a small but rushing river and the patio is the best place to enjoy the ambiance and natural surroundings. Cocktail service and separate lounge. The restaurant offers a children's menu.

Moderate

CAROLINE'S CUISINE, *9921 US Highway 34. Tel. 970/627-9404. American Express, Diners Club, MasterCard and VISA accepted. Dinner served nightly; Sunday brunch.*

Caroline's is a most attractive restaurant with country French decor highlighting each of several comfortable and cozy dining rooms. The menu features mainly Colorado beef prepared in both American and French styles but there is also fish and chicken. Patio dining is available during the warmer months. Full cocktail service and separate lounge. Children's menu.

LEADVILE

Moderate

LA CANTINA MEXICAN RESTAURANT, *1942 US Highway 24. Tel. 719/486-9021. MasterCard and VISA accepted. Lunch and dinner served nightly.*

Good and authentic regional Mexican cuisine served in a cheerful atmosphere by a friendly staff. Especially worth looking into are their homemade tamales and tortillas. The chili is among the best you'll find anywhere. It tends toward the hot side. Cocktail service. Children's menu.

PROSPECTOR RESTAURANT, *3 miles north of town on Colorado Highway 91. Tel. 719/486-3955. Most major credit cards accepted. Dinner served nightly except Monday. Smoke free premises.*

This is as close as you get to gourmet dining in laid back Leadville. The decor is based on the town's mining heritage and contains lots of turn of the century memorabilla in a traditional wooden cabin-like structure. Colorado beef, game and fish are featured. All are well prepared and graciously served by an attentive staff. Cocktail service and lounge.

WILD BILL'S RESTAURANT, *200 Harrison Avenue. Tel. 719/486-0533. Most major credit cards accepted. Lunch and dinner served nightly in summer. At other times it is best to call for hours.*

Although Leadville has numerous restaurants, none of them are anything particularly special. Wild Bill's is a typical example, included here because the western theme and menu are well suited to the frontier atmosphere that is Leadville. The menu includes a good selection of steaks, ribs, and chicken and the staff is friendly and efficient. Cocktail service and separate lounge.

Inexpensive

HOMESTEAD BAKERY & CAFE, *714 Harrison Avenue. Tel. 719/486-0284. No credit cards. Breakfast, lunch and dinner served daily. Smoke free premises.*

The Homestead has wonderful freshly baked goods such as pastries, muffins and bagels, homemade soups and humongous burgers along with a large selection of sandwiches. They also make their own coffe and serve excellent expresso. It's a delightful little place to have breakfast and lunch. Dinner is another matter because they don't serve full course meals. However, if you are in the mood for a smaller evening repast than it fits the bill for that too.

STEAMBOAT SPRINGS

Expensive

L'APOGEE, *911 Lincoln Avenue. Tel. 970/879-1919. American Express, MasterCard and VISA accepted. Dinner served nightly. Smoke free premises.*

An excellent restaurant for French cuisine as well as quite a few other Continental selections. There are two dining rooms, the main one being casually elegant and the other just plain casual. All the food is individually prepared by a knowledgable chef and graciously served by an attentive staff. L'Apogee has a large selection of quality wines. Full cocktail service tableside and in the separate lounge. Children's menu available.

Moderate

LA MONTANA, *Mount Werner Circle. Tel. 970/879-6976. American Express, Discover, MasterCard and VISA accepted. Dinner served nightly, except closed Sunday and Monday from early April through May and late September to mid-November. Reservations are suggested. Smoke free premises.*

For delicious southwestern cuisine it's hard to beat La Montana. Menu items range from authentic southwest to Tex-Mex but all are prepared from scratch with the freshest ingredients and the chef adds his own personal flair to each dish. It may well be the most popular restaurant in Steamboat with the locals, a sure indication of quality and value. The surroundings are pretty and during the summer you can dine outside on the patio in full view of the beautiful mountains that surround the town. Cocktail service and lounge. Children's menu.

SUMMIT COUNTY
Breckenridge, Dillon, Frisco & Keystone
Very Expensive

KEYSTONE RANCH RESTAURANT, *Keystone Ranch Golf Course, Keystone. Tel. 970/468-4386. Major credit cards accepted. Dinner served nightly. Reservations are suggested.*

An unusual gourmet dining experience but one that is, unfortunately, priced above what many travelers can afford (or will want to pay). For a fixed price of $60 (half that for children) you'll be served an outstanding six course dinner featuring American cuisine. Highest quality Colorado beef, game and fish are thoughtfully prepared and lovingly served by a knowledgable and courteous staff. Despite the elegance of the surroundings and the nature of the service the experience is a casual one, although not what I would term everyday "family dining" despite the existance of a children's menu.

The restaurant is located in an historical log home that has an aura of warmth, privacy and home. Excellent views of the mountains or the adjacent golf course can be had from just about any seat in the house. Cocktail service and lounge. The Keystone also has a relaxing living room area where you can chat (and smoke) before or after dinner.

Expensive

CAFE ALPINE, *106 E. Adams Avenue, Breckenridge. Tel. 970/453-8218. American Express, MasterCard and VISA accepted. Lunch and dinner served daily except dinner only in the spring and fall. Smoke free premises. Reservations are suggested.*

Although the price is a lot lower and the nature of the cuisine quite different from the Keystone, the Cafe Alpine provides one of the best dining experiences available in the Summit County resort corridor. Once a gracious 1880's manner home and now sitting in the midst of Breckenridge's historic district, the Alpine features the decor of a ski chalet. A glowing and warm fireplace occupies a central place. The menu consists of a good selection of Continental entrees, all deliciously prepared and nicely served. Cocktail service and separate lounge.

Perhaps one of the things that makes a dinner visit to the Cafe Alpine so special is the unique wine sampling bar where you can get a preview of their excellent selection. Authentic tapas are served with the wine. Just be careful not to fill yourself up with the tapas to the point where you won't be able to enjoy your dinner.

THE GARDEN ROOM, *6 miles east of I-70, Exit 205, in the Keystone Lodge, Keystone. Tel. 970/468-4386. Major credit cards accepted. Dinner served nightly. Reservations suggested. Smoke free premises.*

One of several excellent restaurants in and around the Keystone Lodge, the Garden room is the best of the lot. With a name like the Garden Room you might expect Continental cuisine or maybe even lights salads and vegetarian dishes. But this is a traditional western steak house when it comes to the food. Professionally served in an attractive and casual dining room that overlooks beautiful Lake Dillon, your steaks will be expertly prepared to your exact specifications and barely fit on the plate. The other menu items are primarily regional western beef and game and are just as delicious. The Garden room features an extensive wine list in addition to full tableside cocktail service and a separate lounge. Children's menu. Sunday brunch.

Moderate

ARAPAHOE CAFE & PUB, *626 Lake Dillon Drive, Dillon. Tel. 970/468-0873. American Express, Discover, MasterCard and VISA accepted. Breakfast, lunch and dinner served daily.*

The Arapahoe is, despite the pub in its name, a good family style restaurant serving traditional American favorites prepared in a simple manner. They serve plenty of good tasting food. The staff is friendly and efficient. Cocktail service and full bar.

EL RIO CANTINA & GRILL, *450 W. Main Street, Frisco. Tel. 970/668-5043. Most major credit cards accepted. Lunch and dinner served daily.*

Traditional Mexican cuisine of all sorts including an unusually large number of vegetarian dishes. The atmosphere is casual and fun. El Rio has a surprisingly big selection of excellent microbrews but is equally well known among the local folk for their hefty (18 ounce) margaritas. Children's menu.

SNAKE RIVER SALOON, *located in Keystone Lodge village shops, Keystone. Tel. 970/468-2788. American Express, Discover, MasterCard and VISA accepted. Dinner served nightly. Closed second half of May.*

When you're looking for an old-time western eatery, the Snake River is about as authentic as they come. The decor and atmosphere is traditional western rustic–knotty pine throughout and a casual wait staff that will make you feel right at home. The menu star is their large, tender and tasty steaks but you can also choose from a good selection of other dishes including chicken, ribs, and pasta. Cocktail service and separate lounge. Children's menu.

VAIL/BEAVER CREEK

Very Expensive

BEANO'S CABIN, *several departures nightly from the Beaver Creek Village. Tel. 970/845-7900. American Express, MasterCard and VISA accepted. Dinner served nightly. Closed late September to early December and mid-April to early June. Reservations are suggested; call between 10:00am and 4:00pm. Smoke free premises.*

I'm not as quick to enthusiastically recommend the most expensive restaurants because all too often they aren't worth the extra cost. Happily, though, I can whole-heartedly endorse this most unusual and delicious dining extravaganza! You can also take the restaurant's name literally. However, this is one of the most beautiful and elegant log cabins that you'll ever see. Wonderfully decorated with western pieces, the richly beamed cabin sits tranquilly amid the glory of nature in a remote but gorgeous mountain meadow. Getting there is half the fun. You have a choice. Transportation (included in the price) is either by van or horse!

Even if horseback riding isn't your thing you should consider making one exception in your life and take that method to reach dinner in order to get the full western experience of Beano's Cabin. If you don't, at least the van ride is pleasant. The culinary adventure begins upon arrival. You'll watch the chef's prepare your delicious and imaginative western cuisine in the exhibition style kitchen. The portions are ample and the service excellent. Cocktails are served and there's a separate lounge. Live entertainment is part of the package. Children's menu.

Expensive

ALFREDO'S, *1300 Westhaven Drive, Vail, in the Westin Resort. Tel. 970/476-7111. Most major credit cards accepted. Breakfast, lunch and dinner served daily in summer; dinner only during peak season. Reservations are suggested. Smoke free premises.*

Serving what may at first seem to be a strange combination of cuisines (western American and northern Italian), you'll quickly learn to appreciate the delicious blend that results. The surroundings are beautiful but the atmosphere is casual, the service friendly, and the dining first class. Cocktails and lounge. Entertainment provided except during the spring and fall seasons.

Moderate

GRATZIE, *48 Beaver Creek Blvd., Beaver Creek. Tel. 970/949-3366. American Express, MasterCard and VISA accepted. Dianner served nightly. Smoke free premises.*

Gratzie serves excellent traditional Italian fare in a lovely setting. The casual dining room features windows that are two stories high and provide beautiful mountain vistas. The service is highly professional yet warm and personal. Cocktail service and separate lounge.

SIAMESE ORCHID, *12 South Frontage Road, Vail. Tel. 970/476-9417. American Express, Discover, MasterCard and VISA accepted. Lunch and dinner served daily. Closed May. Reservations are suggested. Smoke free premises.*

Tasty and mild to hot Thai cuisine and an attractive and traditional Oriental atmosphere make the Siamese Orchid a worthwhile dining choice. The menu features a large number of entrees ranging from meat to vegetarian. Many dishes feature noodles or curry as the prime ingredient. Try the delicious and spicy lemon soup as a prelude to your main course. The service is friendly and efficient. Cocktail service. Carryout is available.

THE TYROLEAN, *400 E. Meadow Drive, Vail. Tel. 970/476-2204. American Express, MasterCard and VISA accepted. Dinner served nightly. Closed April and May and Tuesdays from June through November. Reservations are suggested.*

Built in the style of an Austrian hunting lodge, the Tyrolean provides beautiful surroundings to enjoy a bountiful and delicious dinner in casual ambiance. The extensive menu features a good selection of beef, lamb and veal dishes along with chicken and some seafood dishes. However, the fresh Colorado game dishes are the local favorites. All are attractively presented by an excellent wait staff. Full cocktail service, including one of Vail's biggest wine lists, and a separate lounge. Children's menu.

SEEING THE SIGHTS
BOULDER

If you thought that Denver and Colorado Springs were close to the mountains, wait until you see Boulder! It's not only near, it's virtually there. This growing community, blessed with lots of sunshine and a spectacular setting that rivals that of a Swiss Alpine village, is fast approaching 100,000 residents. Initially fueled by the University of Colorado, it has become home to a sizable number of government and private research facilities. It has consistently been rated as one of the best places to live in America and it's easy to understand why. It has the distinction of being the only municipality to have all of its water needs served by a city owned glacier–the nearby **Arapaho Glacier**. Dining, cultural, and entertainment facilities are in abundance and are all out of proportion for a city of its size, which is a real nice plus for visitors. Boulderites love the outdoors as evidenced by the more than 9,000 acres of parks, many of which are part of a huge system of mountain parks.

Coming in from Denver on US 36 your first stop will be at the **National Center for Atmospheric Research** in the southern part of the city. Take Table Mesa Drive westbound and follow it to the end where the

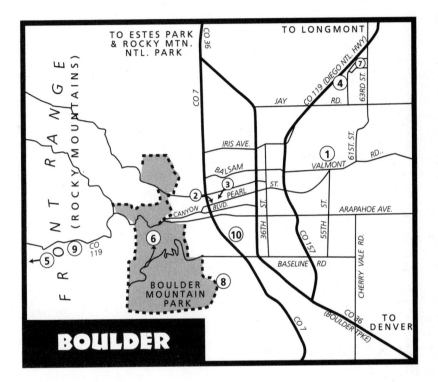

1" - approx. 1 1/4 miles

(1) Boulder Municipal Airport

(2) Boulerado Hotel

(3) Boulder (Pearl Street) Mall

(4) Celestial Seasoning's Tour of Tea

(5) Eldora Ski Area

(6) Flagstaff Mountain

(7) Learning Tree Museum of Western Art

(8) National Center for Atmospheric Research

(9) Peak to Peak Highway

(10) University of Colorado (Main Campus)

HOP & SKIP THROUGH BOULDER

*Denver's Rapid Transit District is helping Boulder, growing by leaps and bounds, to develop a bus system. The **HOP** is a loop shuttle that goes through central Boulder. There's no mistaking these brightly colored buses tha run every 7 to 20 minutes Monday through Saturday from early morning into the wee hours.*

__SKIP__ travels along Broadway and also in the Table Mesa area in the southern part of the city. It runs every 6 to 30 minutes. Each costs only 75 cents (25 cents for seniors) and slightly higher during rush hours. HOP maps and schedules are available by calling Tel. 303/447-8282, while SKIP information is available from the RTD at Tel. 303/299-6000, Ext. 1182.

In addition, there are about a dozen local routes run by the RTD and these don't count the Boulder-Denver services. A few routes that may be of use to visitors include the #200 along Pearl Street, the #209 along Arapahoe Road, and the #204 that runs north to south along the west side of the University of Colorado.

research center is located. The futuristic building was designed by world renowned architect I. M. Pei and is set against a magnificent backdrop of the Boulder Flatiron Mountains. Inside several exhibit areas explain the work of the center which does research on weather, the environment, and atmospheric phenomenon. There's an interesting display about the Cray Supercomputer. Self-guided tours of the facility further enhance visitors' understanding of their work. The grounds of the center are in a park-like setting. *Tel. 303/497-1174. Center open weekdays from 8:00am until 5:00pm and from 9:00am to 3:00pm on weekends and federal holidays. Guided tours are offered daily except Sunday from June 1st to Labor Day at noon. There is no admission charge.*

Head back on Table Mesa as far as Broadway (CO 93) and make a left. Coming up soon on your right will be the beautiful 1,600 acre main campus of the **University of Colorado**. The campus still dominates the city landscape with its many red-tile roof buildings, although not as much as in the past. Folsom Stadium is home to the University's fine football team. Tours are offered but are probably of most interest to potential students. *Call Tel. 303/492-6301 for information.* The **University Museum**, *Broadway between 15th and 16th Streets in Henderson Hall,* is an excellent natural history facility that devotes its collection to the southwestern United States. Special programs for children make this the ideal educational destination if you have youngsters. The **Heritage Center**, *third floor* *of Old Main Building (off of Broadway and Pleasant Street)* has seven different galleries that document the hisory of the University, including possessions of some famous alumni. There are also changing exhibits. *Museum: Tel. 303/492-6892. Open weekdays from 9:00am until 5:00pm; Saturday until 4:00pm; and on Sunday from 10:00am to 4:00pm. Donations are requested. Heritage Center: Tel. 303/492-6329. Operating hours are Tuesday through Friday from 10:00am until 4:00pm. No admission fee.*

Once you've got your education completed drive west from the southeastern corner of the school (Broadway and Baseline Road) on Baseline. This street becomes the **Flagstaff Scenic Highway** and the accompanying **Boulder Mountain Park**. Popular with bicycle riders and joggers, the highway climbs to a summit 1,600 feet above the city and affords great views of the urban area as well as of the mountains and plains. Panorama Point is an especially popular vantage point for taking in the scenery and has picnic tables. Hiking trails of varying lengths are at the summit.

Upon returning from this first excursion into the heights above Boulder, go east on Baseline only as far as 9th Street. Make a left and continue to Canyon Boulevard (just across the Boulder Creek) and you're on the edge of **Downtown**. Park your car in one of the many garages (there's one right at 9th and Canyon) and explore this area the best way–on foot. The thriving nature of Boulder's economic life can be seen in the busy downtown area. Stretching from 8th to 18th Streets, and from Spruce Street to the Boulder Creek, downtown is more than a central business district. Attractive gardens and parks, especially along the waterfront, make it an unusually attractive commercial hub.

The **Downtown Boulder Mall** is a four-block pedestrian only area on Pearl Street. Boulder's government center is amid a park-like setting south of Canyon Boulevard at the intersection of Broadway. Be sure to pay a visit to the ornate **Boulderado Hotel** (described in the *Where to Stay* section). For more information on Boulder's shopping, nightlife and entertainment, see the sections that follow later in this chapter.

The final two Boulder attractions are in the northwest part of town. Take Canyon Boulevard east to Foothills Parkway (CO 157) and then turn right (north). Foothills becomes Diagonal Highway (and also changes to CO 119). Stay on Diagonal until you reach Jay Road, then turn right and proceed one mile to Spine Road. Turn left and go a half mile to Sleepytime Drive. A left here will bring you to the **Celestial Seasonings Tour of Tea**. Celestial offers 45 minute long tours of their factory that shows how everything is crammed into those little tea bags. There's also an art gallery where the original paintings from their packages are on display. An herb garden contains many of the ingredients found in their teas Tastings are offered. Children will delight in meeting *Sleepytime Bear*.

Also on the premises are a cafe with excellent breakfast and luncheon menus and the Tea Shop & Emporium that carries the company's full line of products along with merchandise, gifts, and collectibles. *Tel. 800/525-0347. Tour times are daily on the hour from 10:00am through 3:00pm except Sunday when the first tour is at 11:00am. Closed on state holidays. There is no admission charge.*

Now go back to Spine Road and make a left. In a few blocks you'll come to Longbow Drive. Turn right there to reach the **Leanin' Tree Museum of Western Art**, *6055 Longbow Drive*. The museum is one of the largest private collections of Western art in the country with over 200 paintings and an equally notable collection of bronze sculptures. One is titled "The Marshall" and is a tribute to John Wayne, but perhaps the most impressive statue is outside–"Invocation" is a 15-foot high masterpiece of an Indian atop his steed. The museum features modern artists so don't be disappointed when you don't see such familiar names like Charles Russell or Frederick Remington. *Tel. 303/530-1442. Open Monday through Friday from 8:00am to 4:30pm and Saturday from 10:00am to 4:00pm. Closed on state holidays. Admission is free.*

The best way to get back into the heart of town after the museum is to return to Diagonal Highway and go south. Access to most of Boulder is easy via Foothills Drive.

Wine enthusiasts may be interested to know that Boulder has a couple of wineries that invite visitors. These are the **BookCliff Vineyards**, *Boulder Farmers Market, Tel. 303/499-7301* and **Augustina's Winery**, *4715 North Broadway, Tel. 303/545-2047*. Beer lovers shouldn't fret because the **Rockies Brewing Company**, *2880 Wilderness Place, Tel. 303/444-8448* also offers tours of their facility.

TO ESTES PARK

We'll leave Boulder by heading west on Canyon Boulevard (CO 119). This wonderfully scenic road travels through **Boulder Canyon** for 14 miles. Along the way make a brief stop at pretty **Boulder Falls**. Most of the route through the canyon is part of Boulder's mountain park system so you'll see a lot of locals bicycling, walking, or simply doing their thing in the crisp mountain air. At the town of Nederland (which is close to several major ski areas–see Sports & Recreation) you'll reach the junction of CO 72. This is a simply beautiful mountain road officially designated as part of the **Peak to Peak Scenic Byway**. As you travel north on this road for 23 miles to the junction of CO 7 and then another 23 miles on that road, you'll have excellent views of some of the many towering peaks of Rocky Mountain National Park. Among the most notable are 14,256-foot high **Long's Peak** on your left and the **Twin Sisters Peaks** (11,413 and 11,428 feet) to your right. CO 7 will end on the eastern edge of Estes Park.

Estes Park is a major resort town and the gateway to Rocky Mountain National Park. The town sits at an elevation of more than 7,500 feet and possesses the look and feel of an Alpine village. The "downtown" is busy year round with summer sightseeing tourists and winter skiers and always seems to have a festive atmosphere. Recreation that includes, besides skiing, rafting, fishing, and hiking are as important as the attractions. These can be found listed under Sports & Recreation but among the attractions are the **Aerial Tramway**, *Riverside Drive*. Ten-passenger cars bring visitors to the top of 8,700 foot high Prospect Mountain. Although it certainly isn't the tallest peak in the area it does provide a wonderful panorama of Estes Park and the surrounding area, including large tracts of Rocky Mountain National Park. *Tel. 970/586-3675. Cars operate daily from 9:00am to 6:30pm, mid-May through mid-September. The fare is $8 for adults and $7 for senior citizens and children ages 6 through 11.*

Nearby is the **Estes Park Area Historic Museum**, *200 4th Street*. It's a small museum that chronicles the history of the community and shows the importance of tourism. *Tel. 970/586-6256. Museum hours are daily from 10:00am until 5:00pm (from 1:00pm on Sunday), May through September. Call for hours at other times. The admission is $2.50, $2 for seniors, $1 for children age 5-12. Family rate is $10.* Less than a mile north of downtown on MacGregor Avenue is the 1870's **MacGregor Ranch and Museum**. The furnishings are original. *Tel. 970/586-3749. Open Tuesday through Friday from 10:00am until 4:00pm year round. There is no set admission fee but donations are requested.*

Two points of interest are located to the east of town on US 34. The first is the **Michael Ricker Museum and Gallery**, two miles east at the base of the Lake Estes Dam. In this pretty setting Mr. Ricker has put together "Park City–America Remembered," a remarkable miniature Victorian village made entirely of pewter. Besides the model visitors can take a guided tour that takes you step by step through the pewter casting process. *Tel. 970/586-2030. Open daily from 9:00am until 6:00pm from June 1st to mid-September and until 5:00pm the remainder of the year. The museum is closed on state holidays. There is no admission charge.* The other attraction is US 34 itself as it traverses the wild and scenic **Big Thompson Canyon**. A ride of a few miles out of town and then back will give you a good sampling of the gorge's scenic splendor.

ROCKY MOUNTAIN NATIONAL PARK

The grandeur of **Rocky Mountain National Park** has few rivals in all the world. For alpine mountain scenery it is unsurpassed anywhere in America. Mother Nature has outdone herself in this national treasure. If you came to Colorado only to visit Rocky Mountain National Park it would be a worthwhile journey. The park covers a vast 265,753 acres (415 square miles) of the magnificent Front Range, one of the highest mountain regions in North America.

But it is far more than perpetually snow-clad mountain peaks. The Park has hundreds of rushing streams, natural lakes both large and small, wildflower meadows ablaze with color, waterfalls, precipitous ledges that drop off into deep canyons (some of these gorges are as much as 3,000 feet deep), and much more. Although the greater part of the park is heavily forested, a third of the area consists of Alpine tundra. Glacial features are also prominent. Rocky Mountain National Park is also a wildlife refuge and bighorn sheep, elk, and deer as well as many species of birds are frequently sighted. Less often seen are coyote, black bear, mountain lions, bobcats and many other smaller species.

GEOLOGY 101

As you read, and certainly as you travel through the park, you're going to encounter some terms that relate to the park's glacial features which you may be unfamiliar with. Since I was an A student in high school earth science, I feel eminently qualified to offer this short cram course!

Moraines are areas of rock debris that have fallen as a result of glacial ice action. They tend to increase in size toward the lower end of the glacier. Moraines are characterized as lateral, meaning the rock falls at the sides of the valley walls, medial, where two or more glaciers converge, and terminal, at the end of the glacier. **Cirques** are an area of the headwall of a glacial valley that has eroded into a semi-circular shape, much like the letter U, as opposed to the V-shaped valleys associated with the cutting action of rivers. **Tundra** is an arctic plain with specific plant-life characteristics. The tundra of Rocky Mountain National Park is more specifically an alpine tundra, meaning that it occurs because of the high altitude rather than an arctic location. It is a common feature in elevations that go higher than **timberline** (or **tree line**). Timberline is simply the point where trees no longer grow due to the environmental conditions associated with the altitude. The point where timberline occurs varies depending upon the degree of latitude.

The park has three visitor centers and a museum. Visitor centers are located at each entrance and you should stop there to check for special programs and activities as well as any unusual conditions which may exist in the park. Remember: because of the high altitude the weather can often change quite abruptly. You should also take it easy for a while if you can in order to accommodate yourself to the altitude. While an auto tour is an excellent and popular way to see the park, horseback riding and hiking

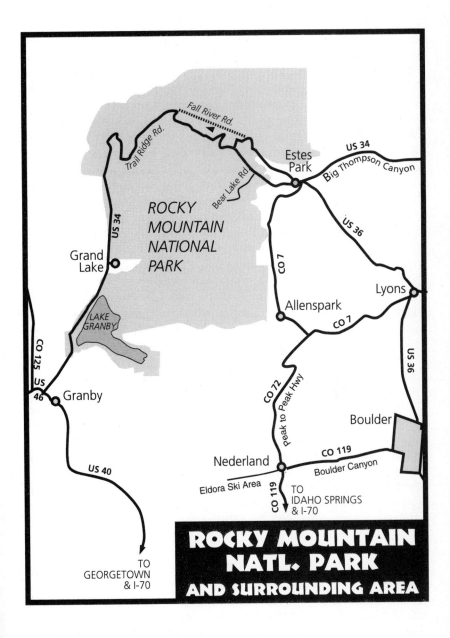

Fall River Rd.

Trail Ridge Rd.

US 34

Bear Lake Rd.

Estes Park

US 34

Big Thompson Canyon

ROCKY MOUNTAIN NATIONAL PARK

US 36

Grand Lake

CO 7

Allenspark

Lyons

CO 7

LAKE GRANBY

US 36

CO 125

US 46

Granby

CO 72

Peak to Peak Hwy

Boulder

CO 119

US 40

Nederland

CO 119

Boulder Canyon

Eldora Ski Area

CO 119

TO IDAHO SPRINGS & I-70

TO GEORGETOWN & I-70

ROCKY MOUNTAIN NATL. PARK AND SURROUNDING AREA

are also available on a system of trails that covers more than 350 miles. All ranges of difficulty are represented.

Okay, now that you have all of this information let's tour the park. From Estes Park head west on US 36 and go through the Beaver Meadows entrance station. Turn left onto **Bear Lake Road**, an easy and quite level road that passes through a glacial valley filled with pretty meadows. Along the route is the **Moraine Park Museum** with exhibits on the area's natural history. At the end of this dead-end 11-mile route is **Bear Lake**, one of the prettiest in the park. Many hiking trails begin from here but the easiest one is the short loop that circles the lake. As you go around it you can almost hear your own heartbeat–it's that quiet. And the reflection of nearby mountain peaks in the water is awesome. Now make your way back north on Bear Lake Road and turn left once returning to US 36.

A little bit up the road you'll reach the junction of US 34 and the beginning of **Trail Ridge Road**, the park highlight for most visitors. (If you don't want to go to Bear Lake you can come in from Estes Park via US 34 west through the Fall River entrance station.) Trail Ridge Road covers 45 miles and exits the southwestern edge of the park. It is open from late May through mid-October. With many elevations on the road being in excess of 12,000 feet it is the highest continuous paved highway in the United States. Eleven miles of the route are above timberline and it climbs a total of 4,200 feet. The road is narrow and twisting with several steep grades and hairpin turns as well as switchbacks. It requires that you pay careful attention to the road. There is plenty of opportunity to see the wonderful scenery at any or all of the more than dozen overlooks, several of which are strategically located in the bend of a turn or switchback.

One option needs to be mentioned before we set out on Trail Ridge. During July and August a one-way unpaved route called the **Fall River Road** is open to traffic. This route parallels Trail Ridge but the scenery is entirely different. The 11-mile uphill trek passes many waterfalls, glaciers, pools of glacial water, and staggering sheer cliffs before rejoining Trail Ridge. The beginning of Fall River Road is between the Fall River entrance station and the junction of US34/36. The road is much more difficult than Trail Ridge Road so less experienced mountain drivers will probably want to stick with Trail Ridge.

Trail Ridge Road quickly climbs in a series of switchbacks (pullouts at **Many Parks Curve** and **Rainbow Curve** are excellent) before straigthening out for a long stretch as it reaches the tundra level of the park. Lookouts at **Lava Cliffs** and **Gore Range** sandwich the highest point on the road–12,183 feet–and precede the crossing of the Fall River Pass at the **Alpine Visitor Center**. There is information and exhibits available here but it is especially noteworth for the view from the promenade at the rear of the center. The panorama of mountains, ice, and tundra from this spot is unforgettable. So, too, is the view of Trail Ridge Road itself as you peer out on the snaking highway as it climbs and drops in a series of several switchbacks. You see toy-like looking cars moving along the road where you came from and where you are headed.

Continuing further along Trail Ridge Road you'll soon reach the **Milner Pass** which marks where the road crosses the Continental Divide. It goes without saying that the view from here is great. After the **Farview Curve** overlook there is a last but dizzying series of switchbacks as you make the major part of the descent back to levels closer to 8,000 feet. The road straightens out all of a sudden and the descent becomes gentle. The western slopes of Rocky Mountain National Park are much less steep than on the east. Alas, the scenery here also lessens although it is still beautiful.

Park information: Tel. 970/586-1206. Mailing address is Superintendent, Rocky Mountain National Park, Estes Park CO 80517-8397. Park Headquarters & Visitor Center (US 36 att west edge of Estes Park) open daily year round, 9:00am to 5:00pm with extended hours in summer; Alpine Visitor Center (on Trail Ridge Road) open daily 9:00am to 5:00pm when road is open; and Kawuneeche Visitor Center (west entrance north of Grand Lake) open daily 9:00am to 5:00pm mid-June through October 31st with extended hours during the summer. Moraine Park Museum, Tel. 970/586-1206, daily 9:00am to 5:00pm mid-May to late September. It seems that the park's visitor center hours are changed almost every year. Therefore, if you plan to be there at any time before 9:00am or after 5:00pm it is best to call in advance to confirm the hours. Admission is $10 per vehicle for persons not possessing a valid park service passport.

Immediately upon leaving the park you'll enter the picturesque and bustling resort community of Grand Lake. The town sits near a narrow neck of land that separates **Grand Lake** and larger **Shadow Mountain Lake**. Just a couple of miles further on is the largest natural body of water in Colorado, **Lake Granby**. At elevations of over 8,000 feet and with plenty of mountains on all sides, it isn't any surprise that all three lakes attract plenty of vacationers for fishing, swimming, and other water sports. The mountains of the **Arapaho National Forest** and other areas provide plenty of other recreational alternatives to the water, some of which will be found in the Sports & Recreation section. Pretty as it all is, the Grand Lake area tends to cater mostly to people who come to stay in the area for a week or two and take advantage of the boating and fishing rather than those just passing through to see the sights.

GRANBY TO STEAMBOAT SPRINGS

A few miles beyond Grand Lake is the town of Granby. At the junction of US 40 take that road west for 70 miles to Steamboat Springs. The scenery is real nice all the way as you traverse several mountain passes in excess of 9,000 feet. Along the way you can make a brief stop in Hot Sulphur Springs to visit the **Grand County Museum**, about a quarter mile east of town. Local history is on the agenda. *Tel. 970/725-3939. Museum hours are daily from 10:00am until 5:00pm between Memorial Day and Labor Day and Wednesday through Saturday from 11:00am until 4:00pm at all other times. It is closed on Thanksgiving and Christmas. The admission is $4 for adults, $3 for seniors and $2 for children ages 6 through 18.*

The Steamboat Springs area contain in excess of 150 mineral springs, many of which are claimed to have medicinal properties. It was these springs that first attracted settlers to the area. The combination of the springs, beautiful scenery and surprisingly mild climate all helped to spur development. It was in this spot that the sport of skiing was introduced into America back in 1913. It seems to have taken quite nicely! The town is at an elevation of 6,700 feet, a number which also approximates the population. While Steamboat Springs is best known for its excellent skiing, the natural surroundings do draw a lot of people at all times of the year.

AN ALTERNATE ROUTE THROUGH THE BERTHOUD PASS

*While Steamboat Springs is lovely, it does involve a considerable extra drive from the main touring area of the central Rockies. An alternative route from Granby is to go east on US 40 for 46 miles to I-70 and then 27 miles west on the Interstate to Dillon. This route cuts off about 75 miles from the routing above and the only attractions missed are those in Steamboat Springs. The scenery is equally good this way, compliments of the amazing 25-mile stretch of US 40 between Winter Park and I-70. The **Berthoud Pass** crosses the Continental Divide at an elevation of 11,314 feet. The highway is good but second gear is a must as the steep grade, especially on the way down, could make you lose control if you go too fast. It is one of the longest climbs and drops on a major highway and provides outstanding scenery as well as a little excitement.*

The I-70 stretch from US 40 to Dillon passes a number of communities where there are many things to see and do. However, skip them for now because we're going to hit them on the way back from the heart of the Rockies to Boulder (or Denver).

During the summer the **Steamboat Springs Ski Area and Gondola** is used to transport visitors as it ascends to an altitude of about 9,000 feet at Thunderhead. From there is a magnificent view of the mountains and the Yampa River Valley. Yampa, by the way, was the Indian name for the region, a word that means "Big Medicine" and proof that the Native

Americans made use of the springs far before the white man did. *Tel. 970/ 879-6111. Summer gondola hours are daily from 10:00am through 4:00pm approximately mid-June to mid-September. Fare is $12 for adults and $7 for seniors and children under age 13.*

Another wonderful sight is located close to town on US 40. **Fish Creek Falls** tumble almost 300 feet through a narrow fault in the rock. An easy footpath leads along the creek from a highway parking area to a bridge at the base of the falls from which the best view is available. Upon leaving Steamboat Springs head back east on US 40 for 46 miles to the junction of CO 9 and then south on the latter road for 38 miles to the junction of I-70 at the town of Dillon.

THE CENTRAL ROCKIES:
DILLON, KEYSTONE, BRECKENRIDGE & FRISCO

These four towns along with nearby Silverthorne, Copper Mountain and Arapahoe Basin resort areas, are in many ways the true heart of the Rocky Mountain resort corridor as much of the area literally sits on top of the Continental Divide. The skiing section later will give you a better idea of why I say that but for now we'll concentrate on other aspects of the region. The scenery alone makes just passing through this part of Summit County an unforgettable experience–the rough texture of the mountains softened by verdant forests of pine, ice cold mountain streams and rivers, and air so marvelously fresh that you can almost taste it. But there's also history here and active resort communities with plenty of special events year-round. And to make things even better, it's all compact. All of these towns and resorts are within 15 miles of one another.

Dillon is a picturesque town on the shore of a beautiful mountain lake of the same name, just a mile or so off of I-70 (Exit 205) via US 6/CO 9. While Dillon hardly qualifies as a metropolis (its population numbers only about a thousand), it is the only place in Summit County with a movie theater or bowling alley, for example. **Keystone** is a couple miles south of Dillon via CO 9 and is a resort rather than a town. Since opening in 1971 the resort has grown and grown to the point that it almost is like a town with its fine selection of shopping, dining, and night life. It's also a great place to view the nearby mountains from.

Breckenridge is another important skiing and year-round resort but it is also an historic area with a classic Victorian style. It began as a small mining camp in 1859 and continued as such until the end of World War II. It would have become a ghost town except for another natural resource–snow, referred to by locals as "white gold" with tongue only partly in cheek. Many of the original Victorian dwellings now house shops of various kinds. I especially like the **Rocky Mountain Chocolate Factory.**

A visitor center on North Main can provide further information on events and other activites that may be taking place.

The most interesting attraction in Breckenridge is the **Country Boy Mine**, *542 French Gulch Road.* The mine dates from the late 19th century. Visitors are transported more than 1,200 feet underground during well thought out 45-minute long guided tours. There are also numerous exhibits on the surface. Real mining enthusiasts may wish to inquire about two hour tours that actually involve using some authentic vintage mining equipment. *Tel. 970/453-4405. Tours are offered daily on the hour from 10:00am until 5:00pm between Memorial Day weekend and the middle of September. Admission to the 45-minute tour is $11. Credit cards.*

The **Peak 8 Fun Park** is an amusement park open only in summer that will provide a needed change of pace for the kids (see Sports & Recreation for further information). Rafting on the Blue River is available in summer and winter. Besides skiing, Breckenridge is known for snowmobile tours. Breckenridge is located on CO 9 a few miles south of Keystone. Then head back north on CO 9, following signs for the Interstate. At the highway you'll reach the town of **Frisco**. Overshadowed by Mount Royal and several mountain peaks of the Ten Mile Range, Frisco is about as pretty a little mountain town as you can find anywhere.

Of notable inteest is the **Frisco Historic Park** *(on I-70 business loop at 2nd & Main Streets)* which depicts the history of the town's mining era. The original structures include an 1881 jail, log chapel, school house, and several homes. The school contains a museum with exhibits and pictures about early Frisco. *Tel. 970/668-3428. The park is open Tuesday through Sunday from 11:00am until 4:00pm (closed on Sunday after Labor Day until before Memorial Day) and the admission is free.*

Now hop on I-70 in a westerly direction for the 25 mile scenic drive to Vail. Use exit 176 to get into town (or #173 if you should be coming from the west).

VAIL

Vail, both as a community and ski resort, didn't exist until around 1960. In the relatively short span of time since then it has grown to a point where it has earned an international reputation for beauty and excellence, not only in skiing, but for lodging, fine dining, and entertainment.

It was the vision of a few men who foresaw the possibilities of the region known as the Vail Valley (which includes, besides Vail, several other resort communities). It was largely a remote wilderness region during World War II when it was used as a training area for ski paratroopers. Several of those paratroopers fell in love with the area and returned years after to begin their dream planned ski resort community.

Vail has about 4,000 people and sits at an altitude of 8,150 feet above sea level. The main town, called Vail Village, is built mostly in the architectural style of an alpine community from the Austrian Tyrol. The year-round center of recreation has Vail Village sitting on the east side and the more contemporary styled Lionshead on the west. Both are confined within the shadows of the eight to 14,000 foot peaks of the Gore Range. Most summer activities (like cycling, mountain biking, river rafting, and others) are within the surrounding **White River National Forest**.

Many of the streets within Vail Village and Lionshead are pedestrian-only malls. Because many Vail resorts only allow registered guests to park, if you're not staying in town it is best to leave your car either in the Vail Transportation Center garage (east side) or the Lionshead Parking Structure (west side). Both facilities charge a fee.

In-town activities during the summer often revolve around one of many music or entertainment festivals (the visitor bureau at *100 East Meadow Drive* will have up to the minute information) or shopping in Vail's many shops and boutiques. Because of the pedestrian only streets, the Tyrolean architecture and the surrounding scenery, just a simple stroll through Vail is a special experience. There are, however, some specific attractions that you should make the time to see. The first is the **Betty Ford Alpine Gardens** (east side about a quarter mile from Vail Village). The gardens have more than 500 different species of alpine and subalpine plants and over 1,500 perennial plants in two separate garden areas. *Tel. 970/476-0103. Open daily during daylight hours. Guided tours are given on Monday and Thursday at 10:00am during the summer months. There is no admission charge.*

The **Colorado Ski Museum and Hall of Fame**, *two blocks east of I-70, Exit 176*, has an extensive collection of exhibits on the history of skiing as well as historical skiing equipment and accessories. Even non-skiers will find it interesting. *Tel. 970/476-1876. Open Tuesday through Sunday from 10:00am until 5:00pm except for the months May and October. Also closed on New Year's Day, Thanksgiving, and Christmas. There is a nominal admission fee of $1 per person.* Finally, the **Vail Ski Area & Gondola** is a must see. The ski area is reputedly the largest single ski facility in the world. There are dozens of lifts to the various ski trails but in summer the gondola takes visitors to the summit for some great scenery and access to several nature and hiking trails. *Tel. 970/476-5601. Open daily from 10:00am until 4:30pm from mid-June through Labor Day and on Saturday and Sunday for the rest of September. The adult fare is $12, $8 for senior citizens and children under 12.*

Leave Vail by going west on I-70 for a few miles to Exit 171 and then east on US 24 (although the road will actually be heading due south at this point). It is 32 miles through beautiful mountain terrain of the White River National Forest to the town of Leadville.

LEADVILLE

Leadville is, from a historic standpoint, probably the most interesting of the mining towns turned resort. Here there is an excellent balance of both that makes it a special place to visit.

At an elevation of 10,188 feet it claims to be the highest incorporated city in the country. At this altitude the residents have to be a hearty breed.

The town was originally called Oro City after a mining camp began with the discovery of gold in 1860. Within a short time there were more than 5,000 miners. Much gold was found but it was hard to get out and once the easiest ore was taken the town's fortunes declined. The reason for the difficulty was a thick black sand that turned out to be lead carbonate. That, with the efforts of H.W. Tabor (see sidebar) led to a mining renewal. The name was changed to Leadville in 1878. Gold, lead, and silver have all been important commodities through the years. During its heyday Leadville, thanks to the extravagant spending of Mr. Tabor, had luxurious facilities and world famous entertainment. Many of that era's structures remain and that's what makes visiting Leadville today such a great time.

I've already mentioned that touring this region is generally a summer activity. That's even more so in Leadville because, as you will see, many attractions have extremely limited off-season hours when they're open at all. So, plan accordingly.

The majority of attractions are located on Harrison Street (which is also US 24) between 3rd and 10th streets, making seeing the sights convenient. Most of the buildings in this area date from the 1870s through 1890s. Begin your activities in Leadville at the **Healy House and Dexter Cabin**, *912 Harrison Avenue*. Although the cabin was moved from its original site to a place next to the Healy House, the two collectively exemplify the great variance in lifestyles during the boom and bust era of Leadville's early years.

Healey House is an elegant Victorian mansion which was a center of Leadville's high society for many years. The house was eventually turned into a boarding house and that is how visitors see it today as costumed guides play the roles of various boarders. The Dexter Cabin is even more interesting: despite the rough log exterior of a simple miner's cabin, the interior had two rooms that were lavishly furnished by its successful mining owner. *Tel. 719/486-0487. Both properties are open daily from 10:00am until 4:30pm between Memorial Day and Labor Day. They also open on weekends for the remainder of September. The admission is $5 for adults, $3 for seniors, and $2 for children ages 6 through 12.*

The adjacent **Heritage Museum** tells the story of Leadville's unusual history through a large diorama, a scale model replica of Leadville's Ice Palace, and numerous artifacts and furnishings from the mining era. *Tel.*

THE FAMOUS EXPLOITS OF H.A.W. TABOR & BABY DOE

*The golden age of Leadville is almost synonymous with the exploits of shopkeeper **Horace Austin Warner Tabor**, who was one of the few people left in Oro City in 1870 after the initial bust. By buying up as many mining tracts as he could at low prices, including the soon to be famous Matchless Mine property, Tabor was in good shape when the next boom started due to the mining of lead carbonate. Within eight years Tabor had become fabulously wealthy as well as the mayor of the renamed community of Leadville.*

*He was known for his generous free spending, something that his wife, Augusta, didn't appreciate. Tabor soon met the young and beautiful **Baby Doe** (real name Elizabeth McCourt Doe) who had an appetite for Tabor and his money. Augusta divorced Horace and moved to Denver and he secretly married Baby Doe. This led to a nationwide scandal (remember that we didn't have O.J. Simpon type trials and other such things to keep us occupied then so this was big news). Tabor died in 1899 but Baby Doe vowed to keep up the Matchless Mine, all that was now left of the Tabor family fortune. That she did, until 1935 when her body was found frozen in a cabin at the mine site.*

719/486-1878. Operating hours are daily from 10:00am through 6:00pm, Memorial Day through October 31st. Adult admission is $3.50, seniors pay $3 and children ages 6 through 12 are charged $2.

On the other side of Harrison at *120 West 9th Street* is the **National Mining Hall of Fame & Museum**. Occupying a 70,000 square foot renovated Victorian schoolhouse which is itself a point of interest, the museum is one of the largest and best of many western museums devoted to the history of mining. Exhibits include an underground mine, mine cars, equipment and more than twenty large dioramas by a noted woodcarver that depict the history of mining. Many works of art, including a larger than life steel welded statue entitled "The Anatomy of a Miner" add to the enjoyment of this fine facility. *Tel. 719/486-1229. The museum is open daily, May to October, from 9:00am until 5:00pm and Monday through Friday from 10:00am until 2:00pm the rest of the year. The admission price is $4 for adults, $3.50 for senior citizens, and $2 for children ages 6 through 11.*

The **Earth Runs Silver**, *809 Harrison Street*, is a half-hour long multi-media presentation that explores the history of Leadville from its origins to the present. The emphasis is on the early years. It's mildly interesting but lacks the vigor of the real thing that is available on the streets of Leadville and the other attractions mentioned here. *Tel. 719/486-3900.*

The film is shown daily, year-round, on the hour from 10:00am through 1:00pm. Inquire for schedule at other times of the year. Ticket prices are $3 for adults and $2 for children ages 2 through 12.

A few blocks down Harrison at 4th Street is the **Tabor Opera House**, Leadville's best known structure since it opened on November 20, 1879 and is one of Colorado's most famous attractions. The opulence of the theater clearly shows how rich Leadville was during its prime. You'll go up the original wide wooden staircrase with the walls covered by autographed pictures of the famous performers from around the world who graced the stage of the Tabor. The theater remains as it was on the night of its last show, at least under the ownership of Mr. Tabor because the opera house is still used for performances of the Victorian style Crystal Comedy Company. The self-guided tour includes a visit to the theater itself, backstage, dressing rooms, and the fabulous five room Tabor Suite. *Tel. 719/486-1147. Open daily (except Saturday), Memorial Day through October 1st, from 9:00am until 5:30pm. The admission charge is $4 for adults and $2 for children ages 6 through 12.*

Now go back to 7th Street and go a few blocks east to the depot for the **Leadville, Colorado & Southern Railroad Company**, *326 East 7th Street*. This is an excellent 2-1/2 hour long trip through the heart of Colorado's mining country. The high route traces the course of the Arkansas River's headwaters and goes up to the scenic Fremont Pass. A stop is made at the historic French Gulf water tower where riders have an excellent photo opportunity of magnificent Mt. Elbert. The line was originally narrow gauge but was converted to regular gauge during World War II as it was used then to haul molybdenum from the Climax Mine. The only disappointment for some people is that a modern locomotive is used to pull the open air cars. Well, you can't have everything. *Tel. 719/486-3936. The train departs daily at 1:00pm from late May through mid-June and again for most of September, and at 10:00am and 2:00pm from mid-June through Labor Day. Always call ahead to confirm the operating schedule. The adult fare is $22.50 for adults and $12.50 for children ages 4 through 12. Credit cards.*

Upon finishing the exciting train ride you can walk or ride a little further east on 7th to the **Matchless Mine**, *414 West 7th Street*. It is symbolic in many ways of the entire Leadville mining area. H.W. Tabor bought it in 1879 for $117,000 but it returned more than a million dollars a year during the 14 years of its peak operation. Today you can see the shaft and headframe of the mine, the hoist room and blacksmith shop, blasting powder magazine, and Baby Doe's cabin (more about her in the Tabor sidebar). *Tel. 719/486-3900. The mine is open daily, June through Labor Day, from 8:00am until 5:00pm. The adult admission price is $3 and children ages 6 through 12 are charged $1.*

The final attraction is located two miles west of town on US 24 and then a short ride on CO 300. This is the **Leadville National Fish Hatchery** which is the second oldest hatchery operated by the government–it opened in 1889. Visitors learn about the operations of the hatchery that propagates millions of brook, brown, cutthroat, lake, and rainbow trout. Also on the grounds are several nature and hiking trails which afford excellent views of the surrounding mountains. *Tel. 719/486-0189. The hatchery is open every day of the year from 7:30am until 4:00pm and admission is free.*

With the above eight attractions I think you'll agree that Leadville packs a mighty wallop for a town of its size. But now it's time to move on. Drive east on US 24 for about 15 miles to the junction of CO 82 and then west for 44 miles to Aspen. There's some stunning scenery along the way, including outstanding views of Mt. Elbert, Colorado's highest peak, and the ride over the 12,091 foot high Independence Pass.

ASPEN

Aspen and the adjacent resort community of Snowmass has rightly become as familiar a name as Vail. Which one is more beautiful is simply a matter of opinion. They're both mountain scenery at its best and resorts par excellence. Unlike Vail, however, Aspen did not develop originally as a ski resort. As in the case of so many other localities in this part of Colorado, Aspen was a mining town. The first small ski facility was developed in the 1930s and soon mushroomed into a world-class resort. While skiing is the most important aspect of Aspen's tourist based economy, all sorts of year-round recreational opportunities abound. And the **Aspen Music Festival**, held throughout the summer, is one of the best known events of its type in the world.

Aspen doesn't have much left of its mining days so it isn't at all like Leadville. However, the **Wheeler-Stallard House Museum**, *620 West Bleeker Street*, is furnished in the style of the 1880's when the house dates from. Walking tours of Aspen are offered daily at 9:30am and leave from the museum. *Tel. 970/925-3721. Museum is open Tuesday through Friday from 1:00pm to 4:00pm from the middle of June through mid-September and again from January through mid-April. The admission is $3 for adults and 50 cents for children under 12.*

The most visited site in Aspen (other than the ski slopes) are actually located about ten miles south of town near CO 82. These are the famous **Maroon Bells**. This is a combination Forest Service and Aspen Center for Environmental Studies tract that encompasses a 14,126 foot double peaked mountain that is said to be the most photographed spot in Colorado. Of course, there's no proof of such a claim but a brilliant picture it will make. Maroon Lake has many trails and recreational facilities. During the busiest times of the year the Maroon Bells access road is not open to private vehicles. A bus provides service from Aspen's Rubey Park Transit Center. *Tel. 970/925-8484. Buses leave every 20 minutes from 9:00am until 4:00pm every day from mid-June through Labor Day. The fare is $5 for adults and $3 for seniors as well as children ages 6 through 16.* Another noted view is available for summer visitors on the **Silver Queen Gondola** which ascends **Aspen Mountain**. *Tel. 970/925-8484. Gondola hours are 900am to 9:00pm daily. Fare for adults is $14 and $10 for seniors and childen ages 6-16. Combination tour tickets that include the Maroon Bells bus tour are available. Credit Cards.*

The Aspen area contains a number of ghost towns. While interesting, they haven't been fully developed for visitors and require caution. The most accessible is Ashcroft, located 11 miles from Aspen via Castle Creek Road. If you like this sort of exploration then the Aspen Historical Society can provide you with further information. Call them at *Tel. 970/925-3721.*

One of the most unusual attractions in the area is not in Aspen but in neighboring Snowmass. **Krabloonik**, *5-1/2 miles west of CO 82 via Brush Creek and Divide Roads,* is a dog kennel which means "big eyebrows" in the Eskimo language. The center raises Toklat sled dogs which are a hybrid of Malamute, Eskimo, and Siberian sled dogs. The result is a hearty breed that is especially well suited to a mountain environment. Many dogs bred at Krabloonik compete in the famous Alaskan Iditarod sled race. Krabloonik offers interesting guided tours of the kennel as well as hand-made sleds. *Tel. 970/923-3953. Tours given Tuesday through Sunday at 11:00am and 2:30pm only, Memorial Day through Labor Day. Adult admission is $4.50, and children under 13 pay $4.*

For something even more unusual, try a half-day dog sled ride. These are given in winter (Thanksgiving through April 1st) at 8:30am and 12:30pm. *Tel. 970/923-4342. Dog sled riders must be at least three years of age. The charge is $185. Credit cards.*

Aspen is the furthest point on our north-central trip, so we'll be heading back now. However, Aspen makes a convenient point to connect with two other touring regions. If you want to see the northwest than you can hook up with the northwest loop at the town of Carbondale. To reach this point simply travel 42 miles west of Aspen via CO 82. At the junction of CO 133 you'll be on the other loop. Similarly, to get to the southwest touring region, head back toward US 24 and then proceed 22 miles to US 285. A distance of about 20 miles south on the latter road will bring you to the town of Poncha Springs which is on the southwest region tour loop.

If you're not connecting to another regional tour then simply retrace your route to Leadville via CO 82 and US 24. At Leadville go north on CO 91 for 24 miles to I-70. A distance of about 35 miles east on the Interstate will bring you to Georgetown, located at Exit 228. Along the Interstate route, however, besides some appealing scenery is the **Eisenhower Tunnel**. This engineering marvel cuts through 1-1/2 miles of Mount Trelease and bypasses the older US 6 route which twisted through the mountains and was often considered hazardous during the winter. Almost 2-1/2 million cubic yards of rock had to be excavated from the mountain in order to build the tunnel.

I-70 CORRIDOR:
GEORGETOWN, IDAHO SPRINGS & CENTRAL CITY

Georgetown's mining days began in 1859. Nestled amid mountains that are almost in the backyard of many of Georgetown's Victorian structures, it is a picturesque and almost idyllic setting. The colorful buildings have been meticulously restored and maintained. Because Georgetown avoided the destructive fires that plagued many mining towns throughout the west, it has an unusual number of original buildings–more than 200 by official count. Although the mining boom ended Georgetown remained as a community, perhaps because of the beautiful setting. Today, although skiing and other forms of recreation are nearby, the town itself is the main attraction. Taking a stroll down its streets is like making a trip to the 19th century.

While almost every building in the historic center of town is worth taking a closer look at, two are especially important to visitors. The first is the famous **Hotel de Paris**, *409 6th Street*, built in 1875 by Louis Dupuy of Alencon, France who was somewhat homesick. While most of Georgetown is Victorian, the hotel is rococo and was renowned at the time for its luxurious appointments. Today the hotel is a museum but it is filled with many original furnishings and visitors can see the wine cellar and other areas. *Tel. 303/569-2311. Museum hours are daily from 10:00am until 5:00pm, Memorial Day through October 1st, and weekends from noon until 4:00pm the remainder of the year. It is closed on New Year's Eve and Day, Easter, Thanksgiving, and Christmas Eve and Day. The adult admission price is $4 while seniors pay $3. The charge for children ages 12 hrough 16 is $2.*

Nearby at *305 Argentine Street* is the **Hamill House**, one of the most notable of the elegant Victorian houses in Georgetown. Owned by one of the richest men in the Territory, Hamill House had such unusual features (for the time) as gas lighting, central heating and a built in bathtub. Even the toilet was most unusual–an outhouse seating six and covered by a cupola! *Tel. 303/569-2840. the house is open daily from 10:00am until 4:00pm, May through September, and on weekends from noon until 4:00pm the remainder of the year. It is closed on state holidays. The admission is $5 for those over age 6 except that seniors and students with proper identification pay only $4.*

The **Georgetown Loop Railroad** has its terminal adjacent to Exit 228 of I-70. This narrow gauge railroad features a steam locomotive from the 1920s that pulls open air cars (some covered) through an area of old mining towns on the way to Silver Plume. Riders can also board at that location. The 70-minute long journey (allow an additional hour for the mine tour) covers seven miles, a highlight of the beautiful mountain scenery being the trip over the breathtaking **Devil's Gate Bridge**. A stop is made at the **Lebanon Mine** and visitors can explore it. The mine is not open to people who do not take the train ride. I thoroughly enjoy all of Colorado's historic train rides and this one is no different, although the price is kind of high considering the length of the trip. *Tel. 800/691-4386. If calling locally the number is Tel. 303/569-2403. Train trips depart daily at 9:00am and then every 80 minutes until 4:00pm from Memorial Day through early October. The mine tour is not offered on departures after 1:00pm. Another option is to take a combination van/mountain bike tour with the train trip. Call for information regarding schedules. Fares vary depending upon itinerary and combination of travel methods but adult prices begin at $13 for the train ride and $5 for the mine tour. Credit cards.*

One last point of interest in Georgetown before we continue onward is an area by Georgetown Lake where you can view bighorn sheep. The viewing station is the only one of its kind in Colorado. When you're ready to leave Georgetown get back on I-70 in an easterly direction for 12 miles to **Idaho Springs** (Exit 240). This is another important mining community and also has a large number of Victorian buildings in its historic downtown area. Two facilities connected with mining are the **Argo Gold Mill**, immediately off of I-70, and the **Phoenix Mine**, following signs from Exit 239 of I-70 via Stanley and Trail Creek Roads.

A visit to the Argo consists of three parts. It begins in the gold mine itself, a hand dug tunnel at the base of a mountain, then proceeds to the old mill where you'll see how gold and silver were processed during the late 19th century, and ends at a small museum that has displays and mining equipment as well as mineral samples. You can even pan for gold or other gemstones but more than likely will come away with nothing of value except for what you learned at the Mill. *Tel. 303/567-2421. The mill is open daily from 10:00am until 7:00pm, year-round. The admission is $10 for adults, $8 for children ages 7 through 12, and $5 for ages 3 to 6.*

The Phoenix Mine is a still operating gold mining facility. Actual miners take visitors on an informative 45-minute long tour of the underground facilities. You are also allowed to pan for gold but I don't know anyone who has found anything of great value. *Tel. 303/567-0422. Tours are offered daily between 10:00am and 6:00pm. The admission fee is $9 for adults, $8 for seniors and $5 for children under age 12. If you only want to pan for gold then the admission cost is $5 per person*

Besides being surrounded by beautiful mountains, like just about every other community in this part of the state, Idaho Springs has other scenic attractions of interest. One is picturesque **Bridal Veil Falls**, which has an old water wheel at the base, and **St. Mary's Glacier**. The first is near town but the glacier is reached by a 12-mile drive on Fall River Road (Exit 238 off of I-70) and then by a three-quarter mile hike. That sounds difficult but this glacier, along with St. Mary's Lake at James Peak, is one of the more accessible glaciers in the United States near major population centers. *Both sites open at all times and are free of charge.*

A popular excursion from Idaho Springs is the **Mt. Evans Scenic & Historic Byway**, a 28-mile round trip south via CO 103 and CO 5. Open during the summer (usually Memorial Day through mid-September but can vary depending upon weather conditions), the road passes beautiful Echo Lake (that portion is open year round) before climbing to the 14,264 foot summit of Mt. Evans. At this point you'll be in a climatic and life zone that is equivalent to the Arctic Circle. Bighorn sheep are commonly sighted. The panorama of the Front Range and the Continental Divide from the summit is stunning. Besides Echo Lake there are several other mountain lakes, including Lincoln and Summit Lakes. The latter is at an elevation of 12,830 feet. Hiking trails are available at all of the lakes. The road is paved all the way and, although the climb is kind of steep in places and there are many sharp turns, it can be done in any kind of car. Mountain driving experience (which you'll have by now) is useful.

The next destination is **Central City** and it can be reached in two ways. The long way is the easy way. Go east on I-70 to Exit 244 and after being on US 6 for a fraction of a mile go north on CO 119 for about five miles. At Black Hawk take CO 279 the last mile into Central City. The other way is to take CO 279 from Idaho Springs north directly to Central City. This shortcut is definitely not for the timid driver. Known affectionately as the **"Oh My God" Road** (I wish I had made up that name), is a dirt and gravel route that traverses Virginia Canyon. Although it only takes about a half hour, the road is extremely bumpy as well as narrow and has loads of sharp turns. It does pass several old mining towns and has a wonderful view of Central City as you descend on the final leg into town.

Either way you get there Central City is our last stop of the tour. It was one of the most successful of the 19th century gold camps. Today it has only a few hundred residents but lots of visitors to its beautiful 8,500-foot setting. Besides the usual outdoor recreation available in Colorado's mountain communities, both Central City and neighboring Blackhawk have several casinos. You might need to unwind there if you take the "Oh My God" route into town!

The main street still looks much as it did in the 1870s and the entire town is part of a National Historic District. This is another place where strolling through town is an experience in itself. However, the two most famous attractions are the Central City Opera House and the Teller House. The **Opera House**, *off of Main Street on Eureka Street*, was built in luxurious style in 1878. World famous performers such as Sarah Bernhardt came to Central City to perform. Of note is the ornate interior which is covered with murals and features many crystal chandeliers. Performances are still given at the Opera House. *Tel. 303/292-6700 for information, including performance schedules and prices. The Opera House can be visited via guided tours daily from 10:00am until 4:00pm, May through October. The admission is $3.*

Whether or not the casinos of Central City are of interest to you, definitely allow at least a few minutes to visit the **Teller House Casino**, *Eureka and Pine Streets*. The historic residence, which cost the staggering sum of $100,000 in 1872 is now a gaming facility but you can still see much of the elegance which made it famous long before the gamblers arrived. It houses an excellent collection of Victorian furniture and you can still see the "Face on the Barroom Floor," a painting of a lady put on the floor instead of a wall (or ceiling, for that matter).

If you're going to be returning to Boulder then upon reaching Blackhawk head north on the Peak to Peak Highway, CO 119. It is under 30 miles to Boulder. Returning to Denver is equally simple. Go back to the Interstate via CO 119 south and then east on I-70. The Denver area is also around 30 miles away.

WINTER TOURING

Since this region has the majority of Colorado's ski resorts it should be no surprise that it receives the greatest number of winter visitors of any part of the state. If the purpose of your winter visit is to ski, that's fine but it doesn't mean that you should overlook the sightseeing possibilities in winter. The snow on the slopes will be there if you take a day or two off. For non-skiers, too, winter presents a unique opportunity to see a side of nature that most people who don't live in the mountains often get to see.

Now, I'm not saying that you should venture out in a driving snowstorm. The fact of the matter is that winter in the Colorado Rockies is quite likely to be filled with day after day of sun filled sky. The major roads are almost all open throughout the winter although even the Interstate highway can be closed for short periods immediately following a major winter storm.

The only important roads that are definitely closed for the winter are a portion of US 34 through Rocky Mountain National Park and CO 82 between Aspen and Leadville. (If you want to get to Aspen during winter you have to approach it from the northwest via CO 82 from I-70.)

I have two suggested routes that will take you through some of the best Colorado scenery, winter or summer. The first itinerary covers only about 160 miles from a base in Denver, Boulder or anywhere else along the route. From Denver take US 36 through Boulder and continue on that highway to Estes Park. From there head south on Colorado state highways 7, 72 and 119 until you reach US 6 or I-70 at Idaho Springs from where you can return to Denver. A little more than a third of this route traverses the entire course of the magnificent Peak to Peak Scenic & Historic Byway mentioned earlier in this chapter.

A second route covers about 260 miles and can be begun at any point on the loop. It begins in Golden where you'll take I-70 westward to past Vail and the junction of US 24. Then go east on US 24 to the small town of Antero and the junction of US 285. Going north on US 285 will return you to Golden.

What will you see in the winter? First of all, many of the historic and other man-made attractions are open year round although often on a reduced schedule. However, those types of activities are more suited to visits at other times of the year. Nature in wintertime is unique and that is what you should be looking for. The Rockies, when only the peaks are covered with snow, are dramatically beautiful because of their rugged-ness. A winter blanket of snow softens them so much that they take on a gentle beauty. However, in many places where the slope is more precipi-tous you'll still see rock of various shading projecting through the snow cover.

Look too at the mountain tops. Even on the sunniest of days you'll likely see a few clouds up at the peaks. The clouds blend almost into the snow so it's hard to tell exactly where one begins and the other ends. The large number of evergreen trees jutting out from the silky white ground adds a splash of color and variety to the landscape of the lower slopes. Watch for people on the ski slopes, whether they're actually skiing or just riding the chairlift. Somehow the vast fields of white make them seem even smaller then they would appear in the warmer months. Finally, the small towns and resort villages of the Central Rockies region also take on a warm glow during winter. Snow covered roofs and the twinkling of lights at night are especially a sight that will always be remembered.

NIGHTLIFE & ENTERTAINMENT

The listings will be arranged, as they were for shopping, alphabeti-cally by location. Night life in localities not listed is mainly limited to larger hotels. If it is a major resort center, as in the case of places like Aspen, Keystone or Vail, then you can usually count on the bigger hotels having a good variety of entertainment and lounges, sometimes featuring well-known names.

COLORADO MUSIC FESTIVALS

Summertime in Colorado brings new meaning to "the hills are alive with the sound of music." Music festivals, many of which have gained international stature, are a big part of the entertainment scene throughout Colorado. Maybe it's the beauty of the surroundings that brings out the music in one's soul. Skeptics would say that it gives the ski resort owners something to make money with once the snow has melted from the slopes. Well, I won't be so cynical. But whatever the reason, there are more than twenty major festivals in Colorado, mainly classical, but with a big smattering of jazz and country. Surprisingly, pop and rock are almost totally missing from the festival scene–what a blessing! Following is a rundown of the biggest Many, but not all, are in the central Rockies region. It is best to check with the local chamber of commerce for exact dates and program information.

American Music Festival (Winter Park). Mid-July. Held at the base of the ski area. Mostly contemporary music.

Aspen Music Festival (Aspen). Late June through August. One of the biggest outdoor concert series in the world.

Aspen-Salida Music Festival (Salida). Early July. Classical series provided by some of the performers appearing at Aspen.

Bach, Beethoven and Breckenridge (Breckenridge). All classical music but not limited to the two B's!

Bravo! Colorado Music Festival (Vail). July and August. If Aspen has a classic music show, so must Vail.

Colorado Music Festival (Boulder). Six weeks beginning in mid-June. Classical music with some of the biggest names from around the world performing two dozen concerts at beautiful Chautauqua Auditorium in view of the Flatiron Mountains.

Country Jam USA (Grand Junction). Big names in country music always on tap.

Gilbert & Sullivan Festival (Boulder). July. What you see is what you get, G&S lovers.

Great Rocky Mountain Brass Band Festival (Silverton). Mid-August. A change of pace from most of the other festivals, but would you expect otherwise from a place like Silverton?

Jazz Festival (Central City). Mid-August.

Jeepers Jamboree and Music in Ouray (Ouray). Anything's possible in little Ouray.

Strings in the Mountains (Steamboat Springs). Six weeks of classical music except one night per week can be almost anything else. Held at the base of the ski slopes. One of the best.

Summer Concert Series (Estes Park). A straight-forward name for this classical concert series held on the grounds of the magnificent Stanley Hotel.

Summer of Jazz (Glenwood Springs). Outdoors in Two Rivers Park for ten weeks starting in early summer.

Telluride Blue Grass and Country Music Festival and Telluride Jazz Festival (Telluride). Held in the town park, the Blue Grass festival is world renowned. Early August. Both famous and up and coming artists.

ASPEN

Most of the major resorts have live entertainment, especially during the ski season. For a change of pace try the **Crystal Palace Dinner Theater**, *300 E. Hyman Avenue, Tel. 970/925-1455*. They've been in business for almost forty years and the entertaining cabaret revue (performed by the waiters and waitresses) is good fun. The setting is as eclectic as you can get–a mixture of Victorian style with a bit of everything else. The main bar area features a Maxwell automobile from 1908 and a Ford Model T a few years younger.

BOULDER

The University of Colorado began Boulder's tradition of cultural events but it has grown far beyond that. The **Boulder Ballet** is an excellent company that has an annual program at the Dairy Center for the Arts, *2590 Walnut Street, Tel. 303/449-1343*. The **Boulder Philharmonic Orchestra** has as its home the marvelous Macky Auditorium at the University of Colorado as well as at other venues from time to time. Call *Tel. 303/449-1343* for performance schedule and ticket information.

For theater you can choose from the **Boulder Conservatory Theatre**, productions at the Dairy Center, *Tel. 303/444-1885*; or the interesting **Boulder's Dinner Theatre**, *Tel. 303/449-6000, Ext. 4,* where dinner is served by the cast. The University of Colorado is a major player in the Boulder entertainment scene. The Department of Theater and Dance stages many performances. Call *Tel. 303/492-8181* for information. Major events include the **Colorado Shakespeare Festival** during the summer. It is held in the Mary Rippon Outdoor Theater, home to numerous other events as well. The **Lyric Theater Festival** presents an annual Artists Series. Finally, outside the university scene is the 8-week long summer music festival held in lovely Chautauqua Park.

For a city of its size Boulder also has a busy nightlife scene, mostly because of the presence of the University because the students are always looking for something to do *after* studying. However, college students are especially prone to change what they like from one day to the next so the list of nightspots is subject to a great deal of fluctuation. The three establishments listed here seem to have at least a measure of staying power:

BENTLEY'S NIGHTCLUB, *555 30th Street, Tel. 303/444-3330*.

Popular dancing and mingling spot featuring wide variety of music that spans the 50's through today's sound.

THE CATACOMBS, *2115 13th Street (in Hotel Boulderado), Tel. 303/443-0486*.

Features blues in its nightly entertainment repertoire. Pool tables, video games are available if you don't like the music.

WEST END TAVERN, *924 Pearl Street, Tel. 303/444-3535.*
This two-level establishment features live entertainment downstairs that ranges from jazz to comedy, depending upon the night of the week, and a popular rooftop deck bar that has excellent views of the Flatiron Range.

There isn't any place that I know of for women looking for a little vicarious thrills, but men can check out the **Bustop Gentlemen's Club**, *4871 N. Broadway, Tel. 303/440-3911.* The club features nubile dancers on four stages.

CENTRAL CITY

The town's dozen or so casinos top the nightlife scene in Central City. They're all easy to find in this tiny town but two of the better ones if you're interested in more than gambling are the **Dostal Alley** with its microbrew pub, and the Blackjack Saloon at the **Glory Hole Casino**. For casino action in an elegant 19th century atmosphere then check out the **Teller House**.

ESTES PARK

There are several local watering holes but among the more popular places for visitors are the lounges of two Estes park restaurants. These are **Chapins**, *101 S. St. Vrain on CO 7 (in the Holiday Inn), Tel. 970/586-2332* and **La Casa**, *222 E. Elkhorn Avenue, Tel. 970/586-2807.* Both feature nightly entertainment (summer only at Chapins).

LEADVILLE

Drawing on its mining era, Leadville offers summer theater by the **Crystal Comedy Company** at the Old Church, *8th and Harrison Streets, Tel. 719/486-1512.* Call the box office for the current season's performance and schedule.

VAIL

Like Aspen, there's plenty going on in the lodges and resorts. Locals, however, will gladly tell you that the best place in town is **Cyrano's**, located just beneath the main ski lifts. They have a varied music program ranging from rock to jazz. Lately it seems that it's different each night so you might want to check in advance to make sure it suits your style. *Tel. 970/476-5553.*

And also like Aspen, Vail has numerous music festivals during the summer. An ongoing venue for all types of music and theater is the **Vilar Center for the Arts**, *46 Avondale Lane (in nearby Avon). Tel. 888/920-ARTS.*

SPORTS & RECREATION

Amusement Parks
- **Peak 8 Fun Park**, *Georgetown. Tel. 970/453-5000 or 800/789-7669.* Single, multi-ride or all day tickets are available. The amusement park is open only during the summer. It is part of the Breckenridge Ski area.

Ballooning
- **Adventures Aloft II**, *Aspen. Tel. 970/925-9497*
- **Camelot Balloons**, *Vail. Call for pick-up. Tel. 800/785-4743 or 970/926-2435*
- **Unicorn Balloon Company**, *Aspen. Tel. 970/925-5752*

Bicycling
You can find many bike trails covering all types of terrain throughout the north-central region. One of the most popular areas is in Boulder and the surrounding mountains. For a trail map contact the City of Boulder Open Space Department, *Tel. 303/441-3440.* If you didn't bring your own bike you can rent in many locations, including the following:
- **Colorado Bicycling Adventures**, *Estes Park. Tel. 800/607-8765 or 970/586-4241*
- **Top of the World Cyclery**, *9th & Harrison Streets, Leadville. Tel. 719/486-8224*
- **University Bicycles**, *839 Pearl Street, Boulder. Tel. 303/444-4196*

Boating
Lake Granby and the adjacent **Grand Lake** are two of the best boating spots for either motorized boating or sailing in Colorado. There are several boat launching sites. Rentals are available from **Highland Marina**, *7878 US Highway 34, Granby. Tel. 970/887-3541.* **Lake Dillon** also has large marina facilities as do some other resorts in that part of the I-70 corridor.

Fishing
In addition to the outfitters and other facilities listed below, the rivers and streams of the area's national forests are prime fishing territory. See the introductory chapter on Colorado fishing license information.
- **Eldorado Canyon State Park**, *CO 170, four miles southwest of Boulder. Tel. 303/494-3943*
- **Fly Fishing Outfitters**, *Vail. Call for pick-up. Tel. 800/595-8090 or 970/476-FISH*
- **Golden Gate State Recreation Area**, *four milels east of Black Hawk on CO 119.*
- **Kinsley Outfitters**, *1155 13th Street, Boulder. Tel. 800/442-7420 or 303/442-6204*

• **Trout Haven**, *US Highway 36 1-1/4 miles west of Estes Park. Tel. 970/586-5525*

Golf

• **Aspen Golf Course**, *22475 West Highway 82, Aspen. Tel. 970/925-2145.* A fine 18-hole municipal course that will challenge all but the most proficient golfers.

• **Breckenridge Golf Club**, *200 Clubhouse Drive, Breckenridge. Tel. 970/453-9104.* 18 hole Jack Nicklaus designed public course with wonderfully varied terrain.

• **Flatirons Golf Course**, *5706 Arapahoe Road at 57th Street, Boulder. Tel. 303/442-7851.* 18 holes.

• **Haystack Mountain Golf Course**, *5877 Niwot Road, Boulder. Tel. 303/530-1400.* Nine holes. Good place for beginners as well as experienced players.

• **Mount Massive Golf Course**, *County Road 5, 3-1/2 miles west of Leadville. Tel. 719/486-2176.* At 9,700 feet, this is America's highest golf course. 18 holes.

• **Sheraton Steamboat Golf Club**, *Clubhouse Drive, Steamboat Springs. Tel. 970/879-2220.* 18 holes. A beautiful course designed by the renowned Robert Trent Jones. Pricey but worth it for true golf lovers.

Horseback Riding

• **A & A Historical Trails Stables**, *2380 Riverside Drive, Idaho Springs. Tel. 303/567-4808*

• **Aspen Lodge at Estes Park**, *6120 Colorado Hwy. 7, Estes Park. Tel. 970/586-8133*

• **Eagles Nest Equestrian Center**, *Silverthorne/Dillon. On CO 9 three miles north of I-70, Exit 205. Tel. 970/468-0677*

• **Hi Country Stables**, *Moraine Park (Rocky Mountain National Park). Tel. 970/586-2327*

• **Pa's & Ma's Stables**, *US Highway 24 at Tennessee Pass (Leadville). Tel. 719/486-4750*

• **T · Lazy 7 Ranch**, *3129 Maroon Creek Road, Aspen. Tel. 970/925-7040*

Off Road & 4-Wheel Drive Vehicles

The Rocky Mountains are heaven for off-roading enthusiasts. If you have your own off-road or 4-wheel drive vehicle (or if you've rented one) the Leadville area has some of Colorado's best (make that the bumpiest) off roading adventures available. The difficulty ranges from moderate to nearly impossible. You can obtain a map from the Leadville Chamber of Commerce. Other good areas for venturing out are around Estes Park, in the vicinity of Mt. Evans (reached from either Idaho Springs or Georgetown) and the Guanella Pass area also south of Georgetown. Another possibility is the White River National Forest near Aspen.

If you want to be "chauffered" through the rough terrain then contact **American Wilderness Tours**, *875 Moraine Avenue, Estes Park. Tel. 970/586-1626* or **Tiger Run**, *Breckenridge, Tel. 970/453-2231.*

Rafting
- **Acquired Tastes Rafting**, *Boulder. Call for pick-up. Tel. 303/443-4120*
- **Clear Creek Rafting**, *Idaho Springs. Call for pick-up. Tel. 800/353-9901*
- **Good Times Rafting**, *Dillon. Call for pick-up. Tel. 970/453-5559*
- **Rocky Mountain Adventures**, *Estes Park. Call for pick-up. Tel. 800/858-6808 or 970/586-6191*

Skiing
Operating dates are approximate based on weather conditions. The telephone number shown is the resort's main information number. See the *Practical Information* section for central reservation numbers for most areas. Explanation of all abbreviations used in this section can be found under *Skiing* in Chapter 8.

- **Ajax**, *Aspen Mountain, Aspen. I-70 to State Highway 82. Tel. 970/925-1220 or 800/525-6200; www.aspensnowmass.com.* Open mid-November through late April. 8 lifts. 76 trails. Terrain: B=0; I=35, A=65. DH, XC, SS. Base elevation 7,945 feet; top elevation 11,212 feet. Vertical drop 3,267 feet. Ski school for adults and children. Programs for the physically challenged. Child care available for ages 2 months through 3-1/2 years.

- **Arapahoe Basin**, *Arapahoe Basin Resort, Arapahoe Basin. 65 miles west of Denver via I-70 to Exit 216. Tel. 970/468-0718 or 888/ARAPAHOE; www.araphoebasin.com.* Open mid-November through end of June. 5 lifts. 61 trails. Terrain: B=15, I=45, A=45. DH, TM, SS, SB. Base elevation 10,800 feet; top elevation 13,050 feet. Vertical drop 2,250 feet. Ski school for adults and children. Child care available for ages 1 through 3.

- **Aspen Buttermilk**, *Buttermilk Mountain, Aspen. I-70 to State Highway 82. Tel. 970/925-1220 or 800/525-6200; www.aspensnowmass.com.* Open mid-December through end of March. 7 lifts. 43 trails. Terrain: B=35, I=39, A=36. DH, XC, SS, SB. Base elevation 7,870 feet; top elevation 9,900 feet. Vertical drop 2,030 feet. Ski school for adults and children. Programs for the physically challenged and visually impaired. Child care available for ages 2 months through 3-1/2 years.

- **Aspen Highlands**, *Aspen. I-70 to State Highway 82. Tel. 970/925-1220 or 800/525-6200; www.aspensnowmass.com.* Open mid-December through end of March. 4 lifts. 109 trails. Terrain: B=20, I=33, A=47. DH, XC,

TM, SS, SB. Base elevation 8,040 feet; top elevation 11,675 feet. Vertical drop 3,635 feet. Ski school for adults and children. Programs for the physically challenged and visually impaired. Child care available for ages 2 months through 3-1/2 years.

- **Beaver Creek**, *Beaver Creek Resort, Vail. I-70 to Vail exit. Tel. 970/949-5750; www.beavercreek.com.* Open mid-November through mid-April. 13 lifts. 146 trails. Terrain: B=34, I=39, A=27. DH, XC, TM, SS, SB. Base elevation 7,400 feet; top elevation 11,440 feet. Vertical drop 3,340 feet. Ski school for adults and children. Child care available for ages 2 months through 6 years.

- **Berthoud Pass**, *Berthoud Pass Ski Area, Winter Park. 50 miles west of Denver via I-70 to US 40. Tel. 303/569-0100 or 800/754-2378; www.berthoudpass.com.* Open early November through mid-May. 6 lifts. 65 trails. Terrain: B=20, I=30, A=50. DH, XC, SS, SB. Base elevation 10,610 feet; top elevation 12,240 feet. Vertical drop 1,630 feet.

- **Breckenridge**, *Breckenridge Ski Resort, Breckenridge. I-70 to State Highway 9. Tel. 970/453-5000 or 800/789-SNOW; www.breckenridge.com.* Open late October through late April. 25 lifts. 139 trails. Terrain: B=15, I=28, A=57. DH, XC, SB. Base elevation 9,600 feet; top elevation 12,998 feet. Vertical drop 3,398 feet. Ski school for adults and children. Child care available for ages 2 months through 5 years.

- **Copper Mountain**, *Copper Mountain Resort, Copper Mountain. 75 miles west of Denver via I-70 to Copper Mountain exit. Tel. 970/968-2882; www.ski-copper.com.* Open mid-November through mid-April. 21 lifts. 125 trails. Terrain: B=21, I=25, A=44. DH, XC, TM, SS, SB. Base elevation 9,712 feet; top elevation 12,313 feet. Vertical drop 2,433 feet. Ski school for adults and children. Child care available for ages 2 months through 4 years.

- **Eldora**, *Eldora Mountain Resort, Nederland. 45 miles northwest of Denver via I-25 to US 36 and then State Highway 119. Tel. 303/440-8700; www.eldora.com.* Open mid-November through mid-April. 11 lifts. 53 trails. Terrain: B=20, I=50, A=30. DH, XC, TM, SS, SB. Base elevation 9,200 feet; top elevation 10,600 feet. Vertical drop 1,400 feet. Ski school for adults and children.

- **Howelsen**, *Howelsen Ski Area, Steamboat Springs. I-70 to State Highway 9 and then US 40. Tel. 970/879-8499; www.ci.steamboat.co.us.* Open late November through late March. 3 lifts. 19 trails. Terrain: B=25, I-20, A=55. DH, XC, SS, SB. Base elevation 6.696 feet; top elevation 7,136 feet. Vertical drop 440 feet. Ski school for adults and children.

- **Keystone**, *Keystone Resort, Keystone. 70 miles west of Denver via I-70 to US 6 at Keystone exit. Tel. 800/258-9553; www.keystoneresort.com.* Open mid-October through early May. 22 lifts. 116 trails. Terrain: B=12,

I=29, A=59. DH, XC, SS, SB. Base elevation 9,300 feet; top elevation 12,200 feet. Vertical drop 2,900 feet. Ski school for adults and children. Child care available for ages 2 months and up.

• **Loveland**, *Loveland Ski Area, Georgetown. 56 miles west of Denver via I-70 to Georgetown exit. Tel. 303/569-3203 or 800/736-3SKI; www.skiloveland.com.* Open mid-October through mid-May. 11 lifts. 70 trails. Terrain: B=17, I=42, A=41. DH, XC, SB. Base elevation 10,600 feet; top elevation 13,010 feet. Vertical drop 2,410 feet. Ski school for adults and children. Child care available for ages 1 through 12.

• **Silver Creek**, *Silver Creek Golf & Ski Ranch, Silver Creek. 79 miles west of Denver via I-70 to US 40. Tel. 970/887-3384; www.silvercreekski.com.* Open late November through early April. 5 lifts. 33 trails. Terrain: B=30, I=50, A=20. DH, XC, TM, SS, SB. Base elevation 8,202 feet; top elevation 9,202 feet. Vertical drop 1,000 feet. Ski school for adults and children. Child care available for ages 1 through 12.

• **Ski Cooper**, *Ski Cooper Resort, Leadville. I-70 to State Highway 91 and then US 24. Tel. 719/486-3684; www.skicooper.com.* Open late November through end of March. 5 lifts. 26 trails. Terrain: B=30, I=40, A=30. DH, XC, SS, SB. Base elevation 10,500 feet; top elevation 11,700 feet. Vertical drop 1,200 feet. Ski school for adults and children. Child care available for ages 2 and up.

• **Snowmass**, *Snowmass Ski Area, Aspen. I-70 to State Highway 82. Tel. 970/ 925-1220 or 800/525-6200; www.aspensnowmass.com.* Open mid-November through late April. 21 lifts. 83 trails. Terrain: B=7, I=55, A=38. DH, SC, SS, SB. Base elevation 8,104 feet; top elevation 12,510 feet. Vertical drop 3,010 feet. Ski school for adults and children. Programs for the physically challenged and visually impaired. Child care available for ages 2 months through 3-1/2 years.

• **Steamboat**, *Steamboat Ski & Resort Corp., Steamboat Springs. I-70 to State Highway 9 and then US 40. Tel. 970/879-6111; www.steamboat-ski.com.* Open late November through mid-April. 20 lifts. 142 trails. Terrain: B=13, I=56, A=31. DH, XC, TM, SB. Base elevation 6,900 feet; top elevation 10,568 feet. Vertical drop 3,668 feet. Ski school for adults and children. Programs for the physically challenged. Child care available for ages 2 through 6.

• **Vail**, *Vail Associates, Vail. 100 miles west of Denver via I-70 to Vail exit. Tel. 970/476-5601; www.vail.com.* Open mid-November through late April. 33 lifts. 193 trails. Terrain: B=18, I=29, A=53. DH, XC, TM, SS, SB. Base elevation 8,120 feet; top elevation 11,570 feet. Vertical drop 3,450 feet. Ski school for adults and children. Child care available for ages 2 months through 6 years.

• **Winter Park**, *Winter Park Resort, Winter Park. 85 miles west of Denver via I-70 and US 40. Tel. 970/726-5514; www.wintepark-resort.com.* Open mid-November through late April. 22 lifts. 134 trails. Terrain: B=9, I=21, A=70. DH, XC, TM, SS, SB. Base elevation 9,000 feet; top elevation 12,060. Vertical drop 2,886 feet. Ski school for adults and children. Programs for the physically challenged (including children). Child care available for ages 2 months through 5 years.

IS ALL WELL IN SKI HEAVEN?

The last several years have seen an escalating battle between the ski resort operators and developers, and increasingly demonstrative environmentalists who do not wish to see any further encroachment on wilderness lands. While skiers never cease to tire of new slopes to explore, the ecologically minded see every new run as a threat to the pristine Colorado wilderness. The result is, of course, the usual logjam in the courts as everyone sues everyone else. That would be fine (especially for the lawyers) if it were not for the actions of some environmental groups who have taken the law into their own hands. There have been several instances of vandalism, arson and other illegal acts against ski properties. For the most part these have been directed against facilities that are being expanded or under new construction. These acts have been only against property and no ski visitor has been injured.

Hopefully, the confrontations will spawn a dialogue between the resort operators and the environmentalists so that a satisfactory compromise can be reached. In the meantime, we'll still probably continue to read about scattered acts of "eco-terrorism," and skiers will have to come to grips with how much wilderness is really necessary to satisfy their urge to swoosh down the mountainside.

Snowmobiling

• **Brush Creek Stables**, *Snowmass Village. Tel. 970/923-3075*
• **Catride**, *920 Grand Avenue, Grand Lake. Tel. 970/627-8866*
• **Good Times Adventures**, *Breckenridge. Call for pick-up. Tel. 800/477-0144 or 970/453-7604*
• **Leadville Ski Country**, *116 East 9th Street, Leadville. Tel. 800/500-5323 or 719/486-3836*
• **On the Trail**, *County Route 491, Grand Lake. Tel. 970/627-2429*
• **Snowest**, *US Highway 24, Ski Cooper area (Leadville). Tel. 719/486-1750*

Spectator Sports

The **University of Colorado** is a member of the "Big 12" Conference, one of the nation's most prestigious inter-collegiate athletic programs. The most important spectator sports are the men's football and basketball teams. Information on tickets for **Colorado Buffalo** games and other events is available by calling *Tel. 303/492-8337.*

Swimming

- **Breckenridge Recreation Center**, *880 Airport Road, Breckenridge. Tel. 970/453-1734*
- **Eagle-Vail Swim Club**, *99 Eagle Drive, Avon (Vail). Tel. 970/949-4257*
- **Iselin Park Complex**, *450 Maroon Creek Road, Aspen.*

Tennis

- **Aspen Meadows Tennis Courts**, *25 Meadows Road, Aspen.*
- **Dillon Public Courts**, *La Bonte Street, Dillon. Tel. 970/468-2403*

The Vail resort provides about two dozen courts that are open to the public. These are located at **Betty Ford Park**, on the frontage road just east of the village, and at Lionshead.

SHOPPING
BOULDER

As a city with a strong economic and cultural base as well as an important tourist trade, it shouldn't be surprising to learn that Boulder has the greatest diversity of shopping opportunities in the central Rockies region. The downtown area bounded by Spruce, Walnut, 8th and 18th streets has the most interesting shopping possibilities. Highlighting the downtown shopping district is the **Pearl Street Mall**, a landscaped outdoor pedestrian corridor extending from 11th through 15th Streets. There are art galleries, apparel stores, fine jewelry shops, loads of gift shops where you can buy a momento of your trip ranging from junk to extremely expensive, and plenty of restaurants serving anywhere from a quick bite to a lavish meal.

Another area that will be of interest to shopophiles is the **University Hill district**, located adjacent to the main campus of the University of Colorado. This section contains more than 80 stores, many of which carry unusual items. Stylish boutiques and eating places are numerous too.

For a little break, try **Boulder Ice Cream**, *1964 13th Street.* **Handmade in Colorado**, *1426 Pearl Street,* is an excellent place to find just the right souvenir to bring back to friends and family. One of the better known art outlets is the **White Horse Gallery**, *1218 Pearl Street.* Away from downtown the best selection of stores is at the 160-store **Crossroads Mall**, *1600 28th Street at Arapahoe.*

ESTES PARK

The usual selection of tourist town shops can be found along the main thoroughfare of Estes Park, Elkhorn Avenue. Some of the better places you might want to patronize are the **Stage Western**, *Elkhorn and Moraine,* which has an excellent selection of western wear for the entire family; **Omnibus**, *239 W. Elkhorn Avenuem,* varied collection of craft items; **Country West City East**, *209 W. Elkhorn*, featuring gifts and home decor items; and the **Glen Comfort Store**, *five miles east of town on US 34.* Open only from May through October, this store has one of Colorado's best selections of authentic Native American items including Navajo rugs and Hopi kachinas.

I-70 CORRIDOR: BRECKENRIDGE, DILLON, KEYSTONE & VAIL

All of the major resort hotels have upscale shops. Ski apparel and equipment are, of course, among the most popular items in this area regardless of the time of the year. Quality and selection are both excellent but don't expect to find any bargains, especially during the winter. The shopping in Aspen, although not on the Interstate corridor, is of a similar nature.

More general shopping can be yours at the **Dillon Factory Stores**, *just east of Exit 205 of I-70*, where **Donna Karan**, **Clothes for Kids**, and **Nautica** are among the stores. North of Dillon on CO 9 is the **Silverthorne Factory Stores**. Stores are divided into three sections (Green, Blue, and Red Villages). The stores include such well known names as **Levi's**, **London Fog**, **Mikasa**, **Nike**, **Izod**, **Eddie Bauer**, **American Eagle Outfitters**, and **Tommy Hilfiger** among the more than 60 stores and eating places.

PRACTICAL INFORMATION
- **Airport**
  Aspen: *Tel. 970/920-5385*
  Steamboat Springs: *Tel. 970/879-1204*
  Vail: Eagle County Airport (32 miles west of Vail in Gypsum off of I-70, Exit 140). *Tel. 970/524-9490*
- **Airport Transportation**
  Boulder Airporter, *Tel. 303/444-0808*
  Service to Denver International Airport (Aspen, Breckenridge, Dillon, Vail): **Colorado Mountain Express**, *Tel. 800/525-6363;* **Discount Shuttle**, *Tel. 800/570-5540;* **Vans to Vail**, *Tel. 800/222-2212*

- **Bus Depot**
  Boulder: *4401 N. Broadway*
  Dillon (Silverthorne) *Tel. 970/468-1938*
  Frisco: *1202 N. Summit Blvd., Tel. 970/668-5703*
- **Hospitals**
  Aspen: **Aspen Valley Hospital,** *200 Castle Creek Road. Tel. 970/925-1120*
  Boulder: **Boulder Community Hospital,** *1100 Balsam. Tel. 303/440-2273*
  Breckenridge: **Breckenridge Medical Center,** *535 S. Park Street. Tel. 970/453-9000*
  Estes Park: **Estes Park Medical Center,** *555 Prospect. Tel. 970/586-2317*
  Leadville: **St. Vincent General,** *4th & Washington Streets. Tel. 719/486-0230*
  Steamboat Springs: **Routt Memorial Hospital,** *80 Park Avenue. Tel. 970/879-1322*
  Vail: **Vail Valley Medical Center,** *181 W. Meadow Drive. Tel. 970/476-2451*
  Winter Park: **Winter Park Medical Center,** *Tel. 970/726-9616*
- **Hotel Hot Line**
  Aspen Central Reservations: *Tel. 800/262-7736*
  Breckenridge: *Tel. 800/858-5885*
  Dillon/Keystone: *Tel. 800/365-6365*
  Estes Park Central Reservations: *Tel. 970/586-4402 or 800/762-596*
  Grand Lake: *Tel. 800/462-5253*
  Snowmass: *Tel. 800/215-7669*
  Steamboat Springs: *Tel. 800/922-2722*
  Vail: *Tel. 800/525-3875*
- **Police** (non-emergency)
  Aspen: *Tel. 970/920-5400*
  Boulder: *Tel. 303/441-4444*
  Breckenridge: *Tel. 970/453-2941*
  Estes Park: *Tel. 970/586-5331*
  Grand Lake: *Tel. 970/627-3322*
  Leadville: *Tel. 719/486-1365*
  Steamboat Springs: *Tel. 970/849-1144*
  Vail: *Tel. 970/479-2200*
  Winter Park *Tel. 970/726-5666*
- **Public Transportation**
  Aspen/Vail: Shuttle service to and from resorts. Inquire at visitor information center.
  Boulder: **Skyride-RTD Bus Service,** *Tel. 303/299-6000 and 303/447-*

8282

Summit County (Breckenridge, Dillon, Frisco, Keystone): **Summit Stage**, *Tel. 970/453-1241*

Steamboat Springs: **Steamboat Springs Transit**, *Tel. 970/879-3717*

· **Taxi**

Aspen: **High Mountain Taxi**, *Tel. 800/528-8294 or 970/925-8294*

Boulder: **Boulder Yellow Cab**, *Tel. 303/442-2277;* **Metro Taxi**, *Tel. 303/333-3333*

Breckenridge: **Around Town Taxi**, *Tel. 970/453-6425*

· **Tourist Office/Visitor Bureau**

Aspen: *425 Rio Grande Place, Tel. 800/26-ASPEN; www.aspenchamber.org*

Boulder: *2440 Pearl Street, Tel. 800/444-0447; www.visitor.boulder.co.us*

Central City: *141 Nevada, Tel. 800/542-2999*

Dillon/Frisco/Keystone: *S. Summit Blvd., Frisco. Tel. 970/668-0376; www.summitchamber.org*

Estes Park: *500 Bigh Thompson Ave., Tel. 800/443-7837; www.rockymtntrav.com/estes*

Georgetown: *Tel. 800/472-8230*

Granby: *Tel. 800/325-1661*

Grand Lake: *Tel. 800/531-1019; www.grandlakecolorado.com*

Idaho Springs: *2300 Colorado Blvd., Tel. 303/567-4382; www.clearcreekcounty.com*

Leadville: *809 Harrison Avenue, Tel. 800/933-3901; : www.leadvilleusa.com*

Steamboat Springs: *Tel. 970/879-0880; www.steamboat-chamber.com*

Vail: *100 East Meadow Drive, Tel. 800/525-3875; www.vail.net/chamber*

Winter Park: *50 Vazquez Road, Tel. 800/903-7275; www.winterpark-info.com*

· **Train Station**

Granby: *438 Railroad Avenue*

Winter Park: *420 Railroad Avenue, in adjacent town of Fraser*

14. NORTHWEST COLORADO - OFF THE BEATEN PATH

This is an unusual region, most of which is "unexplored" for the typical visitor to Colorado. That is a mistake that you should try to avoid because the area has some wonderful attractions, highlighted by the **Colorado** and **Dinosaur National Monuments**. Northwest Colorado is generally a high plateau with elevations ranging mainly in the neighborhood of from 4,000 to 6,500 feet. The western edge of the Rockies ends fairly abruptly and drops to the Colorado Plateau. There are occasional higher mountains along with many river gorges, valleys, and hilly regions. Except for **Grand Junction**, which has a population of nearly 45,000 people, there are few towns of any size. There is some skiing near Grand Junction and especially at **Glenwood Springs**, but this isn't really ski country. Plenty of outdoor action is available in the warmer months, though, as this is largely a near-wilderness area except for the I-70 corridor that traverses the southern portion of the northwest.

Portions of the **White River** and **Grand Mesa National Forests** occupy large chunks of the eastern edge of the area but large expanses are quite arid and surprisingly barren for Colorado. It is contrasts such as these that make the northwest special. Unusual geologic formations are a big part of the attraction here. In many places the landscape is incredible and is more like that found in Utah rather than Colorado. However, since the northwest borders on Utah that shouldn't be so surprising.

Except for a few resorts in the Glenwood Springs area you won't find many fancy accommodations and restaurants in the northwest. What you will find is friendly people and few gimmicks. This is the real west and is suitable more to the traveler who seeks adventure rather than pampering.

ARRIVALS & DEPARTURES

As the biggest city in the region, Grand Junction is the most likely place to arrive if you're coming by common carrier. **Walker Field Airport** is served by AmericaWest Express, Skywest/Delta Connection, and United Express. There are non-stop flights to Denver, Phoenix, and Salt Lake City. Glenwood Springs is served by the Eagle County Regional Airport (see the *North-Central Rockies* chapter for further information). Amtrak has stations in Grand Junction and Glenwood Springs but there's a bigger choice of car rentals and tours from Grand Junction. The same is true for Greyhound bus service.

Travelers coming to the northwest by car are most likely to be arriving via I-70 from either the east or west. If you're coming from the east it's more logical to begin the touring loop in Glenwood Springs. Other major routes coming into this part of the state are US 50 from the southwest and US 40 from either northern Utah or the northern Rockies via Steamboat Springs.

ORIENTATION

My northwest touring region is rectangular in shape with the north-south edges being bigger. I-70 provides the best east-to-west access as it cuts across the bottom of the region from Glenwood Springs to Grand Junction and beyond into Utah. US 40 does the same in the north between Steamboat Springs and Dinosaur, but this is a much more sparsely developed area.

The main north to south routes are CO 13 from Rifle along I-70 north to Craig and CO 139 which runs near the western border of the state from west of Grand Junction to Rangely. Other than Grand Junction and Glenwood Springs the only towns of significance are Rangely, Craig, and Meeker and all of those are far less important than the other two as tourist destinations.

GETTING AROUND THE REGION

Scheduled transportation within the area is minimal once you get away from Grand Junction so except for some bus service between the bigger communities you almost have to have a car in order to easily get around. The roads are generally good. In addition, because most of the northwest is away from major population and visitor centers there are relatively few guided tours, another reason to drive.

WHERE TO STAY

Lodging facilities in the northwest are quite limited except for the Grand Junction and Glenwood Springs areas. Consequently, you may want to refer to the chain property listings in Chapter 6, *Planning Your Trip*, more for this region than in other parts of the state.

CRAIG
Inexpensive

A BAR Z MOTEL, *269 West US Highway 40. Tel. 970/824-7066; Fax 970/824-3641. Toll free reservations 800/458-7228. 42 Rooms. Rates: $39-55 including Continental breakfast. Most major credit cards accepted. Located about 1-1/2 miles west of downtown on the main highway.*

A clean and comfortable roadside motel with mildly attractive rooms that feature good views of the Yampa Valley. Coffee makers are standard in all units while some have microwave ovens or refrigerators. There's even one large "executive suite" with its own Jacuzzi. The A Bar Z doesn't have a swimming pool but there is a hot tub. It also has a game room and a large outdoor area for picnicing or playing horseshoes and volleyball. Restaurants are located nearby.

BLACK NUGGET MOTEL, *2855 W. Victory Way. Tel. 970/824-8161; Fax 970/824-9446. Toll free reservations 800/727-2088. 20 Rooms. Rates: $36-55 including Continental breakfast from mid-May to mid-November. Most major credit cards accepted. Located just west of the junction of CO 13 abou 1-1/2 miles west of town.*

Sitting on a hillside off of the main highway, the Black Nugget has panoramic valley views that, along with a super friendly staff, make this small motel quite an attractive choice. It has basic accommodations but is exceptionally well maintained. Some rooms feature microwave ovens or refrigerator. There is a large outdoor recreation area and deck where guests can enjoy such diversions as basketball or horseshoes. The more cultured can even play croquet! A decent restaurant is located nearby.

GLENWOOD SPRINGS
Expensive

BEST WESTERN ANTLERS MOTEL, *171 West 6th Street. Tel. 970/945-8535; Fax 970/945-9368. Toll free reservations 800/528-1234. 101 Rooms. Rates: High season: $118-170 with higher range on weekends; Low season: $88-118. "Seasons" change frequently so it is best to call for exact rates for the time you plan to visit. Major credit cards accepted. Located to the immediate north of I-70, Exit 116.*

An attractive two-story lodge style roadside motel picturesquely situated at the base of a gently sloping green carpeted mountain, the Antlers property covers five acres. The guest rooms are standard to a little better than most motels and some have refrigerators. There are several two bedroom units available. There's a sizable outdoor heated swimming pool, whirlpool, one tennis court and a playground for children. Although there isn't any on-premise restaurant, the Antler's near downtown location puts it in close proximity to a decent selection of eateries.

Moderate

GLENWOOD HOT SPRINGS LODGE, *415 East 6th Street. Tel. 970/ 945-6571; Fax 970/945-6571. Toll free reservations 800/537-7946; www.hot-springspool.com. 107 Rooms. Rates: High season (mid-March through September): $92-117; Low season (October through mid-March): $72-97. Major credit cards accepted. Located across from the municipal pool to the north of I-70, Exit 116.*

This modern five-story motor inn is one of the newest in town and has better than average bright and cheerful rooms that feature clean and comfortable furnishings with coffee maker and in-room safe. Many rooms have refrigerator. However, if you are a pool lover or require lots of recreational facilities for your stay in Glenwood Springs, than the Hot Springs Lodge is an ideal choice. The main heated swimming pool is more than four hundred feet long (kids will like the water slide) and there is also a mineral pool with a toasty temperature of 104 degrees. In addition the inn has a whirlpool, fully equipped athletic club and miniature golf. There is a restaurant on the premises (no dinner served during the summer) and a cocktail lounge.

HOTEL COLORADO, *526 Pine Street. Tel. 970/945-6511; Fax 970/ 945-7030. Toll free reservations 800/544-3998; www.hotelcolorado.com. 128 Rooms. Rates: $108-178. Major credit cards accepted. Located in the heart of downtown on CO Highway 84.*

This 1893 Victorian structure is a true delight. Listed on the National Register of Historic Places, it was frequented by Teddy Roosevelt on such a regular basis that it was often referred to as his Western White House. The five-story brick building is fronted by a small but attractive flower garden with statuary, fountains and antique lightpoles. Guest accommodations vary considerably from some tiny rooms to better sized single room units all the way up to a dozen individually themed suites. All rooms have video cassette players. There isn't any air conditioning. Some rooms feature such amenities as coffee makers and refrigerators. A few even have Jacuzzi tubs.

The complete health spa includes exercise room, sauna, steamroom and whirlpool. There's also a jogging track. Other facilities and services provided at an additional charge include a tanning salon, massage, rafting trips, and bicycle rentals. The restaurant and cocktail lounge are both pleasant places. Free transportation is provided within a seven mile radius of the hotel.

GRAND JUNCTION
Moderate

ADAM'S MARK HOTEL, *743 Horizon Drive. Tel. 970/241-8888; Fax 970/2412-7266. Toll free reservations 800/444-2326. 264 Rooms. Rates: High season (May through mid-October): $99-220; Low season (mid-October through April): $79-200. Major credit cards accepted. Located just south of I-70, Exit 31.*

The modern eight-story Adam's Mark is Grand Junction's largest and most elaborate lodging facility. The respected Adam's Mark name is the reason why the prices here are considerably more than elsewhere in town, but the quality is worth it for some travelers. Situated on two acres of lovely landscaped grounds and boasting a beautiful courtyard recreation area overlooked by most of the public facilities, the rooms feature outstanding views of either the Colorado National Monument, Mount Garfield or the imposing Grand Mesa. All of the guest rooms are large and attractively furnished. Some rooms have coffee makers, refrigerators and whirlpool tub. The hotel has two good restaurants and in summer you can also dine outside on the patio besides the pretty swimming pool. There is also a cocktail lounge.

Recreational facilities at the Adam's Mark are extensive and include, besides the heated pool, several lighted tennis courts, courts for volleyball, basketball, horseshoes and croquet, exercise room and health club. A sizable playground will keep little children well occupied.

GRAND VISTA HOTEL, *2790 Crossroads Boulevard. Tel. 970/241-8411; Fax 970/241-1077. Toll free reservations 800/800-7796; www.grandvistahotel.com. E-mail: sales@grandvistahotel.com. 158 Rooms. Rates: $72-109 including Continental breakfast. Major credit cards accepted. Located a quarter mile north of I-70, Exit 31.*

Although the exterior of this modern six-story motor inn looks more like a suburban office building, things get much better once you step into the well appointed lobby and other public areas. The rooms, too, are excellent as they are spacious (many are mini-suites) and well decorated. Several have whirlpool tubs. The majority of the guest rooms have wonderful views of the Colorado National Monument and the colorful Bookcliffs. Recreational facilities include an indoor swimming pool and spa. There's a small gift shop on the premises. Oliver's Restaurant offers a decent meal at a fair price, but its strong point is the freshly baked cakes, pies and breads. Bailey's Lounge sometimes offers entertainment.

If you are looking for a combination of quality accommodations and value when it comes to paying the bill, the Grand Vista is my selection as the number one choice when staying in Grand Junction.

Inexpensive
BEST WESTERN SANDMAN MOTEL, *708 Horizon Drive. Tel. 970/ 243-4150; Fax 970/243-1826. Toll free reservaitons 800/528-1234. 79 Rooms. Rates: $48-65. Major credit cards accepted. Located just south of I-70, Exit 31.*

The white exterior of this motel is trimmed with blue and makes a pretty picture. The rooms aren't anything special but considering the price are a nice size and very comfortable. All rooms have refrigerators and hair dryers. There isn't any restaurant but many are locted along Horizon Drive. The heated pool and spa are outdoors during the warmer months but can be enclosed once the cold weather arrives.

PEACHTREE INN, *1600 North Avenue. Tel. 970/245-5770; Fax 970/ 243-2955. Toll free reservations 800/525-0030. 75 Rooms. Rates: $40-89. Most major credit cards accepted. Located near downtown south of I-70, Exit 31 via 12th Sreet to North Avenue and then east.*

A lot of what I said about the Clifton Inn's rooms applies as well to the Peachtree, another bargain buy that will more than adequately serve to keep you comfortable for a night or two. The Peachtree, however, does have an on-premise restaurant as well as a cocktail lounge. It also has a heated outdoor swimming pool. It is situated about eight blocks from the center of town and is close to Mesa State College. A lot of families and friends of the school's students stay there.

RANGELY

Because of the scarcity of accommodations near Dinosaur National Monument, you should also consider staying in Vernal, Utah, especially if you are going to be visiting the Utah section of the Monument. This community is located 30 miles west of the Colorado state line. Among the major chain hotels represented there are Best Western and the Econolodge and Rodeway brands of the Choice group.

Inexpensive
BUDGET HOUSE INN, *117 S. Grand Street. Tel. 970/675-8461. 25 Rooms. Rates: $40-45. Most major credit cards accepted. Located just off of Main Street (CO 64).*

Basic accommodations and few facilities but if you're traveling in this part of the state you might well need to stay in Rangely. The rooms are clean and well kept. Some have microwave ovens and refrigerators. Restaurants are located within a short distance.

FOUR QUEENS MOTEL, *206 East Main Street. Tel. 970/675-5035; Fax 970/675-5037. 32 Rooms. Rates: $45-55. American Express, Discover, MasterCard and VISA accepted. Located near the center of town on the Colorado Highway 64.*

Another place that I wouldn't usually recommend but it gives you another choice besides the Escalante Trail. Rooms are simple but clean and at the prices the Four Queens is charging you couldn't expect much more. Guests receive free passes to a nearby recreation center. Restaurants are close by.

CAMPING & RV SITES
• **Arni's Acres**, *50235 US Highways 6 & 24, Glenwood Springs. Tel. 970/945-5340*
• **Blue Mountain RV Park**, *800 Dakota Avenue, Dinosaur. Tel. 970/374-2747*
• **Craig KOA Campgrounds**, *US Highway 40 East, Craig. Tel. 970/824-5105*
• **Junction West RV Park**, *793 22 Road, Grand Junction. Tel. 970/245-8531*
• **Lamplighter Estates**, *2210 W. 3rd Street, Craig. Tel. 970/824-8550*
• **RV Ranch at Grand Junction**, *3238 I-70 Business Loop. Tel. 970/434-6644*
• **Rock Gardens**, *1308 County Road 128, Glenwood Springs. Tel. 970/945-6737*

WHERE TO EAT
CRAIG
Moderate/Inexpensive
   SIGNAL HILL, *2705 W. Victory Way. Tel. 970/824-6682. Most major credit cards accepted. Lunch and dinner served daily.*

   Standard steak house with an attractive atmosphere and a decent selection of nicely prepared beef, chicken and ribs. The portions are generous, especially considering the prices. Friendly service. Cocktails are served.

   VIRGINIA'S CACTUS GRILL, *420 Yampa Avenue. Tel. 970/824-9966. Discover, MasterCard and VISA accepted. Lunch and dinner served daily except Sunday.*

   This is a pleasant little place if you like Mexican cuisine (there are also a few items that can be considered Southwestern on the menu). Like the previous listing, it isn't anything special but you won't find that in Craig. Cocktail service provided by Mather's Bar, which is in the same "room," so to speak, but not a part of the restaurant.

GLENWOOD SPRINGS
Moderate
   THE BAYOU, *West Glenwood Highway. Tel. 970/945-1047. Most major credit cards accepted. Dinner served nightly.*

   A popular and attractive casual restaurant that features excellent Cajun style cooking. The decor is charmingly southern and so is the deliberate accent of some of the friendly staff that provides warm and personal service. The portions are so generous that some grown-ups have been known to order from the children's menu–The Bayou allows that by calling it their menu for "Wimps and Kids." A large outdoor patio open during the warmer months provides a splendid view of the massive mountain wall that lies just beyond the town. Full cocktail service and separate bar with live entertainment.

CHINA TOWN, *2830 S. Glen Ave. Tel. 970/945-0307. MasterCard and VISA accepted. Lunch and dinner served daily. Smoke free premises.*

This is actually two restaurants in one. The Panda Room specializes in chinese food and serves first rate dishes in both Mandarin and spicy Szechuan styles. The Fuji Room boasts a large selection of Japanese cuisine including tempura, teriyaki, miso and sushi. Each dining room is attractively decorated to reflect the cuisine and is staffed by a friendly staff that will enhance your casual dining experience. Tableside cocktail service.

THE FIRESIDE, *West Glenwood Highway. Tel. 970/945-6613. Most major credit cards accepted. Breakfast or brunch on Sunday only; lunch served Monday to Friday; dinner served nightly.*

The Fireside is a large, popular and casual family restaurant that serves a big selection of steaks, ribs, fresh fish and seafood in an attractive dining room. The salad bar is really big and features a nice array of fresh and wholesome items along with several hot soups. Portions are on the humongous side. The service is good. Sunday brunch and lunch on Monday through Thursday is in the form of a buffet. Cocktail service and separate lounge. Children's menu.

RESTAURANT SOPRIS, *7215 State Highway 82. Tel. 970/945-7771. American Express, Discover, MasterCard and VISA accepted. Dinner served nightly. Reservations are suggested.*

When the word restaurant comes before the name you usually know that the eatery is upscale and probably serves European cuisine. That is the case at Sopris where some entrees go into the Expensive category. The atmosphere is casual in this fine restaurant with a Victorian atmosphere and excellent service. The varied menu is highlighted by an outstanding selection of appetizers, but you won't be disappointed with the main courses either. There is table side cocktail service and a separate lounge. Surprisingly, this is a place that is casual enough for the whole family to enjoy and they even offer a children's menu.

Inexpensive

VILLAGE INN, *Located at I-70, Exit 116. Tel. 970/945-9275. Most major credit cards accepted. Breakfast, lunch and dinner served daily.*

A contemporary style family restaurant that doesn't look too different on either the outside or inside from a number of national chain restaurants like Denny's. However, the food is a lot better and there's also more of it, especially when you consider the value oriented pricing. It's nothing fancy but is often what you'll be looking for after sampling so many unusual places to eat while on vacation. The desserts are excellent. Children's menu.

GRAND JUNCTION
Moderate
THE WINERY, *642 Main Street. Tel. 970/242-4100. Most major credit cards accepted. Dinner served nightly. Reservations are suggested.*

This downtown restaurant (on street parking only) is popular with the locals and with good reason. The attractive decor is an interesting combination of western casual and classic elegance–it's rough wood with abundant use of stained glass. The atmosphere and service are casual. The chefs prepare a variety of steak and seafood dishes. Many entrees are prepared either grilled or teriyaki style. The prime rib is excellent. All dinners are accompanied by trips to their ample salad bar. Cocktail service and lounge.

W.W. PEPPERS, *759 Horizon Drive. Tel. 970/245-9251. American Express, MasterCard and VISA accepted. Lunch served Monday through Friday; dinner served nightly.*

Another casual and popular place, W.W. Peppers has a pretty southwestern style and cuisne to match. You can also opt for some traditional western American dishes. The service is warm and friendly. Cocktail service and separate lounge.

Inexpensive
REDLANDS DOS HOMBRES, *421 Brach Drive. Tel. 970/242-8861. Most major credit cards accepted. Lunch and dinner served daily.*

Traditional Mexican cuisine in an attractive setting at a most modest price makes Redlands a good choice for family dining. During the warmer months you can dine outside on the patio in view of the Colorado National Monument. The main courses don't have any surprises but everything is quite tasty. For dessert I recommend either their excellent fried ice cream or sopapillas. Cocktail service and lounge. Childen's menu.

MEEKER
Inexpensive
MEEKER CAFE & HOTEL, *560 Main Street. Tel. 970/878-5255. MasterCard and VISA accepted. Breakfast, lunch and dinner served daily.*

Located off the lobby of a nicely restored hundred year old facility, the cafe features simple and unpretentious home-style cooking (beef, chicken and seafood) that is tasty and served in generous amounts. In towns like this, that's about all you can expect. Cocktails served.

As the name indicates, the Meeker is also a hotel. While I don't consider it as meeting the standards set for a lodging listing in this book it could do in a real pinch should you need to stay in Meeker.

RANGELY
Inexpensive/Moderate
MAGALINO'S FAMILY RESTAURANT, *124 W. Main Street. Tel. 970/675-2321. Most major credit cards accepted. Breakfast, lunch and dinner served daily.*

What can be said for the Meeker Cafe also applies here, although it would be unfair to characterize it as the best place to eat in Rangely because it's the only place. Actually, the menu is quite varied and the atmosphere much more contemporary compared to the previous entry and you shouldn't have any complaints with their American cuisine or friendly and efficient service. Cocktail service. Children's menu.

SEEING THE SIGHTS
The suggested itinerary through the northwest is a loop so the starting point doesn't matter. Grand Junction or Glenwood Springs, both along I-70, is the logical starting point for the majority of visitors.

GRAND JUNCTION
The important agricultural community of **Grand Junction** is located at the confluence of the Colorado and Gunnison Rivers. At one time the Colorado was known as the Grand River, hence the name. The fertile soil of the Grand Valley is largely a result of those two rivers and the area is a major producer of several crops, especially fruits. In fact, on the western side of Grand Junction is a small town called Fruita. The Grand Valley is bordered on the east by an impressive geological feature known as the Grand Mesa. More about that later as I've scheduled that for the return end of the loop.

In addition to the many sights in and around Grand Junction the area is popular for rafting, biking, golf, and even skiing. A system of riverfront trails on the Colorado is also part of the recreation scene. More about that later. Several of the city's sights have to do with dinosaurs in one way or another. Although Grand Junction is more than a hundred miles from Dinosaur National Monument, the Grand Valley was at one time home to many dinosaur species as well. It ranks in importance, from a paleontologist's standpoint, only slightly behind the latter as a place for scientific research on these prehistoric creatures. However, because

Grand Junction covers a fairly big area I'll group the attractions by location rather than subject.

A good place to start touring Grand Junction is at the visitor center off of Exit 31 on I-70. You can get up to the minute information there about what's going on. As you wander around downtown Grand Junction you'll notice a large number of sculptured art on the streets, many in lifelike poses. This **Art on the Corner** program is the largest outdoor display of sculpture in Colorado.

The first four attractions are all in the downtown area and can be done on foot if you like. From Exit 31 take Horizon Drive to 7th Street and then south a few blocks into the city center. The **Western Colorado Center for the Arts**, *1803 N. 7th Street*, features permanent and changing exhibits by Southwestern artists including works by the Navajo such as rugs and pottery. *Tel. 970/243-7337. The gallery is open Tuesday through Saturday from 9:00am until 4:00pm except Thanksgiving and Christmas. Admission is $2 for those age 12 and older.* A few blocks away at 4th and Main is the **Dinosaur Valley Museum** *(362 Main St.)* which has a large collection of fossilized dinosaur bones found in the vicinity of Grand Junction. It is also a working paleontology laboratory. Children, and maybe a lot of adults, will especially enjoy the animated life-size dinosaurs. With the popularity of dinosaurs these days the museum's extensive gift shop inventory of dinosaur items will be sure to please. *Tel. 970/241-9120. The museum is open daily from 9:00am until 5:00pm (to 4:00pm on Sunday), Memorial Day through Labor Day; and Tuesday to Saturday from 10:00am to 4:00pm the rest of the year. The adult admission price is $4, $3.50 for seniors and $2 for children.*

Nearby is the **Museum of Western Colorado** at *248 South 4th Street, corner of Ute.* It has exhibits on regional history from the mid-1880's until the present time. Of interest is the turn-of-the century schoolroom. *Tel. 970/242-0971. Museum hours are Monday through Saturday from 10:00am until 4:45pm (closed Monday after Labor Day until Memorial Day) except for state holidays. The admission is $3 for adults and $2.50 for children ages 2 through 12.* The final downtown stop is only for those of you traveling with children. They'll enjoy the **Doo Zoo Children's Museum**, *635 Main Street between Main and Colorado*, not a zoo at all but a hands-on learning center. *Tel. 970/241-5225. The hours are daily from 10:00am until 5:00pm except for state holidays. The admission is $3 for children over 2 and $1 for adults.*

The **Cross Orchards Historic Farm** is east of downtown at *3073 Patterson ("F") Road.* Take any numbered street north to Patterson and then drive east (right turn). Operated by the Museum of Western Colorado, the farm recreates agricultural life of the early 1900's through costumed guides, demonstrations, and tours of the barn, bunkhouse and orchards. There is also a large display of heavy farm equipment and narrow gauge railroad cars. *Tel. 970/434-9814. Operating hours are Tuesday through Saturday from 10:00am until 4:00pm and on Sunday from noon until 4:00pm during the summer. The season usually runs from May through September but inquire as to exact dates. Admission is $4 for adults, $3.50 for senior citizens, and $2 for children ages 2 through 12.*

The area around Grand Junction is the heart of the Colorado wine country, so while you are on the east side of town you might want to visit one of the area's numerous wineries. The largest number of wineries are located in the community of Palisade. That town can be reached from Grand Junction via Patterson ("F") Road to US 6 eastbound. All of the wineries feature tours of the wine making process as well as tasting sessions and retail shops. Among the wineries inviting visitors are:

- **Canyon Wind Cellars**, *3907 N. River Road, Tel. 970/523-5500*
- **Colorado Cellars**, *3553 E Road, Tel. 800/848-2812*
- **Grand River Vineyards**, *I-70 at Exit 42, Tel. 970/464-7586*
- **Plum Creek Cellars**, *3708 G Road, Tel. 970/464-7586*
- **Rocky Mountain Meadery**, *3701 G Road, Tel. 800/720-2558*
- **St. Kathryn Cellars**, *785 Elberta Avenue, Tel. 970/464-9288*

Call for information on operating hours. All of the wineries offer free admission and most do not charge for tastings. One additional winery is located within Grand Junction itself. This one is the **Two Rivers Winery**, *2087 Broadway, Tel. 970/255-1471.*

All the way over on the west side of Grand Junction are **Riggs Hill** and **Dinosaur Hill**. Take Broadway westbound from town (also designated as CO 340). Along the way you'll have an excellent view of the plateau on which the Colorado National Monument is located. You don't have to visit both sites because they're quite similar but each is an example of a site where dinosaur remains were found.

THE COLORADO NATIONAL MONUMENT

I have always wondered how something as beautiful as the **Colorado National Monument**, conveniently situated within minutes of a major interstate highway, has remained so relatively unknown to the traveling public. It is truly a gem of the national park system and something which is worth going out of the way to see. It's an ideal way to spend anywhere from two hours to a whole day.

Its beauty is both awesome and strange, the product of erosion which has left thousand foot deep canyons and monolithic sandstone formations towering hundreds of feet above the valley floor. Brilliant colors and rugged terrain dominate the scene. The 20,454 acre (about 32 square miles) monument sits on the south side of the Colorado River, 2,000 feet above the valley floor as if it were one massive building rising above Grand

Junction. And best of all, the sights of the Colorado National Monument are easily seen by car and short walks (there are seven trails of a mile or less in length) along the 23-mile long **Rim Rock Drive**. Bicycles are permitted on the road and that is also a popular way of getting around the monument. Adventure travelers will find longer back-country trails ranging from two to over eight miles in length. More than twenty overlooks along Rim Rock Drive provide plenty of opportunities to take in the monument's wonderful rock formations as well as the view of the valley below.

You can enter the monument from either the east or west sides. It doesn't matter which way you come in but I'll take you from the west entrance only because the visitor center is located on that side and it's always helpful to stop there before embarking on your journey. The easiest way to get to the West Entrance is to take I-70 west to the Fruita Exit (#19) and then follow CO 340 directly into the monument.

Rim Rock Drive starts climbing as soon as you enter the monument. You'll encounter several switchbacks that are easy enough for anyone to drive on but exciting enough to provide some feeling of adventure during the climb along with two tunnels as well as several overlooks before reaching the Visitor Center. But before you get to there do stop at **Balanced Rock View**, an amazing sight–a 600-ton bolder sits perched in apparent comfort atop a large rock pedestal. Nearby is the half-mile **Canyon Rim Trail** which is a level walk along the cliff edge above a colorful canyon. The first overlook after the Visitor Center is **Independence Rock**, the largest single formation in the monument at over 450 feet. **Monument Canyon View** is also outstanding. At the **Coke Ovens Overlook** there is a staggering view of these two massive and rounded rock formations that look every bit like what they're named. There is also a half-mile trail at this point that makes a gradual descent from the parking area to a point closer to the formations.

After the Coke Ovens the overlooks are a litle more spread out for about 12 miles. However, **Artists Point**, **Highland View**, **Ute Canyon View** and **Red Canyon Overlook** are all worth at least a brief stop. Just before Ute Canyon the road reaches its highest elevation at 6,640 feet. (The entrance stations are 4,690 feet and 4,930 feet.) Soon after passing **Cold Shivers Point** the road begins its main descent via another series of switchbacks and a tunnel. Your last stop should be at the **Devil's Kitchen** where a 3/4-mile trail easily descends to a natural grotto amid huge boulders. *Tel. 970/858-3617. The monument is open at all times. Visitor Center hours are daily from 8:00am until 7:00pm, June through Labor Day; and 9:00am until 5:00pm the rest of the year.. Admission is $4 per vehicle but free if you have a park service passport.*

DINOSAUR NATIONAL MONUMENT

Leave Grand Junction by heading west on I-70 to Exit 15. Then go north on CO 139 for 73 miles to Rangely. The drive, although long, is pleasant because the road is good and it takes in the mildly interesting scenery of the Roan Plateau along with distant mountain peaks. Rangely is the town closest to Dinosaur National Monument that has a good selection of visitor services, so it's likely that you might stay here. From Rangely go west 18 miles on CO 64 to the small town of Dinosaur, the gateway to the national monument.

Dinosaur National Monument covers more than 211,000 acres (325 square miles) of spectacular canyons as well as one of the biggest area of dinosaur remains ever found anywhere in the world. The monument extends across the Colorado-Utah state line and has two distinct sections, one in each state. Unfortunately, the park road system doesn't provide a direct connection between them. Although I don't intend to make this a Utah guide, I will cover that section because a visit to Dinosaur isn't complete without doing both parts.

We'll go to the Utah section first. From the town ride west on US 40 for 25 miles to Jensen and then north for seven miles on Utah 149 into the **Dinosaur Quary** section of the park. This is probably the part of the monument that visitors most associate with its name as the Colorado section is primarily scenic. At the quary you can see many dinosaur bones in a staggering array of sizes. Almost all of the bones were removed from a single sandstone cliff. There are some exhibits as well but most of the complete skeletons removed from the quary are on display at various museums throughout the country. During the summer you'll have to take a shuttle bus from the parking area to the quary but you can drive all the way there at other times. *Tel. 435/789-2115. Quary open every day of the year except New Year's, Thanksgiving, and Christmas from 8:00am to 7:00pm in summer and to 4:30 the remainder of the year.*

Return to Dinosaur and you're ready for the Colorado section of the monument. The Visitor Center is located two miles east of Dinosaur on US 40. From that point the **Harpers Corner Scenic Drive** travels 31 miles through magnificent canyon country. There are several overlooks which provide easy viewing of this natural wonderland. The road ends at Harpers Corner from which there is a trail (not for the physically challenged) that has even better views of the canyons.

The main road is paved and easy but if you have a high clearance vehicle you might want to try some of the othe roads, such as the **Echo Park Road** that lead to more remote areas and even better sights. River running at Dinosaur National Monument is first class. If you want to experience the canyons in that manner stop at the Visitor Center for further information. *Tel. 970/374-3000. The Monument is open at all times.*

Headquarters Visitor Center in Dinosaur open daily from 8:30am-7:00pm in summer and daily from 8:00am until 4:30pm during the rest of the year. It is closed on New Year's Day, Thanksgiving, and Christmas. Admission is $10 per vehicle to those not holding a park service passport.

Retrace your route back to Dinosaur and then continue the northwest loop by traveling east on US 40.

BROWN'S PARK COUNTRY

*One of the most remote areas of Colorado is located in the extreme northwest corner of the state above the Green and Yampa Rivers. It is often called **Brown's Park**, a high desert valley. Once home to some famous outlaws such as Butch Cassidy, it looks much the same today as it did more than a hundred years ago.*

*A visit to Brown's Park is mainly for the adventurous because of the nature of the roads (mostly unpaved) and the relative scarcity of visitor services. Among the beautiful sights that those who venture in will find are the **Vermillion Falls**, **Irish Canyon**, the towering rocky walls known as the **Gates of Lodore** and the **Brown's Park National Wildlife Refuge**. Outdoor recreation such as rafting and four wheel touring is especially popular.*

Access to the area is mainly by CO 318 west from Maybell. That comunity is located about 30 miles west of Craig via US 40. Further information can be obtained from the Moffat County Visitors Bureau (see "Craig" in the Practical Information section).

THROUGH THE WILDERNESS

This section, from Dinosaur to Glenwood Springs, covers some 205 miles through territory that, while not officially wilderness, is sparsely populated and lacking major visitor facilities. Fortunately, the drive is on decent roads. The scenery isn't as spectacular as you might have become accustomed to in Colorado, but it isn't bad either. The major communities along the way are Craig and Meeker, both of which have all the necessary services. The first leg on US 40 to Craig covers 88 miles with only a few really small towns along the way. Craig has about 9,000 people and is the county seat. It is home to several outfitters that provide trips on the Yampa and Green Rivers.

In town is the **Museum of Northwest Colorado** located on CO 13. The small but interesting museum has Native American artifacts, exhibits on area history, and a good collection about famous western gunfighters that little boys will especially enjoy. *Tel. 970/824-6360. Open daily except*

Sunday from 10:00am until 8:30pm during the summer and until 5:00pm the rest of the year. There is no admission charge but donations are requested.

Head south from Craig on CO 13. About 50 miles down the road is Meeker, a good place to stop and rest and fill up your tank as well as the car's. Of mild interest is the **White River Museum**, *265 Park Avenue, 2 blocks off of CO 13.* The museum occupies the former officer's quarters of the army garrison that was stationed here to assist with the relocation of the Ute Indians from this location. *Tel. 970/878-9982. The museum is open daily from 9:00am until 5:00pm during the summer and Monday through Friday from 11:00am until 3:00pm the remainder of the year. It is closed on state holidays. There is no charge for admission but donations are appreciated.*

Continue south from Meeker on CO 13 for 40 miles until you reach I-70 at the town of Rifle. Then head east on the Interstate to Exit 116 which will bring you right into Glenwood Springs.

GLENWOOD SPRINGS

The town of **Glenwood Springs** numbers about 7,,000 residents and lies on the western slopes of the Rockies at an elevation of 5,758 feet. The medicinal qualities of the many mineral springs in the area were known to the Ute Indians long before the arrival of white settlers. There are several vapor caves that are also said to provide benefits. By the latter part of the 19th century many rich miners were coming from other parts of Colorado by special trains to "take the cure." So did other people including the famous gunslinger Doc Holliday who suffered from tuberculosis. Visitors then and now not only took to the springs and vapor caves but enjoyed the beautiful mountain and valley scenery. Contemporary Glenwood Springs is a jumping off point for skiing, white-water rafting, hiking, and four-wheel drive adventuring on back roads. Many trails begin in town.

While most of the spas aren't around these days you can sample the thermal waters at the **Glenwood Hot Springs Pool**, *Grand Avenue at I-70,* which is said to be one of the largest outdoor mineral pools in the world. The main pool has a constant temperature of 90 degrees while the therapy pool is a toasty 104 degrees. To make things more amusing for people who don't just want to sit around in the water, the complex also has a slide and mini-golf. *Tel. 800/537-7946. Pool open daily from 7:30 until 10:00pm (from 9:00am, October through May). It is closed on the second Wednesday of some months. The admission is $8 for adults and $5 for children ages 3 through 12.*

Glenwood Caverns, *508 Pine Street near I-70, Exit 116,* is one of the most unusual caverns you're likely to visit from both a geological and historical perspective. First, some interesting history. The caverns were known as the Fairy Caves when they received their first visitors in 1886. Tours ceased in 1917 and it wasn't until 1999 that the caves were again opened to visitors after their "rediscovery" by some local spelunkers. Now for the geology. During your tour you will see some of the largest cave rooms in Colorado and the usual assortment of pretty cave formations. However, the most unusual part of the tour is when a cave passageway comes to an opening on the side of the cliff in which Glenwood Caverns is located. The view of Glenwood Canyon is a sight you'll always remember. *Tel. 800/530-1635. Guided tours depart on the hour between 9:00am and 5:00pm from late April through the end of October. Admission is $12 on weekends and $10 on weekdays for adults, $11/10 for senior citizens and $7 for children ages 5 through 15. Credit cards. Reservations are recommended. A "wild" tour is also offered for those with spelunkering experience.*

The **Pioneer Cemetery** (sometimes known as **Linwood Cemetery**) is the final resting place of Doc Holliday. To see it requires a hearty and fairly steep climb from the trailhead at *12th and Bennett Streets*. Actually, you won't know if you see his grave since the exact location of his resting place isn't known. What you definitely will see are fantastic views of Glenwood Springs and the old fenced cemetery with history engraved on its many markers. There is a small memorial to Doc Holliday and visitors often leave such things as playing cards in his memory.

One of Colorado's most scenic areas is the twelve mile stretch east of town called **Glenwood Canyon**, now easily traversed by I-70. The highway is one of the most awarded stretches of road to be found in the nation, not only because of the difficulty of its construction, but for the way it does not interfere with the beauty of nature. In fact, there are those who say that it even enhances the scene. Four rest areas along the highway allow you to stop and appreciate nature's handiwork. **No Name** (Exit 119) is wheelchair accessible and provides the best overall panorama of the canyon. **Hanging Lake** rest stop is the starting point for a difficult 1.2 mile trail (ascent of 900 feet) that will reward the fit with views of a beautiful waterfall. The other areas where you can stop are called **Grizzly Creek** and **Bair Ranch**. All have trails and are interconnected by a system of paths along the Colorado River.

Some more great scenery and area history can be found south of Glenwood Springs as we continue on our northwestern loop. Leave town via CO 82. At Carbondale get on CO 133 which soon enters the White River National Forest and the scenic **Crystal River Valley**. The road enters a mountainous area of spruce and aspen forest. Hikers and campers will find many trails that lead into the backcountry and which can literally take days to explore. Past Avalanche Lake the narrow river valley gets even narrower. Then you suddenly emerge from the valley. Stop at the gravel pullout to view the old cabins of historic **Penny Hot Springs**, a former resort.

Look for the signed short cutoff to the town of Redstone so that you can visit **Redstone Castle.** One of several original Victorian structures in the small community, it was built as a manor house by a wealthy relative of President Grover Cleveland named John Osgood. Today the castle is a bed and breakfast facility but visitors can see it on a tour that is usually given once a day. Inquire at the general store on the main street.

GRAND MESA COUNTRY

CO 133 ends at the town of Hotchkiss where you should continue west on CO 92. About 14 miles up the road you'll have to make a choice as to one of two routes to take back to Grand Junction. Both will provide access to the area's best known scenic attraction–the Grand Mesa.

The first route is about 30 miles longer but goes by a more scenic route through a portion of the **Grand Mesa National Forest.** There are many recreational opportunities along this route which, for some people, will be a factor in determining the best route to take. After the town of Austin drive north on CO 65. The lush forest has a delicious aroma. Just past the town of Skyway is a cutoff on the left to a gravel road that leads to Lands End (described in the next paragraph) via an easier means than if you take the other route. The **Grand Mesa** is the world's largest flat-topped mountain. ("Mesa" is Spanish for table and has come to be used to name most flat mountains in the west.) It is sometimes refered to as a 10,000 foot high island in the sky. Covered by pine forests, the mesa contains more than 200 lakes of all sizes. They constitute an angler's paradise but are a pleasant scene for anyone passing through. After Lands End make your way back to CO 65, turn left and you'll soon reach I-70. Head west on the Interstate for the short ride back to Grand Junction.

The second route continues on US 92 a few miles further to the town of Delta. **Fort Uncompahgre**, *west of US 50 via Gunnison River Drive*, is an authentic recreation of an 1826 fur-trading post. The fort features costumed guides that take visitors on guided tours. *Tel. 970/874-8349. The fort is open from the early part of March through mid-December. The hours are Tuesday through Saturday from 10:00am until 5:00pm. The admission is $3.50 for adults and $2.50 for seniors and children under 17.* Then return to US 50 westbound.

About 25 miles later there will be a cutoff for an unpaved road that leads to **Land's End.** This is a projection at the western tip of the Grand Mesa and provides a spectacular view of a large section of western Colorado. The trip to Land's End is almost as good as the view–a series of spectacular and dizzying switchbacks with a different panorama at every turn. Care should be exercised in driving this road. Four-wheel drive is helpful. Use low gear.. Then return to US 50 and continue westbound for the short ride into Grand Junction and the end of the northwest regional tour.

NIGHTLIFE & ENTERTAINMENT

Grand Junction again heads the list in this category. The **Avalon Theater** is a renovated 1923 downtown structure that hosts plays, concerts and other events. *Tel. 970/245-2926* for a schedule of events and ticket information. The **Grand Junction Symphony** has been around for more than 20 years. The 65-piece orchestra has a varied program that often features noted guest artists. *Tel. 970/243-6787.* For more liquidy nightlife the lounges at the Hilton and Holiday Inn hotels have the most going on, including entertainment. Otherwise you'll have to join the locals at a neighborhood bar.

Glenwood Springs usually hosts a considerable number of seasonal art and music festivals. It is best to contact the chamber of commerce for current information. The larger hotels in Glenwood Springs feature lounges, some with entertainment.

SPORTS & RECREATION

Bicycling

Information and maps on biking trails in and around the Grand Junction area are available from the **Bureau of Land Management**, *Tel. 970/244-3000*; the **Colorado Plateau Mountain Bike Trail Association**, *Tel. 970/241-9561*; and local bike shops. Glenwood Canyon is a popular place for biking and much of it is on easy, level terrain, although there are certainly challenges for those who want more adventure.
- **Bicycle Outfitters Touring & Adventures**, *Grand Junction. Tel. 800/464-6426*
- **Canyon Bikes, Inc.**, *319 6th Street, Glenwood Springs. Tel. 970/945-6183*

Boating
- **Highline State Park**, *14 miles norhwest of Grand Junction on CO 139*

Fishing

Two of the most productive areas for fishing in the northwest region (and in all of Colorado for that matter) are located close to Glenwood Springs. The **Frying Pan** and **Roaring Fork Rivers** are likely to yield trophy sized trout, among other treasures. Both rivers have been designated by the state of Colorado as *Gold Medal Waters*, meaning that the fishing is great! **Highline State Park**, aforementioned under boating, is also a good fishin' hole.

Golf
- **Lincoln Park Golf Course**, *12th & North Avenue, Grand Junction. Tel. 970/242-6394.* Nine holes.

• **Tiara Rado Golf Course**, *2063 South Broadway, Grand Junction. Tel. 970/ 245k-8085*. 18 Holes. Spectacular setting at the base of the Colorado National Monument.

• **Westbank Golf Club**, *Glenwood Springs. Tel. 970/945-7032*. Nine holes.

Off Road & 4-Wheel Drive Vehicles

Popular in the Glenwood Springs area. Contact the Visitors Bureau for maps and information.

Rafting

• **Adventure Bound River Expeditions**, *2392 H Road, Grand Junction. Call for pick-up. Tel. 800/423-4668*

• **Good Times Rafting Tours**, *1308 County Road, Glenwood Springs. Tel. 800/808-0357*.

Skiing

Operating dates are approximate based on weather conditions. The telephone number shown is the resort's main information number. See the *Practical Information* section for central reservation numbers for most areas. Explanation of all abbreviations used in this section can be found under *Skiing* in Chapter 8.

• **Powderhorn**, *Powderhorn Resort, Mesa. I-70 to State Highway 65. Tel. 970/ 268-5700; www.powderhorn.com*. Open early December through March. 4 lifts. 27 trails. Terrain: B=20, I=50, A=30. DH, XC, SB. Base elevation 8,200 feet; top elevation 9,850 feet. Vertical drop 1,650 feet. Ski school for adults and children. Child care available for ages 3 and up.

• **Sunlight**, *Sunlight Mountain Resort, Glenwood Springs. I-70 to State Highway 82 and then County Road 117. Tel. 970/945-7491 or 800/445-7931; www.sunlightmtn.com*. Open December through mid-April. 4 lifts. 66 trails. Terrain: B=20, I=55, A=25. DH, XC, TM, SB. Base elevation 7,886 feet; top elevation 9,895 feet. Vertical drop 2,010 feet. Ski school for adults and children. Child care available for ages 9 months through 6 years.

Swimming

• **Highline State Park**, *14 miles northwest of Grand Junction on CO 139*

Tennis

• **Lincoln Park**, *14th Street and Gunnison Avenue, Grand Junction*.

SHOPPING

The northwest isn't the place for the shopper on a rampage given its generally small communities and out of the way location. What shopping there is that is worth mentioning is all located in Grand Junction. It's concentrated in two locations. The first is downtown along the tree lined **Shopping Park**. There are several art galleries, souvenir shops, and plenty of restaurants. The **Mesa Mall** is the region's biggest shopping mall with more than 120 stores. It is located at *2424 US Highways 6/50.*

PRACTICAL INFORMATION

- **Airport**: *Walker Field Airport, Grand Junction. Tel. 970/244-9100*
- **Bus Depot**
    Craig: *470 Russell Street. Tel. 970/824-5161*
    Glenwood Springs: *118 W. 6th Street. Tel. 970/945-8501*
    Grand Junction: *230 South 5th. Tel. 970/242-6012*
- **Hospital**
    Craig: *Memorial Hospital, Tel. 970/824-9411*
    Glenwood Springs: *Valley View Hospital, 6535 Blake Avenue. Tel. 970/945-6535*
    Grand Junction: *Grand Junction Community Hospital, 12th & Walnut Streets. Tel. 970/242-0920*
    Meeker: *Pioneers Hospital, 785 Cleveland. Tel. 970/878-5047*
- **Police** (non-emergency)
    Craig: *Tel. 970/824-8111*
    Glenwood Springs: *Tel. 970/945-8566*
    Grand Junction: *Tel. 970/244-3500*
    Meeker: *Tel. 970/878-5555*
- **Taxi**
    Grand Junction: *Sunshine Taxi, Tel. 970/245-TAXI*
- **Tourist Office/Visitors Bureau**
    Craig: *360 E. Victory Way, Tel. 800/864-4405; www.craig-chamber.com*
    Glenwood Springs: *1102 Grand Avenue, Tel. 800/221-0098; www.glenwoodchamber.com*
    Grand Junction: *740 Horizon Drive, Tel. 800/962-2547; www.grand-junction.net*
    Meeker: *710 Market Street. Tel. 970/878-5510; www.colorado-west.com*
- **Train Station**
    Glenwood Springs: *413 7th Street, Tel. 970/945-9563*
    Grand Junction: *339 South 1st Street, Tel. 970/241-2733*

15. SOUTHWEST COLORADO - NATURE'S MAJESTY & ANCIENT CIVILIZATIONS

While the heart of the Rocky Mountains may be synonymous with and symbolic of Colorado, the **southwest region** has a far greater diversity than any other area of the state. Diversity, however, is not a word that does it proper justice. Spectacular and diverse is more appropriate. Towering mountains vie for attention with huge plateaus, deep canyons, rushing rivers and waterfalls, and there is even an area of giant sand dunes. Historical attracations, spanning the time from the ancient **Anasazi** to the mining days of **Silverton** and other towns add to the adventure and excitement. There are a couple of scenic vintage train rides including one that is simply the best in the United States.

Some of the southwest's names are famous, like **Mesa Verde National Park**, and the **Durango and Silverton Narrow Gauge Railroad**. Others, like the **Black Canyon of the Gunnison** and the **Great Sand Dunes** are not as commonly known, even though they are equally wonderous. And that sense of discovery is part of what makes this area of Colorado so special.

The southwest is generally high country, home as it is to the **San Juan Mountains** and the **Uncompahgre Plateau**, although the peaks aren't as tall as in the central Rockies. But they're high enough, given the climate, to include a couple of places that have become important ski resorts. White-water rafting and jeep tours into the back country are also first rate. Although some of those four-wheel roads are well off the main roads and require a degree of skill to negotiate, the good news is that the majority of the southwest's countless scenic highlights are within easy reach via an excellent system of United States and Colorado highways. The Million Dollar Highway (US 550) and US 50 over the Monarch Pass are just two fine examples.

So get your binoculars out, your cameras loaded, and your sense of adventure ready–we're going to explore southwest Colorado!

ARRIVALS & DEPARTURES

There are lots of towns in the southwest but you'll be hard pressed to find any with a population more than 15,000. Consequently, there isn't a lot in the way of public transportation into the area. Places like Cortez, Durango, Montrose, Alamosa, have bus service but to get from one to another is difficult because of the infrequency of service. There isn't any Amtrak service in the southwest (although Trinidad and Grand Junction are reasonably close by). Daily year-round air service is available from Denver to Cortez, Durango, Gunnison, Montrose and Telluride via United Express while America West serves Durango, Montrose and Telluride from Phoenix. During the winter ski season there is additional service to Montrose via Continental Airlines from Houston or New York.

By now you must have gotten the idea that most people will be arriving in the southwest by car. Access is provided from the east by taking either US 50 west from either Pueblo or Colorado Springs (CO 115 to US 50) or US 160 from the Walsenburg exit of I-25 in south-central Colorado. If you're connecting from the northwest section of Colorado US 50 also is the entry route. US 285 heads through the mountains from Denver to US 50 at Poncha Springs and US 24/US285 provides access from the Aspen/Vail/Leadville vicinity. Finally, if you're coming from Arizona or Utah via the Four Corners area, then US 160 leads into the southwest area at Cortez.

ORIENTATION

The suggested tour through the southwest is a loop so it doesn't matter where you begin or end. (For our purposes I'll begin in Alamosa at the southeastern corner of a more or less rectangular loop. Regardless of your origin point there are only a few major roads that you have to be familiar with, save for a few side trips that will be described and routed for you later.

GETTING AROUND THE REGION

The southern side of the loop is US 160 and it runs from Alamosa, through Durango and by Mesa Verde to Cortez. CO 145 and CO 62 form the western edge and link up with US 550 south of Montrose near the northwest corner of the loop. At Montrose US 50 heads east and forms the northern portion of the route all the way to Poncha Springs/Salida. The eastern edge is CO 17.

While there are some tours from Durango and a few other of the major tourist communities, you can't rely on public transportation to get to most of the attractions. If you aren't going to drive upon getting to the southwest than a comprehensive guided bus tour would probably be the best alternative.

WHERE TO STAY
ALAMOSA
Moderate

BEST WESTERN ALAMOSA INN, *1919 Main Street. Tel. 719/589-2567; Fax 719/589-0767. Toll free reservations 800/528-1234. 121 Rooms. Rates: High season (June through August): $79; Low season (September through May): $65. Major credit cards accepted. Located a mile west of the center of town on US Highways 160 and 285.*

Considering that Alamosa isn't such a small town the choices for lodging are rather sparse. You almost have to stay in a chain to get decent accommodations and the local Best Western is probably the best. The two-story motel is situated well back from the road on a spacious shaded and nicely maintained lawn. The rooms are about average in quality. Some have refrigerators. A good family style restaurant is located adjacent to the inn. Indoor swimming pool and whirlpool on the premises.

CORTEZ
Moderate

KELLY PLACE, *14663 Road G. Tel. 970/565-3125; Fax 970/565-3540. Toll free reservations 800/745-4885; www.kelly-place.com. 10 Rooms. Rates: High season (summer): $89-125; Low season (winter): $65-89, including full breakfast. Most major credit cards accepted. Located 2 miles west of town via Main to Road G then west in direction of Hovenweep National Monument for ten miles. Follow signs for last mile on gravel road.*

A quaint little bed & breakfast in a quiet location with a real homey feel. Old fashioned style without looking old, Kelly Place provides comfortable rooms that are a bit on the small side. Few facilities although some rooms do have kitchens. The nicest part about staying at Kelly Place is that guests can leisurely explore the almost 100 acres of grounds that have significant archaeological remains along with a variety of local flora. Good breakfast served but it does require a short drive to reach restaurants.

Inexpensive

ANASAZI MOTOR INN, *640 South Broadway. Tel. 970/565-3773; Fax 970/565-1027. Toll free reservations 800/972-6232. 87 Rooms. Rates: High season (June through September): $71; Low season (October through May): $55. Most major credit cards accepted. Located one mile southwest of the center of town on US Highways 160 and 666.*

Convenient jumping off location for points of interest in all directions, the Anasazi is a comfortable facility with nice sized rooms, some with refrigerator or full kitchen. It has a full service restaurant, cocktail lounge with live entertainment, heated outdoor swimming pool and hot tub. Free transportation to area casinos is provided.

TOMAHAWK LODGE, *728 South Broadway. Tel. 970/565-8521; Fax 970/5654-9793. Toll free reservations 800/643-7705. 39 Rooms. Rates: High season (summer): $69; Low season (winter): $47. Most major credit cards accepted. Located about 1-1/2 miles from downtown on US Highways 160 and 666.*

Basic roadside motel that will serve your requirements if you're just looking for a place to hit the pillow after a day exploring the area's many sights. The rooms are a little small but comfortable and well maintained. There is an outdoor swimming pool. Restaurants are located within a short distance.

DURANGO (see also **Purgatory**)

Very Expensive

GENERAL PALMER HOTEL, *567 Main Avenue. Tel. 970/247-2600; Fax 970/247-1332. Toll free reservations 800/523-3358; southwestdirectory.com/palmer. E-mail: gphdurango@yahoo.com. 39 Rooms. Rates: High season (April through December): $250-275; Low season (January through March): $145-199, all rates including Continental breakfast. Major credit cards accepted. Located adjacent to the Durango & Silverton train terminal near the foot of Main Avenue.*

Durango has a number of well known Victorian style hotels dating from the town's wild early days and the General Palmer is one of the best of this distinguished group. Built in 1898 it is a place of elegance and warmth, filled with history and offering great service by a caring staff. It is considered by some travel sources as a Bed & Breakfast but I think of it more in terms of a small hotel. Either way it is a place that will make your stay in Durango something special.

Entering through the main entrance with its tiffany stained glass window over the doors and into the public areas is like walking back in time over a hundred years. From the dark wooden counters and paneling to the rich and darkly upholstered furnishings, and from the brass lamps and colorful wallpaper to the richly textured carpets, the General Palmer has a charming atmosphere that is hard to match. The lobby is a comfortable place to relax and people watch or you can play board games in the lounge, browse the library or soak up some Colorado mountain sunshine in the solarium.

The guest rooms are all uniquely decorated and feature beds of brass or pewter or wooden four-posters with hand crocheted canopies. Brass lamps and colorful wallpaper are in abundance here too. The bathrooms are thoroughly modern but have beautiful traditional fixtures. All rooms have ceiling fans (no air conditioning) and some have refrigerator, video cassette player, and Jacuzzi tub. There are also a few multi-bedroom units, some with wet bar and refrigerator. The delicious chocolate placed on the nighttable beside your bed is a General Palmer tradition.

Breakfast at the Palmer isn't large (another reason I don't consider it a B&B) but features some of the most delicious muffins you'll ever taste along with fresh juice and coffee. There isn't any restaurant but many are located within a short walk. An authentic old time western saloon is located right next door. Guests traveling by car have to use on street parking but there usually isn't any problem getting a good spot.

SHERATON TAMARRON RESORT, *40292 US Highway 550 North. Tel. 970/259-2000; Fax 970/259-0745. Toll free reservations 800/678-1000; www.tamarron.com. 310 Rooms. Rates: High season (May through mid-October and mid-December through early January): $139-459; Low season (mid-October to mid-December and early January through April):$99-339. Full breakfast included during the winter months. Major credit cards accepted. Located betwe Durango and Purgatory.*

In a setting par excellence along the San Juan Skyway, Tamarron nestled in the Animas River Valley, hemmed in by gorgeous toweri mountain peaks on all sides. It consists of a main building and thr separate lodges, some on grassy meadows and others perched atop ro outcroppings. The placement of the buildings and their architectu style are designed to complement the natural surroundings rather th interfere and the designers have done a most admirable job in that regar The Tamarron was until recently affiliated with Hilton and was cons tently ranked as one of the five best hotels worldwide in that chain. I'm sure it will do the same under the Sheraton name

The spacious guest rooms range from 900 to 2,200 square feet, in single rooms to multi-bedroom loft units, all beautifully furnished and containing all of the comforts of home. Tamarron also has two excellent restaurants, a deli, and cocktail lounges.

The wide range of recreational facilities includes a complete health spa that, in addition to the usual exercise and steam rooms, offers professional massage and even aroma therapy. Golf lovers will salivate at the sight of Tamarron's championship level golf course, *The Cliffs,* considered to be one of the top courses in the United States. They even have a summer golf institute. Grown-ups needn't worry about what to do with the children if they want to venture off either day or night. The Tamarron's "Kids Korral" and "Kampfire Kids" programs provide supervised fun for the little ones.

Selected as one of my Best Places to Stay (see Chapter 10 for details).

Expensive

APPLE ORCHARD INN, *7758 County Route 203. Tel. 970/247-0751. Toll free reservations 800/426-0751. 4 Rooms. Rates: High season: $125-180; Low season $85-135. Discover, MasterCard and VISA accepted. Located about 9 miles north of town via US 550 then just west on County 252 and north on County 203.*

A charming little bed and breakfast inn located in a secluded setting amid the forested lower mountain slopes yet close enough to the many activities of Durango. It has a small but attractive common area with a warm fireplace and a friendly staff. Cozy but comfortable accommodations, some of which have their own Jacuzzi. Excellent breakfast. The only potential problem with Apple Orchard is a lack of restaurants in the immediate vicinity. However, you can always eat in Durango before returning for the evening. The inn has some restrictions on young children.

DOUBLETREE HOTEL DURANGO, *501 Camino del Rio. Tel. 970/259-6580; Fax 970/259-4398. Toll free reservations 800/222-TREE. 159 Rooms. Rates: High season (May 1st to mid-October): $139-179; Low season (mid-October to April 30th): $89-109. Major credit cards accepted. Located on US 160/550 to the immediate west of the Durango & Silverton train terminal at Durango's southwestern edge.*

Contrasting sharply with Durango's many historic buildings and lodging properties, the Doubletree is a sleek and modern affair perched in a lovely spot at the southern end of town overlooking the Animas River and walking distance to the heart of Main Avenue's shopping and restaurants. The four-story motor inn has attractive public areas and large guest rooms with pretty decor, some with excellent views of river and mountain. Among the many amenities in each room are iron with ironing board and coffee maker. Many rooms have refrigerators and Jacuzzi tubs.

The Edgewater Grill & Lounge is a good restaurant with separate lounge. It is noted for the Sunday brunch that includes live entertainment. During the summer breakfast is a bountiful buffet. The recreational facilities consist of a heated indoor swimming pool; and spa with sauna, whirlpool and exercise room. There is a good gift shop on the premises and the hotel's tour desk will be glad to arrange all sorts of vigorous outdoor activities in the Durango area.

LELAND HOUSE BED & BREAKFAST SUITES, *721 East 2nd Avenue. Tel. 970/385-1920; Fax 970/385-1967. Toll free reservations 800/664-1920. E-mail: leland@frontier.net. 10 Rooms. Rates: $109-169 including full breakfast. Major credit cards accepted. Located one block east of Main Avenue between 7th and 8th Streets.*

The Leland House was originally a small apartment building and was built back in the 1920's. It has been lovingly restored to its original elegance with the apartments being converted into seven one-bedroom suites with separate sitting area and three smaller studio style efficiencies. Over half the units have kitchens but all have at least a coffee maker and refrigerator. The rooms feature lovely decor that's somewhere between Victorian and modern. In addition to the delicious gourmet breakfast that is served daily in the attractive restaurant to guests only, the Leland's dining facility is open to the public for other meals. No recreational facilities are located on the premises but for a place to sleep and eat it's so nice.

ROCHESTER HOTEL, *726 East 2nd Avenue. Tel. 970/385-1920; Fax 970/385-1967. Toll free reservations 800/664-1920; www.rochesterhotel.com. 15 Rooms. Rates: High season (all months except April and November): $149-199; Low season (April and November): $119-159; all rates including full breakfast. Major credit cards accepted. Located one block east of Main and 7th Street.*

This place has such a fun theme that it's a shame that they have restrictions on small children. Another cross between B&B and hotel, the Rochester dates from 1892 and has been restored relatively recently. The guest rooms each have an Old West decor that is based on a movie that was filmed in the Durango area. It's like a little bit of Hollywood in Colorado.

Beyond the theme and attractive furnishings, some rooms have efficiency kitchens, refrigerators or whirlpool tubs. The breakfast is a gourmet experience but you'll have to go elsewhere for other meals. Many restaurants are located within walking distance.

STRATER HOTEL, *699 Main Avenue. Tel. 970/247-4431; Fax 970/259-2208. Toll free reservations 800/247-4431; www.strater.com. E-mail: rod@frontier.net. 93 Rooms. Rates: High season: $169-245; Low season: $99-225. Major credit cards accepted. Located several blocks north of the Durango & Silverton train terminal.*

Perhaps Durango's most famous Victorian era hotel, the Strater has been a tourist attraction as much as a hotel for many years. You'll probably be at the Strater during the course of your visit to Durango for some entertainment if not just to see the place even if you don't stay here. It dates from 1887 and the furnishings in both public areas and guest rooms are authentic Victorian antiques with attractive walnut wood being predominent among red and black papered walls. The rooms have been thoroughly modernized and include air conditioning (somewhat rare in usually cool Durango) but retain the original old time flavor.

The dining and entertainment at the Strater are special too. There are a couple of restaurants but the best is Henry's at the Strater which is described in the Where to Eat section. Two of Durango's top night spots are also located here. These are The Pelican's Nest with live jazz in a nautical setting (how that got into Durango I'll never know), and Diamond Belle Saloon. The latter is an authentic old west watering hole with live ragtime piano player and colorfully dressed saloon girls. During the summer the Strater also is home to the Diamond Circle Melodrama.

Moderate

IRON HORSE INN, *5800 N. Main Avenue. Tel. 970/259-1010; Fax 970/385-4791. Toll free reservations 800/748-2990. 141 Rooms. Rates: High season (summer): $109-119; Low season (winter): $79-89. All rates include Continental breakfast. Most major credit cards accepted. Located downtown just west of main street and adjacent to the Durango & Silverton Narrow Gauge Railroad tracks.*

Not only is this *the* closest lodging to the train, it's one of the nicest places in town if you don't want to go the historic hotel route. And the relative value is among the best too. The rooms are unusually large and well decorated. All units have fireplaces and many are bi-level loft rooms or suites. The facilities are quite varied and include a heated swimming pool, spa with sauna and whirlpool, exercise room, game room, gift shop, ski shop and even a small general store. The on-premises restaurant and lounge is more than adequate if you don't feel like heading over to Main Street after a long day on the train.

JARVIS SUITE HOTEL, *125 West 10th Street. Tel. 970/259-6190; Fax 970/259-6190. Toll free reservations 800/824-1024. E-mail: jarvis@frontier.net. 22 Rooms. Rates: High season (April through December): $119-169; Low season (January through March): $79-129. Most major credit cards accepted. Located a block west of Main and four blocks north of the Durango & Silverton train terminal.*

A beautifully restored turn of the century building that is listed on the National Register of Historic Places, the Jarvis consists entirely of studio units or one and two bedroom suites, all with fully equipped kitchen. The rooms are spacious and nicely decorated. A small courtyard contains a pretty patio and an outdoor hot tub. The Jarvis doesn't have a restaurant but it is located within walking distance of the heart of Durango.

GUNNISON
Moderate

MARY LAWRENCE INN, *601 N. Taylor. Tel. 970/641-3343; bbonline.com/co/mlawrence. E-mail: marylinn@gunnison.com. 5 Rooms. Rates: $79-134 including full breakfast. MasterCard and VISA accepted. Located north of US 50 on Colorado Highway 135.*

An intimate and charming historic bed & breakfast inn dating from 1885 that's located on a quiet residential street with a number of other homes from the same period. The guest accommodations are spacious (two of the units are two bedroom suites) and colorfully furnished with antiques and unusual collectibles. It's almost like staying in a museum! Restaurants are located within a short distance.

Inexpensive

WATER WHEEL INN, *US Highway 50 West. Tel. 970/641-1650. Toll free reservations 800/642-1650. 52 Rooms. Rates: $45-85 including Continental breakfast. Major credit cards accepted. Located about 2-1/2 miles west of town on the main highway.*

Attractive roadside motel with spacious grounds featuring a large pond and pretty trees. The guest rooms are equally pretty and have much nicer furniture than you usually get in small private motels of this type. A few units have full kitchens. The inn has a small exercise room and hot tub as well as a picnic area with barbecue facilities. Restaurants are located within a five minute drive.

MESA VERDE NATIONAL PARK
Moderate

FAR VIEW LODGE, *near the Park Visitor Center. Tel. 970/529-4421; Fax 970/529-4411; www.vistmesaverde.com. 150 Rooms. Rates: $82-98. Open from late April to mid-October only. Major credit cards accepted. Located about 15 miles from the park entrance station.*

Sometimes lodging facilities located within national parks leave something to be desired. Not so in this case–the Far View Lodge is a beautiful facility with excellent accommodations and services, even more so when you take into account the reasonable price charged for "the only place in town" (that isn't a town). Majestically situated at the top of Navajo Hill, the single story lodge is spread out over a wide area. The simple but attractive exterior houses colorfully decorated rooms in a modern southwest style. Each room features huge picture windows and a spacious sun balcony that provides outstanding vistas that stretch up to a hundred miles. Some rooms have refrigerators but none have air conditioning, television or phones. That's actually for the better because it enables you to have an undisturbed stay that will make your appreciation of the surroundings even greater.

When you get hungry the Far View Lodge offers two choices. First, The Metate Room is an outstanding southwestern restaurant that is described further in the Where to Eat section. If you're looking for something more casual (and quick if you're on the go), the lodge's cafeteria is more attractive and serves a better variety and quality of food than you often get from national park cafeterias. There is also a cocktail lounge. An interpretive slide show about Mesa Verde and its early inhabitants is offered in the evening.

MONTROSE
Moderate

BEST WESTERN RED ARROW, *1702 East Main. Tel. 970/249-9641; Fax 970/249-8380. Toll free reservations 800/528-1234. 60 Rooms. Rates: High season (May through October): $82-119; Low season (November through April): $72-98. Major credit cards accepted. Located a mile east of the center of town on US 50.*

This is an attractive modern motel facility with pretty and lots of nicely cared for grounds. The rooms are equally spacious and feature coffee makers and refrigerators. Most have either a balcony or patio and some have their own Jacuzzi tub. There's a heated swimming pool and hot tub as well as a small fitness center. The on-premise restaurant serves decent family style fare at very reasonable prices.

COUNTRY LODGE, *1624 East Main. Tel. 970/249-4567. 22 Rooms. Rates: $62-85. Most major credit cards accepted. Located a mile east of the center of town on US 50.*

The nicest part about this little motel is its lovely grounds that boasts a tranquil courtyard with a genuine redwood deck, swimming pool and hot tub, all amid a beautiful and well tended flower garden. That loving care extends to the more than adequate rooms which feature knotty pine construction. Among the amenities in some units are efficiency kitchens or microwave oven and refrigerator, and patios. Restaurants are locted in close proximity to the motel.

Inexpensive

WESTERN MOTEL, *1200 East Main. Tel. 970/249-3481. Toll free reservations 800/445-7301. 28 Rooms. Rates: High season (late May to mid-November): $40-58; Low season (mid-November to late May): $36-45. Most major credit cards accepted. Located about three quarters of a mile east of the center of town on US 50.*

Another small motel, the Western has fairly basic accommodations but at a real budget price. For that you'll get a clean and comfortable room (some with refrigerator) and use of the heated swimming pool. Several restaurants are located within a short distance.

OURAY
Moderate
ALPENGLOW CONDOMINIUMS, *215 5th Avenue. Tel. 970/325-4972. 16 Rooms. Rates: Studio units $100-129; $136-264 for multi-bedroom units. Discover, MasterCard and VISA accepted. Located one block west of Main Street at the corner of 2nd Street.*

Consisting entirely of studio to three bedroom units, all with full kitchen, private deck and fireplace, these attractive condominium style accommodations offer spacious and comfortable home-like facilities in a modern but rustic looking three-story lodge. The all wood exterior blends in nicely with the surrounding abundance of trees and the mountain backdrop to provide a truly eye pleasing picture. Larger units have two bathrooms and all feature queen size beds. The largest suites have pretty sitting rooms in the loft with great views. The prices are quite reasonable for the large and well equipped units but can be a real bargain for larger families or couples traveling together. Many units can occupy as many as six people and the biggest can handle up to ten.

The Alpenglow has an indoor/outdoor spa area with sauna and hot tubs. There is also a small picnic area with barbecue pits. Restaurants are located within a short walk. They offer many package plans year round including skiing at Telluride.

BOX CANYON LODGE, *45 3rd Avenue. Tel. 970/325-4981; Fax 970/325-0223. Toll free reservations 800/327-5080. E-mail: bcm@rmii.com. 38 Rooms. Rates: High season (late May through September and late December to early May) $69-95; Low season (early April to late May and October to late December): $55-70. Most major credit cards accepted. Located about two blocks west of Main Street (US 550) at the entrance to Box Canyon Falls.*

Ouray's only lodging establishment with its own mineral hot spring, the Box Canyon Lodge is an extremely attractive wooden chalet style structure with a wonderful mountain backdrop on one side and near plenty of towering trees on the other that's picture perfect winter or summer. The rooms are spacious and attractive and some multi-bedroom suites with or without kitchen are available. The units with fireplaces are especially nice. The furnishings are better quality and more comfortable than in most motels in this price range. Complimentary coffee and tea are available in the lobby. Several restaurants are located within a short distance.

Although the lodge doesn't have a swimming pool it does have one of the most unusual hot tubs around. Actually, there are four separate mineral springs that allow you to take in the scenery year-round in 108 degree warm comfort. They're beautifully set into a series of terraces low on the mountain.

CHINA CLIPPER INN, *525 2nd Street. Tel. 970/325-0565; Fax 970/325-0565. Toll free reservations 800/315-0565; www.colorado-bnb.com/clipper. 11 Rooms. Rates: $95-125 including full breakfast. MasterCard and VISA accepted. Located a block west of Main Street (US 550) between 5th and 6th Avenues.*

Take a quick look at the China Clipper and you would think it was another well cared for and restored Victorian era home. But it was actually built in 1995 deliberately in a classic style that immediately generates a feeling of home style warmth. The three story multi-peeked structure is painted a dazzling white and the many balconies add to the pleasing exterior. This unusual B&B inn has a pretty garden with hot tub; afternoon beverages are served in addition to the most enjoyable breakfast. Room accommodations vary in size and amenities but all also have the look and feel of an earlier era with colorful wallpaper, four poster beds and other traditional furnishings. Among the facilities in some rooms are fireplaces, decks or balconies, Jacuzzi tub for two and full kitchens. All have ceiling fans and excellent views. Restaurants and shopping are just a short walk away. Some age restrictions on children may apply.

DAMN YANKEE COUNTRY INN, *100 6th Avenue. Tel. 970/325-4219; Fax 970/325-0502. Toll free reservations 800/845-7512. 12 Rooms. Rates: High season (mid-May to mid-October and late December to early January): $119-200; Low season (mid-October to mid-May except late December to early January): $72-102; all rates including full breakfast. American Express, Discover, MasterCard and VISA accepted. Located two blocks west of Main Street (US 550) at Munn Court.*

Here's another of Ouray's delightful B&B's. Located alongside the pretty Uncompahgre River, the Damn Yankee is an attractive country style home with a massive brick chimney fronting the wooden exterior. The structure is basically two stories high but a small third story in the central part of the house contains a wonderful observatory lounge that affords great views in a most relaxing atmosphere. The downstairs public area is dominated on the interior by a huge fireplace. The parlor has a piano and is filled with leather furniture. Guest rooms are large, bright and airy. Many feature vaulted ceilings and almost wall to wall windows. The furniture is old fashioned in style and pleasing to the eye. Some rooms have fireplace and/or whirlpool tub. Stereo music is piped into each room (but you can turn it off anytime). Outside there are tables and chairs on the attractive grounds.

Breakfast is wonderful but so is the "afternoon snack" which consists of fresh fruit, wine and cheese or soft drinks. During the winter season guests can also have dinner at the inn (not open to the general public). The inn doesn't have its own pool but offers free passes to the municipal hot springs pool. No children are allowed to stay at the Damn Yankee. A most pleasant experience at an affordable price.

MATTERHORN MOTEL, *201 6th Avenue. Tel. 970/325-4938; Fax 970/325-7335. Toll free reservations 800/334-9425; www.ouraycolorado.com/ matthorn. 25 Rooms. Rates: High season (late May to late September): $82-99; Low season (May 1st to late May and late September to October 31st): $58-73. Closed November 1st to April 30th. Discover, MasterCard and VISA accepted. Located one block west of Main Street (US 550) at the corner of 2nd Street.*

The Matterhorn is a typical two-story roadside motel in way of accommodations and facilities but it is more attractive than most with its pretty Alpine inspired architecture. The mountain backdrop is, as is the case with almost all Ouray lodging, magnificent. All of the modern and comfortable rooms feature coffee maker and some larger family units have their own Jacuzzi. The motel has a nice swimming pool and surrounding patio with whirlpool. You can easily walk to a number of restaurants and Ouray shopping.

OURAY HOTEL, *303 6th Avenue. Tel. 970/325-0500. Toll free reservations 800/A1-OURAY. 14 Rooms. Rates: High season (summer): $85-190; Low season (winter): $54-89. MasterCard and VISA accepted. Located at the corner of Main Street (US 550).*

A unique and historic building dating from 1893 and surrounded by many other old structures in Ouray's historic downtown, the Ouray Hotel was completely renovated in 1993. The exterior has a true old west flavor and although not beautiful, it does project a certain charm. The rooms are mainly simple but comfortable and have king or queen beds and large windows. Unfortunately, most of the rooms face away from the best scenery. There are also some multi-room suites. It is one of the few hotels in Ouray that is entirely air conditioned (even though you probably won't need it). There aren't any dining or recreational facilities but restaurants are close by and you can even walk to the municipal hot springs pool.

OURAY VICTORIAN INN AND TOWNHOMES, *50 3rd Avenue. Tel. 970/325-7222; Fax 970/325-7225. Toll free reservations 800/84-OURAY. E-mail: info@ouraylodging.com. 38 Rooms. Rates: (late May to early October and at Christmas holiday time): $85-190; Low season (early October to late May except for Christmas season): $54-89. Rates include full breakfast except mid-June to September 30th and Christmas season. Located a block west of Main Street (US 550).*

Stylish and beautiful, the Ouray Victorian has been awarded for its architecture by a prestigious historical society. Nicely situated alongside the Uncompahgre River, the inn consists of two sections. The first is the main lodge, a low-rise motel type structure of white and gray with a lot of elegant Victorian touches that make it a lot difference from the ordinary motel. Then there are the nearby townhomes with their multi-room family style accommodations. Between the two are lovely landscaped grounds that include two hot tubs on redwood decks within full view of the mountains and a playground.

Most of the spacious rooms have a view of either the river or mountains and some have both. All have coffee makers and comfortable furnishings. The townhome units have either one or two bedrooms. The upstairs units have the best views and are equipped with full kitchen and fireplace in the living room. Downstairs townhome units have kitchenettes and countertop dining area. Larger units have private garages. The Ouray Victorian doesn't have any restaurant, something that for some reason is the general rule in this town, but it is located within walking distance of a good selection of dining spots.

Inexpensive

OURAY CHALET INN, *510 Main Street. Tel. 970/325-4331. Toll free reservations 800/924-2538. 32 Rooms. Rates: High season (July through September): $69-80; Low season (October through June): $50-70. American Express, Discover, MasterCard and VISA accepted. Located on US 550 at the corner of 5th Avenue.*

While Ouray isn't a particularly expensive place to stay it does lack a variety of budget accommodations. I am, however, willing to recommend the Chalet as fitting the bill for the low price category. The rooms are a good size and range from slightly better than adequate to very nice. You might want to check them out and get one of the better ones for the few extra dollars it costs. All rooms have coffee makers. The only on-site recreation is a whirlpool and, once again, you can walk to restaurants.

PAGOSA SPRINGS

Moderate

INN AT THE PASS, *157649 East US Highway 160. Tel. 970/264-7100. 10 Rooms. Rates: $85-120. American Express, Diners Club and MasterCard accepted. Located 12 miles northeast of town on US 160 at the base of the Wolf Creek Pass.*

A small and immaculately kept rustic lodge, the Inn at the Pass is located in a setting of dramatic natural beauty, nestled in a high valley of the San Juan Mountain range and surrounded by towering mountain peaks. Also overlooking two rivers, the inn consists of a main lodge and several cabin units. All are built of native wood in a pleasing rustic style. The main lodge is a two-story structure with the upper floor consisting of bedroom units that jut out from the steeply sloping slate roof. It is located in an area known for its abundance of outdoor recreation, including winter skiing at Wolf Creek, just 12 miles away.

The accommodations, whether in the lodge or cabins, are clean and comfortable. They aren't anything fancy but are in keeping with the get-away-from-it-all atmosphere that dominates a stay at the Inn at the Pass. A large outdoor deck with spectacular views contains a hot tub. The views from inside are equally impressive from the large meeting room with its cathedral ceiling. Get a look if it's not being used for one of the inn's frequent river study seminars or fishing institutes, the latter of which might be of special interest to anglers. The inn has a small but attractive dining room with roaring fireplace.

SPA MOTEL, *317 Hot Springs Blvd. Tel. 970/264-5910; Fax 970/264-2624. Toll free reservations 800/832-5523. 18 Rooms. Rates: High season (summer): $69-87; Low season (winter): $40-59. American Express, Discover, MasterCard and VISA accepted. Located in town directly across from the public hot springs pool.*

The Spa has been owned and operated by the Giordano family for over forty years and they certainly have become experts in the art of being gracious hosts. Many of their guests come here to take advantage of the natural mineral bath and large mineral water swimming pool. There are a lot of people who swear that it has remarkable therapeutic benefits. I don't claim to know one way or the other but some of the ingredients in the water don't sound so great to me–like sulfated residue, alumina oxide, and lithium for example. The baths and pools are both indoor and outdoor and there are also steam rooms. As far as the motel units are concerned they're decent sized (some larger family units available) and five units have kitchen facilities. The motel is located close to several downtown restaurants.

Inexpensive

HIGH COUNTRY LODGE, *3821 East US Highway 160. Tel. 970/264-4181. Toll free reservations 800/862-3707. 29 Rooms. Rates: $60-90 including Continental breakfast. Most major credit cards accepted. Located about three miles east of town on the main highway.*

A small and rather basic motel with rooms ranging from cozy to comfortable. However, it is clean and well maintained and at the price being asked represents a worthwhile bargain. In addition to the motel units there are a few larger cabins with fireplaces and kitchenettes. Most rooms have ceiling fans. The lodge has a whirlpool but no swimming pool. A restaurant is located in close proximity.

PURGATORY (see also **Durango**)
Expensive

CASCADE VILLAGE, *50827 US Highway 550. Tel. 970/259-3500. Toll free reservations 800/525-0896; www.cascadevillage.com. 8 Rooms. Rates: High season (mid-November through early April): $79-150; multi-bedroom units from $149-470; Low season (early April through mid-November): $62-90; multi-bedroom units from $103-340. 2 night minimum stay. Most major credit cards accepted. Located one mile north of Purgatory on the main highway. (26 miles north of Durango.)*

Surprisingly affordable given the location and luxury level, the Cascade sits in the forested and mountain-rimmed valley of the Animas River. It's a wilderness experience with all the comforts of home. The setting is simply spectacular and walking through the brilliant wildflower meadows down to the Cascade Creek is alone almost reason enough to consider staying here. You might see deer, elk or even a peregrine falcon. The lodge is constructed of wood and brick and looks like an oversized cabin. That's not meant as a knock—in fact, it fits in perfectly with the natural surroundings.

The accommodations are diverse. There are studio units, two bedroom suites and a three bedroom unit, all named. Studios have kitchenettes while the multi-bedroom units have full kitchen with separate dining room. Two other standard features (except in one studio) are a warm fireplace and Jacuzzi tub. Units range in size from 400 square feet (about a standard motel room) to a spacious house sized 1,425 square feet. Some units have a loft with the best views. The furnishings are modern and the decor is color and attractive as well as comfortable. I especially like the wooden shutter blinds on the windows that give you maximum privacy but open up to reveal magnificent vistas. Of course, the views are even better from your own private balcony!

For dining you can head to the nearby Purgatory Ski area for the biggest selection or stay right at Cascade Village for the excellent Cafe Cascade featuring seafood and steaks. The Flume Lounge with its A-one view is a great place for a nightcap. The Cascade also has a huge heated indoor swimming pool, Jacuzzis, full service ski shop and general store. Snowmobiling tours are offered right on the property. The front desk will also assist guests in making reservations for the almost unlimited outdoor activities of the surrounding San Juan National Forest.

SALIDA
Moderate

TUDOR ROSE BED & BREAKFAST, *6720 Paradise Road. Tel. 719/ 539-2002; Fax 719/530-0345. Toll freee reservations 800/379-0889; www.thetudorrose.com. E-mail: tudorose@amigo.net. 6 Rooms. Rates: $70-145 including full breakfast. American Express, MasterCard and VISA accepted. Located west of town via US 50 to County Route 104 and then a half mile following signs up the hill.*

There have been a lot of places to stay where I've said that staying there is like traveling back to another era. That certainly applies at the Tudor Rose, a delightfully small B&B perched on a hilltop and gazing out upon some mighty fine scenery. The 37-acre estate is covered with stately pinon pine trees and the old fashioned country manor house built, as would be expected from the name, in classic Tudor style.

The six rooms and suites are comfortable with many touches of home and most have excellent views. One is a suite with its own Jacuzzi tub. Note that a couple of units have shared (semi-private) bath facilities, something that keeps me from giving the Tudor Rose my highest recommendation. The public facilities are lovely and spacious. There's a Queen Anne furnished living room where guests often gather in the evening and a less formal den. Outside on the wooden deck is a hot tub. There is also a small exercise room.

Breakfast is excellent and restaurants for other meals are located via a short drive into town or along the main highway. Unlike many B&B's the Tudor Rose's warm staff welcomes children and pets. While there probably will be few readers who are traveling with their own horse, you might be interested to know that this inn has horse boarding facilities available at an additional charge.

Inexpensive

ASPEN LEAF LODGE, *7350 US Highway 50 West. Tel. 719/539-6733. Toll free reservations 800/759-0338. 18 Rooms. Rates: High season: (summer, Christmas and Easter holiday periods): $59-69; Low season (winter except Christmas and Easter holidays): $39-59. Major credit cards accepted. Located in town on the main highway.*

For a bargain rate you can get a large, comfortable and well maintained motel unit at the Aspen Leaf. The rooms all have either king or queen beds but are far from fancy. The nicest part of this motel is its spacious outdoor "island" area with attractive landscaping and benches for sitting and watching the fountain. There is also a sundeck with hot tub. Restaurants are located within close proximity.

GAZEBO COUNTRY INN BED & BREAKFAST, *507 East 3rd Street. Tel. 719/539-7806. Toll free reservations 800/565-7806. 3 Rooms. Rates: $80-95 including full breakfast. American Express, MasterCard and VISA accepted. Located downtown. Take Hunt Street north from US 50 to Third and turn left.*

If you're looking for privacy, quiet, comfort and for absolutely nothing to do but relax after you've checked in for the evening, then this three unit 1901 restored Victorian style home will be exactly the right choice. Each unit is spacious and furnished with interesting period pieces. The large deck and porch which surrounds the entire house has magnificent views. There are no recreational facilities; restaurants are located within walking distance.

RAINBOW INN, *105 US Highway 50 East. Tel. 719/539-4444. Toll free reservations 800/539-4447. 21 Rooms. Rates: $45-75; higher end of range during the summer. American Express, Discover, MasterCard and VISA accepted. Located on main highway near center of town.*

A warm and friendly little roadside motel, the Rainbow has decent accommodations at a remarkably low price. The rooms aren't anything special but will do nicely for a few nights as they are clean and comfortable and feature king or queen size beds. There are four two-bedroom units for families and five units have kitchenettes. The grounds have lovely landscaping with colorful flowers, trees and a picnic area. There are also excellent mountain vistas. The Rainbow Inn has a hot tub but no swimming pool. Located on the premises is a pottery studio where you can get quality items at a reasonable price. Restaurants and shopping are nearby.

SILVERTON
Moderate

WINGATE HOUSE, *1045 Snowden Street. Tel. 970/387-5520; www.silverton.org/wingate. E-mail: 110120.2201@compuserve.com. Rooms: 10. Rates: High season (suammer): $99-124; Low season (winter): $64-79; all rates including full breakfast. Most major credit cards accepted. Located east of US 550 via Greene Street to 10th Street and then north two blocks to Snowden.*

Stately Victorian elegance characterizes this turn of the century manor house. The rooms are spacious, bright and airy with nice furnishings. Especially inviting are the real down comforters and pillows that are covered either with elk hide or satin. The breakfast is a gourmet affair that includes home ground coffee. From the front porch (as well as some of the guest rooms) you have an excellent view of towering Kendall Mountain which towers beyond the southern edge of town. All of Silverton's restaurants and shopping are within walking distance.

WYMAN HOTEL & INN, *1371 Greene Street. Tel. 970/387-5372; Fax 970/387-5745. Toll free reservations 800/609-7845. E-mail: thewymann@frontier.net. 19 Rooms. Rates: High season (late May to mid-October>: $85-170; Low season (mid-October to late May): $55-89; all rates including Continental breakfast. American Express, Discover, MasterCard and VISA accepted. Located about seven blocks east of US 550 between 13th and 14th Streets.*

The Wyman is a charming historic hotel dating from 1902 and has a style that well epitomizes Silverton itself. The public areas and guest rooms are filled with historic furnishings or excellent reproductions. Accommodations vary from cozy to quite spacious. The two-story hotel has several multi-bedroom units and a few have whirlpool tubs. All rooms have plushg carpeting, ceiling fans and video cassette players. The hotel boasts a collection of more than 500 videos which you can borrow should you want to spend the night in. Restaurants are located within a short walk.

TELLURIDE
Very Expensive
THE PEAKS RESORT & SPA, *136 Country Club Drive. Tel. 970/728-6800; Fax 970/728-9522. Toll free reservations 800/789-2220; www.thepeaksresort. 181 Rooms. Rates: High season (mid-December to late March): $300-505; Low season (late March to mid-December): $195-325. Multi-bedroom suites available at higher rates. American Express, Discover, MasterCard and VISA accepted. Located in Telluride Mountain Village about 2 miles south of CO 145/Spur 145.*

A magnificent setting surrounds this self-contained full service resort. Although it is nine stories high, the hotel is simply dwarfed by the immense mountains that virtually surround it on three sides. While Telluride is certainly first and foremost a ski resort, summer activities are equally plentiful and the beauty of the countryside is hard to surpass.

The rooms are all quite large, comfortably furnished in a modern style and have many amenities. All feature honor bar and safe while most have a private balcony and ceiling fan. Some have their own whirlpool tub. Service at the Peaks is first class and the staff will help you plan outdoor activity and area tours of any kind. The hotel has a good dining room as well as a cocktail lounge with live entertainment.

Recreation is the name of the game at the Peaks regardless of the time of the year. A number of ski packages are offered and the hotel features ski-in/ski-out facilities. They also offer helicopter skiing for the more adventurous. Other recreational venues are a wading pool as well as a lap pool (complete with indoor water slide), complete spa with sauna, steamroom and whirlpool, fitness center, 18-hole golf course, and five tennis courts as well as courts for racquetball and squash. Among the activities that can be arranged in the immediate vicinity are horseback riding, fishing, white water rafting and more. You can rent bicycles and arrange for a professional massage. Or you can simply relax with a video or maybe take a leisurely walk along a pretty nature trail. Children can take advantage of a well equipped playground and the hotel also offers child care. Free area transportation is provided. This hotel is now a member of the Wyndham Hotels chain.

PENNINGTON'S MOUNTAIN VILLAGE INN, *100 Pennington Court. Tel. 970/728-5337; Fax 970/728-5338. 12 Rooms. $200-225 including full breakfast. Rates change frequently within season depending upon exact dates. American Express, Discover, MasterCard and VISA accepted. Closed beginning of May to before Memorial Day and again for the early part of November. Located in Telluride Mountain Village about 2 miles south of CO 145/Spur 145.*

A large and decidedly modern bed and breakfast inn, the Pennington offers a high standard of luxury, service and facilities for its genre. The guest rooms are spacious and attractively furnished. All have private balcony from which the views are exceptional and mini-bar. Surprisingly, the mini-bar is complimentary, which is something you don't see very often. Public areas are equally attractive.

Besides serving an excellent breakfast (reservations are required), you can snack on complimentary hors d'oevres in the late afternoon and beverages in the evening. With all of that you'll hardly need a restaurant but there are several located within the Mountain Village. Recreational facilities include a steamroom and Jacuzzi as well as billiards. Pennington's also offers access to Telluride's excellent ski facilities and has storage area for your ski equipment.

Expensive

BEAR CREEK BED & BREAKFAST, *221 E. Colorado Avenue. Tel. 970/728-6681; Fax 970/728-3636. Toll free reservations 800/338-7064. 10 Rooms. Rates: High season (late December to late March): $135-235; Low season (late March to late December): $80-125; all rates including full breakfast. Discover, MasterCard and VISA accepted. Located in center of town via Main Street.*

Sorry that I can't find an adequate place to stay in Telluride during the high season in the moderate price range. This is as close as it gets. The rooms are all nicely furnished and extremely comfortable but vary in size from small to about average. Some have balconies that are shared with other units and almost all have great unobstructed mountain views. The inn has three stories but no elevator. It has a sauna and steamroom and is located close to restaurants.

WALSENBURG

Moderate

BEST WESTERN RAMBLER, *At I-25, Exit 52. Tel. 719/738-1121; Fax 719/738-1093. Toll free reservations 800/528-1234. 32 Rooms. Rates: High season (March through October): $79-89; Low season (November through February): $59-69. Major credit cards accepted. Located one mile north of the center of town.*

This is just an average one-story roadside motel but is convenient for those of you who will be traveling on the southern stretch of I-25. The rooms are a fairly good size and are well maintained. The motel's nicest feature is its large and attractive outdoor heated swimming pool. Restaurants are located within a short distance.

CAMPING & RV SITES

- **Alamosa KOA**, *6900 Juniper Lane, Alamosa. Tel. 800/562-9157*
- **Alpen Rose RV Park**, *27847 US Highway 550 North, Durango. Tel. 970/247-5540*
- **Black Canyon of the Gunnison National Park**, *Tel. 970/249-7036*
- **Centennial RV Park & Campground**, *70455 Buckhorn Road, Montrose. Tel. 970/249-6320*
- **Cortez-Mesa Verde KOA**, *27432 East US Highway 160, Cortez. Tel. 970/565-9301*
- **Cozy Comfort RV Park**, *1501 Central, Dolores. Tel. 800/757-1723*
- **Curecanti National Recreation Area**, *Tel. 970/641-2337*
- **Four J + 1 + 1 RV Park**, *790 Oak St., Ouray. Tel. 970/325-4418*
- **Hangin' Tree RV Park**, *17250 US Highway 550, Montrose. Tel. 970/249-9966*
- **Hermosa Meadows Camper Park**, *31420 US Highway 550 North, Durango. Tel. 800/748-2853*
- **Lazy G Campgrounds**, *Highways 160 & 145, Cortez. Tel. 970/565-8577*
- **Lightner Creek Campground**, *1567 County Route 207, Durango. Tel. 970/247-5406*
- **Mesa Campground**, *36128 West US Highway 50, Gunnison. Tel. 800/482-8384*
- **Mesa Verde Point Kampark**, *35303 US Highway 160, Mancos. Tel. 800/776-7421*
- **Montrose KOA Campground**, *200 N. Cedar, Montrose. Tel. 800/562-5734 or 970/249-9177*
- **Morefield Campground**, *Mesa Verde National Park. Tel. 970/533-7731*
- **Ouray KOA**, *225 County Route 23, Ouray. Tel. 970/325-4736*
- **Ridgway State Park**, *Ridgway. Tel. 800/678-2267 or 970/626-5822*
- **Silver Summit RV Park**, *Empire Street, Silverton. Tel. 970/387-0240*
- **Sundance RV Park**, *816 East Main, Cortez. Tel. 800/880-9413*

WHERE TO EAT
CORTEZ
Moderate

DRY DOCK LOUNGE & RESTAURANT, *200 W. Main. Tel. 970/ 564-9404. American Express, Discover, MasterCard and VISA accepted. Dinner served nightly.*

A pleasant and attractive dining room near the heart of town with patio dining available during the summer. The menu is quite varied with both traditional American and southwest regional cuisine. The steaks and fresh seafood dishes are always good. Service is efficient. Cocktail service and lounge.

NERO'S ITALIAN RESTAURANT, *303 W. Main. Tel. 970/565-7366. American Express, MasterCard and VISA accepted. Dinner served nightly. Reservations are suggested.*

This is a casual restaurant that should appeal to the whole family. The traditional Italian cuisine is well prepared and includes many beef, fowl, seafood and veal dishes. Nero's linguini specialties are popular with the locals. Excellent and fresh baked garlic bread is brought to each table and usually disappears quickly but is so good you'll find yourself asking for refills. You can eat outside on the patio or in the comfortable dining room. Cocktail service and separate lounge. Children's menu.

Inexpensive

M&M FAMILY RESTAURANT, *7006 US Highway 160 South. Tel. 970/565-6511. Discover, MasterCard and VISA accepted. Breakfast, lunch and dinner served daily*

Considering the low prices M&M serves very nicely prepared and tasty selections from a diverse menu of American fare along with a smattering of southwestern items. They also have a really good salad bar. The atmosphere is a casual with a contemporary style and fast, friendly service. Children's menu. Take out service available.

DURANGO
Expensive

ORE HOUSE, *147 E. College Drive. Tel. 970/247-5707. American Express, MasterCard and VISA accepted. Dinner served nightly.*

The Ore House features excellent steaks along with fresh fish and seafood in an authentic old southwestern atmosphere enhanced by the works of local artists. A few southwestern entrees also appear on the menu. Generous portions are served by an excellent wait staff and there's also a large salad bar. The Ore House has been around for almost 30 years now and has developed quite a local following. As a result you might have to scrounge around to find a place to park on the street as they have no lot. Cocktail service either tableside or in the separate lounge. Children's menu.

Moderate

EDGEWATER GRILLE ON THE ANIMAS, *501 Camino de Real, in the Red Lion Hotel. Tel. 970/259-6580. Major credit cards accepted. Breakfast, lunch and dinner served daily; Sunday brunch. Reservations are suggested.*

One of the most attractive dining rooms in Durango is matched by excellent food and service. The location overlooks the Animas River and also affords beautiful mountain views. The cuisine is mainly southwestern although a few standard American fare items are always a good alternative if you've had your fill of regional food. The Edgewater also boasts one of Durango's bigger and better salad bars. Full cocktail service and lounge with periodic entertainment. Live entertainment is also a feature of their popular Sunday brunch. During the summer months breakfast consists of a lavish buffet.

FRANCISCO'S RESTAURANTE Y CANTINA, *619 Main Avenue. Tel. 970/247-4098. American Express, Carte Blanche, MasterCard and VISA accepted. Breakfast served Sunday only; lunch and dinner served daily.*

If you like tasty authentic Mexican food then Francisco's will delight you. They serve a large vaiety of chicken, fish and steak dishes as well as pasta and bountiful salads. A pleasant atmosphere and efficient service add to the overall dining experience. Cocktail service and lounge.

HENRY'S AT THE STRATER, *699 Main Avenue, in the Strater Hotel. Tel. 970/247-4431. Major credit cards accepted. Breakfast and dinner served daily; Sunday brunch. Reservations are suggested.*

One of the most popular restaurants in Durango because of its location in the Strater as well as great food, Henry's has a diverse menu of southwestern cuisine, steak and prime rib, fresh fish and seafood as well as pasta. Dinner can be ordered from a regular menu or you can opt for the buffet. Either way the food is delicious. Those ordering from the menu can also partake of the extensive salad bar. Cocktail service and separate lounge, sometimes offering live entertainment. Children's menu. On street parking only.

LADY FALCONBURGH'S BARLEY EXCHANGE, *640 Main Avenue. Tel. 970/382-9664. Most major credit cards accepted. Lunch and dinner served daily.*

You have to hunt just a little bit to find this place because it's located downstairs in an arcade like mall. Lady F provides a fun dining experience in a pub like atmosphere. It's well known for the huge selection of beers– 135 at the latest count but the food is also good and served in ample portions. The menu features mainly beef but also some chicken and pasta dishes. The service is friendly and so are the patron's–it's one of the most casual places around. Cocktail service and bar. You will see plenty of family's here for dinner but I don't consider it the best spot in Durango for traditional family dining.

LORI'S FAMILY DINING, *2653 Main Avenue. Tel. 970/247-1224. MasterCard and VISA accepted. Breakfast, lunch and dinner served daily.*

Unlike the Barley Exchange, this place caters mainly to families with its casual atmosphere, friendly service and diverse menu. The specialties, however, are barbecued ribs, big tender steaks and several chicken entrees. The roast ham is excellent too. Children's menu.

GUNNISON
Expensive

THE TROUGH, *US Highway 50 West. Tel. 970/641-3724. American Express, Discover, MasterCard and VISA accepted. Dinner served nightly. Reservations are suggested.*

This is a casually elegant place with a western decor, style and service. The ambiance is warm and the food well above average. The menu features steak, fresh seafood and a number of Colorado wild game entrees. Cocktail service and separate lounge. Children's menu.

MESA VERDE NATIONAL PARK
Moderate

METATE ROOM, *in Far View Lodge, near the Visitor Center. Tel. 970/ 529-4421. Major credit cards accepted. Dinner served nightly. Smoke free premises.*

The Metate ranks as one of the best restaurants to be located inside of a national park. Casual but beautiful, with authentic southwestern decor, and featuring service that is both friendly and efficient, the Metate offers spectacular views of the Chapin Mesa from its oversized windows. The menu is southwestern with beef, fowl and seafood dishes all prepared in a unique manner by an imaginative chef. Cocktails served tableside or in the separate lounge. Children's menu.

MONTROSE
Expensive

GLENN EYRIE RESTAURANT, *2351 S. Townsend. Tel. 970/249-9263. Major credit cards accepted. Dinner served Tuesday through Saturday. Reservations are suggested.*

Situated in a former colonial style farmhouse overlooking a magnificently cared for garden, Glen Eyrie offers a casual and cozy dining experience featuring a diverse menu of Colorado beef, duck, lamb, trout and wild game dishes along with some vegetarian items. The nightly specials are always delicious. All of the baking is done on the premises. The excellent service is professional but friendly. Cocktails are served. Children's menu.

Moderate

CAMP ROBBER CAFE, *228 E. Main. Tel. 970/240-1590. American Express, Discover, MasterCard and VISA accepted. Lunch and dinner served Tuesday through Saturday; Sunday brunch. Smoke free premises.*

Just about everything in this small but attractive dining room is prepared on a mesquite grill that gives a distinctive and delicious flavor to whatever you order. Cocktail service. Children's menu and take out service.

PASTA GARDEN, *33 N. Cascade. Tel. 970/249-7896. Most major credit cards accepted. Lunch and dinner served daily except Sunday.*

Owners Frank and Renee Cork serve up a wide assortment of fresh pasta dishes as well as fish and salads in this attractive little restaurant. The home like casual atmosphere and service that makes you feel like you're one of the family will leave as good a taste in your mouth as the food does.

RED BARN RESTAURANT, *1413 E. Main. Tel. 970/249-9202. Major credit cards accepted. Lunch served Monday through Saturday; dinner served nightly; Sunday brunch. Reservations are suggested.*

Established for over thirty years, the Red Barn is one of Montrose's more popular restaurants and offers good value for your money. It's mainly a "meat and potatos" kind of place with first quality fresh Colorado beef being the menu's star attraction. Also worthy of note is their excellent salad bar which is bountiful enough to make a meal from. Try the daily special for extra good value. Cocktail service.

SAKURA, *411 N. Townsend. Tel. 970/249-8230. MasterCard and VISA accepted. Lunch and dinner served Tuesday through Saturday.*

I was surprised to find an excellent Japanese restaurant in this neck of the woods, but Sakura is just that. Authentic Japanese decor enhances the large menu of well prepared entrees that includes sashimi, sukiyaki, sushi and tempura as well as Japanese style steak and shrimp. Sakura also has a real tatami room. Full cocktail service is available but I suggest you try one of the many Japanese beers or wines that are available.

STOCKMEN'S CAFE & BAR, *320 E. Main. Tel. 970/249-9946. Discover, MasterCard and VISA accepted. Breakfast, lunch and dinner served daily except Wednesday.*

Although the name makes it sound like this is another Colorado steakhouse, it is more than that as a wide assortment of Mexican dishes that you would find in a south of the border cantina are also offered. All of the food is well prepared and nicely served in ample portions by an efficient staff. Full cocktail service either tableside or at the attractive western style bar. The dining room has been newly remodeled and is quite attractive.

Inexpensive
JIM'S TEXAS STYLE BBQ, *1201 S. Townsend. Tel. 970/249-4809. Discover, MasterCard and VISA accepted. Lunch and dinner served daily except Sunday. Reservations are suggested.*

There are a lot of good Texas BBQ places in Colorado but Jim's is one of the best and at a surprisingly low price. The friendly western atmosphere and decor gets you in the mood for great mesquite smoked beef and ribs as well as turkey and chicken. Patio dining is available during the warmer months in this semi-cafateria style eatery. If you're not in the mood for a big meal try one of Jim's many specialty half-pound hamburgers that give new meaning to this otherwise ordinary dish. Children's menu.

OURAY
Moderate
BON TON RESTAURANT, *426 Main Street. Tel. 970/325-4951. American Express, Discover, MasterCard and VISA accepted. Dinner served nightly; Sunday brunch.*

Perhaps Ouray's best locale for fine dining, this award winning Italian restaurant serves a variety of traditional Italian entrees, including beef and fresh seafood. They also have an excellent wine list. The portions are generous and the service is excellent. Some entrees inch into the expensive category.

BUEN TIEMPO RESTAURANT, *206 7th Avenue. Tel. 970/325-4544. American Express, Discover, MasterCard and VISA accepted. Dinner served Thursday through Monday.*

Located in the historic Western Hotel the Buen Tiempo has an authentic old west decor and feel. It serves outstanding Mexican and southwestern cuisine in a casual and fun atmosphere with friendly and efficient service. Their chile (either red or green) offers great taste in a variety of strengths prepared to your tolerance. Other good choices are the blue corn enchiladas, carne asada or adovada, fajitas and the tostadas. Cocktails are available tableside or at the wonderful Old West wooden bar with a stuffed mountain lion prowling around on the mantle. A delightful place that's also a good value.

OUTLAW STEAKHOUSE, *610 Main Street. Tel. 970/325-4366. MasterCard and VISA accepted. Dinner served nightly. Reservations are suggested.*

Recommended by just about every travel and restaurant authority, I have to add that a stay in Ouray without visiting the Outlaw Steakhouse would be a big mistake. For casual western ambiance and friendly service it's hard to beat. The rustic decor features wood paneling and several giant wagonwheel chandeliers. Some of the decor is rather eclectic, such as the round red topped stools at the bar which are reminiscent of a 1950's roadside diner. The Outlaw, which claims to be the longest operating restaurant in town, is also the home of a hat worn by John Wayne. They seem to be almost as proud of that as of their wonderful food which features generous portions of steak, chicken, fish, and pasta. Full cocktail service. Children's menu.

For something even more different you can opt to try their Outlaw Mountain Cookout, an outdoor meal of steak and pan-fried potatoes served from the grill alongside a lovely stream in the mountains high above Ouray. Dinner price includes round-trip transportation.

Inexpensive

CECELIA'S FAMILY RESTAURANT, *630 Main Street. Tel. 970/325-4223. No credit cards. Breakfast, lunch and dinner served daily. Closed from mid-October to mid-April.*

Located along Ouray's main thoroughfare (on street parking only), Cecelia's is, as the name says, another good place for friendly family dining. The Victorian style decor is quite attractive. The menu features traditional homemade style beef, chicken and fish. Especially noteworthy, though, are Cecelia's delicious soups (types vary by day) and their wonderful fresh baked goods. You must try their fresh baked cinnamon rolls. The doughnuts and pies are also yummy.

SILVER NUGGET CAFE, *940 Main Street. Tel. 970/325-4100. Most major credit cards accepted. Lunch and dinner served daily.*

Although some entrees do head into the moderate price category, the Silver Nugget is a most reasonably priced establishment that serves unpretentious but well prepared American favorites, especially western beef and a few southwestern items. The atmosphere is typically western and the service is downright friendly. Cocktails are served.

PAGOSA SPRINGS

Moderate

OLE MINERS STEAKHOUSE, *3825 US Highway 160 East. Tel. 970/264-5981. MasterCard and VISA accepted. Dinner served nightly. Smoke free premises.*

The unique decor of this very good steak place is designed to recreate the appearance of a mine shaft. Maybe not your choice of atmosphere for a romantic dinner but, nevertheless, interesting and appropriate to the area's history. There is also outside patio dining during the summer in full view of the surrounding mountains. Ole Miners serves a variety of steaks, fowl and seafood. The kabob dishes are especially good. All entrees include a visit to the salad bar. The service is better than average. Cocktails. Children's menu.

PURGATORY
Moderate

DINING ROOM IN THE LODGE AT PURGATORY, *US Highway 550 in the Best Western Lodge at Purgatory. Tel. 970/247-9669. Dinner served nightly. Closed in April and November.*

This unpretentious restaurant serves a good variety of American and southwestern regional dishes in an attractive contemporary atmosphere. The service is efficient and pleasant and is, surprisingly, not overpriced considering the location. Cocktail service tableside or in the adjacent lounge.

SALIDA
Expensive

ANTERO GRILL, *14770 Highway US 285. Tel. 719/530-0301. MasterCard and VISA accepted. Lunch and dinner served daily except Monday during the summer. There are reduced hours at other times of the year so call in advance.*

The Antero has a delightful setting about ten minutes north of town in the Arkansas Valley. A fairly large restaurant (150 seats) for the area, the simple but pleasant interior has a real western look, especially the plain wooden beams that separate the various dining room sections. Antero bills its cuisine as "modern American cowboy" and there's a lot of that on the menu, including a variety of steaks and Southwestern fare.

However, the menu is much more diverse. Here's a typical meal – Pueblos-style tortilla soup and an appetizer of rock shrimp with cheddar enchiladas followed by a main course of open fire bone-in pork loin. Some of the non-cowboy fare you might want to try are the paella or New Zealand rack of lamb. All of the cooking is done from scratch right on the premises, including the breads and delicious desserts. A children's menu is available. Full table side cocktail service and a separate lounge.

Moderate

FIRST STREET CAFE, *137 East 1st Street. Tel. 719/539-4759. American Express, Discover, MasterCard and VISA accepted. Breakfast, lunch and dinner served daily; Sunday brunch.*

For bistro like ambiance and charm it's hard to beat the First Street Cafe. Mexican dishes share the menu with steak and seafood but you can also select from a number of vegetarian dishes. All are nicely prepared from scratch. The Cafe's desserts are outstanding. There's full cocktail service and a separate bar but the most popular drinks are fantastic margaritas or one of several microbrews. Children's menu and carry out service.

GOURMET CHEF CHINESE RESTAURANT, *710 Milford Street. Tel. 719/539-6600. American Express, MasterCard and VISA accepted. Lunch and dinner served daily.*

Despite the name this Chinese eatery presents only adequate oriental cuisine in a typical atmosphere. The portions are ample and the service is quite good. The menu does offer a few out of the ordinary Chinese delicacies and they're also known for serving some of the most exotic cocktail drinks.

SHAVANO GRILL, *1220 US Highway 50 East. Tel. 719/530-0700. American Express, MasterCard and VISA accepted. Dinner served nightly.*

Dine in an authentic western style grille or outside on the patio amid the splendors of nature. The Shavano cooks up excellent first quality steaks, ribs and seafood as well as some pasta entrees. The service is friendly. Cocktail service tableside or in a small but cozy lounge. Wine is served by the glass and they also have a number of microbrews. Children's menu.

Inexpensive

WINDMILL RESTAURANT AND COUNTRY STORE, *720 US Highway 50 East. Tel. 719/539-3594. Most major credit cards accepted. Lunch and dinner served nightly.*

The Windmill offers a good variety of American cuisine, especially steak and seafood dishes, along with several Tex-Mex options and salad platters. There's also a nice salad bar. All of the food is well prepared–nothing fancy, just homestyle goodness that is in keeping with the restaurants casual country store atmosphere. Cocktails and lounge. Children's menu. The Windmill has a large gift shop on the premises where you can get everything from ordinary souvenir junk to fine quality Native American crafts.

SILVERTON
Moderate

BROWN BEAR CAFE, *1129 Greene Street. Tel. 970/387-5630. Discover, MasterCard and VISA accepted. Breakfast, lunch and dinner served daily.*

Standard fare American and southwestern cuisine along with simple food such as burgers and sandwiches can be found at this pleasant old time street cafe. It's a friendly place and the service is quick–a plus if you're in town via the Durango and Silverton Narrow Gauge Railroad and only have a few hours to dine and explore the town. The locals (few as they may be) also seem to like the Brown Bear.

GOLD KING RESTAURANT, *in the Grand Imperial Hotel, Greene & 12th Streets. Tel. 970/387-5527. Most major credit cards accepted. Breakfast, lunch and dinner served daily.*

An adequate full service restaurant located inside of an historic hotel. The centerpiece as far as the decor is concerned is the hundred year old wooden bar. The food is good but nothing special. It is, however, one of the few restaurants in Silverton that offers what I would term as "tranquil" dining–that is, without the deliberate raucous old-time western atmosphere. Not that I find that a problem but some people do. If you're one of them you might want to try the Gold King. The food is western American and the service is good. Cocktails and lounge.

HANDLEBARS FOOD & SALOON, *117 East 13th Street. Tel. 970/387-5395. Discover, MasterCard and VISA accepted. Lunch and dinner served daily, May through October. Reservations are suggested.*

My favorite Silverton restaurant, Handlebars doesn't refer to the things you hold on a bike but to the famous western style mustache that is their logo. This is a wonderful recreation of an old west saloon from the 1880s period. The rustic wooden decor is so filled with western memorabilla that the place could almost be a museum. You can't miss the fully stuffed elk that watches over patrons. There's also a cozy fireplace that adds to the warmth, just as the friendly and efficient staff does.

The extensive menu features excellent prime rib, steaks, ribs and chicken fried steak. On the lighter side are burgers (including delicious buffalo burgers) and sandwiches. Cocktail service and lounge. Handlebars also offers live entertainment, typically in the form of a guitar player. Children's menu. Lots of fun for everyone and a decent value.

TELLURIDE
Very Expensive
LA MARMOTTE RESTAURANT FRANCAIS, *150 West San Juan. Tel. 970/728-6232. American Express, MasterCard and VISA accepted. Dinner served nightly, except Tuesday during the summer. Closed from mid-April to the end of May and October 1st to mid-November.*

A beautiful but still casual dining room located inside an historic structure that once served as an ice house. The French provincial cuisine is expertly prepared and graciously served. The menu changes with the season. Always a good choice, however, is the superb roast duck, served in a number of different sauces depending upon when you visit. Cocktail service and separate lounge. Not a place that children are likely to enjoy.

Expensive

FLORADORA, *103 W. Colorado. Tel. 970/728-3888. Most major credit cards accepted. Breakfast, lunch and dinner served daily.*

The Floradora is located in the heart of "downtown" Telluride which means that you shouldn't be surprised when you first see it — the exterior looks like a saloon from a western movie. That kind of atmosphere extends inside in this popular establishment that has been in business since 1974. The food is nicely prepared and served by a most gracious and friendly staff. Try one of their several appetizers prepared with red chili. Entrees include a wide variety of steaks prepared in just about every way you could imagine. There's also ribs, pork chops, meat loaf, chicken, pasta and trout, but one of my favorites is the teriyaki glazed salmon. There is table side cocktail service and a separate bar that serves several microbrews. Floradora also has an excellent wine list.

Moderate

McCRADY'S RESTAURANT, *115 W. Colorado Avenue. Tel. 970/728-4943. American Express, MasterCard and VISA accepted. Lunch and dinner served daily. Closed mid-April to late May and the first half of October. Reservations are suggested.*

Moderate priced restaurants in Telluride are hard to find but, fortunately, McCrady's comes to the rescue. They serve a wide variety of American entrees with a Continental flair. Beef, fresh fish and seafood and pasta are always on the menu. The contemporary atmosphere is attractive and the service is professional. Cocktail service and lounge.

SEEING THE SIGHTS
THE ALAMOSA AREA
& GREAT SAND DUNES NATIONAL MONUMENT

The first part of our southwestern adventure is a loop from **Alamosa**. Head east from Alamosa on US 160. About two miles from town, then south on El Rancho Lane is the **Alamosa National Wildlife Refuge**. The refuge is an important haven for various shore birds as well as ducks and geese. The winter season also sees many bald eagles in the area. The refuge has an auto route and several easy trails. An overlook along the car route provides excellent viewing conditions. *Tel. 719/589-4021. Open daily dawn to dusk. Visitor Center open weekdays from 7:30am until 4:00pm. Closed on holidays. There is no admission charge.* Upon your return to US 160 continue east for 14 miles and at the junction of CO 150 go north until you reach the monument entrance.

Nestled in the San Luis Valley between the San Juan and Sangre de Cristo mountain ranges, the **Great Sand Dunes National Monument** appears to be a natural anamoly–great dunes of fine colored sand measuring as high as 750 feet in some places. It seems oddly out of place amid the surrounding mountains and forests because we usually associate sand dunes with either the shore or desert regions. However, earth scientists tell us that they are right at home because the area possesses three key ingredients for the formation of dunes–sand, wind, and the slow passage of time. Winds blow finely eroded sand particles across the San Juan Mountains and into the San Luis Valley. They are deposited at the base of the higher Sangre de Cristo and eventually form the dunes you see today. The monument covers more than 38,000 acres and the major dune area is spread out over almost 39 square miles of the valley. The beautiful color of the dunes – pink, cream, brown, tan or even gold if you're lucky – depends upon the angle of the sun. Some of the dunes reach a height of 700 feet. Their own immensity is somewhat dwarfed by the spectacular backdrop of the Sangre de Cristos mountain range.

A SIDE TRIP OFF THE BEATEN PATH

This trip covers a number of interesting historic and scenic sights in a 210-mile loop from the junction of US 160 and CO 150 south of the Great Sand Dunes. I've made it a sidebar because the sights may not justify the mileage if you have limited time. However, if you're coming from the Trinidad-Walsenburge area along I-25 then it only adds a little extra mileage and is definitely worthwhile seeing.

The route takes US 160 east to CO 12 near the town of La Veta, follows that road through the mountains of the San Isabel National Forest, reaches I-25 at Trinidad, and heads north to Walsenburg. At Walsenburg you get back on US 160 and go west, soon returning to your point of origin.

*The sights along this excursion begin with the **Fort Garland Museum** in the town of the same name and the **Fort Francisco Museum** in La Veta. CO 12 through the **San Isabel National Forest** is the highlight of the route as you pass beautiful scenery that includes **The Spanish Peaks, Cordova Pass**, and **Monument Lake**. Trinidad is home to the **Trinidad History Museum** and a western art museum.*

Once you enter the monument the road travels along the edge of the main sand dunes until reaching the Visitor Center where exhibits graphically explain the story of the dunes and the people who have lived in the area for generations. There is also a four-wheel drive road that continues further north along the dunes but if you don't have such a vehicle the views are just as good from the paved portion of the road. No motor vehicles of any kind are allowed to drive on the dunes. From the visitor

A CAR RIDE TO A TRAIN RIDE

Less than thirty miles south of Alamosa via US 285 is the tiny community of Antonito. It's claim to fame is that is the eastern depot of the **Cumbres & Toltec Scenic Railroad.** *The journey covers about 60 miles of excellent scenery that zig-zags across the Colorado and New Mexico state line on its way to Chama, New Mexico. It is one of the longest remaining segments of the original Denver & Rio Grande narrow gauge railroad that was built to serve mining and logging operations in the 1880's. Among the highlights of the train ride through the San Juan and Sangre de Cristo Mountains, which features both closed and open air cars pulled by a coal-burning locomotive, are a mountain tunnel and trestles overlooking deep gorges.*

The all-day trip is highly enjoyable and is probably a must for train ride lovers. However, I will state flatly that it isn't as spectacular as the Durango & Silverton which you'll be encountering later in this chapter. So, if time permits doing both, fine–if not, go for the D&S.

A variety of journeys are offered. Some involve going all the way from Antonito to Chama by train and returning by bus. Others go to the half-way point and then return by the train coming in the other direction. You can bring your own lunch or add on either a buffet western style or Mexican lunch that is served at the mid-way point of Osier. Tel. 719/376-5483. Departures from Antonito at 9:15am, 10:00am, and 10:30am. Returns between 4:00 and 6:00pm depending upon departure time and routing. Always call to confirm exact departure times. Reservations are highly advisable. Fares range from $34 to 52 for adults and $17 to $27 for children under age 11. Credit cards.

center you can take a short side road or walk the nature trail (about a half mile long) to a parking area right at the dune's edge. To get close to the highest dunes requires walking across a shallow creek in some places. It's safe even for the smallest child but you might want to protect your footwear by removing your shoes.

Visitors are encouraged to walk on, climb, slide down, or do just about anything else they want to on the soft sand dunes. However, be advised that in the summer the sand can become quite hot so it's best to have some protection. Don't worry about leaving footprints–the frequent valley winds will soon erase all traces of your visit as the dunes are constantly renewed and reshaped by the forces of nature. On the other hand, despite the continual effects of wind, many of the largest dunes are remarkably consistent in their overall size and shape. *Tel. 719/378-2312. The Monument is open all the time but the Visitor Center hours are daily from*

8:00am until 6:00pm between Memorial Day and Labor Day; and from 8:30am until 4:30pm the remainder of the year. Admission is $4 per vehicle for persons without a park service passport.

Unless you're going to be doing one or both of the detours described in the sidebars, head back toward Alamosa via Six Mile Lane to Mosca (a few miles of the road are unpaved but not a problem in good weather). A bit north of Mosca on CO 17 is the **San Luis Valley Alligator Farm**. Strange to have alligators in Colorado you say? Well, there's a good reason for it. Alligators were brought in to do away with animal remains in the area that could have contaminated operations from a nearby fish hatchery. Then someone got the great idea to charge visitors for seeing the alligators. That's two examples of American ingenuity! And the alligators seem to thoroughly enjoy the view of mountains as they keep comfy in the near 90-degree warm water from the natural hot springs. *Tel. 719/378-2612. Farm open daily from 7:00am until 7:00pm June throug Labor Day, and from 10:00am until 3:00pm the remainder of the year. The admission is $5 for adults and $2.50 for children ages 6 through 12.*

Upon returning to Alamosa via CO 17 south, pick up US 160 westbound for the next leg of the journey.

THE SOUTHERN FRONTIER

It is 150 miles from Alamosa to Durango, all via US 160. Although there aren't any major attractions on this stretch, the entire route is quite scenic and makes for a pleasant drive. The route first parallels the northern part of the Rio Grande and then turns toward the southwest through the **Rio Grande National Forest** and the **San Juan Mountains**. The road is excellent and shouldn't present any problem for drivers, at least not during the summer, even when it crosses the Continental Divide at the **Wolf Creek Pass** (elevation 10,550 feet). In this vicinity, which is the most scenic portion, are views of the highest peaks of the San Juans. Eagle, Pagosa, Sheep, and Gray Back Mountains are all in excess of 12,000 feet so you'll be confronted with rocks that tower more than 3,000 feet above you.

The road drops to an elevation of about 7,000 feet by the time it reaches the town of Pagosa Springs, only about 22 miles from the Wolf Creek Pass. Pagosa meant "healing" in the language of the Indians who orginally inhabited the area. It is about half-way to Durango and makes a good stopping point to relax and have a bite to eat. Approximately 20 miles further west in the town of Chimney Rock are some ancient Indian ruins. US 160 skirts the northern border of the Southern Ute Indian Reservation from this point on. The last forty miles or so into Durango are largely uneventful but give you time to catch your breath before experiencing the wonders of the trip's next leg.

DURANGO

A visit to **Durango** is like receiving a blast from the past–the late 19th century to be exact. Durango sits majestically alongside the Animas River at the base of the San Juan Mountains in a setting of great beauty. The elevation is 6,500 feet. Durango has about 14,000 residents but during the summer season it is always bustling and seems to have twice that many visitors. The city was founded in 1879 during the heady days of the gold and silver mining era. Much of the downtown section along Main Avenue still features original Victorian style structures. There are many old style saloons and even hitching posts to provide visitors with an old west flavor.

The Durango area, thanks to the surrounding **San Juan National Forest**, is a major center of outdoor activity. White-water rafting, horse-back and jeep tours of the mountains, mountain biking, and even skiing are all nearby. Rodeo is popular, too. On a more esoteric note visitors can spend the evening taking in a 19th-century style melodrama or vaudeville program. Or a chuckwagon supper with cowboy entertainment. All of these are detailed later in the chapter.

A stroll along Main Avenue (which is also US 550) is a good way of getting to know the town. The old buildings are colorfully painted and now house many restaurants and interesting shops. There are also more than twenty galleries as Durango has been consistently placed among the top ten of America's small art towns. One of the most interesting structures on Main is the **Strater Hotel**, *699 Main Avenue*, which was built in 1887. It still functions as a hotel (and was described in the Where to Stay section) but should be seen regardless of where you stay. The hotel exudes the elegance of its early days and has one of the world's largest collections of antique walnut furniture.

The **Animas Museum**, *31st Street and West 2nd Avenue (one block off of Main)*, has a number of exhibits which depict local history. *Tel. 970/259-2402. The museum is open daily except Sunday from 10:00am until 6:00pm, May through October. Donations are requested.*

Part of the fun of visiting Durango is that you can get involved in activities that bring back memories of the old west. These include the **Diamond Circle Melodrama** at the Strater Hotel and a chuckwagon supper. More information can be found in the *Nightlife & Entertainment* section. On a more modern note, you can tempt your taste buds while in Durango by stopping in at the **Rocky Mountain Chocolate Factory**, *265 Turner Drive*. Guided tours take you through the process of creating these delicious morsels. *Tel. 970/259-0554. Tours depart daily on the half hour between 9:30am and 1:30pm between June 1st and early September. At other times the tours are given only at 10:30am and 1:30pm. It is closed on state holidays. Admission is free but tickets must be picked up in advance at the company's retail store in downtown Durango at 561 Main Street.*

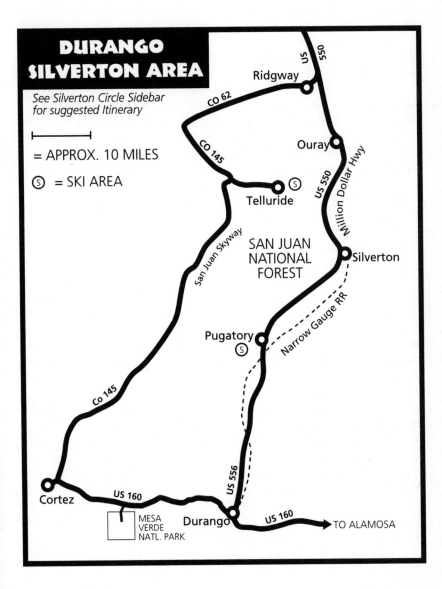

DURANGO SILVERTON AREA

See Silverton Circle Sidebar for suggested Itinerary

= APPROX. 10 MILES

Ⓢ = SKI AREA

Ridgway

US 550

CO 62

CO 145

Ouray

Telluride Ⓢ

US 550

Million Dollar Hwy

San Juan Skyway

SAN JUAN NATIONAL FOREST

Silverton

Narrow Gauge RR

Pugatory Ⓢ

Co 145

US 556

Cortez

US 160

MESA VERDE NATL. PARK

Durango

US 160 → TO ALAMOSA

The atmosphere in Durango makes it a fun place to visit. However, there is no doubt that the town's real claim to travel fame is the incomparable ride on the **Durango & Silverton Narrow Gauge Railroad**, *depot located at 479 Main Avenue at the south end of town.* The line has been in use continuously since 1882. More than $300 million in ore was hauled by the D&S before it was turned into one of the greatest of tourist attractions. The coal-burning steam locomotives currently in use were built in the 1920's and are meticulously cared for.

Your journey on *The Silverton*, as it is known for short, covers a round-trip distance of 90 miles and takes the entire day. The route goes through the San Juan Mountains following the course of the Animas River all the way to Silverton. (Although US 550 roughly parallels the train route, the scenery by train is far superior– too much of the view on the road between Durango and Silverton is blocked by the thick forest cover.) The long trains wind through the terrain, often on a narrow ledge and seemingly clinging to the precipitous cliffs. It also goes near the rushing river and past several waterfalls. It is quite a sight to look out the window (especially good if you're near one end of the train) and see the other end snaking around a turn.

The train makes stops at several secluded resorts, such as Purgatory, some of which are only accessible by *The Silverton*. There are also two stops to take on water. When it finally reaches the town of Silverton it has climbed almost a mile higher than from its departure point in Durango! The layover in Silverton is approximately two hours but the exact time depends upon which train you're on. That's enough time to have lunch and explore most of what the town has to offer. However, my description of Silverton will be later in this section when the southwest tour reaches there by car.

Which train car to select can be a consideration in the enjoyment of your trip. There are open cars and closed; some of the closed cars offer special services such as beverages for an additional fee. Keep in mind that there is a great deal of soot and smoke from the locomotive. You are more subject to them if you sit in an open car or towards the front of the train. It won't do you any harm but it is better to wear dark color clothing–it won't show the dirt as much if you do get hit by cinders. A jacket is also helpful, even during the middle of summer, since it can sometimes be kind of chilly when the train is moving.

While most travelers prefer to return to Durango from Silverton the same way they came (by the train), you do have the option of coming back by bus. This isn't nearly as much fun and is inadvisable if you are going to be on that stretch of road for other purposes at another time during your journey in the Durango area. The only possible advantage is if you are pressed for time since it is faster than the train.

Tel. 888/872-4607 or 970/247-2733. Reservations are required. The train operates year-round on a daily basis. During the summer (mid-May through mid-October) there are departures at 8:15am and 9:45am. Additional departures are scheduled at 7:30am and 9:45am between June and late September. Return times are between 4:45pm and 7:00pm, depending upon departure time. At other times of the year the train only operates as far as Cascade Canyon (about a 50-mile round-trip). It departs at 10:00am and returns around 3:00pm. Seating for disabled travelers is available. The summer fare is $53 for adults ($88 for parlor car seating) and $27 for children under 12. There is an additional $10 charge if you return by bus. The winter fare is $45 for adults ($75 for parlor car seating) and $22 for children. Credit cards. Boarding begins 45 minutes prior to departure. It is always a good idea to confirm scheduled departures.

Note that your fare on the train includes admission to two small museums at either end of the line. These are the Durango Railroad Museum and the Silverton Freight Yard Museum. They aren't anything special but if you have a few extra minutes while waiting to board, give them a try.

THE SILVERTON CIRCLE

If you look at the accompanying Durango-Silverton area map you should quickly spot a possible routing problem–US 550 runs across two points on the loop. Since there are so many important things to see along all portions of the route, you could run into a situation where you have to back-track several times to see everything, adding a lot of mileage. I have a good solution although there are certainly other combinations that you may want to try.

From Durango we'll take the train up to Silverton and return. We won't drive on the accompanying part of US 550. Then we'll head out to Mesa Verde and Cortez before traveling north to Telluride. At the junction of CO 62 and US 550 we'll then head south to Ouray and further via the Million Dollar Highway back to Silverton. The only doubling back this way is the highly scenic 40 mile stretch between Silverton and Ridgway.

MESA VERDE NATIONAL PARK

To reach **Mesa Verde National Park** from Durango drive 35 miles west on US 160 to the park's entrance road. A visit to Mesa Verde can require anywhere from several hours to a few days (most visitors should count on spending at least five hours there) so many people like to leave Durango (or Cortez to the west) in the morning and come back to stay in the same place at the end of the day. There are also lodging facilities within the park.

Mesa Verde is one of the most remarkable facilities in our National Park system. It is, first and foremost, one of the world's most significant archaelogical preserves as it contains more than 600 examples of the amazing cliff dwellings of an ancient culture. But it also has some of the most beautiful scenery you could ever imagine. Mesa Verde means "green table" in Spanish, an appropriate name for this flat-topped 80-square mile plateau that is blanketed by forest. The plateau top is 2,000 feet above the valley to the north, from where visitors enter, while the southern slope is more gradual. The plateau top is seamed with numerous deep steep-walled canyons that from the air would resemble fingers. It is in the upper reaches of these canyons, protected by natural overhangs, that the inhabitants of Mesa Verde built their homes. Mesa Verde represents the period from about 550 through 1250AD. The sidebar has more information on the houses and the people who inhabited them.

Upon entry into the park the road begins to climb gently and fairly straight for about five miles before you encounter a ten mile stretch of more severe grades, turns, switchbacks, and even tunnels. This isn't meant to scare you away–the road is easy enough if you take it slow and each turn in the road provides a new and beautiful panorama. There are several overlooks over the valley but the best one is **Park Point**, reached by a short spur road. From this elevation of more than 8,500 feet you can see a great expanse of the southwest covering parts of four different states. Soon after you'll reach the top of the plateau at the **Far View Lodge** and **Visitor Center**. Tickets for tours of some of the ruins as well as the Wetherill Mesa tour are sold here.

Continuing south from Far View onto **Chapin Mesa**, the best known area of Mesa Verde, you'll soon come to a short spur that leads to the first ruin viewing point known as the **Far View Ruin**. Then stop at the park headquarters area which contains an excellent museum on the ancestral Puebloans. Within walking distance of the museum is the impressive **Spruce Tree House**. A trail descends into the canyon so that you can actually walk through this large and well-preserved ruin. Only by going into at least one ruin can you truly appreciate the architectural genius of the ancestral Puebloans. This is the most accessible of the major ruins. The trail is easy going down but may represent a problem on the return climb for aged or physically challenged visitors. The view from the top of the trail is, however, outstanding.

Just below the museum begins the **Ruins Road Drive**, two six mile loops that provide access to many of the highlights of Mesa Verde. Besides taking you to the cliff dwellings, the western loop of Ruins Road passes many small "pit" dwellings that were built on top of the mesa. There are more than 3,000 of these located in Mesa Verde. Also on the west loop is the **Square Tower House** ruin. The east loop contains two of the best

= APPROX. 3 MILES

(1) Balcony House   (7) Park Point

(2) Camp Ground   (8) Museum & Park H.Q.

(3) Cliff Palace   (9) Spruce Tree House

(4) Far View Lodge   (10) Square Tower House

(5) Far View Ruins

(6) Far View Visitor Center

THE ANCESTRAL PUEBLOANS OF MESA VERDE

Up until very recently the native inhabitants of the Four Corners region were known as the Anasazi, or ancient ones. Another interpretation of the word is that it meant "ancient enemies." Thus, in this time when everything has to be politically correct, Anasazi has suddenly become objectionable to some of the Hopi descendents of that culture. Therefore, the term "ancestral Puebloans" is finding its way into the archaeological lexicon. So much for titles–let's learn more about them.

*The ancestral Puebloan arrived in the southwest around 1AD. They had a simple agriculture based society and also hunted. As they grew in numbers so did the complexity of their society. They began to diversify into different groups depending upon where they lived. Those in this part of present-day Colorado reached a high cultural level by as early as 500AD. They were descendents of the "Basketmakers," so called because of their excellence in weaving. They soon learned how to make pottery and construct dwellings with roofs. It was around this time that the Basketmakers started constructing pit houses on the mesa top. Several hundred years later they began clustering their homes into what can be termed the first pueblos (Spanish for village). The houses became larger and larger and added ceremonial chambers called **kivas**. By the first century of the millenium their culture had reached its highest stage of development. Many of the greatest structures in Mesa Verde today are from that era.*

Then the ancestral Puebloan suddenly abandoned their cliff-top cities. The reasons aren't known for sure but a prolonged period of drought is thought to have forced them to move to a location where water was more readily available. Invasion by nomadic Indian tribes is also believed to be a factor. Many settled in present-day Arizona and the Hopi claim to be direct ancestors of the Pueblo people.

ruins–the **Cliff Palace** and **Balcony House**. Each of these can be seen from the top of the mesa but requires joining a guided tour to gain access. Cliff Palace is the easier of the two to reach but is still not recommended for those with impaired ambulatory skills. It is the largest of Mesa Verde's cliff dwellings. To view it from the rim use the overlook at **Sun Temple**. The Balcony House is reached only via a strenuous walk that involves scaling several 20-foot ladders and crawling through a tunnel. On the other hand, it is considered to be the best example of the high-point of ancestral Puebloan architecture and civilization.

Until recently summer visitors were able to take a bus tour of the adjacent and less developed Wetherill Mesa. However, due to recent forest fires and a growing concern for protecting primitive sites, these tours have been suspended at least for the time being. Therefore, your visit to Mesa Verde will be complete once you have finished the two loops. However, if you're going to be staying overnight in Mesa Verde or plan to be around in the evening between 6:30 and 9:30pm (April through mid-October), then do plan to see the excellent multimedia presentation called "Anasazi" that is given at the Far View Lodge. *Admission is $3 for adults and $1.50 for children ages 5 through 12.*

The park also has many trails of various lengths and difficulty. One of the most popular is the three-mile long **Petroglyph Point Trail**.

For additional information write to: Superintendent, Mesa Verde National Park, PO Box 8, Mesa Verde N.P. CO 81330; or call Tel. 970/529-4465 for general information. The park is open all year but facilities and activities are limited or closed during the winter months. The visitor center is open daily from 8:00am until 5:00pm from May through September. The Chapin Mesa Museum is open daily from 8:00am until 6:30pm between April and the middle of October and from 8:00am until 5:00pm the remainder of the year. Tel. 970/533-7731. Admission to the park is $10 for each vehicle to those not holding a park service passport. There is a $1.75 per person charge for guided tours of either Cliff House or Balcony House.

CORTEZ TO TELLURIDE

The city of **Cortez** is located only ten miles west of the Mesa Verde entrance road via US 160. It is the hub of several roads and the most important community in the Colorado section of the Four Corners region. The **Cortez Center**, *25 Market Street*, is in the heart of town in a building dating from 1908. The center promotes archaeological investigation and understanding of Native American culture. It has a number of interpretive exhibits that are open to the public but of most interest to visitors are the colorful and authentic **Native American Dances** that are performed to the delight of audiences of all ages. *Tel. 970/565-1511. Dance performances nightly except Sunday at 7:30pm from Memorial Day through Labor Day. Donations are greatly appreciated.*

Cortez is also a good base for several excursions in the extreme southwestern corner of Colorado. A popular one is the 40-mile drive via US 160 west (the first part is also US 666 southbound) to the **Four Corners Monument**. This is the point where Colorado, Arizona, Utah, and New Mexico meet–the only place in the United States where four states adjoin. There is a monument on the ground marking the spot and Native Americans sell their wares around the perimeter. It's mildly interesting but unless you are coming in from Arizona by that route I doubt if it is worth an 80-mile round-trip to take a picture of your traveling companion contorted in such a way as to be in four states at one time. A more worthwhile trip (and a shorter one) is to get off of US 160/US 666 about ten miles south of Cortez in Towaoc at the **Ute Mountain Tribal Park** on the Ute Mountain Indian Reservation. The tribe offers full and half day tours of archaeological sites with emphasis on creating an understanding of their heritage. *Tel. 800/847-5485 or 970/565-3751, Ext. 282 for more information and reservations.*

If it's more ruins you want you can also venture out on your own to the **Hovenweep National Monument**. It is located 43 miles west of Cortez by a mostly unpaved road which can be difficult or impassable during or after bad weather, so inquire locally before setting out. Hovenweep (translation is "deserted valley") was constructed around 1200 and consists of six different ruins. Only the Square Tower ruin is readily accessible. All of the Hovenweep ruins are characterized by towers that are either oval, circular, or D-shaped. Keep in mind that Hovenweep is not a developed site and requires a sense of adventure to visit. *Tel. 970/749-0510 or 970/529-4461. The monument is accessible during daylight hours and there is no admission charge.* Also nearby and similar to Hovenweep is the smaller **Yucca House National Monument**.

Our journey now heads north from Cortez via CO 145, another immensely scenic moutain route part of a system of roads in this region known as the **San Juan Skyway**. Some of the mountain peaks in this area are as high as 14,000 feet but most are more in the 12,000-foot range. There are also brilliant red rock canyons and spruce forests to be seen as the road traverses the Dolores River Valley. After 73 miles on this road there is a side road of four miles that leads to the resort community of Telluride.

Telluride is located in a magnificent box canyon with only one way in or out. The deep and hidden valley provides a remarkable setting for this tiny town that is dwarfed by the 13,000-foot high peaks and glaciers which surround it. The entire town has been designated as a National Historic District. Begun as a mining camp, Telluride still retains many of its original Victorian style buildings. Among the most notable is the 1913 **Sheridan Opera House** on North Oak Street (see *Nightlife & Entertainment* for more information) with its hand painted curtain containing a Venetian scene.

Boasting some of the finest in Colorado's winter sports facilities, Telluride is now more than the "most beautiful place you'll ever ski," to borrow from their own catchy marketing phrase. It has numerous delights for summer visitors too. One of the best ways to see both the town and surrounding area is to take the *free* **Station Telluride Gondola**. How often can you get a free ride these days? Exploring the area around the town has also become a favorite activity either by foot or by jeep/4WD vehicle. You can get information on all of these activities by contacting **Telluride Visitor Services**, *Tel. 888/605-2578.* Be aware that if you are going to be driving around in your own vehicle that many of the roads are extremely difficult and are only for the most experienced drivers. Likewise, trails in the surrounding mountains tend to be long and difficult. Beginners should stick to hiking in the canyon or the trail to the 365-foot high **Bridal Veil Falls**.

After Telluride go back to CO 145 and continue on to the junction of CO 62. A turn to the right and 23 more miles of scenic highway will take you to the town of Ridgway and the junction of US 550. Go south for 11 miles to Ouray.

OURAY, THE MILLION DOLLAR HIGHWAY, & SILVERTON

Ouray, pronounced you-RAY, was named for a Ute Indian chief and has such a magnificent valley setting that it is often called the "Switzerland of America." The valley itself is more than 7,700 feet above sea level and is surrounded by perpetually snow-clad peaks. The population is only about 700 people and the residents are proud of their community that is "9 blocks long and 6 blocks wide." That's not only because of the small number of residents–it would be hard to be larger given how it is sandwiched in between the mountains. It is typical of so many of Colorado's former mining towns, having been the site of silver discoveries in 1875 and gold in 1893.

Ouray is a popular starting point for jeep and off-road tours. Some of the more popular jeep excursions are listed in the *Sports & Recreation* section below. The best view of Ouray and the adjacent mountains is from south of the town on US 550. A scenic overlook in this area by **Bear Creek Falls** is a marvelous sight– the thundering torrent of water passes under the highway bridge on its way into the canyon below. But we're jumping a little bit ahead by telling you something that's south of town. A mile north of Ouray and then another mile east on County Road 14 is the long established **Bachelor-Syracuse Mine**. An interesting train tour brings visitors more than a half mile inside famous Gold Hill where about $100 million worth of ore has been recovered. The temperature in the mine is a constant but cool 52 degrees. The price is as steep as the mountain so unless you're especially fascinated by this type of attraction you may not feel it's worth the cost of admission. *Tel. 970/325-0220. Tours are given on the hour between 9:00am and 5:00pm every day from mid-June to late August and until 4:00pm late May to mid-June and during the first half of September. Tour price is $11 for adults, $6 for children ages 3-11. Gold panning costs an additional $6 per person. Credit cards.*

You can relax for a while before resuming the tour by taking a swim at the **Ouray Hot Springs Pool**, a spring fed muncipal pool in a park at the north end of town. Also in the park is the **Caboose in the Park**, an original Denver & Rio Grande caboose used from the 1880's until as recently as the 1950's. It has been painstakingly restored. Three blocks south of the park is Eighth Avenue. Turn left and follow it to **Cascade Falls**. The 300-foot high falls can be seen from just about any point in Ouray but there's no better spot than from the base of the falls.

The **Ouray County Museum**, *420 Sixth Avenue*, is housed in an 1887 building that was originally a hospital for miners. The many exhibits include a mine reconstruction, jail, medical office, and general store. *Tel. 970/325-4576. The museum is open daily from 9:00am through 4:00pm, May through mid-October; and Saturday through Monday from 10:00am until 4:00pm during the remainder of the year. Adult admission is $3 and children are charged $1.00.* **Main Street** between 4th and 7th Avenues is worth doing some exploring on as most of the buildings are of historic significance.

Perhaps Ouray's highlight (except for the setting itself) is the **Box Canyon Falls and Park** at the south end of town. A narrow canyon is hemmed in by granite walls. It's almost always dark in the canyon because it is only 20 feet wide and the walls are more than 200 feet high. In addition, the slope of the walls almost makes it more of a natural tunnel than a canyon. Two waterfalls, made extra-loud by the enclosed setting, are quite beautiful. They are reached by a suspended walkway and bridge that traverses the gorge. The base of the falls can be reached via a stairway. You can't see the "outside" world when you're in the box canyon–you might as well be on a journey to the center of the earth! *Tel. 970/325-4464. The park is open daily from May through the middle of October between 8:00am and 8:00pm. It may be open at other times but call for information. The admission is a bargain at $2 for adults, $1.50 for seniors, and $1 for children ages 5 through 12.*

The 23-mile stretch of US 550 from Ouray south to Silverton is known as the **Million Dollar Highway**, although some non-purists consider the portion from Silverton to Durango to be part of it. The origin of the name is related to one of three things–depending upon who you talk to: the high cost of building this fete of road engineering, the value of ore that was carried over the original unpaved route, or the fantastic scenery that your eyes will feast on every mile of the route. Maybe it's just best to say that it is a combination of all three although I'm certainly partial to the million dollar view theory. The route starts just south of Ouray at the aforementioned Bear Creek Falls. Other notable sights include a view of **Mt. Adams** through a tunnel portal, mountains of incredible reddish and orange color due to the presence of iron and other minerals, and deep, narrow gorges. In many places on the road you won't be able to see the top of the canyon or the bottom on the opposite side. The road is generally easy to drive but requires that you take it slow, especially if you are new to mountain driving.

If Durango was taking a step back in time then **Silverton** must be the equivalent of two steps. There's something unreal about the place as if it weren't an actual town at all but a movie set or theme park. You almost expect some cowboys and Indians to come riding down the main street, although it would be more historically accurate to see a group of weary miners returning to town after a day of prospecting. Actually, it has and still is used for movie production with its old-time style false fronts on Blair Street, the former notorious red-light district during the town's $65 million period between 1873 and 1918. The street is now filled with gift shops and art galleries. About 800 people call Silverton home these days.

Amid the San Juan Range, Silverton is another prime territory for hiking and off-road adventuring. A number of ghost towns and and jeep roads criss-cross the surrounding mountains. You can get maps to do some exploring on your own from the Silverton Visitor Center as you come into town on US 550 from the north. There is a fantastic view of this tiny community along with the approach of the Durango & Silverton Railroad from the **Christ of the Mines Shrine** located in the Elephant Hills above town. Access is via 15th Street north of Greene Street by the San Juan County Courthouse.

The **Historical Society Museum**, *next to the Courthouse on Greene Street,* is housed in the former county jail. There are a variety of exhibits on Silverton's mining history and several of the original cells still occupy an upper floor. *Tel. 970/387-5838. The musuem is open daily from 9:00am until 5pm, Memorial Day through mid-September, and from 10:00am until 3:00pm through the middle of October. The admission is $2 for ages 12 and older.* A walk through "downtown" Silverton can start at the Courthouse Square and proceeds down Greene Street for four blocks to 12th and then back via 12th and Blair Streets. Bronze plaques are placed on historic buildings to make your tour easier and more educational. You can also get a detailed description of each historic structure by picking up a copy of the walking tour guide at the visitor center.

For an interesting little excursion take CO 110 east from downtown past the museum for two miles to Howardsville and right on County Road 4. Or just follow the clearly marked signs to the **Old Hundred Gold Mine Tour**. The last three miles to the mine are gravel surface. A one hour guided tour takes you more than 1,500 feet inside Galena Mountain. Your guide will point out the ore veins and actual drilling demonstrations will be given. Everyone enjoys putting on their yellow jacket to keep them clean and donning a real miner's helmet for the train ride into the mine. You'll also be allowed to pan for gold. The mine temperature is a constant 48 degrees so wear a jacket or sweater. *Tel. 800/872-3009 or 970/387-5444. Tours are given daily on the hour from 10:00am through 4:00pm from the middle* *of May through the middle of October. The admission is $13 for adults, $12 for seniors, and $7 for children ages 5 through 12. Credit cards.*

If you don't want to go on the unpaved road then you can visit the **Mayflower Gold Mill** just east of town off of CO 110. I think the Old Hundred is better but movie nostalgia buffs might recognize the Mayflower from the 1957 Jimmy Stewart film, *Night Passage. Tel. 970/387-0294. Tours are given daily only during the months of June through August. between 10:00am and 3:00pm. The price is $6 for adults and $3 for children ages 11 through 16.*

BLACK CANYON OF THE GUNNISON NATIONAL PARK

From Silverton, return via US 550 through Ouray and Ridgway but this time continue on US 550 all the way to Montrose (about 25 miles north of Ouray). Montrose is the gateway community to the Black Canyon and has a few points of interest worth seeing. The first is the **Ute Indian Museum & Ouray Memorial Park**, located on US 550 about four miles south of the center of town. It is one of only a handful of museums in the country that is devoted to a single tribe. The site is the former farm of the Ute Chief Ouray who we met earlier. Many of the items in the museum belonged to Ouray and his wife Chipeta. Displays depict everyday Ute life. Chipeta is buried in the memorial park. *Tel. 970/249-3098. The museum is open daily from 9:00am until 5:00pm from mid-May through Labor Day. At other times of the year it is best to call to confirm hours. The admission is $2.50 for adults, $2 for seniors, and $1.50 for children ages 6 through 16.*

The **Rocky Hill Winery**, *1230 S. Townsend, in town,* produces a variety of wines. (Montrose isn't that far from the fruit producing region around Grand Junction.) *Tel. 970/249-3765. Free tours and tastings are offered daily from 10:00am until 6:00pm except Sunday when the hours are 1:00pm to 4:00pm.*

A final stop in Montrose can be made at the **Montrose County Historical Museum** in the former Denver & Rio Grande train station, *Main and Rio Grande Streets.* Besides railroad memorabilla the museum depicts pioneer life in early Montrose and has an extensive collection of farm equipment as well as recreations of homesteader's cabins and other structures from 19th century Montrose and the surrounding area. *Tel. 970/249-2085. The museum is open daily except Sunday from 9:00am until 5:00pm, mid-May through the end of October. The admission is $2.50 for adults and 50 cents for children ages 5 through 12.*

Eight miles east of Montrose via US 50 there is a cutoff (CO 347) that winds upward for six miles to the fantastic **Black Canyon of the Gunnison National Park**. It was redesignated from a national monument to park status in 2000. Not that it should make a difference, but as a gleeful hotel

AUTUMN IN COLORADO

Maybe because of the wonderful sights in summer and the skiing in winter Colorado doesn't have the same reputation as New England does in the minds of a lot of people when it comes to the brilliant colors of fall. But it should. The fall foliage in many parts of Colorado is on a par with the best that can be found anywhere in the world. The past few years have finally seen a growing awareness of what is to be found here in the fall.

The colors of autumn in Colorado are dominated by glowing gold, flaming red and bright orange. Set against mountains tinged with the first snows of the season and a sky of brilliant blue, the scene before you is one of indescribable beauty. As the day wears on and the sun begins to set the color of the sky almost seems to take on the radiant golden glow of the aspen leaves.

There isn't any best spot to see Colorado's fall foliage but the most spectacular areas are in the immense national forests that cover more than half of western Colorado. Altitudes below 10,000 feet are the wisest choice because of the more limited number of trees in the highest elevations. Trees are such a part of the landscape that you'll see the changing colors from any main or secondary road in the forests. The season starts early in Colorado. Count on September in the higher elevations. What makes things even better is that the fall colors last longer in most parts of Colorado–usually several weeks or even longer.

operator in the area pointed out, business does increase when it's called a National Park as opposed to a Monument. In any event, I've seen a lot of wonderful places in my own travels but this has to rank right up there with the most awesome sights you'll ever behold! Oh, sure, there are canyons that may be deeper, longer, or narrower, but no canyon anywhere in the world so remarkably combines these three attributes in such a relatively compact area. The 20,766 acre monument encompasses twelve miles of the deepest section of the Gunnison River Gorge. In some places the canyon is as deep as 2,700 feet. The top is only 1,100 feet across at its narrowest point but is only an incredible 40 feet wide at one point on the bottom. The name has two origins. First is the dark color granite and other rocks that comprise the sheer walls of the canyon. The other reason is that because of the narrowness of the canyon sunlight has a difficult time penetrating its depths.

The rim road is a relatively flat and easy road to negotiate although there are several sharp turns. The overlooks are all within a short distance of the parking areas. Upon entering there is one view point before you reach the Visitor Center at **Gunnison Point**. The center is small but has a few exhibits on the forces of erosion that created this masterpiece of nature. Several rim-top trails are in the vicinity of the Visitor Center. Only the first section of the road is open during the winter. **Pulpit Rock Overlook** and **Cross Fissure View** come up in quick succession as do **Rock Point** and **Devils Lookout**. The latter two are the furthest viewpoints from the road but require only about a five or ten minute walk each way from the parking area. At Devils Lookout you will be near to the narrowest portion of the gorge. In fact, the depth of the canyon is greater than its width across at this point.

After a sharp turn in the road come two of the best viewpoints– **Chasm View** and **Painted Wall View**. The Painted Wall rises 2,200 feet straight up and can also be seen from **Dragon Point**. **Sunset View** and **High Point** round out the overlooks. The majority of overlooks enable you to see the course of the surging Gunnison River. Although the road only extends less than ten miles to High Point (where you have to turn around and head back) you should take in as many view points as time permits. Careful examination of the sheer canyon walls will, despite the overall somber color, reveal clearly marked rock strata and fascinating streaked patterns of lighter color rock as if the canyon were the immense canvas of a race of artistic giants. The view at each one is no less than spectacular and breathtaking.

While the overlooks are all short walks there is ample opportunity for those who wish to stretch their muscles more. The **Warner Point Nature Trail** extends from road's end at High Point for another mile along the canyon rim to one last overlook. Climbing into the canyon is allowed but it is an arduous task to say the least. For the non-experienced climber it is also potentially dangerous, so be forewarned. *All* canyon climbers must register at the Visitor Center and have a back country permit.

One last touring possibility in the park is to hang a left immediately before leaving the monument onto the **East Portal Road**. This road is paved (but only open in the summer) and is more difficult than the main road. It leads to the **East Portal** at the beginning of the Gunnison gorge and provides views of not only the gorge itself, but of the Gunnison Diversion Dam.

Tel. 970/240-5300. The park is open at all times. Visitor Cener hours are daily from 8:00am until 7:00pm from Memorial Day through Labor Day and from 9:00am until 3:30pm the remainder of the year. Admission is $7 per vehicle to those not holding a park service passport.

THE BLACK CANYON'S NORTH RIM

*Just like the Grand Canyon, the most visited part of the Black Canyon is the south rim. But it does have an almost wilderness-like **north side** that can be reached if you have a little spirit of adventure. And that's what it requires since the views, although equally wonderful, aren't all that much different from the south rim.*

The easiest way to get to the north rim is to follow the route in the main text below to the junction of CO 92 in the Curecanti National Recreation Area. At the town of Crawford an unpaved road leads to the north rim road which is also not paved. There are several overlooks. The north rim road and overlooks are less developed and have no guard rails. Combined with the rougher surface and other mountainous conditions, this route is only for the experienced mountain driver. The distance from the south rim to the north is about 80 miles one way.

CURECANTI NATIONAL RECREATION AREA, US 50 CORRIDOR, & MONARCH PASS

Upon completing the Black Canyon and returning via CO 347 to US 50, travel east for the short ride to Cimarron where US 50 meets the **Curecanti National Recreation Area**. The recreation area covers a narrow tract of land extending for more than thirty miles on either side of several lakes formed by the impoundment of the Gunnison River. Crystal, Morrow Point, and Blue Mesa Lakes vary in width from little more than a river to more than a mile. With a backdrop of high mountain peaks and rugged country it is a beautiful sight that adds to the enjoyment of the recreation area's boaters, fishermen, hikers, and other outdoor enthusiasts.

The Cimarron Visitor Center at the west end has several old railroad cars and a locomotive displayed on a trestle dating from 1891 as well as several other historic exhibits. Then take the side road that leads about 1-1/2 miles off of the main road to the **Morrow Point Dam**. The road twists through a narrow canyon where you can practically reach out and touch the steep rock walls. From the parking area at the end of the road is an impressive view of the 469-foot dam that straddles the narrow gorge. A footpath leads beside the Gunnison River so you can get a closer look at the force behind the creation of Black Canyon. The dam itself is usually open during summer days for self-guiding tours of the power house.

Back on US 50 the next stop is **Morrow Point Lake**, reached by a short spur at Pine Creek Trail. From this point you can reach a dock where boat tours on the lake are conducted by naturalists who describe the history of the region. However, it isn't that easy to get to–the trail to the dock involves a mile long descent with more than 230 steps. Given the altitude you have to be in pretty decent shape to attempt it. *Tel. 970/641-0402 for information on boat tours which depart daily at 10:00am and 12:30pm from Memorial Day weekend through Labor Day. The fare is $8.50 for adults, $6.50 for seniors, and $5.00 for children ages 2 through 12. Reservations are required.*

Just beyond the Pine Creek Trail stop US 50 reaches the Blue Mesa Dam that crosses over to the north side of the lake. This is CO 92 (the route to the north rim of the Black Canyon if you are so inclined) and immediately upon crossing over you'll reach one of the nicest views in the entire recreaion area: the **Blue Mesa Dam Overlook**. If you have time you might want to drive a few miles further on CO 92 as this entire area has some of the best scenery in Curecanti. Continuing back on the south side, US 50 skirts Blue Mesa Lake, winding around a bend and then crossing a bridge to the north side of the lake at Cebolla Basin. The lake is quite beautiful at this point and if it's sunny (a good liklihood in summer) the sparkling water beneath the towering mountains is a sight to remember. You'll also catch a quick view of some unusual rock formations known as the **Dillon Pinnacles** as you reach the north side. A two-mile hiking trail leads through the pinnacle area.

The **Elk Creek Visitor Center**, a few miles past the pinnacles, is the main visitor center for the Curecanti recreation area. Nature walks and fish feedings are held periodically–the schedule is posted. The east end of the lake is where most of the boat ramps are located. Pleasant scenery continues as you traverse the final few miles of the Curecanti. *Tel. 970/ 641-2337. The recreation area is open at all times. Visitor center hours vary but are generally open daily during the summer from at least 8:30am to 4:30pm. There is no charge for entering the area.*

Gunnison lies near the east side of the recreation area. After that US 50 continues to be a scenic route as it crosses the mountainous **Gunnison National Forest**. The best scenery along the route comes in the vicinity of the **Monarch Pass**, at 11,312 feet atop the Continental Divide. The pass is reached by a long ascent and an equally long descent. The road is good but lower gear is advisable during the trip up and down. The Monarch Pass covers part of the Sawatch Range which has 15 nearby peaks in excess of 14,000 feet. Monarch Pass is a winter skiing center but in the summer you can ride the **Monarch Crest Tram**, a thrilling climb to a view that extends more than a hundred miles in every direction. To the northeast you can even see Pikes Peak. The starting point of the tram is one of the highest of any such facility in the world. The vertical ascent on the enclosed tram ride is about 700 feet. *Tel. 719/539-4789. The tram operates daily, mid-May through the end of September and the fare is $7 for adults, $6 for senior citizens, and $4 for children under the age of 13.*

A little more than 20 miles east of the Monarch Pass you will come to the adjacent towns of Poncha Springs and Salida. Both are centers for white-water rafting and other outdoor adventure outfitters. Salida especially has many buildings dating from the late 19th and early 20th centuries and a walk through downtown can be of interest.

From Poncha Springs you can return to the beginning of the loop in Alamosa via US 285 and CO 17 south, a distance of about 75 miles. If you've already done the entire loop and you want to get back to either Colorado Springs or Denver, it's easily done from Poncha Springs. US 50 continues east to the Royal Gorge and on into the Colorado Springs area. Denver can be reached in approximately three hours via US 285 north. Or you can take US 285 and US 24 to Leadville if you want to hook up with the central Rockies region.

NIGHTLIFE & ENTERTAINMENT

Considering that southwest Colorado is dominated by small towns, there are a surprisingly large number of theater experiences that travelers can take advantage of. Some combine modern entertainment with historic surroundings while others have entertainment in the style that was popular in the mining camps. Either way it can make for a most memorable evening. Here are the best to choose from.

Alamosa: **Adams State College**, *Tel. 719/589-7121.* Presents a variety of musical and dramatic programs.

Durango: **Diamond Circle Melodrama**, at the historic **Strater Hotel**, *690 Main Avenue, Tel. 970/247-3400.* A throwback to the days of Vaudeville, the Melodrama has been leaving audiences smiling for 40 years!

Ouray: During the summer there are a series of musical performances known as the **Accoustic Mountain Series**. In addition, various types of theater performances are frequently held at the historic **Wright Opera House** on Main Street. Information and schedules on either venue can be obtained from the town's visitor information center.

Silverton: **Miners Union Theater**, *1069 Greene Street, Tel. 800/752-4494.* The resident program puts on about a half-dozen different programs each year ranging from well known plays to some quite obscure works. The surroundings are historic.

Telluride: **Sheridan Opera House**, *110 N. Oak Street, Tel. 970/728-6363.* This opulent turn-of-the-century theater plays host to a varied calendar of events ranging from concerts to plays.

Just outside of **Towaoc** (11 miles south of Cortez) is the **Ute Mountain Casino**. With almost 400 slot machines it is one of Colorado's biggest casinos. Although it is on the reservation the stakes are limited to $5 per bet as in all Colorado casinos. Bars and lounges with entertainment are easily found in Durango. Try the Strater Hotel for Victorian ambiance.

The pickings are slimmer in other parts of the southwest but the larger lodging establishments on the main routes are generally your best shot for a nightcap.

Chuckwagon dinner shows, which include a western style barbecue and entertainment, are usually loads of fun, especially for families. You can find them in most of the bigger visitor destinations in the southwest. One is the **Z-Bar Chuck Wagon Supper and Show**, *22047 Highway 550 in Ouray, Tel. 970/240-8210*. Another, and possibly the most popular in the state, is the **Bar-D Chuckwagon,** *nine miles north of Durango on County Route 250, Tel. 970/247-5753*. Reservations are required for both. (If a chuckwagon dinner has the word "bar" and a letter in it then you can expect the best–it means they're part of an association which promotes this genre of dining and entertainment.)

SPORTS & RECREATION
Ballooning
• **Rocky Mountain Balloon Adventures**, *Pagosa Springs. Call for pick-up. Tel. 970/731-8060*

Bicycling
Maps showing bike trails are available at visitor centers in Montrose, Ouray, Silverton, and Durango.
• **Hassle Free Sports**, *2615 Main Avenue, Durango. Tel. 800/835-3800*
• **Pedal the Peaks**, *520B Main Avenue, Durango. Tel. 970/259-6880*

Boating
Vallecito Lake, *23 miles northeast of Durango on County Route 501*, has a variety of water sports. Boat rentals are available at several places along the lake, including **Angler's Wharf**, *Tel. 970/884-9806* and **Mountain Marina**, *Tel. 970/884-9450*.

Fishing
The Gunnison River is another of Colorado's Gold Medal Waters.

McPhee Reservoir and the **Dolores River** (especially the ten miles immediately south of the **McPhee Dam** is another "can't miss" area for fishing. The easiest to reach fishing access point is at the west end of the town of Dolores, 11 miles north of Cortez.
• **Anasazi Angler**, *Durango, Tel. 970/385-4665*
• **Browner's Guide Service**, *228 F Street, Salida. Tel. 719/539-4506*
• **Don Oliver Fishing Guide Service**, *Durango. Tel. 800/484-2349*
• **Fly Fishing Durango**, *Durango. Call for pick-up. Tel. 970/382-0478*

Lake Capote, *43 miles east of Durango on US 160*, is a good place for trout fishing and no state license is required. General information and fishing conditions throughout the southwestern part of Colorado can be obtained by calling *Tel. 970/291-7539.*

Golf

- **Cattails Golf Club**, *Alamosa. Tel. 719/589-9515.* 18 holes.
- **Conquistador Golf Course**, *Cortez. Tel. 970/565-9208.* 18 holes.
- **Dalton Ranch Golf Course**, *US 55 6 miles north of Durango. Tel. 970/247-8774.* 18 hole championship level course.
- **Hillcrest Golf Club**, *2300 Rim Drive, Durango. Tel. 970/247-1499.* 18 holes.
- **Montrose Golf Club**, *1350 Birch Street, Montrose. Tel. 970/249-8551.* 18 holes. Excellent views of the San Juan Mountains.
- **Salida Golf Club**, *Crestone and Grant Streets, Salida. Tel. 719/539-1060.* 18 holes.
- **Tamarron**, *40292 US Highway 550, Purgatory. Tel. 800/678-1000.* 18 holes. Rated by *Golf Digest* as one of the top courses in the United States.

Horseback Riding

- **Echo Basin Ranch**, *Highway 160, Mancos. Tel. 800/426-1890*
- **Ouray Livery Barn**, *834 Main, Ouray. Tel. 970/325-4606*
- **Rapp Guide Service**, *US 550, 20 miles north of Durango. Tel. 970/247-8454*
- **Southfork Riding Stables**, *US Highway 160 East, Durango. Tel. 970/259-4871*
- **Telluride Outside**, *1982 Highway 145, Telluride. Tel. 970/728-3895*

Off Road & 4-Wheel Drive Vehicles

Perhaps no other part of Colorado offers the variety of rugged terrain that off-road lovers thrive on. The San Juan Mountains provides the best of the southwest. There are literally dozens of routes you can follow with the majority being accessible from either Ouray or Silverton. The chamber of commerce in either locality can provide you with a map showing not only jeep roads and off-road areas, but many interesting ghost towns that can only be reached via these routes. A popular loop from Silverton covers about 35 miles. The mountains around Durango are also good places for off-roading.

If you're adventurous, but not quite enough to go it alone, then you can hook onto one of the many jeep or off-road tour operators. Some of the more popular ones are:

- **Colorado West Jeep Rentals & Tours**, *440 Main, Ouray. Tel. 800/648-JEEP*

• **Outlaw Jeep Tours**, *700 Main Avenue, Durango. Tel. 970/259-1800*
• **Rocky Mountain High Tours**, *Durango. Call for pick-up. Tel. 800/530-2022*
• **San Juan Scenic Jeep Tour**, *824 Main, Ouray. Tel. 800/324-4385*
• **Switzerland of America Tours**, *226 Seventh Avenue, Ouray. Tel. 800/432-5337*

Rafting

• **AAE's Mild to Wild Rafting**, *701 Main Ave., Durango. Tel. 800/567-6745*
• **American Adventure Expeditions**, *228 N. F Street, Salida. Tel. 800/288-0675*
• **Canyon Marine Whitewater Expeditions**, *Salida. Call for pick-up. Tel. 800/643-0707*
• **Durango Rivertrippers**, *720 Main Avenue, Durango. Tel. 800/292-8885*
• **Mountain Waters Rafting**, *Durango. Call for pick-up. Tel. 800/748-2507*
• **Peregrine River Outfitters**, *64 Ptarmigan Lane, Durango. Tel. 800/598-8852*
• **River Runners Ltd.**, *11150 US Highway 50, Salida. Tel. 800/525-2081*
• **Riverswest**, *Durango. Call for pick-up. Tel. 800/622-0852.* Also features family oriented rafting trips (not white-water)
• **Whitewater Voyageurs**, *Poncha Springs. Call for pick-up. Tel. 800/255-2585*

Skiing

Operating dates are approximate based on weather conditions. The telephone number shown is the resort's main information number. See the *Practical Information* section for central reservation numbers for most areas. Explanation of all abbreviations used in this section can be found under *Skiing* in Chapter 8.

• **Crested Butte**, *Crested Butte Mountain Resort, Mt. Crested Butte. US 285 to US 50 and then State Highway 135. Tel. 970/349-2333; www.crestedbutteresort.com.* Open late November through early April. 14 lifts. 85 trails. Terrain: B=15, I=44, A=41. DH, XC, TM, SB. Base elevation 9,375 feet; top elevation 12,162 feet. Vertical drop 2,787 feet. Ski school for adults and children. Child care available for ages 6 months through 7 years.
• **Cuchara**, *Cuchara Mountain Resort, Cuchara. I-25 to US 160 and then State Highway 12. Tel. 719/742-3163 or 888/282-4272; www.cuchara.com.* Open mid-December through late March. 5 lifts. 28 trails. Terrain: B=40, I=40, A=20. DH, XC, SS, SB. Base elevation 9,248 feet; top elevation 10,810 feet. Vertical drop 1,562 feet. Ski school for adults and children. Child care available for ages 9 months through 8 years.

- **Durango Mountain**, *Durango Mountain Resort, Durango (Purgatory). US 285 to US 160 and then US 550. Tel. 970/247-9000; www.durangomountainresort.com.* Open late November through late April. 11 lifts. 75 trails. Terrain: B=23, I=51, A=26. DH, XC, TM, SS, SB. Base elevation 8,793 feet; top elevation 10,822 feet. Vertical drop 2,029 feet. Ski school for adults and children. Programs for the physically challenged. Child care available for ages 2 months through 3 years.
- **Monarch**, *Monarch Ski & Snowboard Area, Monarch. US 285 to US 50. Tel. 719/539-3573 or 888/996-7669; www.skimonarch.com.* Open mid-November through early April. 5 lifts. 54 trails. Terrain: B=21, I=37, A=42. DH, SS, SB. Base elevation 10,790 feet; top elevation 11,961 feet. Vertical drop 1,170 feet. Ski school for adults and children. Child care available for ages 3 months through 6 years.
- **Telluride**, *Telluride Ski & Golf Co., Telluride. I-70, US 50, US 550 to State Highway 62 and then State Highway 145. Tel. 970/728-6900; www.telski.com.* Open late November through mid-April. 12 lifts. 66 trails. Terrain: B=21, I=47, A=32. DH, XC, SS, SB. Base elevation 8,725 feet; top elevation 12,247 feet. Vertical drop 3,522 feet. Ski school for adults and children. Child care available for ages 2 months through 6 years.

Swimming
- **City Park**, *830 E. Montezuma Avenue, Cortez. Tel. 970/565-7877*
- **Durango Municipal Swimming Pool**, *2400 Main Avenue, Durango.*

Tennis
- **Fort Lewis College**, *Durango*
- **Memorial Park**, *Silverton*

SHOPPING

Because of the small-town nature of the southwest region you might not expect to find much in the way of sophisticated shopping. Think again. Besides Native American and Western crafts which can easily be found in a number of localities, a number of southwestern communities are art towns of sorts. When purchasing Native American craft items the authenticity and quality are generally high but you always have to be on your guard for inferior imitations. Fine arts and other haute shopping can be found, surprisingly, in one of the tiniest of towns–Silverton. About a dozen merchants formed the **Silverton Handcrafters and Artists Guild** in the early 1990's. You can count on high quality merchandise in any of their shops which are concentrated in the vicinity of Grene and Blair Streets from 10th through 13th Street.

You can purchase watercolors (**Silver San Juan Gallery**); pottery (**Silverton Artworks**); jewelry (**Michael P. Geryak, Inc.**); wordworking (**Fisher Woodworking**); furniture (**Signature Furniture**); unusual three-dimensional Souhwestern images (**Bob Watkins**) and many other fine arts and crafts.

Durango is another great little art town. In fact, it has been rated as the fourth best small art community in America. The **DACRA** is a local association of galleries like the Guild in Silverton and ensures excellence but, alas, usually also means you pay top dollar. You can pick up a brochure outlining all of the member stores at the Durango Visitor Center. Salida and Ouray also have a number of art galleries. In Ouray especially try the 500 through 700 blocks of Main Street for the best selection. The same area has good gift shops. The **Columbine Gifts and Jewelry** shop is especially good for Indian jewelry and pottery. Many local artists produce goods that are on sale at **Hidden Treasures**.

An additional good source of Native American goods can be found on the Ute Mountain Indian Reservation, south of Cortez. Go to the main settlement area of the reservation at Towaoc for the best choice. The Ute Indians also sell their wares within Cortez and you can probably find something real nice there if you don't want to go out to the Reservation itself.

PRACTICAL INFORMATION

• **Airport**
   Alamosa: **Alamosa Muncipal Airport**, *Tel. 719/589-9446*
   Durango: **La Plata Field**, *Tel. 970/247-8143*
• **Bus Depot**
   Durango: *275 East 8th Avenue. Tel. 970/247-2755*
   Montrose: *132 North 1st. Tel. 970/249-6673*
• **Hospital**
   Alamosa: **San Luis Valley Medical Center**, *106 Blanca Avenue. Tel. 719/589-2511*
   Cortez: **Southwest Memorial Hospital**, *1311 N. Mildred. Tel. 970/565-6666*
   Durango: **Mercy Medical Center**, *375 E. Park Avenue. Tel. 970/247-4311*
   Montrose: **Montrose Memorial Hospital**, *800 S. Third Street. Tel. 970/240-7399*
   Salida: **Heart of the Rockies Regional Medical Center**, *448 E. 1st Street. Tel. 719/539-6661*
   Trinidad: **Mt. San Rafael Hospital**, *410 Benedicta. Tel. 719/846-9213*

- **Hotel Hot Line**
  Durango: *Tel. 800/525-0892*
  Telluride: **Telluride Visitor Services**, *Tel. 888/783-0264*
- **Police** (non-emergency)
  Alamosa: *Tel. 719/589-2548*
  Cortez: *Tel. 970/565-8441*
  Durango: *Tel. 970/247-3232*
  Montrose: *Tel. 970/249-6609*
  Salida: *Tel. 719/539-2814*
  Trinidad: *Tel. 719/846-4441*
- **Public Transportation**
  Durango: **LIFT bus service**, *Tel. 970/259-LIFT*
  Salida: **The Ride Transit Services,***Tel. 719/221-7433*
- **Taxi**
  Durango: **Durango Transportation**, *Tel. 970/259-4818*
  Montrose: **Western Express**, *Tel. 970/249-8880*
  Telluride: **Skip's Taxi**, *Tel. 970/728-6667*
- **Tourist Office/Visitors Bureau**
  Alamosa: *Cole Park. Tel. 800/BLU-SKYS; www.alamosa.org*
  Cortez: *928 E. Main Street, Tel. 970/565-3414; www.swcolo.org*
  Durango: *Gateway Drive off of US 160. Tel. 800/GO-DURANGO; www.durango.org*
  Montrose: *435 South 1st Street, Tel. 800/873-0244; www.montrose.org*
  Ouray: *1222 N. Main (US 550), Tel. 800/228-1876; www.ouraycolorado.com*
  Pagosa Springs: *402 San Juan Street, Tel. 800/252-2204; www.pagosa-springs.com*
  Salida: *406 West US 50, Tel. 719/539-2068; www.salidacolorado.com*
  Silverton: *US 550 at Greene Street. Tel. 800/752-4494; www.silverton.org*
  Telluride: *666 W. Colorado Avenue, Tel. 800/525-3455; www.telluridemm.com*

16. EASTERN COLORADO - THE GREAT PLAINS

It would be stretching it by a long shot to claim that **eastern Colorado** has the same level of "must see" scenery and attractions as the rest of the state. That isn't to say, however, that there aren't places of unusual interest in the high plains that cover roughly the eastern third of the state from the Wyoming border in the north to the New Mexico and Oklahoma line in the south. The places to see here are mainly historic in nature but of a type different than that found elsewhere in Colorado. You've already seen that, with the exception of ancient Indian cultures, history in the Colorado we've explored up to now is largely tied in with the mining era of the second half of the 19th century and early 20th century. Eastern Colorado's historic sites deal more with the general westward expansion of the United States–more in keeping with the "cowboy and Indian" theme popular with the young ones, although that is far from the whole story.

In addition, many of the communities on the western edge of the region are near to the mountains and have some places to see that are of a scenic nature. Just as important are the attractive and uniqueness of several of the towns–Loveland and Sterling, for example, have some unusual attractions. The Plains have their own type of scenery–not spectacular but different if you haven't been through the mid-western states of the nation. Outdoor recreation is also plentiful, much of it in state parks centered around the many lakes and rivers of the Plains region.

Because the Great Plains portion of Colorado covers a huge area and the attractions in the southern portion are far from those in the north, I've deviated from the format of the earlier regional destination chapters. Here you'll encounter the places to visit in three separate sections each of which is treated as an entity of its own. The east, consequently, lends itself to the "home base" approach I mentioned early in the book. Of course, you could link them together into a circle trip if you wanted to.

The three areas are a relatively short corridor located due north of Denver; another corridor along the South Platte River that is close to the first; and a final section in the south along the Arkansas River.

THE I-25 NORTHERN CORRIDOR: LOVELAND, FORT COLLINS & GREELEY

ARRIVALS & DEPARTURES

All of the places in this section are quite close to Denver. So if you're planning on flying or training into Denver it is just a matter of heading north on I-25 for about an hour until you reach Loveland. Those coming in from the north via I-25 can also go to Loveland (Exit 257) or begin with Fort Collins which comes first from that direction (Exit 269). There is bus service from Denver and other points to all three communities.

If you are coming in from the east via I-76, get off at Exit 66 on that road and take US 34 westbound into Greeley.

ORIENTATION & GETTING AROUND

The communities in this section and their immediate surroundings comprise the smallest geographic area of the three parts of this chapter, so you won't be dealing with any significant distances. By car you really only need to be familiar with I-25 (Loveland and Fort Collins lie within a few miles west of the highway) and US 24, which Greeley is on. Loveland and Fort Collins are also connected by US 287. Together the three form a neat "L" that covers a mere 33 miles.

You could also take a bus from Denver to any three of them and then go from one to the other by bus without too much of a hassle. Both Fort Collins (Transfort, *Tel. 970/221-6620*) and Greeley ("The Bus," *Tel. 970/350-9287*) have public transportation that will take you to most of the sights. However, a car would still be useful to see some of the surrounding areas, especially around Fort Collins.

Any one of the three would make a convenient base for seeing the others. Denver and Boulder are also possibilities if you don't mind driving an extra ninety minutes or so each day.

WHERE TO STAY
FORT COLLINS
Moderate

EDWARDS HOUSE BED & BREAKFAST, *402 W. Mountain Avenue. Tel. 970/493-9191; Fax 970/484-0706. Toll free reservations 800/281-9190; www.edwardshouse.com. E-mail: edshouse@edwardshouse.com. 6 Rooms. Rates: $109-149 including full breakfast. American Express, Discover, MasterCard and VISA accepted. Located about a half mile west of US 287 (College Avenue).*

An historic old house dating from 1904, the Victorian style Edwards House has been fully refurbished. Located on a quiet street and shaded by large mature trees, the property has a dignified and elegant appearance. The rooms almost can be termed luxurious given their rich and comfortable furnishings, working gas fireplace and standard video cassette player (video library is available). A few units have their own Jacuzzis. Those that don't have unique and interesting claw foot bathtubs. For recreation you can use the sauna or exercise room. A delicious gourmet breakfast is served each morning in an attractive dining room and there are refreshments every evening in an equally pretty sitting room. The Edwards House is within walking distance of the many shops and restaurants of Old Town.

FORT COLLINS MARRIOTT, *350 E. Horsetooth Road. Tel. 970/226-5200; Fax 970/282-0651. Toll free reservations 800/548-2635; www.marriott.com. 230 Rooms. Rates: $129-145. Most major credit cards accepted. Located about 3 miles south of center of town off of US 287.*

A full service hotel with well designed and impressive public areas, the Marriott underwent an extensive renovation in late 1996 when all the guest rooms were redone. The rooms are large and furnished with tasteful class. Some of the rooms in the six-story facility have refrigerators and video cassette players. The Marriott features a good restaurant as well as a cocktail lounge. Recreational facilities include both indoor and outdoor heated swimming pools, hot tub, and a well equipped exercise room.

MULBERRY INN, *4333 E. Mulberry. Tel. 970/493-9000; Fax 970/224-9636. Toll free reservations 800/234-5548; www.mulberry-inn.com. 120 Rooms. Rates: $44-110 all year for regular rooms and $85-175 for suites. Major credit cards accepted. Located just east of I-25, Exit 269A.*

The Mulberry Inn offers better than average motel quality at a reasonable rate and may well represent the best overall lodging value in Fort Collins. The attractively furnished rooms have enough space for you to spread out on either king or queen sized beds. Among the variable amenities and features of the guest rooms are private balcony, coffee makers, and hot tubs. There are some family suites available. For recreation the motel features a heated outdoor swimming pool and hot tub. A restaurant is adjacent.

GREELEY
Moderate

    GREELEY GUEST HOUSE, *721 13th Street. Tel. 970/353-9373; Fax 970/353-9297. Toll free reservations 800/314-3684; www.greeleyguesthouse.com. 19 Rooms. Rates: $109-159 including Continental breakfast. Most major credit cards accepted. Located near the center of town via US 34 Business Route to 7th Avenue and south to 13th Street.*

    This is a pretty country style inn with attractive and comfortably furnished guest rooms. Several suites offer more space than the standard room and also have Jacuzzi tubs. There are nicely furnished public areas and decent mountain views. The breakfast is called Continental but will probably be more than adequate except for those who like to start off the day with a really big meal. Restaurants are located within close proximity. There aren't any public recreational facilities on the premises.

CAMPING & RV SITES
- **Conejos River Campground**, *317 Park Place, Fort Collins. Tel. 970/352-0754*
- **Fireside RV Park**, *6850 W. US Highway 34, Loveland. Tel. 970/667-2903*
- **Greeley RV Park & Campground**, *East US 34, Greeley. Tel. 970/353-6476*
- **Loveland RV Village**, *4421 E. US Highway 34, Loveland. Tel. 970/667-1204*
- **Riverview RV Park & Campground**, *7806 W. US Highway 34, Loveland. Tel. 970/667-9910*

WHERE TO EAT
FORT COLLINS
Moderate

    BISETTI'S, *120 S. College Avenue. Tel. 970/493-0086. Most major credit cards acceped. Lunch served Monday though Friday; dinner served nightly. Smoke free premises.*

    Located downtown (on street parking), Bisetti's is an attractive family owned and family style Italian restaurant with great food and excellent service. The intimate dining room is casual and relaxing. The generous portions of food feature southern Italian style cooking–lots of pasta dishes. But whatever you have for dinner be sure to leave room for their absolutely fantastic authentic Italian style cheesecake. Cocktail service and a huge selection of wine. Children's menu.

    CANINO'S ITALIAN RESTAURANT, *613 S. College Avenue. Tel. 970/493-7205. American Express, Discover, MasterCard and VISA accepted. Dinner served nightly.*

    A little bit fancier in style and cuisine than Bisetti's, this is another good family owned Italian eatery. Serving Fort Collins for over twenty years, Canino features veal, seafood and chicken dishes along with excellent home baked bread and desserts. Cocktail service.

JAY'S BISTRO, *151 S. College Avenue. Tel. 970/482-1876. Most major credit cards accepted. Lunch and dinner served Monday through Friday; dinner only on Saturday. Reservations are suggested.*

Eclectic is the one word that best describe's this unusual American bistro located, like so many of Fort Collin's better restaurants, in the city center near Old Town. The food is beautiful to look at and served on colorful and attractive plates that are too huge for the amount of food you get (the only drawback to Jay's). Beef and seafood are specialties. Desserts are absolutely delicious. Jay's also has an extensive wine list in addition to the full cocktail service which is known for their martini's.

Inexpensive
COOPERSMITH'S PUB & BREWING, *5 Old Town Square. Tel. 970/223-5271. American Express, MasterCard and VISA accepted. Lunch and dinner served daily.*

A beer lover's delight. That's because, in addition to having their own brewpub as well as a huge selection of lagers, Coopersmith's has a most interesting menu of eclectic foods that almost always have beer as a major ingredient! Right, this place is not necessarily for kids despite the presence of a children's menu. Attractive pub decor in the heart of town (on street parking only) with patio dining available during the warmer months.

LOVELAND
Moderate
THE BLACK STEER, *436 N. Lincoln Avenue. Tel. 970/667-6679. Most major credit cards accepted. Lunch and dinner served daily.*

The Black Steer has been serving some of the best steaks in Colorado for more than thirty years. Proprietors Janice and Hamid Eslami take great pains to insure that you feel at home in this attractive dining room with a casual ambiance. In addition to plate filling steaks they also serve a number of excellent fish and seafood entrees. For lunch you should try one of their great overstuffed sandwiches. Cocktail service and lounge.

THE SUMMIT RESTAURANT, *3208 W. Eisenhower Blvd. Tel. 970/669-6648. Major credit cards accepted. Lunch and dinner served daily; Sunday brunch. Reservations are suggested.*

Consistently considered to be "the restaurant" in Loveland by the locals, I would have great difficulty challenging that. With tables either inside or out on the patio that have splendid views of the not too distant mountains and a pleasant casual country atmosphere, the Summit is already off to a good start as soon as you sit down. The menu features an excellent variety, highlighted each night by the outstanding Colorado prime rib. There's also steak, seafood, chicken, and even a smattering of Northern Italian. The chef also has a nightly special that will be sure to please. No matter what you order it will be prepared to perfection and delicious. The Summit also has a better than average salad bar. The service is also quite good. Cocktail service and separate lounge. Children's menu.

SEEING THE SIGHTS

I won't be going out on a limb to say that you'll probably be coming into **Loveland** via I-25. From Exit 257 go west on US 34 (named Eisenhower Boulevard) and you'll be in town in a matter of a few blocks. Known as the "Sweetheart City," Loveland has more than a lovely name. It is, in a sense, where the bountiful Great Plains meet the majestic Rockies. It's 40,000 residents don't have to look east or west to enjoy the scenery because it is right in the city itself–more than a dozen lakes lie within the city limits or immediately adjacent to it. **Lake Loveland**, the third largest, lies within a few blocks of downtown. **Boyd** and **Horseshoe Lakes** are the biggest.

Loveland's origins go back to 1858 but it did not receive its current name until 1877 when it was named after the Colorado Central Railroad's president, one W.A.H. Loveland. Then and now it has been a shipping point for agricultural goods as well as lumber and other natural resources.

The **Loveland Museum & Gallery**, *Fifth Street and Lincoln Avenue in downtown* (eight blocks south of US 34) is both a museum of local history as well as an art gallery that displays the works of local and national artists. The museum has a number of rooms that have reconstructions of shops from various eras in the town's history. The Valentine Re-mailing Program (see the sidebar) is chronicled in an exhibit called Sweetheart Town USA. *Tel. 970/962-2410. Museum hours are Tuesday hrough Friday from 10:00am until 5:00pm; Saturday from 10:00am to 4:00pm, and Sunday from noon until 4:00pm. It is also open during the evening on Thursday. There is no admission charge.*

The **Benson Park Sculpture Garden**, *29th Street and Taft Avenue (north of US 34)* is a pretty park with pathways that lead around two small ponds and over forty different pieces of life-like sculpture. And, speaking of sculpture, Loveland's streets are filled with it. The Civic Center and downtown areas have the greatest concentration of it but you can get a map from the chamber of commerce that will direct you through a driving tour of the city to more than a dozen locations with sculpture in the street.

US 34 west of Loveland marks the beginning of the **Big Thompson Canyon**, a scenic route that leads all the way to Estes Park.

VALENTINE GREETINGS FROM LOVELAND

Elmer Ives was the local postmaster back in the days immediately following World War II when he, along with the head of the chamber of commerce, realized that the name of their community could be a great promotional opportunity. No matter that it was a railroad president and former general's name, "Loveland" certainly had a romantic ring to it. So they established the **Loveland Valentine Re-Mailing Program.**

Here's how it works. Lovers all around the country mail their valentine greeting to the Loveland Post Office where dozens of volunteers place it in an annually revised cachet and remail it to the intended recipient with the special official Loveland post office valentine cancellation. There are also plenty of other "official" Valentine products which are sold throughout the city by participating merchants. Anyhow, the program continues to be a rousing success: more than fifty years later a total of over seven million valentine greetings have been re-mailed from the Sweetheart City.

From Loveland you can get to **Fort Collins** by going north on US 287 (Lincoln Avenue within Loveland city limits) for about 12 miles. Or you can go back to the Interstate and take that north to Exit 269 and then drive west into Fort Collins.

Fort Colllins began in 1864 with the establishment of a military post to protect travelers on a branch of the Overland Trail. With approximately 100,000 residents, today's Fort Collins is one of the state's largest cities, a manufacting center, and home of Colorado State University, the second largest institution of higher education in the state.

From I-25 take CO 14 west into the city. You'll arrive in the heart of downtown via Mulberry Street. The **Fort Collins Museum**, *Mulberry and Matthews Streets*, is a regional history museum with diverse exhibits. Of most interst are three 19th century structures–two cabins and a schoolhouse–located in the museum courtyard. One of the cabins is among the oldest in Colorado still in existence. *Tel. 970/221-6738. Museum hours are Tuesday through Saturday from 10:00am until 5:00pm and Sunday from noon to 5:00pm. There is no admission fee but donations are requested.*

A few blocks to the west and then north on College Avenue is the **Historic Old Town Square**. This area contains many of Fort Collin's original and earliest structures. The Square has been converted into an attractive shopping center. During summer weekends a nice way to spend some time is to take the **Fort Collins Municipal Railway** (Route #21), an old time electric trolley that connects the downtown area with attractive **City Park**, a nice place to relax and unwind. The main campus of

Colorado State University is located nearby off of College Avenue between Laurel Street and Prospect Road. The campus boasts several art galleries and a visitor center. *Tel. 970/491-6444.*

A last attraction within Fort Collins is in the northeast section of town. Go back to the Interstate and take it north two miles to Exit 271. Adjacent to the exit is the **Anheuser-Busch Brewery**. Like just about all Busch facilities it features tours of the brewing, packaging, and storing process, and a beer garden with free tastings for adults (soft drinks for the kids). A highlight is a visit to the barn where a team of the famous Clydesdale horses is kept. *Tel. 970/490-4691. Tour hours are daily from 9:30am until 5:00pm, May through October; and Thursday through Monday from 10:00am until 4:00pm the remainder of the year.*

If you have some time and haven't quite yet had your fill of mountain scenery then you will be interested in taking a half-day tour of the foothills to the west of Fort Collins. Among the sights are **Horsetooth Mountain** and **Arthur's Rock**. The route contains several parks with picnic areas and short hiking trails that afford excellent views of the Front Range. There's also a fish hatchery. The route follows several county routes and you can obtain a map from the Fort Collins Convention & Visitors Bureau which is located downtown at *420 South Howe Street.*

The final city in our northern corridor trio is **Greeley**. To get there from Fort Collins go back south on I-25 to Exit 257 and then travel east on US 34 for 17 miles. If you don't want to double back on the Interstate you can also head east from Fort Collins on CO 14 for 18 miles to US 85 and then turn south for 11 miles into Greeley, which is named for Horace Greeley (see the sidebar). Greeley is an attractive community of about 65,000 people that sits close to the confluence of the South Platte and Cache la Poudre Rivers. It was water from these sources that helped to sustain Greeley in its early days and helped it to flourish.

Stay on US 34 business route until you reach 14th Avenue. Take a left turn there and proceed north to "A" Street (or, if coming in via US 85, bear onto 11th Avenue to "A"). The **Centennial Village Museum**, *1475 "A" Street*, is Greeley's best known attraction. Established on the hundredth anniversary of the city's founding, this is a living museum that chronicles the history of life and architecture in Greeley. There are some thirty different varieties of architecture represented and the buildings include a blacksmith shop, church, home, schoolhouse, fire station, and more. The architectural styles run the gamut from an Indian tepee to Spanish adobe to Victorian. The lovely park-like grounds include attractively landscaped gardens and winding pathways. Living history demonstrations are offered throughout the day and you can see the village on your own or by guided tour. It is an enjoyable and educational way to spend several hours. *Tel. 970/350-9220. Village hours are Tuesday through Saturday* *from 10:00am until 5:00pm, Memorial Day through Labor Day. From mid-April to before Memorial Day and after Labor Day to the middle of October it is open Tuesday through Saturday from 10:00am until 3:00pm. Guided tours are presented at 11, 1 and 3. It is closed on state holidays. The admission is $4 for adults, $2.50 for seniors, and $2 for children ages 6 through 12. The price also includes the admission to the Meeker House described below.*

The **Municipal Museum & Archives**, *917 7th Street*, is just a few blocks away and has photographs that document the history of Greeley. Not nearly as good as Centennial Village but worth a few minutes of your time. *Tel. 970/350-9220. Hours are Monday through Friday from 10:00am until 4:00pm except for state holidays. There is no admission charge.* The **1870 Meeker Home**, *1324 9th Avenue*, was the personal residence of Nathan Meeker who was, despite his obscurity to most people, as instrumental in establishing Greeley as better known Horace G. was. The luxurious family furnishings date from the turn of the century and depict life on the frontier for the well-to-do. *See Historic Centennial Village for phone, time, and admission information, which is all the same for the Meeker Home.*

"GO WEST, YOUNG MAN"

*Oh, so you've already heard that line. It was coined by **Horace Greeley**. Hmm, any connection to Greeley, Colorado? You bet there is. Mr. Greeley was the editor of the New York Tribune, and though he was the one who gets all of the credit, the inspiration for his message probably came from Nathan Meeker, the paper's agricultural editor.*

They asked for people with high moral standards and finances to help establish an agricultural community much in the style of the religious-based eastern colonies of two centuries earlier. More than 3,000 responded to the call and a stock company was formed in 1869. A town was established the following year. In October 1870, Horace Greeley was to pay his first and only visit to the community which was to bear his name. The foundations had already been laid and a system of irrigation ditches were in place. A school was built in 1872 and a college in 1889. Education was an important component of Greeley's and Meeker's plan for a stable community.

Many similar ventures were tried in parts of the west during the last quarter of the 19th century but most failed. Greeley succeeded, partly because the people involved had the necessary finances to weather the initial storms, but also because Greeley and Meeker had put together the ingredients for stability. The rest is, as they say, history.

If you're going to be heading back to Denver from Greeley you can either continue south on US 85 or return to I-25 via US 34. The latter route will also connect you with the central Rockies regional tour at Estes Park. While the preceding three city tour and the next one along the South Platte can be done separately they can also be easily combined into a longer trip. From Greeley simply continue east on US 34 and in about 50 miles you'll reach Fort Morgan. That locale could conceivably be used as a home base for seeing both sections.

NIGHTLIFE & ENTERTAINMENT

For all of its romanticism, Loveland doesn't have much nightlife but that shouldn't be too surprising given its small town character. If you're looking for western style entertainment you could check out the **Lazy B Ranch**, *1915 Dry Gulch Road, Tel. 970/586-5371.* It features a chuckwagon-style supper that kids are sure to enjoy.

Fort Collins, bigger and with a large university population, has more diverse and sophisticated options. The **Bas Bleu Theater Company**, *216 Pine Street, Tel. 970/498-8949,* offers plays, music, poetry readings and other programs in a delightfully small and intimate theater. Broadway style entertainment along with good food is available at the beautiful **Carousel Dinner Theater**, *3509 S. Mason Street, Tel. 970/225-2555.* Various forms of entertainment are also presented at the **Lincoln Center**, *417 W. Magnolia Street, Tel. 970/221-6730.* Many of Fort Collins' most popular bars and nightspots are within proximiy of the campus of Colorado State University. Downtown features **Linden's Brewing Company**, *212 Linden Street, Tel. 970/482-9291,* with live jazz and blues music. **CooperSmith's Pub & Brewing**, *5 Old Town Square, Tel. 970/498-0483,* is considered to be one of the country's premier brew pubs by publications who rate such things.

Greeley is big enough to have several local bars but none of them appear to be especially popular with visitors. On the more cultural side the **Union Colony Civic Center**, *10th Avenue & 8th Stree, Tel. 970/356-5555,* offers a program of music, ballet and other dance forms, and Broadway and community theater productions. Greeley also has a philharmonic orchestra, *Tel. 970/356-6404* for further information. The **University of Northern Colorado** has a program of musical and dramatic performances throughout the year.

SPORTS & RECREATION
Boating
• **Horsetooth Reservoir**, *3 miles west of Fort Collins on County Route 52*

Fishing
• **Horsetooth Reservoir**, *3 miles west of Fort Collins on County Route 52*

Golf
• **Boomerang Links**, *7304 W. 4th Street, Greeley. Tel. 970/351-8934.* 18 holes.
• **Cattail Creek**, *2116 W. 29th Street, Loveland. Tel. 970/663-5310.* Nine-hole course.
• **City Park Nine Golf Course**, *411 S. Bryan Ave., Fort Collins. Tel. 970/221-6650.* Considered to be Colorado's premier nine hole public course.
• **Collindale Golf Course**, *1441 E. Horsetooh Road, Fort Collins. Tel. 970/221-6651.* 18 holes.
• **Highland Hills**, *2200 Clubhouse Drive, Greeley. Tel. 970/351-8934.* 18 holes.
• **Marianna Butte Golf Course**, *701 Clubhouse Drive, Loveland. Tel. 970/667-8308.* Highly rated by Golf Digest magazine, the course features excellent views of the nearby mountains. 18 holes.
• **Olde Course at Loveland**, *2115 W. 29th Street, Loveland. Tel. 970/667-5256.* 18 holes.
• **South Ridge Golf Course**, *5750 S. Lemay Ave., Fort Collins. Tel. 970/226-2828.* 18 holes.

Horseback Riding
• **Ellis Ranch, Inc.**, *2331 Waterdale Drive, Loveland. Tel. 970/667-3964*

Rafting
• **A-1 Wildwater**, *317 Stover Street, Fort Collins. Tel. 800/369-4165*
• **A Wanderlust Adventure**, *3500 Bingham Hill Road, Fort Collins. Tel. 800/745-7238*

Swimming
• **City Park Pool**, *1599 City Park Drive, Fort Collins. Tel. 970/484-7665.* Outdoor pool open in summer only.
• **Horsetooth Reservoir**, *3 miles west of Fort Collins on County Route 52.*
• **Mulberry Pool**, *424 W. Mulberry Street, Fort Collins. Tel. 970/221-6657.* Year-round indoor swimming pool and spa.

SHOPPING
Loveland continues to attract visitors to its many art galleries. The majority are located along North Lincoln between 4th and 10th Streets.

Fort Collins also has a considerable number of shops catering to the art lover. Among the most popular is **Michael Ricker Pewter**, *213 Jefferson Street*, in downtown. Unique handcrafted country gifts can be found at the

Creator's Unlimited Craft Shoppe, *116 East Foothills Parkway*. The main shopping areas for Fort Collins are in the historic **Old Town Square Plaza**, *College and Mountain Avenues* and at northern Colorado's largest regional shopping center, the **Foothills Fashion Mall**, *215 East Foothills Parkway near College*. It has four department stores, 120 specialty shops and a food court. Several stores specialize in Colorado goods.

In Greeley, many of the nicest shops are concentrated along pedestrian plazas in the downtown area.

PRACTICAL INFORMATION
- **Airport Transportation** (to Denver)
  Fort Collins/Loveland: **Airporter Express**, *Tel. 970/482-0505*
- **Bus Depot**
  Loveland: *1027 E. Eisenhower Blvd.*
- **Hospital**
  Fort Collins: **Poudre Valley Hospital**, *1024 S. Lema;y Avenue. Tel. 970/482-4111*
  Greeley: **Northern Colorado Medical Center**, *1801 16th Street. Tel. 970/352-4121*
  Loveland: **McKee Medical Center**, *2000 N. Boise Avenue. Tel. 970/ 669-4640*
- **Police** (non-emergency):
  Fort Collins: *Tel. 970/221-6540*
  Greeley: *Tel. 970/350-9605*
  Loveland: *Tel. 970/667-8222*
- **Public Transportation**
  Fort Collins: **Transfort**, *Tel. 970/221-6620*
  Greeley: **"The Bus,"** *Tel. 970/350-9287*
- **Taxi**
  Fort Collins: **Shamrock Transportation**, *Tel. 970/686-5919*
  Greeley: **Shamrock Yellow Cab**, *Tel. 970/686-5555*
- **Tourist Office/Visitor Bureau**
  Fort Collins: *420 South Howes Street, Tel. 800/274-3678; www.ftcollins.com*
  Greeley: *902 7th Avenue, Tel. 800/449-3866; www.greeleycvb.com*
  Loveland: *5400 Stone Creek Circle, Tel. 970/667-5728; www.loveland.org*

ALONG THE SOUTH PLATTE RIVER: FORT MORGAN & STERLING

ARRIVALS & DEPARTURES

From Denver or just about any other part of Colorado and other points to the west the route into Fort Morgan and Sterling is via I-76 eastbound. Exit 80 provides easy access into Fort Morgan. Travelers from the east can take I-80 to the junction of I-76 at the Nebraska-Colorado line near Julesburg and then I-76 west to Sterling. From the southeast it gets a little more complicated. US 385 runs along the eastern border of Colorado but is a long haul to go at non-highway speeds. You may be better off using I-25 to Denver and then proceeding as above via I-76.

There is no scheduled air service to this part of the state but you can take a bus from Denver to either Fort Morgan or Sterling, or Amtrak to Fort Morgan.

ORIENTATION & GETTING AROUND

Fort Morgan and Sterling both sit alongside the South Platte River about 50 miles from one another, connected by I-76. You could visit both in an overnight trip from Denver since Colorado's transportation hub is there and it is only 70 miles to Fort Morgan.

WHERE TO STAY
FORT MORGAN
Inexpensive

BEST WESTERN PARK TERRACE INN, *725 Main Street. Tel. 970/ 867-8256; Fax 970/867-8257. Toll free reservations 800/528-1234. 24 Rooms. Rates: $57-78. Most major credit cards accepted. Located a half mile south of I-76, Exit 80.*

A pretty little motel conveniently located to downtown and the Interstate highway, the Park Terrace features clean and comfortable rooms with coffee makers. There is a heated swimming pool and whirl-pool out front. Memories Restaurant is a very good low cost family-style restaurant that also serves cocktails.

STERLING
Moderate
BEST WESTERN SUNDOWNER, *Overland Trail Street. Tel. 970/522-6265; Fax 970/522-6265. Toll free reservations 800/528-1234. 29 Rooms. Rates: $84-105 including Continental breakfast. Major credit cards accepted. Located off of I-76, Exit 125.*

The Best Western is definitely the best lodging choice in Sterling. The modern and attractive two-story motel features attractive landscaping with many colorful flowers and guest rooms with excellent furnishings and pretty decor that isn't sterile looking like so many motels. Some rooms feature balconies with pleasant views. The park-like grounds include a small picnic area, heated swimming pool and wading pool as well as a whirlpool. The Sundowner also has an exercise room. Restaurants are located within a short distance.

Inexpensive
COLONIAL MOTEL, *915 S. Division. Tel. 970/522-3382. 14 Rooms. Rates: $40. American Express, Discover, MasterCard and VISA accepted. Located about a mile southwest of I-76, Exit 125 via US 6.*

Nothing exceptional or unusual to rave about here but I couldn't resist including a decent motel where you can get away with less than a fifty dollar bill including tax! All of the clean and comfortable rooms have coffe makers. Some have microwave oven and refrigerator. There's a small playground on the premises. You can reach several restaurants in less than five minutes.

CAMPING & RV SITES
• **Buffalo Hills Park**, *I-76 & East US Highway 6, Sterling. Tel. 970/522-2233*
• **Wayward Wind Campground**, *I-76, Exit 75, on South Frontage Road, Fort Morgan. Tel. 970/867-8948*

WHERE TO EAT
FORT MORGAN
Moderate
COUNTRY STEAKS OUT, *19592 E. 8th Avenue. Tel. 970/867-7887. American Express, MasterCard and VISA accepted. Lunch and dinner served Tuesday through Saturday; Sunday brunch.*

A casual western style steak house feating excellent prime rib and a salad bar. The service is friendly and efficient. A buffet style lunch is offered on Tuesday. Cocktail service and separate lounge. Children's menu.

STERLING

Inexpensive

COUNTRY KITCHEN, *At I-76, Exit 125 (US Highway 6) in the Ramada Inn. Tel. 970/522-2625. Most major credit cards accepted. Breakfast, lunch and dinner served daily.*

A plain and simple family restaurant with a very good variety of traditional American fare served by a friendly staff in a relaxing and casual setting. Bountiful breakfasts, tasty sandwiches for lunch and large portions for dinner, all at a most affordable price. Cocktail service and separate lounge. Children's menu.

SEEING THE SIGHTS

Fort Morgan is supported today by ranching and farming activities, much as it has been since the latter part of the 19th century. It began as a military post and then was a station on the Overland Trail. The original fort is no longer in existance–only a small historical marker notes its former location on Riverview Avenue. The early days of the post and town can best be explored at the **Fort Morgan Museum**, *414 Main Street in City Park*. Exhibit topics include the Plains Indians and the history of Morgan County. The museum also has a tribute to Fort Morgan's most famous resident, Glenn Miller. Of particular note is an early 20th century soda fountain. *Tel. 970/867-6331. Museum hours are Monday through Friday from 10:00am until 5:00pm and Saturday from 11:00am. The museum reopens from 6:00 to 8:00pm on Tuesday through Thursday. It is closed on New Year's Day, July 4th, Thanksgiving, and Christmas. There is no admission charge but donations are requested.* In the attractive park is a pretty gazebo. The bandstand was the location of a concert given by Glenn Miller after he had become famous.

Along Main Street (the 100 through 400 blocks) are a number of Fort Morgan's original buildings. You can pick up a brochure that describes each one at the museum. A few blocks to the east on Sherman Avenue is another historic district. Four houses here date from the period 1886 through 1926. A final point of interest in Fort Morgan is the historic **Rainbow Bridge** that crosses the South Platte River. It is considered to be of architectural significance because it represents the transition from old-time bridge building methods to more modern ones. The bridge is only open to pedestrian traffic these days and is easily recognizable by the series of arches on either side of the roadway.

From Fort Morgan it is just 48 miles further east on I-76 until you reach **Sterling**. Use Exit 125 to get into town. Sterling was another stopping point for people traveling to the west in the final stages of the great western migration. Accordingly, a good place to make your first stop in town is at the **Overland Trail Museum**, *on US 6 just off of I-76*. One of the reasons that this route became an important route to the west was the South Platte River itself. By following the river you were less likely to get lost (it ultimately led to near the goldfields further into Colorado) and it was a steady supply of water. I-76 today follows a good portion of the course of the Overland Trail. The museum building is designed to resemble an old fort. Many examples of pioneer farm equipment as well as a Concord stagecoach are on display outside while the interior has exhibits and artifacts that belonged to early pioneers. Several displays are also devoted to the Indians of the Plains. The complex also has some historic buildings that have been moved to the site. Unusual is the large collection of branding irons. *Tel. 970/522-3895. Museum hours are daily from 10:00am until 5:00pm (Sundays and state holidays from 10:00am), April 1st through October 31st; and Tuesday through Saturday from 10:00am until 4:00pm the remainder of the year. Donations are requested in lieu of a set admission charge.*

Sterling's historic downtown is centered on both sides of Main Street between 2nd and 4th Streets. Many of the structures are private dwellings so you are requested to respect the rights of property owners. Most downtown businesses will be happy to provide you with a free brochure that describes almost twenty historic structures. Six of them are listed on the National Register of Historic Places. These include the **Logan County Courthouse**, **Old Union Pacific Depot**, **Old Town Hall and Fire Station**, and the **Post Office · Federal Building**. The buildings were erected in the period between 1910 and 1930.

A wonderful aspect of Sterling and the thing that most impressed me about it is their outdoor sculptures–16 carvings by town resident Brad Rhea that have given Sterling the name the **City of Living Trees**. Each is named and among the best are "Skygrazers," five interconnected giraffes that seem to be feeding on the treetops; "Seraphim," a most unusual lion; "The Butterfly," and "Plainsman Pete." All of the sculptures have an amazing life-like quality and vivid colors. Sterling isn't a big place and you'll definitely bump into more than a few of these as you explore the above attractions and other parts of town. However, if you must see all of them (and I wouldn't blame you for wanting to do that) you can get a map that will direct you to each one. It's available from the chamber of commerce, at the museum, and at many downtown business locations. Sterlingites are justly proud of Mr. Rhea's works of art.

The Sterling area is near a lot of recreation facilities including boating, fishing, and hunting. At **North Sterling Reservoir State Park** you can enjoy many of those activities while at the same time taking in a panoramic view of a series of bluffs that frame the high plains just to the northwest of town. The lake which comprises the reservoir covers more than 3,000 acres and has many picturesque coves. Take CO 14 west to 7th Avenue, then north to Country Route 46 and 33. *Tel. 970/522-3657. The park is open at all times. Visitors must purchase a daily Colorado State Park pass unless you already possess at annual pass. The passes are good at all state park facilities.*

Your return to Denver or other areas of Colorado beyond will be via I-76 into the Denver area at which point you can connect to either I-70 or I-25.

NIGHTLIFE & ENTERTAINMENT

Nightlife is limited to some of the local taverns and cocktail lounges of the larger motels.

SPORTS & RECREATION

Boating
- **Jackson Lake State Park**, *20 miles northwest of Fort Morgan on CO 144*
- **North Sterling Reservoir**, *10 miles north of Sterling via N. 7th Ave.*

Fishing
- **Jackson Lake State Park**, *20 miles northwest of Fort Morgan on CO 14.*
- **North Sterling Reservoir**, *10 miles north of Sterling via N. 7th Ave.*

Golf
- **Fort Morgan Municipal Golf Course**, *17586 County Road, Ft. Morgan. Tel. 970/867-5990*
- **Riverview Golf Course**, *Sterling. Tel. 970/522-3035*

Swimming
- **North Sterling Reservoir**, *10 miles north of Sterling via N. 7th Ave.*

PRACTICAL INFORMATION

- **Hospital**
  Fort Morgan: **Colorado Plains Medical Center**, *1000 Lincoln. Tel. 970/867-3391*
  Sterling: **Sterling Regional Medical Center**, *615 Fairhurst. Tel. 970/522-0122*
- **Police** (non-emergency)
  Fort Morgan: *Tel. 970/867-5678*
  Sterling: *Tel. 970/522-3512*

• **Tourist Office/Visitors Bureau**
Fort Morgan: *300 Main Street, Tel. 800/354-8660; www.fmchamber.org*
Sterling: *Tel. 800/544-8609*
• **Train Station**: *South Ensign Street, Fort Morgan. Station is unstaffed.*

ALONG THE EASTERN RUN OF THE ARKANSAS RIVER: LA JUNTA & LAMAR

ARRIVALS & DEPARTURES

The towns on this route are reached by US 50 from either the east or west. From Denver and Colorado Springs you will go south on I-25 to Pueblo and then east on US 50. Both La Junta and Lamar have Amtrak stations with daily service.

There is also limited scheduled commuter airline service into Lamar (as well as Pueblo which is about 65 miles from La Junta) but you would probably be better off with the choice of flights into Colorado Springs. Bus service to both towns is available.

ORIENTATION & GETTING AROUND

If you know how to recognize US 50 you won't have any trouble getting around. Both towns and the other sights in this section are all close to the Arkansas River. Bus service connects Lamar and La Junta. The sights can be seen on an overnight trip from either Colorado Springs or Pueblo.

You could also do it in a two-day loop beginning in Denver. Once you reach Lamar you can then go back to Denver via US 287 and I-70 since that saves some mileage over doubling back by US 50 and I-25.

WHERE TO STAY
LA JUNTA
Inexpensive

STAGECOACH INN, *905 W. 3rd Street. Tel. 719/384-5476; Fax 719/384-9091. 31 Rooms. Rates: $45-50 including Continental breakfast. Most major credit cards accepted. Located in the center of town on US 50/350.*

There isn't a great deal of choice in lodging when you stay in La Junta. This is about the best unless you want to stay in a decent but cookie-cutter same Quality Inn or a typical Super 8. The Stagecoach is a two-story basic motel with adequate rooms and good housekeeping. Some rooms have microwave oven and refrigerator. It also has a small swimming pool. Restaurants are located nearby.

LAMAR
Inexpensive

BLUE SPRUCE MOTEL, *1801 S. Main Street. Tel. 719/336-7454; Fax 719/336-4729. 24 Rooms. Rates: $40. Most major credit cards accepted. Located about 1-1/2 miles south of the center of town on US Highways 287 and 385.*

Pretty much the same story as in La Junta. The Blue Spruce is located by a nice creek and there is a trail that runs alongside it. That's about the extent of the recreation offered except for a small swimming pool. The rooms here are quite large but rather drably decorated. Several dining spots are located within a short distance.

CAMPING & RV SITES
• **La Junta KOA,** *26680 US Highway 50. Tel. 719/384-9580*

WHERE TO EAT
LA JUNTA
Moderate

CHIARAMONTE'S, *208 Santa Fe Avenue. Tel. 719/384-8909. American Express, Discover, MasterCard and VISA accepted. Lunch and dinner served daily.*

Unless you like Mexican food (see the El Camino below) you're not going to find a big choice of good restaurants in La Junta. Chiaramonte's offers nicely prepared Italian and some American cuisine in a relaxed and attractive atmosphere. The service is excellent and the quantity of food is generous. Cocktail service.

Inexpensive

EL CAMINO INN, *816 W. 3rd Street. Tel. 719/384-2871. MasterCard and VISA accepted. Lunch and dinner served Tuesday through Saturday.*

Now in its 35th year of service under the same family ownership, the El Camino serves good and authentic Mexican fare in a small but unusually attractive south of the border atmosphere. All of your favorite Mexican dishes are likely to be on the menu but their chile rellenos is the star attraction. Cocktail service and carry out available.

SEEING THE SIGHTS
The first and most important town on this little tour is **La Junta**, a Spanish term meaning junction or meeting place. La Junta dates from

1881 although the area was previously occupied by several Native American tribes including Pueblo, Apache, Ute, Commanche, and Cheyenne among others. It's history is closely related to the arrival of the Santa Fe Railroad. Cattle and produce production are the mainstays of the region today.

Near the west edge of town as you arrive on US 50 will be Anderson Avenue. Turn right and proceed to the **Otero Museum**, *on Anderson between 2nd and 3rd Streets*. The museum is a complex of historic buildings that were saved from the wrecking ball by some foresighted local citizens. One of the museum buildings with exhibits on local history is known as the **Sciumbata House & Store**. The grocery store is stocked as it would have been during the 1920's. Other components of the complex are the **Hiatt Building** with its 1916 dodge touring car and 1920's gasoline filling station among other exhibits; the **Boyd Coach House** with a Concord stage, chuck wagon, and surrey (complete with fringe on top, of course); a shed containing many farm implements, and an 1890's boarding house filled with period artifacts. This is really one of the better museums of its type and warrants careful examination. *Tel. 719/384-7406. The museum is open daily except Sunday from 1:00pm until 5:00pm, June 1st through September 30th. At other times you can call to arrange seeing it. There is no admission charge to enter the museum but donations are greatly appreciated.*

From the museum go east on 3rd Street to Colorado Avenue. Turn right and proceed to 18th Street. Another right will lead you to the **Koshare Indian Museum**, *115 West 18th Street*. This attractive museum is home to an excellent collection of Native American Art and the **Koshare Indian Dancers** (who are actually members of a local Boy Scout Troop). The group has been performing traditional American Indian songs, dances, and crafts since 1933. Performances take place in a ceremonial round *kiva* made famous by the Pueblos. Constructed with more than 620 logs, the room is one of the largest self-supported wooden roofs in the world.

The museum collection is also of note as it has works from seven of the artists who founded what is probably the nation's greates art community–Taos, New Mexico. Authentic pottery, quilting, jewelry, and musical instruments from several Native American tribes is also on display. The Kiva Trading Post is the museum's excellent gift shop. *Tel. 719/384-4411. Museum is open Monday through Saturday from 10:00am until 5:00pm and on Sunday from 12:30pm to 5:00pm, June through August; and Tuesday through Sunday from 12:30 until 4:30 the rest of the year. Closed on state holidays. The dances are performed evenings at 8:00pm from mid-June through early August only, although the kiva is open for inspection during museum hours. The museum admission is $1 and dance performances are $5 for adults, $3 under age 17.*

The next attraction is located about eight miles east of town. Work your way back to US 50 eastbound and take that to the junction of Adams Avenue (CO 109). Go north across the Arkansas River (the street changes name to Main) and proceed to Trail Road, CO 194. Turn right and follow that route to **Bent's Old Fort National Historic Site**, possibly the highlight of this southeastern tour for many people. The fort, which was more of a fortified trading post, was built in 1833 by William Bent, his brother, and Charles St. Vrain. The location was on a branch of the Santa Fe Trail and the three men soon had an extremely profitable business. William Bent was trusted by the various Native American tribes in the area so the post also served as an Indian Agency for several years. The famous scout, Kit Carson, was on the payroll of Bent's Fort for a time. Worsening relations with the Indians and a cholera epidemic turned the lucrative trade business sour and the fort was abandoned in 1849. It had housed between 40 and 60 permanent residents as well as many traders and travelers just passing through.

A visit to Bent's Fort today allows visitors to explore every aspect of its construction and daily life in a reconstruction that is authentic in every detail. The adobe style structure is an impressive sight, maybe even beautiful. Perhaps the best description of it came from George Gibson, a soldier who was passing through in 1846 and noted in his journal that the fort "at a distance it presents a handsome appearance, being castle-like with towers at its angles." Many visitors, then and now, seemed to find a favorable comparison between it and a medieval European castle. There is some resemblance but to me it looks more like a French Foreign Legion post.

The areas to be seen include rooms used for trading and meetings, dining and kitchen facilities, warehouses, and quarters for laborers (located downstairs) and the upstairs trappers' and hunters' quarters as well as a billiards room. When you are upstairs take a few moments to look out on the interior courtyard. The view encompasses the entire complex and it's easy to imagine how it looked on a busy day during the 1840's. The site is furnished with period pieces and costumed guides give living history demonstrations periodically through the day. *Tel. 719/384-2596. The fort is open daily from 8:00am until 5:30pm, Memorial Day through Labor Day, and from 9:00am to 4:00pm the remainder of the year. It is closed on New Year's Day, Thanksgiving, and Christmas. Admission is $2 for individuals over age 16 with a $4 family rate or free to holders of park service passports.*

Continue east on CO 194 after visiting the fort and you'll soon return to a junction with US 50 at the town of Las Animas. The **John Martin Dam** is located 15 miles east of town and then three miles south of US 50 on the Arkansas River. In addition to flood control the dam is a major recreation area. *Tel. 719/336-3476. Free tours are given by reservation only on weekdays from 8:00am until 2:30pm.*

Back on US 50 east for one last time for the final leg of the trip into **Lamar**. It was in Lamar that William Bent was eventually to build Bent's New Fort to replace the one he abandoned in La Junta. There is not a trace of it today. However, the **Big Timbers Museum**, *located at the junction of US 50 and CO 196*, depicts everyday life during the era from the latter part of the 19th century through the 1930's. The museum also houses a good collection of guns and Native American artifacts. *Tel. 719/336-2472. The museum is open daily from 10:00am until 6:00pm from June through August and from 1:00pm until 5:00pm the remainder of the year. It is closed on New Year's Day, Good Friday, Thanksgiving and Christmas.*

From Lamar you can head back to other parts of Colorado by heading west on US 50. If you're heading directly to Denver you can take US 287 north to I-40 west and then I-70 west. There isn't much to see along this route (except for the growing presence of the Rockies as you head westward) but it avoids retracing the same exact route.

NIGHTLIFE & ENTERTAINMENT

The options are extremely limited to say the least. Your best bet for a drink and some conversation is probably in the lounge of the **Quality Inn Capri** in La Junta, *1325 East 3rd Street.*

SPORTS & RECREATION

Boating
• **John Martin Reservoir**, *Las Animas, 15 miles east off of US 50. Tel. 719/336-3476*

Fishing
• **John Martin Reservoir**, *Las Animas, 15 miles east off of US 50. Tel. 719/336-3476*

Golf
• **La Junta Golf Club**, *27696 Harris Road, La Junta. Tel. 719/384-7133*

Swimming
• **John Martin Reservoir**, *Las Animas, 15 miles east off of US 50. Tel. 719/336-3476*
• **Wipe Out Water Slide & Pool**, *3rd & Grant, La Junta. Tel. 719/384-7531*

PRACTICAL INFORMATION

• Hospital
    La Junta: *Arkansas Valley Medical Center, 1100 Carson Avenue. Tel. 719/384-5412*

Lamar: *Prowers Medical Center, 2101 S. Memorial Drive. Tel. 719/336-4343*
• **Police** (non-emergency)
La Junta: *Tel. 719/384-2525*
Lamar: *Tel. 719/336-4341*
• **Tourist Office/Visitors Bureau**
LaJunta: *110 Santa Fe. Tel. 719/384-7411; www.coloplains.com*
Lamar: *Tel. 719/336-4379*

• **Train Station**: *1st Street & Colorado Avenue, La Junta. Tel. 719/384-227*

FINAL THOUGHTS ON EASTERN COLORADO

Just about the only section of the state I haven't touched on is a wide swath in the middle of the eastern section along I-70 from Burlington near the Kansas line, and Limon, about 90 miles southeast of Denver. I wouldn't recommend a special visit to the area, but if you're doing an "eastern Colorado" tour or coming into Colorado from the east via I-70, that's another matter.

Both Burlington and Limon have regional history museums and the former also boasts a 1920's carousel at the county fairgrounds, with nearly fifty unusual hand-carved animals.

17. COLORADO FOR COWBOYS & COWGIRLS

The great American (and worldwide) fascination with the "cowboys and Indians" aspect of the American west during the 19th century continues unabated. In fact, if anything, it is growing by leaps and bounds. The emphasis has, fortunately, been shifting to a more realistic view of what actually happened during that time. At least part of the growth can be attributed to a longing for a simpler way of life that is more in harmony with nature. No doubt many readers will associate these aspects of the west with Arizona and other more westerly destinations.

The reality, however, is that Colorado has as much of this sort of experience as any place in America. Other than a chuckwagon dinner or two, I haven't emphasized this aspect of Colorado too much up to this point. That will be atoned for now, because this chapter will be devoted to **guest ranches** and another great American tradition, **rodeo**.

GUEST RANCHES

Long known as dude ranches (the term *dude* was originally used by cowboys to denote a guest at the ranch as opposed to someone who lives and works there), these facilities are more often today called **guest ranches**. That may be partially due to films like *City Slickers* which made some people feel uncomfortable being called dude. Although it's not meant to be a derogatory term, some people tend to feel like a country bumpkin when called that. Regardless of what you call them, there are in excess of 50 guest ranches throughout Colorado offering a variety of activities in many price ranges and at all luxury levels. The most common activity, of course, is horseback riding which is sought after by almost every ranch guest regardless of his or her prior riding experience. Almost all guest ranches have extensive children's programs. This makes a guest ranch vacation a great idea for families.

While you'll likely to be satisfied with any guest ranch you select, a guarantee of authentic ranch quality can be assured by verifying that the ranch is a member of the highly respected **Colorado Dude & Guest Ranch Association**. All of the ranches contained in the following alphabetical list are members. Although the majority of ranches are located in the North Central and Southwest areas, I have included at least one ranch in each of the touring regions. Consequently, wherever your Colorado journey takes you, you'll have the opportunity to sample a guest ranch experience if you so desire.

A note of caution before you flip ahead and start looking at the rate information. The rate system quoted here is that used most frequently by the Colorado Dude & Guest Ranch Association. Rates are quoted *per adult person* (even if the room will be on a double occupancy basis) usually for *seven days*. It is common for this to be from Sunday through Saturday without the option for variation. You will see, however, that some of the quoted rates are for six days. Shorter stays are available at most ranches but at a higher daily rate. Children's prices are generally between 25 and 50 percent lower than that for an adult. The rate includes all meals. However, some ranches have additional charges for certain activities. Also pay attention to the period when each ranch is open since this does vary considerably from one location to another. It is also important to note that even when a ranch is open all year, the riding season may be restricted to certain months. Always make sure you understand what you're getting before booking.

Finally, a few suggestions and precautions to make your ranch visit more enjoyable. Casual clothing is, of course, the rule at all ranches. However tee shirts and shorts aren't always the right way to dress. Horseback riding and many other forms of outdoor activity do require more protection. It is best to wear sturdy full length jeans, boots and long sleeved shirts in these cases.

Be aware that all of the ranches listed here are at altitudes of 7,000 feet or more. Since some of the activities can be quite strenuous you should be in fairly decent shape. If there is any question in your mind consult your family physician. Although every ranch will have a full schedule of activities for each day of your stay, you are by no means required to participate in every one of their programs. Many ranch guests, especially those staying for a week, decide to take a day or two off and see the surrounding area sights. Keep an open mind and a flexible schedule.

C LAZY U RANCH, *State Highway 125, Granby. Tel. 970/887-3344. Rates: $2,700 per adult for seven days including all meals. Open year-round. No credit cards accepted. Located approximately 8 miles from Granby via US 40 west and CO 125.*

Billing itself as "America's highest rated guest ranch," the C Lazy U is indeed the recipient of more top ratings from more sources than any other ranch of its type. It's certainly deserved and contributes to the sky high prices charged. But, if you have to ask what they charge then you probably can't afford to stay there. Accommodations are varied, ranging from cottages to lodge units, to luxurious duplexes. All are huge and beautifully furnished. Many have their own fireplace. The setting is in a gorgeous mountain meadow and the majority of units feature excellent views. The ranch also has its own private lake. The food is first class and is served in an elegant dining room that is only open to ranch guests. They also have a cocktail lounge. Although the experience at the C Lazy U is one of luxury it is also designed to let you get away from it all–thus, guestrooms do not have TVs or telephones or even air conditioning. It isn't likely that you'll need any of them. Some units have refrigerators and whirlpools.

Facilities: Heated swimming pool, sauna, and whirlpool; tennis and racquetball courts (instruction is available); TV room.

Activities: Area and wilderness tours, trap and skeet shooting, nature program, fishing, horseback riding, paddleboats, children's program and social program for all ages. Winter activities include cross country skiing and ice skating.

COLORADO TRAILS RANCH, *12161 County Road 240, Durango. Tel. 970/247-5055; Fax 970/385-7372. Toll free reservations 800/323-DUDE. Rates: $1,500 per adult for seven days including all meals and gratuities. Open from June through October only. Most major credit cards accepted. Located just off of US 550 about 12 miles north of Durango.*

Pleasing guests since 1960, the Colorado Trails Ranch occupies a lovely mountain setting adjacent to the magnificent San Juan National Forest. The 400 acre ranch is near several rivers that have some of the best fishing waters in Colorado. In addition to the Florida, Pine and Piedra Rivers, a portion of the Shearer Creek runs through the ranch's property. They also have their own two-acre stocked pond. The attractive mountain lodge's interior is dominated by a floor to ceiling rock fireplace.

The beautiful dining room also has a fireplace and colorful table-cloths provide contrast against the light natural wood shades. Not all of the dining is indoors–the Colorado Ranch has, among other things, a weekly chuckwagon dinner. The menu includes traditional western steaks and roasts as well as more healthful and lighter choices along with homemade breads and great desserts. They even have an old fashioned soda fountain. Other buildings are made to look like an old western town.

RANCHES WITH FLAIR

*A quick examination of the dude ranch listings will reveal a lot of similarities in the activities that are available to guests. That shouldn't be surprising since all of them are trying to appeal to the same type of guest and all take advantage of what the Rocky Mountains offer. But there are some ranches that offer things that are far from par for the course at a dude ranch. For instance, if you're interested in archery than the **Elk Mountain Ranch** (Tel. 719/539-4430) is for you.*

*For something really different how about a ranch stay that lets you get a bird's eye view from the basket of a hot air balloon? It's available at the **Vista Verde Ranch** (Tel. 800/526-RIDE). Maybe it's a bit of history you're looking for. Then check out the historic **Cherokee Park Ranch** (Tel. 800/628-0949) that dates from 1886. You get the idea. The possibilities are almost endless.*

The Opera House is the scene of entertainment and dancing while the 800 square foot parlor is filled with interesting antiques. The ranch has one of the most widely acclaimed riding programs and certified riding instructors for all experience levels. Service by the warm and friendly staff is like family. There are 38 employees for a maximum weekly guest load of 77 visitors.

Colorado Trails accommodations are either hotel style in the main lodge or in larger separate multi-room cabins. All have a warm rustic feel and are quite comfortable.

Facilities: Swimming pool, hot tub and Jacuzzi; two tennis courts, basketball and volleyball court and game room.

Activities: Complete horseback riding program, fishing, archery, trap and rifle shooting range, horseshoes, hiking, hayrides, river rafting and entertainment. Children's and teen's program including camping.

COULTER LAKE GUEST RANCH, *Rifle. Tel. 970/625-1473; Fax 970/625-1473. Toll free reservations 800/858-3046. Rates: $1,248 per adult for seven days including all meals and gratuities. Open year-round except for May and November through early December. Most major credit cards accepted. Located about 21 miles northeast of the town of Rifle (I-70, Exit 90) and then via CO 325 into the White River National Forest.*

With a maximum of only 30 guests at one time, the Coulter Lake Guest Ranch provides one of the most intimate and personalized ranch vacations in Colorado. The surrounding White River National Forest provides abundant scenery and the beautiful aspen-filled meadows in which the ranch are located are ideal for horseback riding. The ranch has a rustic look and feel, much the same as it did when it first opened back in 1936. However, the comfortable accommodations have a good number of modern amenities should you start longing for the real world. But, overall, this is definitely for the individual who is looking for a return to the simple life, far away from everything. The home-cooking here is nothing fancy, as is usually the case, but it's fresh, bountiful and delicious. Your hosts — Don, Russ and Susan — are as nice a bunch of folks as you're likely to come across in your travels.

Facilities: Private lake, games and other diversions in common lodge room.

Activities: Horseback riding, overnight pack trips, 4WD trips, optional trips to surrounding areas, snowmobiling and hunting in season, fishing, swimming, and the ever-popular sing-alongs.

DROWSY WATER RANCH, *Granby. Tel. 970/725-3456; Fax 970/725-3611. Toll free reservations 800/845-2292. Rates: $1,265 per adult for seven days including all meals. Open from June through September only. No credit cards accepted. Located about six miles west of Granby via US 40 and then 1-1/2 miles on the ranch's private road–look for sign.*

Picturesquely located on 640 acres of verdant green valley near the Arapahoe National Forest along a creek of the same name, the Drowsy Water is a haven away from modern life. The rustic log buildings have red paint trim. The main lodge building has massive timbered ceilings, a fireplace, wagonwheel chandeliers and Navajo rugs. Cuisine varies from gourmet to simple and hearty western fare in a family style dining room. Many meals can be taken outdoors. Guest rooms are in the form of cabins or lodge units and all have been recently remodeled. They're a pretty western style with either full wall paneling or half panels and half painted. Most ceilings are exposed wooden timbers. All are spacious and airy. Riding is the main activity like at most ranches and the Drowsy water has more than a hundred horses in their stable.

Facilities: Heated swimming pool and hot tub, playground, game area and library.

Activities: Extensive riding program for all ages and experience levels with instruction, fishing pond, barbecues and other cookouts, entertainment in the form of a staff show, horseshoes, square dancing, jeep tours, campfires, hayrides, movies, rodeo and hunting. A full program for children and pre teens is also available.

KING MOUNTAIN RANCH, *11845 Highway 125, Granby. Tel. 970/887-2511; Fax 970/887-9511. Toll free reservations 800/476-5464. Rates: $1,400 per adult for seven days including all meals. Open year-round. Most major credit cards accepted. Located 12 miles off of US 40 via CO 125 north to King Mountain Ranch sign and then four miles via gravel road.*

Set in the middle of a lovely valley with its own private lake, King Mountain was once a luxury conference center and resort retreat. Surrounded by the Arapahoe National Forest, it offers a delectable mix of ranch living with luxury touches at a rate that is affordable to more than the upper class traveler. Wildlife on the ranch is abundant and you'll likely see deer, elk and more. Gourmet and western cuisine is served in a beautiful western themed dining room with a native stone fireplace overlooking the valley. A Ranch Store has unusual items as well as things you might need on a ranch but didn't bring along. The Library has a warm fireplace, big screen television and a video library. Accommodations, including roomy family suites, are attractive and comfortable. All have ample decks that provide a great place to relax and take in the scenery and crisp mountain air. Some have fireplaces. The Trail's End Bar is where the grown-ups gather to exchange stories and have a great time.

Facilities: Heated indoor swimming pool and hot tub, sauna, bowling alley, two lit tennis courts, recreation center with ping pong and pool table, shuffleboard

Activities: Horseback riding, trap and skeet shooting, fishing, hiking, trail lunches and other cookouts, rodeo and board games. The "Foxes Den" is the King Mountain Ranch's program for children ages 4 through 12.

LAKE MANCOS RANCH, *42688 County Route N, Mancos. Tel. 970/533-7900; Fax 970/533-7858. Toll free reservations 800/325-9462. Rates: $1,300 per adult for six days including all meals and gratuities. Open from June through September only. Discover, MasterCard and VISA accepted. Located approximately 35 miles west of Durango via US 160 to Mancos and then north for about a third of a mile on CO 184 to County Road 42. Take that road four miles to County Road N and the ranch will be a quarter mile further on the left.*

Owned and cared for with love by the Sehnert family since 1956, the Lake Mancos Ranch is one of the oldest guest ranches in Colorado that has been operating continuously. Set on a pine top ridge amid an aspen forest with many crystal clear streams, it is in view of the mighty La Plata Range of the San Juan Mountains. The wonderful western dining room serves one of the best buffet breakfasts you'll find anywhere along with wholesome meals and great desserts. But if you still manage to come up hungry the snack bar with its bottomless cookie jar is always open. Some meals are also served outdoors in pretty Rendezvous Canyon. The main lodge boasts a big circular fireplace and a Trading Post for all your shopping needs. The eighty horses owned by the Ranch ensures that you'll have your own private horse for the length of your stay since there is a maximum weekly guest capacity of only 55 people. Individual service and attention is a hallmark of the Lake Mancos Ranch. Two events at the ranch that are especially popular with guests are the weekly Roundup Party and Skit Night where everyone (who wants to) can participate.

The clean and comfortable wood panelled cabins have a separate living room, refrigerator, king size beds and either one, two or three bedrooms with most having two baths. All feature a spacious covered porch for enjoying the tranquility of the ranch environment.

Facilities: Heated outdoor swimming pool with hot tub, sauna, basketball and volleyball courts, recreation room, library and VCR room.

Activities: Horseback riding on a variety of trails, fishing, off-road jeep tours, cookouts, hayrides, entertainment, hiking, nature programs, mountain biking, horseshoes and gold panning. The ranch also offers a complete activity program for children and teens.

LOST VALLEY RANCH, *29555 Goose Creek Road, Sedalla. Tel. 303/647-2311; Fax 303/647-2315. Rates: $1,740 per adult for seven days including all meals. Open from March through September only. No credit cards. Located 7 miles west of I-25, Exit 183 (Castle Rock) to Sedalia then via CO 67 west to Deckers via a gravel road; or US 285 south from Denver to CO 126 and then left 25 miles to Deckers.*

Unlike most of the other guest ranches, the Lost Valley is an authentic working cattle and horse ranch that covers a huge tract of land and adjoining areas of the Pike National Forest. Set amid beautiful scenery, the last nine miles of the trip to the ranch are on an unpaved road that will quickly make you forget civilization and ready you for an outdoor experience. While it is a working ranch it has the same range of facilities and activities of all the others, including about 130 horses as part of its extensive riding program. For those who do seek the true cowboy experience, Lost Valley has several weeks where guests can participate in actual round-ups. If that is your desire be sure to inquire as to their schedule. The accommodations are almost in the luxury level and consist of individual mountainside multi-room cabins with fireplace and plush furnishings. Dining at Lost Valley is also a wonderful experience with their "home cookin' from scratch" be it in the spacious main dining room with its huge vaulted ceiling and wall-to-wall picture window, in a meadow, or even from your saddlebag while out on the trail.

Facilities: Heated swimming pool, whirlpool, two tennis courts

Activities: Horseback riding, cattle roundups, fishing, trap shooting, hiking, cookouts, square dancing, campfires, hayrides, entertainment and social functions. Supervised children's program except during one week each season when the ranch is reserved for adults only.

PEACEFUL VALLEY RANCH, *475 Peaceful Valley Road, Lyons. Tel. 303/747-2881; Fax 303/747-2167. Toll free reservations 800/955-6343. Rates: $1,502 per adult for seven days including all meals. Open all year. Most major credit cards accepted. Located 15 miles north of Boulder to Lyons and then west on CO 7 for 17 miles to CO 72. Turn south and follow that road for three miles.*

Beautifully situated near some of the Rockies highest peaks, yet only a modest 60 mile drive from Denver, the Peaceful Valley Ranch has been operating for almost 50 years. At an elevation of 8,500 feet and in a pine- and aspen-covered valley, the ranch is a picture-perfect setting for a vacation. Recently remodeled, guests can choose between rooms in one of three lodges or ten private cabins. The latter have fireplaces and hot tubs. The authentic western cooking is always first rate, whether it's taken in their nicely wood paneled indoor dining room or outside during a cookout. Although the ranch itself isn't particularly large by Colorado standards, the extensive recreational program takes full use of parts of the adjacent 800,000 acre national forest. The ranch also has a lovely chapel if you're planning on having a guest ranch hitchin' or just want to renew your vows.

Facilities: Indoor swimming pool, game room, saloon (cocktail service).

Activities: Horseback riding (including indoor riding area), hiking, cookouts, swimming, fishing, square dancing, 4x4 or jeep backcountry trips, hayrides, guest rodeo, snowshoeing, talent show, and overnight pack trips. The ranch has an extensive supervised program for youngsters.

SAN JUAN GUEST RANCH, *2882 Highway 23, Ridgway. Tel. 970/626-5360. Toll free reservations 800/331-3015. Rates: $1,250 per adult for six days including all meals. MasterCard and VISA accepted although other form of payment is preferred. Located six miles north of Ouray via US 550 and then left at the ranch sign onto a gravel road. Cross the river and turn immediately to the left. The ranch is one mile further.*

One of the smallest Colorado dude ranches, this is an intimate vacation experience with personalized service that is both friendly and excellent. Your hosts, Pat MacTiernan and her son Scott, have been operating the ranch since 1970. It is located in one of the most rugged areas of the beautiful San Juan Mountains on the banks of the Uncompaghre River in a delightful valley between Ridgway and Ouray that provides beautiful vistas no matter what direction you look. The owners take pride in pointing out to visitors that photographs of the area taken a hundred years ago show that little has changed in all that time. This is a wonderful near-wilderness experience. Each of the nine guest units in the spacious lodge is uniquely decorated and has modern amenities. Downstairs you'll find a Jacuzzi and a porch where you can relax and enjoy the view. Meals are served family style (the MacTiernans will join you for all meals); you'll find a bountiful selection of well prepared home cooking. Then retreat into the den with its cozy fireplace and works by local artisans. Coffee, tea and lemonade are available at any time of the day.

Facilities: Hot tub.

Activities: Comprehensive horseback riding program, fishing, wagon rides, overnight camping, horseshoes, trap shooting, rifle range, cookouts, jeep tours, children's program. Winter activities are cross country skiing and ice skating.

SYLVAN DALE GUEST RANCH, *2939 N. County Road 31D, Loveland. Tel. 970/667-3915; Fax 970/635-9336. Rates: $1,219 per adult for six days including all meals and gratuities. Open year-round. No credit cards. Located seven miles west of Loveland via US 34 to County Road 31D and then just north.*

A Loveland area fixture since 1946, the Sylvan Dale is another working ranch that's loads of fun for the whole family. Located only an hour from Denver but a world apart, the nearly 5,000 acre ranch is a place to enjoy nature, have fun, and learn to appreciate the great Western heritage that attracts so many people to Sylvan Dale as well as the competition. The main lodge building is the center of indoor activities with its attractive and traditionally furnished dining room of rich, dark wood and the large and comfortable recreation room. New in 1998 is "The Heritage," a dramatic lodge structure with multi-purpose gathering room and fireplace, as well as recreational facilities. Guest accommodations take the form of attractive individual cabins. Larger families can stay at the Wagon Wheel Barn with its own lounge, fireplace, and kitchen. Although children are usually welcome the ranch does feature one week each season that is for adults only.

Facilities: Swimming pool, hot tub, tennis courts, recreation room.

Activities: Horseback riding, ranching chores, cattle drives, nature trails, fishing, entertainment, hayrides, cookouts, square dancing, parties and social program as well as an extensive children's program.

WILDERNESS TRAILS RANCH, *1766 County Road 302, Durango. Tel. 970/247-0722; Fax 970/247-1006. Toll free reservations 800/52-RANCH. Rates: $1,600 per adult for seven days including all meals and gratuities. Open from June through September only. Discover, MasterCard and VISA accepted. Located northeast of Durango via Main Avenue to 32nd Street and then Florida Road (County Route 240) for 14 miles to County Route 501. Turn left and follow the west side of Vallecito Lake until you reach the northeast side. Take the gravel road for 4-1/2 miles via directional signs.*

Owned and operated by the same family for almost 30 years, Wilderness Trails sits in the Pine River Valley near one of the largest designated wilderness areas in Colorado. Rugged mountains, thick forests, dazzling blue lakes and streams as well as large open meadows dominate the scene. It is one of the most beautiful locations of any guest ranch and will certainly give you lasting memories. An expert staff of 33 attends to the needs and wants of the maxium 50 weekly guests, a ratio that (like most of the ranches) surpasses most luxury cruise liners. Meals run the gamut from buffet to individually served, from indoors to cookouts and all feature complete on-premise cooking right down to the breads and desserts.

Accommodations are either in two-bedroom, two-bath Ponderosa cabins or three-bedroom, three-bath Cabin Suites. All are built from logs from the ranch (mostly cut during the 1940s) and feature pretty country furnishings and porches. The cabin suites have a separate living room with wood burning stove, bar, refrigerator and coffee maker. One month during each season is for adults only (usually September) and there is also an annual cattle round-up week.

Facilities: Swimming pool and hot tub, game room.

Activities: Horseback riding, fishing, 4-wheel area tours, staff entertainment, campfires, hayrides, overnight pack trips, hiking, mountain biking, and cookouts. Full children's and teens program except during adult month.

WHAT DID YOU SAY, DUDE?

If you stay at a guest ranch you'll likely to wonder if English is being spoken. That's because the cowboys and other ranch workers and residents have a lingo all their own. "Dude" is only the start. You're sure to encounter some of these other terms. Cookie refers to the ranch cook, regardless of gender. Cookies, of course, serve grub–any type of grub can also be called vittles. When you're hungry for grub (or vittles) you're said to have a hankerin'.

Not all the cowboy talk refers to food. Calves are referred to as doggies Doggies and all types of cattle leave behind something you don't want to step in–cow pie, which is certainly not food! A stampede string is the strap on your hat that is tied underneath the chin to keep your hat from falling off during a stampede or any other time for that matter.

Now be sure to throw in as many of these terms as often as you can during your guest ranch stay. Then the hired help won't think you're a dude.

RODEO

Whether you pronounce it *roh-dio* or *row-day-oh*, this sport holds a special place in the heart of many Coloradans. The sport certainly has its share of detractors who claim that it is cruel to animals. I'm not going to get involved in that argument. Suffice to say it is a sport that attracts large

A RODEO ROUNDUP

The term rodeo comes from the Spanish verb "rodear" which means to surround. In southwestern usage surround had the same connotation as roundup, which is how rodeo got started in the first place. The origins of rodeo go back to the early days of America's cattle industry when cowboys would celebrate the conclusion of once or twice annual roundups and put on demonstration roundups to show off the skills they used. The practice became more formalized over time and the first actual modern rodeo was held in 1872.

*Today rodeo is guided by the **Professional Rodeo Cowboys Association**. The PRCA is headquartered in Colorado Springs (you recall the Pro Rodeo Hall of Fame and Museum, don't you?). A rodeo can consist of many different events but five are basic to all rodeo contests. These are saddle bronco riding, bareback bronco riding, bull riding, steer wrestling, and calf roping. In the riding events the objective is to remain mounted for a prescribed amount of time while the roping and wrestling competitions are awarded to the best elapsed time achieved. There are often huge prizes awarded in PRCA sanctioned championship events but the rewards are much smaller at local rodeos.*

crowds throughout the west and a legitimate topic to be included in this book. If you feel it isn't for you on moral or other grounds, no one is forcing you to take part.

The biggest Colorado rodeo events are listed below. While other types of festivities often take place in conjunction with these rodeos, the competition itself is the star attraction.

- **Brush Rodeo** (Brush), in July. An "open" class rodeo celebrated around the Fourth of July.
- **Collegiate Peaks Stampede Rodeo** (Buena Vista), in July. This is a major PRCA sponsored event.
- **National HS Finals Rodeo** (Pueblo), in July. With more than 1,500 contestants from almost 40 states as well as Canada, this may well be the biggest rodeo in the world.
- **"Pikes Peak or Bust" Rodeo** (Colorado Springs), in August. A Springs tradition for almost 60 years, this event fills Penrose Stadium with avid followers and the curious alike.
- **Rooftop Rodeo** (Estes Park), in July. Another event that has a long history. Celebrates Estes Park's Heritage Days.
- **SLV Ski-Hi Stampede** (Monte Vista), in July. Major PRCA event.

Rodeos are also often part of the festivities celebrating all sorts of things throughout Colorado. The following events have a big rodeo although it may not be the featured attraction:

- **Baca County Fair** (Springfield), in August.
- **Colorado State Fair** (Pueblo), in August. PRCA events occur over a seven day period.
- **Cowboy Roundup Days** (Steamboat Springs), July 4th holiday period. This one has been occuring every year for almost a hundred years.
- **Greeley Independence Stampede** (Greeley), in late June and early August.

Now, don't expect to see a lot of bronco bustin' going on if you attend Winter Park's **Chocolate Rodeo**. That's because it's a cooking festival!

INDEX

THINGS CHANGE!

Phone numbers, prices, addresses, quality of food, etc, all change. If you come across any new information, we'd appreciate hearing from you. No item is too small! Drop us an e-mail note at: Jopenroad@aol.com, or write us at:

Colorado Guide
*Open Road Publishing, P.O. Box 284
Cold Spring Harbor, NY 11724*

TRAVEL NOTES

TRAVEL NOTES

TRAVEL NOTES

TRAVEL NOTES

TRAVEL NOTES

TRAVEL NOTES

TRAVEL NOTES

TRAVEL NOTES

TRAVEL NOTES

TRAVEL NOTES

OPEN ROAD PUBLISHING

U.S.A.

America's Cheap Sleeps, $16.95
America's Grand Hotels, $14.95
America's Most Charming Towns &
    Villages, $17.95
Arizona Guide, $16.95
Boston Guide, $13.95
California Wine Country Guide, $12.95
Colorado Guide, $17.95
Disneyworld With Kids, $14.95
Florida Guide, $16.95
Hawaii Guide, $18.95
Las Vegas Guide, $14.95
Las Vegas With Kids, $14.95
National Parks With Kids, $14.95
New Mexico Guide, $16.95
San Francisco Guide, $16.95
Southern California Guide, $18.95
Spa Guide U.S.A., $14.95
Texas Guide, $16.95
Utah Guide, $16.95
Vermont Guide, $16.95

MIDDLE EAST/AFRICA

Egypt Guide, $17.95
Israel Guide, $17.95
Jerusalem Guide, $13.95
Kenya Guide, $18.95

UNIQUE TRAVEL

Celebrity Weddings & Honeymoon
    Getaways, $16.95
The World's Most Intimate Cruises, $16.95

SMART HANDBOOKS

The Smart Home Buyer's
    Handbook, $16.95
The Smart Runner's Handbook, $9.95

LATIN AMERICA & CARIBBEAN

Bahamas Guide, $13.95
Belize Guide, $16.95
Bermuda Guide, $14.95
Caribbean Guide, $21.95
Caribbean With Kids, $14.95
Chile Guide, $18.95
Costa Rica Guide, $17.95
Ecuador & Galapagos Islands Guide, $17.95
Guatemala Guide, $18.95
Honduras & Bay Islands Guide, $16.95

EUROPE

Austria Guide, $15.95
Czech & Slovak Republics Guide, $18.95
France Guide, $16.95
Greek Islands Guide, $16.95
Holland Guide, $16.95
Ireland Guide, $17.95
Italy Guide, $19.95
Italy With Kids, $14.95
London Guide, $14.95
Moscow Guide, $16.95
Paris Guide, $13.95
Portugal Guide, $16.95
Prague Guide, $14.95
Rome & Southern Italy Guide, $14.95
Scotland Guide, $17.95
Spain Guide, $18.95
Turkey Guide, $18.95

ASIA

China Guide, $21.95
Japan Guide, $19.95
Philippines Guide, $18.95
Tahiti & French Polynesia Guide, $18.95
Tokyo Guide, $13.95
Thailand Guide, $18.95
Vietnam Guide, $14.95

To order any Open Road book, send us a check or money order for the price of the book(s) plus $3.00 shipping and handling for domestic orders, to: **Open Road Publishing**, PO Box 284, Cold Spring Harbor, NY 11724